I am almost twenty-five years old. My mum died of cancer when I was twenty-one. I have a two-and-a-half-year-old boy and am not far off delivering my second baby.

I'm the only person I know, literally,  ny friends had their children young, and all ng your book felt like someone had taken all m em on paper. Some parts of it were word for w

There are not enough words in the Eng........ .ow appreciative I am to have read your book. It hasn't healed all the wounds or filled all the voids, but it has been an immense help in my grieving process, not to mention a huge help with the way I see my relationship with my son and my future relationship with my next child. I will keep your book forever.

—Julie Gibson

I have never recovered from the loss of my mother when I was eighteen. She was my best friend, my confidante, my everything. Having my own babies brought up so many emotions surrounding her absence. Now I find myself scared to death that my girls may lose me. On each birthday cake, on every wishing star, my only wish is to be here for them until I am very old. Reading your book has helped me sort out some of these complex feelings and has helped me feel less alone.

On my forty-fifth birthday, the year that my mother didn't live to see, I too am going to have a big bash and raise my glass to myself and to this crazy, beautiful life. Needless to say, I am very grateful to you for giving me that idea. Thank you from the bottom of my heart for sharing your life with me.

—Paige Morrow Kimball

I was fortunate to have had my mother in my life until I was thirty-four, but not yet a mother myself. I believe the words I used to tell my mother that my husband and I were expecting our first child were ". . . and it's okay if it is cancer, because you're going to be here to help me deliver this baby!" I was two weeks pregnant. Six days later it was confirmed that my mother's breast cancer was in her lungs, liver, bones, and spleen. She made it almost four months, to my fifth month of pregnancy.

I now have a four-and-a-half-month-old daughter who is so completely tied to the final moments of my mother's life and the hollowness I felt after her death that I sometimes feel she has been cheated. I am haunted by the notion that I could either *have* a mother or *be* a mother—for me there doesn't feel like any in between, and it's a horrible thing to choose from. Not that there was ever any choice, of course, but it haunts me all the same. I appreciate your presence as a support.

—Valerie Milner

I am the daughter of a motherless mother. In 1945, when my mom was barely two, her father died of a heart condition. In 1960, when she was sixteen, her mother died of cancer.

Although my early childhood, at least for me, was quite normal, my mom's life has been very, very impacted by the early deaths of both her parents. In recent years I discovered she suffered from a severe bout of depression during the early years of my life—particularly in the postpartum period. Although I have thought about this often, it was with some shock that I read in your book about the intense grief that might accompany the birth of a first child, especially a girl child who would reestablish the mother-daughter relationships.

I am forty years old and have only seen a few pictures of my maternal grandparents and know but a handful of stories about their lives. When I read the one small paragraph in the book where [the daughters of motherless mothers] are described as chronic nail-biters, I laughed out loud (once I took my finger away from my front tooth)!

I wanted to tell you that your book struck a chord for me and gave me insight into the dynamics of my own family and myself. Thank you.   —Lorie Gehrke

I am now fifty-three years old. I lost my mother when I was sixteen, to rheumatic heart disease. At that time, in 1969, death was not discussed and I really struggled.

I have been listening to your book on my way to work, and so many things are now making sense, especially the terrible depression I felt after the birth of my first child, a wonderful experience mixed with the sadness of not having my mother to share it with.

One statement in the book that really hit home for me was about not knowing your mother as an adult, and losing her before things in your life were settled. I take comfort in knowing that my mother did understand that the teenage years were horrible, and that had she survived we would have resolved our differences.

Thank you for writing these books. You make me feel as if I am not so alone and help explain so many of my feelings and actions over the years.

—Myra Katz

© Uzi Eliahou

About the Author

HOPE EDELMAN has a bachelor's degree in journalism from Northwestern University and a master's degree in creative nonfiction writing from the University of Iowa. She is the author of the *New York Times* bestseller *Motherless Daughters* and its companion volume, *Letters from Motherless Daughters*. She lives in Topanga Canyon, California, with her husband and their two daughters.

ALSO BY HOPE EDELMAN

Motherless Daughters

Letters from Motherless Daughters

Mother of My Mother

Motherless Mothers

How Losing a Mother
Shapes the Parent You Become

HOPE EDELMAN

HARPER

NEW YORK • LONDON • TORONTO • SYDNEY

HARPER

A hardcover edition of this book was published in 2006 by Harper-Collins Publishers.

Most names have been changed to protect the identity of the individuals whose stories are told.

FIRST HARPER PAPERBACK PUBLISHED 2007.

Designed by Laura Kaeppel

The Library of Congress has catalogued the hardcover edition as follows:
Edelman, Hope.
 Motherless mothers: how mother loss shapes the parents we become / Hope Edelman.—1st ed.
   p. cm.
 Includes bibliographical references and index.
 ISBN-10: 0-06-053245-9
 ISBN-13: 978-0-06-053245-1
 1. Mothers—Psychology. 2. Adult children—Psychology.
3. Maternal deprivation. 4. Loss (Psychology) 5. Mothers and daughters. 6. Motherhood I. Title.
HQ759.E25 2006
155.9'370852—dc22   2005052812

ISBN: 978-0-06-053246-8 (pbk.)
ISBN-10: 0-06-053246-7 (pbk.)

 14 15 ❖/RRD 10 9 8 7 6 5

For Maya and Eden
love beyond words

They call me mother and my voice
answers, sounding the joy I feel in
my ability to do just this—what for
many lucky women may come naturally or simply, but which for me was
so difficult to learn.

—Linda Sexton,
Searching for Mercy Street

Contents

Acknowledgments

*H*eartfelt gratitude and thanks to all the friends, family, and colleagues who offered insight, support, and companionship over the three years it took to write this book. Without you, it would have been a much longer and lonelier journey, and far less fun. I am blessed by knowing you all.

Elizabeth Kaplan, my agent, always first on my list. Agent among agents, friend among friends.

Gail Winston, the kind of editor an author dreams of. Always patient, exceedingly intelligent, eternally kind. Katherine Hill and Katherine Beitner at HarperCollins. You make things happen.

The women of Motherless Daughters of Orange County, especially Casey Enda, Cami Black, Mary Felix, and Laurie Lucas; the women of Motherless Daughters of Metro Detroit, especially Mary Ann McCourt; Linda Hardy in Tucson; Colleen Russell in Mill Valley, California; Julie Rahav and Shoshanit Feigenberg of the Motherless Mothers Foundation in Tel Aviv; and Shelly Cofield in New York. You do essential, beautiful work.

Gina Mireault, PhD, and Jama Laurent, PhD. Women of insight and encouragement.

The 1,322 women who participated in the online Motherless Mothers Survey, the 73 mothers in the control-group study, and especially the 78 women who shared their stories with me in person. You've made this the book it is.

The women on my e-mail hit list, who responded with such honesty, thoughtfulness, and humor to all my urgent, last-minute requests. If I hadn't promised you anonymity, I would gladly acknowledge you all by name.

Bruce Bauman, Leslie Schwartz, Kate Vrijmoet, Susan Ulintz, Susan and Larry Laffer, Katherine Alteneder, Jennifer Lauck, Lisa Solovay, Sharon Herbstman, Monica Buckley-Price, Jonathan Greenberg & Loretta Mijares, Muppe & Avri Glick. Friends who support spirit and soul.

The Amigos of Topanga: Doug, Gretchen, Jack, Claudia, Matt, Thea, and all our kids. For the welcome distraction of Baja. What a year we're about to have.

My students at Antioch University-Los Angeles and West Coast Writers Workshops. You constantly remind me what it means to be brave and real and true.

Amy Margolis and everyone at the Iowa Summer Writing Festival. July wouldn't be July without you.

Joyce Vuong, Linda Laucella, and Tynette Solomon. For invaluable research assistance.

Sherry Raouf, Paula Duke, Jillian Maliszewski, and the staff at Palisades Montessori Center. For loving my girls as you do.

The Clocktower Inn in Ventura, California, where I spent numerous kid-free weekends in 2004 and 2005. Large portions of this book were written there.

Anna, Shelley, and Shaunnie. For the little miracles you perform every day.

Michele Edelman; Glenn Edelman; Allyson Edelman; Amy Jupiter; Noa & Dror Avisar; Haskel & Rachel Eliahou; Gali Eliahou; and Ruth Eliahou. Family.

My father, who died before this book was complete. A man of courage and dignity when it mattered most.

My mother, whose love and patience still sustain me.

Uzi. My husband, my partner, my prince. For the way you keep us all so calm and safe. Everything is possible because of you.

Maya Bear and Didi Girl. Every hour. Every day. You rock your mommy's world.

Introduction

wo little girls live in my house now. The eight-year-old has the temperament of a sprite; the four-year-old the countenance of an angel. When I return home at the end of a workday, the older one lunges at me in the entryway—*"Mommeee!"*—entwining her body around me in a simian display of unity. The four-year-old races over with her arms raised, bleating "Mommy-mommy-mommy," her halo of dark gold hair backlit by the acute, setting California sun.

I reach down for the little one, trying to keep my balance with the older one wrapped around my right leg. "How's my bunny?" I say to Eden, nuzzling my face into her smooth neck. I grip Maya's gangly third-grade body tight against my upper thigh in the best facsimile of a hug I can manage. "How's my bear?" I ask.

It is an uninhibited spectacle of adoration, an almost embarrassing display of abundance. *Two* little girls whose afternoon cracks open with joy and relief when I walk through the door. Has anyone ever felt so necessary, or so beloved?

My mother felt this way once. At least, I imagine she must have. Or at least I hope she did. There were three children who would have greeted her when she returned home from a PTA meeting or from a long weekend away with my father, though I can't remember a specific time all of us leaped on her as my children leap on me. We weren't a family prone to physical displays of affection, or verbal expressions of love. The only time I remember telling my mother I loved her was in the summer of 1981, when I was seventeen. She was lying in a hospital bed, and I gripped the side bars as I said the words.

"I love you, too," she said, but her voice was distracted, already on its way somewhere else.

She died two days later, of a cancer that had begun in her breast and spread to her liver. That was more than twenty years ago, but the images of her final days have never lost their clarity. It's my memories of her as a mother that have started to dull. I can't remember any of the piano lessons she gave me, or if I ever saw her face in the audience at a school play. Has our time together receded too far into the past for me to retrieve these images? Or are they instead being replaced by the memories I'm building now, with my own daughters, day by day?

For a long time, when people said, "Tell me about yourself," my first impulse was to begin with, "My mother died when I was seventeen." It felt like the most authentic description of myself I could give. Now, when I'm asked this question, I automatically start with, "I have two daughters. They're eight and four." Few events in a woman's life assume such dominance over her identity, but mother loss and motherhood are two.

A mother isn't all I am, of course—I'm also a wife, and a writer, and a teacher, and a homeowner, and an amateur backyard landscaper every year from April to June. But because I've chosen, very deliberately, to place my daughters at the center of my world, my role as their mother eclipses nearly everything else I do. Once I defined myself by an absence. Now I define myself by the presence of two very short people who demand most of my time.

And yet my identity as their mother is influenced by more than just the relationship we three share. It exists in a complex matrix of intergenerational love and loss, colored by what I remember of my own mother's life and death, and complicated by the survival techniques I relied on afterward to manage on my own. My relentless self-sufficiency, my fear of dying young, my love of all things predictable and safe—all of the thoughts and behaviors I'd been trying to shrug off on therapists' couches for years stubbornly solidified after my first daughter was born. And some of them started getting in the way.

You'd think I would have expected this, I who'd spent the prior three years speaking and writing about the significance of transitional events such as marriage and motherhood in a motherless daughter's life. Still, I wasn't prepared for how similar the frustration and anger I felt in 1997, when Maya screamed nonstop for her first ten weeks, would feel to the global despair that consumed me after my mother's death in 1981. I also hadn't anticipated the sort of existential aloneness I felt during the postpartum period, even with my cousin and my mother-in-law providing help. Once I became a mother, my own mother was suddenly nowhere and everywhere all at once. Even the most mundane elements of infant care brought her into the room. *How had she managed with cloth diapers?* I wondered as I struggled with the disposable kind. As I paced the floor with Maya at three A.M., I'd involuntarily muse, *This must have been how she held me in the middle of the night.*

When I wrote *Motherless Daughters* in the early 1990s, I included a chapter on motherless mothers, but writing it was more of an intellectual endeavor than an engagement with emotional truth. As a single, childless woman, I didn't yet appreciate—how could I possibly have appreciated?—how the experience of early mother loss would one day shape me as a parent in virtually every way. It has influenced everything from the partner I chose (someone who I was certain would care for children attentively in the event something bad happened to me); to the obsessive baby books I keep for my daughters (recording every small detail, so they'll have that information in the event something bad happens to me); to my decision to take Maya to France by myself when she was three (so she'd have an early memory of travel with her mother, in the event something bad happens to me); to the way I brush the girls' hair every morning (in styles easy for my husband to replicate, in case something bad happens to me soon).

It has also made me, I believe, a much more conscientious mother than I would otherwise be, one who tries hard to anticipate my children's needs and constantly attempts to shield them from disappointment or despair. Because I know what it feels like to long for a mother, I try to compensate for my daughters by always being there. True, aiming for Supermom status can be exhausting for a working mother, and it definitely cuts into a workday when you stubbornly insist on doing the half-hour preschool drop-off and pick-up each day even though a husband or babysitter would gladly make the trip. But I know how precious our time together is, mainly because I know how suddenly it could be taken away. At forty-one, I'm only one year younger than my mother was when she died, and that mental math figures into the background of most parenting decisions I make.

It isn't exactly a palpable fear of dying young that steers me as much as the constant background awareness that such a thing could happen. Like most of the motherless mothers I've met while researching this book, I don't go through the day obsessing about my health or my mortality, and I've even gotten pretty lax about doing monthly breast self-exams. Who has time for all that anymore? I do, however, invest a considerable amount of energy in self-preservation. One woman I know, a mother of three who lost her father in a car accident when she was eight, describes her parenting style as one that emphasizes "economy of movement." Knowing from an early age that crisis can appear without warning, she shies away from unnecessary risk. I know exactly what she means. I always drive the speed limit. I won't fly in small planes. Bad things can happen to mothers, I know. The most important part of my job as a parent, I believe, is to stick around.

* * *

My story isn't unique. I've heard it from many women by now.

A mother dies of breast cancer when her daughter is seventeen. The father, though well-meaning, retreats into his own world. The daughter, already a chronic overachiever, throws herself into school-work. One year later, she escapes to college. Years of staunch self-sufficiency follow, along with a string of romantic relationships, each of which abruptly ends when one partner or the other gets overly attached, panics, and flees. Then there's graduate school, and several stints in therapy to wrestle with all those years of unresolved grief. A move to the big city. More relationships. A high-powered career. Then comes a man, unlike the others, who is not afraid to pledge eternal love. There's an unexpected pregnancy, a wedding, a birth, and—suddenly, like the miracles she long ago stopped believing in—a new family is born.

I've often thought that if my first daughter hadn't arrived as a surprise I might never have had a child at all. Though I'd passionately wanted to create the mother-child bond I'd lost, the immense responsibility of parenthood unnerved me. How would I possibly find the patience and devotion I'd need, given that I'd been unmothered by anyone but myself for so long? How could I find enough faith to believe that what happened to my mother so young wouldn't also happen to me?

"It takes a lot of courage for motherless daughters to have kids," says Irene Rubaum-Keller, MFT, a Los Angeles therapist who lost her mother at age seven and who now has an eight-year-old son. "Because it's a means of saying, 'We're going to live.' If we really believed we were going to die young, would we have kids? No. Why would we do that to them? So, having a child is a leap of faith. It's saying, 'I'm going to live, therefore I'm going to have children and have a long life with them.' I've seen many motherless daughters who are too afraid to even get married, who won't even get that close to someone, because they think they're going to die or lose someone else they love."

Loss—real and imagined—is a part of a motherless mother's landscape in a way that most friends, husbands, and coworkers can't understand. A baby's high fever, or a mother-in-law's offhand critical comment, or a teenaged daughter's struggle for independence triggers a response in a motherless daughter that might not be triggered in her peers. When Maya was three months old, I joined a Mommy & Me group, and every Tuesday we twenty new mothers sat in a sloppy circle talking about breast-feeding and bottle feeding, motor development and preschool wait lists. While all this was undeniably helpful, I had an additional list of urgent subjects to discuss: Can you get a mammogram if you're breast-feeding, or do you have to wait? Whom should you name as the legal guardian for your child in your will? How do you even draft a will? I could imagine the response I'd receive if I were to blurt out spontaneously, "Ever since Maya's birth, I've been nearly overcome with fear that one of us is going to die." Just the idea of the sudden silence, the polite smiles, and the quick change of subject was enough to keep me quiet. Mommy & Me is many good things, but it's not a good place to discuss dying young.

Which is not to say that thoughts like these don't occur to all new mothers. They do. They just don't surface with the same frequency or intensity, or with the same emotional charge. As Gina Mireault, PhD, an associate professor of psychology at Johnson State College in Johnson, Vermont, who lost her own mother at age three, explains, "All engaged mothers—meaning all those who are engaged in the process of mothering—worry. But motherless mothers worry for different reasons. Most of my girlfriends who have kids still have their mothers, and we talk a lot about what we're doing with our kids and about the different issues we have with them. But the reasons I worry are filtered through the lens of having lost a parent, whereas that's not the case for them."

"Being a good mother" ranks high among most motherless mothers' goals—to be the mothers they didn't get to have, and to be the mothers their mothers didn't get the chance to become.

When Mireault compared thirty motherless mothers with twenty-six mothers whose mothers were still alive, she found that the mother-loss group was more preoccupied with their roles as mothers than the other women were, and were also more focused on how well they were doing as mothers.

"They were more concerned that maybe they weren't doing a good job—but that didn't mean they weren't," Mireault says. "They also reported they were trying hard. They wanted to do it right, because they feared so much that they wouldn't. So, it seemed as if they had a compensatory behavior, and because their children looked okay in comparison with the other children, there was some evidence that perhaps these mothers *were* compensating. In other words, they were kind of hard on themselves, but they seemed to be doing the good job they were afraid they *weren't* doing."

This impulse to overcompensate is a common trait among motherless mothers. From the start, many of them feel somehow less able, less equipped, or less prepared for parenting than their peers. If I haven't received mothering in such a long time, they reason, how will I know how to give it? How will I know what decisions to make, and which to avoid? Without a living mother to rely on for guidance or advice, they feel as if they're starting out with a deficit other mothers don't have to overcome.

At least some of this perception is grounded in fact. Most women who have living mothers do receive parenting support from them, especially during the postpartum weeks. When I surveyed seventy-three mothers who hadn't experienced early mother loss, two-thirds of the respondents said they had received emotional support from their mothers after their first child was born, and more than half had received practical help from her, such as babysitting or assistance with infant care. Only 15 percent had to manage without help from anyone other than a husband or partner.

In a similar survey I conducted with motherless mothers, however, 52 percent—more than half—said they and their husbands or partners had received no outside help after their first child was born. The motherless women were also eight times more likely than other women to report they often worried about not knowing how to be a mother.

"These women often are not totally devoid of nurturing caretakers, but imbedded in their thinking is that if it isn't the mother, they are devoid of a role model for mothering," explains Cynthia Pill, LICSW, PhD, a Boston-area counselor who has led more than fifteen support groups for motherless daughters over the past eight years. "It's as if they need to connect with their mothers in order to feel they have mothering skills."

What does it mean to connect with one's mother, especially twenty years after she died? Sometimes I suspect I'm longing more for *a* mother than for *my* mother, for the archetypal wise woman who would swoop into my household at exactly the right moment, bearing a scrubber sponge in one hand and a tube of diaper cream in the other. "Go lie down," she'd say. "I've got everything under control. And when you wake up, I'll show you how to do it all."

After my first daughter was born, I would sit in the rocking chair nursing her in the dim morning hours, watching the sun slowly rise over Los Angeles down the hill. I was so tired. *So* tired. So full of uncertainty about this new role, and so impossibly sad that I didn't have a mother to help me figure it out. It was a new experience to mourn my mother as an absent grandmother, but that's what I did those first months, when I watched my friends turn to their mothers for reliable child care, or for moral support, or for parenting advice, if not in person then at least by phone. I longed for a mother who would love my daughter, who would be adored by my daughter, and who would take her—who would offer to take her, without even being asked—once in a while just because she noticed I needed a break.

Dream on? That's what my other friends, the ones who have difficult relationships with their mothers, tell me. Even though their mothers are living, they're still not getting that kind of support. Still, what's the harm in dreaming? Imagination has been my constant, silent partner these past eight years. Like most motherless mothers,

I'm making it up day by day, hoping that the confident mask I wear in public obscures the simple fact that most of the time I don't know what I'm doing, and I don't know whom to ask. Instead, I buy books. I read a lot of parenting magazines. I pray for patience, and for guidance, and for good ideas. When all else fails, I get creative. As fifty-five-year-old Louise, who was six when her mother died, explains, "With us, parenting is a process of invention."

I wish I could take credit for the term "motherless mothers," but a man who spent time among monkeys deserves that honor. In the 1970s, psychology professor Harry Harlow and his associates at the Primate Laboratory at the University of Wisconsin set out to study what happened to infant monkeys who were separated from their mothers soon after birth and were raised instead with surrogate "mothers" sculpted either from wire or cloth. When these infant monkeys grew up and gave birth, these "motherless mothers," as Harlow called them, were either negligent or abusive to their firstborn offspring. They showed no ability to nurse, rock, or comfort their young. Some even violently and fatally bit their babies. Deprived of an emotional connection since birth, these monkeys were unable to bond with their firstborn infants.*

In its simplest reduction, this theory suggests that children completely deprived of affection or nurturing are likely to grow into adults who have impaired or nonexistent bonds with their own firstborn children. But what about those who did receive good mothering, only to lose it? Or those who received inconsistent or unpredictable mothering from the start—inadequate, but still more than nothing? What effect might this have on the way they raise children of their own, and on the children they raise?

There is little doubt that early parent loss affects the way daughters interact with their own offspring. As Maxine Harris, PhD, a clinical psychologist in Washington, D.C., and the author of

---

* The monkeys' maternal behaviors, however, did improve with subsequent births. Their difficulties seemed to lie only with caring for a firstborn.

The Loss That Is Forever, has explained, "The struggles of raising the next generation are the struggles of the human race. They become even more complicated when a mother or father has lost a parent in childhood. That person brings to motherhood or fatherhood not only the usual expectations, dreams, and fears but also a host of fantasies born from the experiences of an orphaned child."

Yet only a handful of researchers have spent time studying this group. Erna Furman, the Cleveland child analyst who conducted extensive research with bereaved children in the 1960s and 1970s, was one of the first. She observed that parents who'd lost a parent during childhood frequently had difficulty when raising their own children, but managed fine in other areas of life. Some parents, she wrote in her landmark 1974 book, *A Child's Parent Dies*, lost empathy for their children when the children reached the same age at which the parent had lost a mother or father. Others had minor problems during that year, but could later resume parenting. Furman also saw adults who'd had a certain parenting style before that critical year and then adopted a different style. She speculated this was a result of having been raised one way up to a certain point in their own lives, and then a different way, by a different person, afterward.

At about the same time, Rita Rogers, MD, a Los Angeles psychiatrist, found some startling similarities among seventy-one parents who'd experienced early mother or father loss. Many had trouble accepting their children's age-appropriate behaviors, due to their own lack of experience with an uninterrupted childhood. While most of them had good intentions as parents, their own desire to be parented often got in the way. A few years later, Sol Altschul, MD, and Helen Beiser, MD, two of the founding members of Chicago's Barr-Harris Children's Grief Center, found that parenting problems were most dramatic in those who'd lost a same-sex parent at an early age. These individuals lacked the experience of having been raised by that parent in the later stages of childhood, Altschul and Beiser explained, and tended to identify too much with both the dead parent and with their children, especially those of the same sex.

Furman, Rogers, Altschul, and Beiser were working mainly with clinical populations, meaning that the majority of motherless mothers they encountered were either staying in psychiatric hospitals or were receiving some type of therapeutic help for themselves or for their kids. This was a problem with many early studies of the parentally bereaved. Far fewer studies have been conducted with what's called the "normative" population—meaning the mother next door who looks and acts like a regular mom but happens to have a history of early mother loss in her past—even though most motherless mothers can be described that way.

Donald Zall, DSW, a psychotherapist in Concord, Massachussetts, is among the few researchers who's looked at this specific group. In the early 1990s, Zall, who was then a doctoral candidate, wanted to see how losing a mother young might affect a daughter's future parenting behaviors. He conducted in-depth interviews with twelve mothers from working-class backgrounds whose own mothers had died when they were between five and eleven years old, and who had at least one child between the ages of one and ten. Zall assumed that women who'd lost mothers during childhood would have a poor sense of themselves as parents, would perceive their children as having emotional and behavioral problems, and would view the lack of a maternal role model as a major influence on their experience as parents.

That third assumption was the only one that turned out to be true. None of the motherless mothers Zall met saw themselves as poor parents, and they didn't see their children as problematic, either. But in those interviews, and others he conducted later, Zall uncovered distinct parenting traits the women shared. These included an overprotective parenting style; an increased determination to be a good mother; an emphasis on cherishing time with their children; and a belief in the fragility of life.

These same topics appeared—and reappeared—in the seventy-eight one-on-one interviews I conducted for this book. On living-room couches, in hotel meeting-rooms, in crowded urban cafés, I heard women of diverse backgrounds and accomplishments talk about their intense fears of leaving their children motherless, their efforts to keep their children happy and safe, and about how the caring they had lost influenced the caring they were now trying so hard to provide. It soon became clear to me that even though many of these motherless daughters felt they had lost their guide for parenting, most of them had relied on their experiences of loss or abandonment to create a set of guiding principles they then relied on as mothers.

Eight themes appeared in so many of these interviews, and with such similarity across racial, ethnic, and socioeconomic lines, that I began to call them the "Eight Themes of Motherless Mothers." They are:

1. A strong desire to reactivate the mother-child relationship, while consciously acknowledging that this time one would be approaching the connection from the opposite direction

2. A concern about not knowing how to "be a mother," particularly with regard to raising a child beyond the age one was when mother loss occurred

3. An intense preoccupation with the possibility that they, the child, or the spouse might suffer an untimely death

4. A parenting style, often labeled "overprotective," which involves trying to shield the child from physical or emotional harm, restricting the child's behavior to keep him or her safe, and worrying excessively about the child's happiness and security

5. A commitment to being a good mother by being both emotionally and physically available to the child, and in many cases becoming the mother one lost or never had

6. Difficulty tolerating a child's feelings of sadness, anger, grief, or loneliness, which often activate the earlier memory

of these feelings during the mother's own childhood or adolescence

7. A sensitivity toward age-correspondence events, such as reaching a mother's age at time of death or having an eldest or same-sex child reach the age one was when the loss occurred

8. The belief that having and raising a child has been an unparalleled healing experience with regard to the ongoing mourning process

These themes are at the very core of what it means to be a motherless mother, and I've written about them all in this book. But because *Motherless Mothers* is meant to be a parenting book rather than a bereavement book, chapter 1 is the only place where mourning for a lost mother is discussed. The rest of the text follows a chronological parenting experience, starting with pregnancy and new motherhood, then moving through sections about the first four years of motherhood, raising school-age kids, and parenting teenagers and young adults.

Along the way, I've tried to address the very specific practical and emotional questions readers are most likely to ask, such as: What triggers might I encounter at each of my child's developmental stages, and how can I best manage them? How much parenting (in an attempt to protect my children) is too much? How little (in an attempt to ensure their independence, and therefore their survival without me) is too little? What issues are likely to come up with my mother-in-law? What role does my need for control play in my family's life? How might my parenting be affected if my mother is still alive but was emotionally or mentally impaired during my childhood? How might my kids be affected by my attitudes toward life and death? And, perhaps most important of all, how can I make sure my parenting isn't about me and what I feel I missed, but about my children and their unique needs?

To first identify and then answer these questions, I spent three years interviewing women who had lost mothers to death, abandonment, or impairment before their own children were born. I found these women through the mailing lists of Motherless Daughters organizations in Chicago; Detroit; San Francisco; Los Angeles; and Orange County, California; as well as through word of mouth and through an Internet site designed for motherless mothers. I spoke with Caucasian women, African-American women, Hispanic women, and Asian women; women who'd been raised by widowed fathers and stepmothers, by grandparents or aunts and uncles, in foster care and in orphanages; women who grew up in the United States, Mexico, Cuba, France, and England; women who'd been married for two years and for fifty years; women raising biological children along with stepchildren; single mothers who'd raised children on public assistance; and upper-middle-class mothers of five. The majority of interviewees were white, college-educated women in their thirties and forties, although the interviews included women of various ages, educational backgrounds, and childbearing experience. Although I placed no upper limit on a woman's age at the time of mother loss, requiring only that it occurred before her first child was born, the vast majority of interviewees were younger than twenty when their mothers died or left the family.

In addition to the interviews, which were done almost exclusively in person, I conducted a worldwide Internet survey of 1,322 motherless mothers, and a comparison survey of 73 mothers who had not experienced early mother loss.* The latter group helped me learn which behaviors and characteristics were unique to motherless mothers, and which were shared by all mothers. And I spoke extensively with two dozen experts in the fields of parenting, bereavement, childbirth, psychology, psychiatry, and sociology, all of

---

* Because of the problems inherent in comparing a very large group with a smaller one, whenever I needed to examine how motherless mothers are similar to or different from the control group, I compared all 73 control-group responses with 73 randomly selected responses from the larger Motherless Mothers Survey pool.

whom generously shared their insights about this particular parenting group.

There is no single, uniform mothering experience, not even among a group of women who share so many of the same thoughts, triumphs, and fears. The parenting stories I heard varied across cultures and ethnicities, and maternal behavior often changed character over time as new children entered the family and as all the children grew. Some women were close to their children; others had strained or even nonexistent relationships with them. Some women had been close with their mothers and referenced them frequently; others spoke bitterly of their mothers or hardly remembered them at all.

To write this book, I've needed to find the similarities among the women I interviewed, while at the same time acknowledging their differences. While many motherless mothers share a distinctive set of behaviors and concerns—some of which are shared by other mothers, some of which are not—each woman is also the product of other life experiences and cultural influences that predate or are unrelated to early mother loss. Sorting out which present-day behaviors were the probable effect of lost maternal care and which probably were not has been one of the most challenging aspects of writing this book.

It's been equally challenging to find the right balance between emphasizing the differences between motherless mothers and their peers, and pointing out the similarities. Although my data indicate that motherless mothers are more intense and focused on certain subjects than other mothers are, I don't want to overpathologize them as a group. These are determined, committed mothers with a special set of sensitivities, not a group of women with problems they can't overcome. At the same time, stressing how similar they are to other mothers in many ways doesn't accurately convey the degree to which these women stand out as a unique population. Ultimately, I decided that instead of writing a book about motherless mothers, with a goal of explaining how different they are from other women,

I would think of this as a book for motherless women, who already have a sense of how and when their behavior differs from others around them.

Writing *Motherless Mothers*, like writing that single chapter in *Motherless Daughters*, has been a weighty intellectual task, but this time I've had the benefit of eight years of parenting experience from which to draw. Eight years. It is a lifetime. It is nothing at all. It has spanned the hugest learning curve in my life, and yet, after eight years, I'm often stunned by how much more there still is to learn.

Only now I have teachers. Among the women interviewed for this book, I found my most relevant and sympathetic role models for parenting and my most educated guides. Women like Cleo, a mother of four, who told me how she and her husband co-slept with their children because it broke her heart to hear a child cry out for its mother in the night, and who helped me feel all right about doing the same. Bethany, whose thoughtful responses to her eight-year-old son's questions about his missing grandmother gave me a template for answering those questions myself. And Ruth, a seasoned mother of three, who maintains that 90 percent of successful mothering is having a good attitude and showing up, and whose cheerful, matter-of-fact approach to parenting has helped me lighten up. A lot.

These women understand what I mean when I tell them that motherhood has done more than mature me. It's repaired and restored something essential inside me. For many years, I was stuck in an ongoing adolescent battle with the memory of my mother, frozen in time at the emotional age I was when she died. Separating from her and establishing myself as an autonomous woman was a paramount goal throughout my twenties and into my thirties, just as it had been at seventeen. But motherhood has reunited us in a way I never expected, allowing me to see the world through a set of eyes more similar to hers. Only now can I understand how much she must have loved her three children, and how devastated she must have been to leave us. It explains a great deal about the relentless optimism and the blatant denial she relied on to face her disease. Who knows? I might do the same if I thought it could buy me and my daughters just a few more days.

Motherhood clearly isn't for everyone. I offer no illusions here. It's a noisy and messy and uncompromising enterprise, and it requires a selflessness more extreme than any reasonable person should have to bear. On the days when Maya screams "You're a mean, bad, *mean mother*!" and slams her bedroom door in my face, or when Eden wakes me three times during the night and I can barely drag myself through the following day, I'm almost ready to admit defeat. Almost. But on those other days, when the three of us are driving south on Pacific Coast Highway with the *Shrek* CD blasting out of our open windows, Maya and I shouting the words to "I'm a Believer," and Eden dancing uninhibitedly in her car seat, with the whole Southern California coastline arcing out before us in all of its promise and splendor, I look in the rearview mirror and see my two girls laughing, and—finally, blessedly, completely—my world is right again.

Motherless
Mothers

1

Motherhood and Mourning

THE POWER TO HEAL

*I*t's 7:40 A.M., and the house is cranked up to full volume. We've got twenty minutes till Maya and Uzi have to leave for the bus stop, then another half hour before I drive Eden down to preschool. Between now and then, I've got a snack bag and a lunchbox to prepare, a backpack to fill, breakfast dishes to rinse, two kids and one adult to dress, and two heads of hair to brush. Three, if you include mine, but sometimes that one gets skipped.

"Mom!" Maya shouts from upstairs. "Where are my pink high-tops?"

"In the basket by the front door! Bring a hair clip when you come down!"

Uzi walks down the stairs, rubbing his freshly shaved chin. He stops in front of Eden's chair and kisses her on the top of her head.

"Twenty minutes," I tell him.

"You need help with that?" He nods toward the array of bread and turkey breast slices and condiments spread across the kitchen counter. I consider the offer. If he makes Eden's lunch, I can brew a cup of tea for myself. Otherwise, I won't bother. But I'm the one who knows exactly how to cut the crust off Eden's bread, and how many slices of turkey to use. Those are the details mothers know. From first through eleventh grade, my mother made my sandwich every morning. That's what mothers do.

"I'll do it," I say.

"Have you seen my wallet?" Uzi asks.

"It's probably still in your pants from yesterday."

Maya catapults into the kitchen, pink high-top sneakers on her feet. "Mom!" she says. "Where's my hair clip with the gold bow on it?"

"On the counter in your bathroom, where you left it last night."

Homework. Snack bag. Backpack. The gold barrette, a zip-up sweatshirt, a good-bye kiss for Uzi and they're out the door. I lift Eden out of her chair and shift her to my right hip.

"Made it," I say.

"Made it," she says.

"Whew," I say.

"Whoo," she says.

When I went to school in a New York suburb, the bus picked me up at 8:05 A.M. Every morning, when I walked out the door at 8:04, I stopped on the front step and stuck my head back inside for a final good-bye. It was a little ritual I had.

"Mom!" I'd shout. "Good-bye!"

"Have a good day!" she'd call back from inside.

If she told me to have a good day, I had a good day. If she didn't, my day turned out bad. I'm still not quite sure how that worked, but it was true.

Now I'm the mother left in the sudden vacuum of silence when a child leaves for school. How can that be, when I'm still the daughter stuck in the good-bye?

Eden and I stand quietly in the living room and listen to the soft ticking of the kitchen clock. It's not over yet.

We hear the explosion of noise before we see her. The front door bursts open and Maya hurls herself into the room, a four-foot cyclone of brown curls and pink sneakers and Helly Kitty backpack.

"Mom!" she gasps, making an urgent beeline for us. "I forgot hug and kiss."

I lean down so she can grab my neck. We kiss on the mouth, and she plants one on Eden's forehead. "Bye," she says, hurrying back out the door.

"Have a great day!" I call after her.

"Bye, Maya!" Eden shouts.

"I will!" Maya yells from the front path.

Uzi opens the car's back door for her and I watch them drive off between the palm trees that line our driveway. It's more than two thousand feet down to the bus stop on Pacific Coast Highway, a fifteen-minute drive. When I was a kid, the bus stopped right in front of our house. And palm trees! To get to the nearest palm tree, we had to take a three-hour flight.

Eden and I wave through the window as Uzi's car winds down the hill and out of sight. Every morning it's the same routine. And every morning it ends with the same sweet, odd feeling of wonder, how in this house in the Santa Monica mountains, this place of wildfires and hot tubs and no snow, my California daughters manage to bring the best parts of my mother right back to me.

What is it about motherhood that's so healing for a motherless daughter, mending something inside her in a place deeper than scalpels or medication or therapy can reach? Many of the women interviewed for this book spoke of motherhood as an experience that restored their equilibrium, their self-esteem, or their faith. "Having my kids is like discovering the missing link," explains thirty-five-year-old Sharon, a mother of two who was eleven when her own mother died. "There's a completeness in my life that wasn't there before."

"The first time my son put his hand in my hand when we were

walking," remembers thirty-eight-year-old Corinne, who lost both parents by age eleven, "and the first time he ran to me and threw his arms around my neck, showing that he preferred me over anyone else, for him to love me back so uninhibitedly and unconditionally, filled some part of me that I didn't expect would ever be filled again."

It paints a rosy view of motherhood, but there's more than just a simple idealization going on here—although God knows our culture tacks enough of that onto mothers these days. For these daughters, motherhood is the final repair in their process of mourning and recovery from early mother loss. What was broken in their pasts is once again made whole; what was subtracted has been added back again.

When motherhood interfaces with the long-term mourning process, the result is exponential. Becoming a mother can give a motherless daughter access to a more enhanced, more insightful, deeper, richer, and, in some cases, ultimate phase of mourning for her mother, one that may initially be painful but eventually leads her to a more mature and peaceful acceptance of both her loss and herself.

Bereavement experts now recognize mourning as a fluid, cyclical, and lifelong process rather than a rigid four- or five-step path to recovery like those popularized in the 1970s and 1980s. While most adult mourners do pass through discrete stages of anger, denial, disorganization, and reorganization immediately following a loss, it isn't a one-time deal. This same sequence of emotions is likely to recycle and repeat at various, specific, and often predictable points in the future when the loved one is missed.

Children, on the other hand, don't go through a structured mourning process after a parent dies. Instead, they mourn in bits and pieces scattered throughout childhood and adolescence as their emotional and cognitive abilities mature. A girl who loses a mother at age seven isn't yet capable of thinking about death abstractly, and can't tolerate the kind of intense emotion a fourteen-year-old might be able to handle. That seven-year-old is more likely to have periodic grief reactions throughout the teen years as she becomes better able to understand and process new aspects of the loss over time. Likewise, it's impossible for a sixteen-year-old high school student to mourn a lost mother from the perspective of a mother or a wife. It might take her another fifteen years to marry and have a child and develop those points of view. That's why so many motherless daughters report having intense grief episodes after the births of their first children. You can't mourn *as* a motherless mother until you *are* a motherless mother.

This type of emotional resurgence is called a STUG reaction, an acronym for Subsequent, Temporary Upsurge of Grief. During the adult years, STUGs are usually stimulated when a reminder—such as a date, a piece of information, or a significant event—ushers in a new realization of what was lost, lifting the mourner to a level of awareness she wasn't able to reach before. When STUGs result from life-cycle events (such as marriage or motherhood) or from new experiences (such as divorce or illness), they're considered a form of "maturational grief." Transitions such as these often trigger a wish to regress and be cared for, and the longing for a lost mother can be intense and painful at these times. Instead of being labeled pathological, as they once were, STUGs are now considered universal for bereaved persons, especially those who lost a parent at an early age. They're also considered beneficial in the long term. Because STUGs allow women to work on the loss from new and different angles over time, they're considered a healthy mechanism for working through grief.

Painful as they are, these upsurges won't leave you stuck in a bad place, assures J. William Worden, PhD, the co–principal investigator of the landmark Harvard Child Bereavement Study and the author of several books, including *Children and Grief*. "They process pieces of unfinished business for you," he explains. "These feelings are important to pay attention to, and it can be useful to indulge in them and see what thought or image or memory they take you to."

Unfortunately, when STUGs coincide with new motherhood, they arrive at a terribly inconvenient time. The postpartum period is enough of an upheaval without adding grief to the mix. If a woman feels that she just can't handle a grief reaction at this time, Worden suggests she try "bracketing" off the feelings for a while. "Bracketing isn't a bad thing to do in a case when following the feelings [of grief] would make you less competent with your child," Worden says. "Instead, you need to acknowledge these are important feelings, but recognize this isn't the time to deal with them." Later, when circumstances change or when emotional equilibrium returns, the daughter can revisit the distress and work through it then.

One of the biggest paradoxes of the long-term mourning process is that when you allow yourself to feel the pain of separation and loss, you often wind up feeling more connected to the lost loved one when you're done. That's one reason why a missing mother can feel so present and so absent at the same time. Longing for her brings memories of time spent together into sharper focus, and she's in the forefront of your consciousness once more.

"Becoming a mother is the way, par excellence, to have a sense of connectedness with your mother again," says Therese Rando, PhD, a bereavement counselor in Warwick, Rhode Island, and the author of several books, including *How to Go On Living When Someone You Love Dies*. Rando speaks from both professional and personal experience: she lost both parents in her teens and is now the mother of two young children. "Identifying with your mother, as a mother, is part of the experience, but it's more than that," she says. "There's also a sense of participating in this mother-child bond that is so special. And if we felt that bond once, when we feel it again—even if it's as a mother instead of as a child—it's a very fulfilling experience. That helps with the mourning, not because it brings deeper sadness but because it brings a sense of . . . does it sound too spiritual to say a sense of communion? Communion with someone you've loved and who you think loved you in a good way."

Most psychologists agree that the mother-child bond is the most primal and essential bond a human can experience, and its loss is one of the most emotionally painful events a child can endure. There's been little discussion, however, about the impact that re-creating this bond has on a parent. Most mother-child research focuses on the effect mothers have on children, rather than on how mothers are affected by their children, creating the impression that a woman's psychological growth has already been completed before her children were born.

Developmental theorists, however, believe otherwise. Life, they say, is a continuous process of change and adaptation, in which major adult milestones such as marriage, parenthood, retirement, and widowhood allow our personalities and self-concepts to con-tinuously evolve. Every mother knows that parenthood changes you in fundamental, dramatic ways. Once you've pushed a child into the world or been wholly responsible for an infant's survival, how could it not?

Pregnancy, childbearing, and child-raising transform all mothers, but for motherless mothers, motherhood and mourning are likely to be intertwined. When motherhood ushers in a new stage of healing, it's usually for one or more of the reasons described below.

Repairing the Story

Before motherhood, a mo
before-and-after quality: al
all that has come after. M
frame around the loss. Fir
then she became a mother
story in two. Motherhood r

A break in the middle of
ruption," explains Brown
PhD, which causes someon
tional, linear life story most

interviewed sixty motherless men and women for her 2000 book *Motherless*, she found that not only were these individuals' daily lives disrupted when their mothers died, but that they also constructed their narratives in a way that conveyed something had gone tragically wrong with their stories.

Davidman noticed, however, that these sons and daughters were trying to fix their disrupted stories—a process called "biographical repair"—by taking action both at the real-life level, such as having families of their own, and at the narrative level, by talking about how they'd tried to fix the break. For more than half of Davidman's interviewees, particularly the women, having children and nurturing them was a powerful form of biographical repair.

"It was a way of recreating what they had lost," Davidman says. "And what they said they'd lost was a 'nice, happy family.' By trying to recreate family, they were repairing precisely what had been taken away." Mother love, which had been abruptly removed from these women's stories, reappeared as a central theme when they became mothers themselves. "It's not a perfect reproduction," Davidman explains, "because you're obviously not getting mother love. Your mom is gone. But in reenacting what she gave you, or the idealization of what she gave you, you bring it forth again. Not precisely, but nonetheless overall."

Twenty-eight-year-old Samantha, who lost her mother to cancer when she was twenty-three, deeply mourned the loss of their close mother-daughter bond. A few months later, she became pregnant with her first child. She remembers the moment she first learned news.

as really happy, but I also felt a wave of relief for the first my mom died," she explains. "A mother-child relation- ing in my life, and I thought the only way I'm going nship again is to be on the other side of it. I won't get the relationship back. I thought that maybe it would fill the void of that relationship. nd again with someone. Now I have two sons, and my bonds with them are stronger than any other relationships I have in my life. It's not with daughters, and I'm on the flip side of it, but it's as close as I'm going to get, or maybe a little closer if I have a daughter one day."

Does a motherless daughter have to become a mother to experience this form of repair? Not necessarily. Davidman discovered that adults who had chosen not to have children or who didn't yet have children found other ways to fix their stories. Breaking the silence that surrounded a loss—either through talking about it or by getting other family members to talk—helped many of her interview subjects. Giving lost mothers a symbolic presence by visiting the grave regularly, displaying photographs or cherished items, and performing family religious rituals were other common forms of repair. Nurturing nieces and nephews, students, pets, or clients also brought forth a maternal element that had been missing in these women's lives for so long.

Reactivating the Original Connection

It's nearly impossible for a motherless daughter to go through pregnancy or enter motherhood without thinking about her own mother's experiences. Did she have morning sickness? Did it hurt her to hear her infant cry?

Most motherless daughters didn't get the chance to relate to their mothers as women. They knew them only as mothers, from a daughter's point of view. But motherhood creates an avenue for a new and expanded relationship with one's mother. The relationship, frozen in time when the mother died, becomes dynamic again as the daughter consults with her mother in memory and imagines the kind of updated relationship they might have shared as mothers and as peers.

"Most people are not confronted on a regular basis with the kinds of triggers that allow memories to surface," Maxine Harris says. "So, the time you had with your mother sometimes feels very lost. One thing that happens when you parent a child is that you're immersed in a world of triggers, where lots of things call up little fragments of memory. It becomes a way for a woman to realize she still has much more connection to her mother than she imagined."

After a woman becomes a mother, she never sees her own mother in quite the same way again. The "Why did she do this?" and "Why didn't she do that?" accusations of the daughter are replaced by the "Ah, that's why she did it" and "So *that's* why she didn't do that" awareness of the mother. More (or, in some cases, less) of her behavior is understood. More (or fewer) of her actions are forgiven.

More than half of all women surveyed, motherless and not, said they had more admiration for their mothers after becoming mothers themselves. More than 40 percent also said they had more sympathy for their mothers now. Fewer than 5 percent of both groups said they had either less admiration or less sympathy for their mothers, who should have done a better job. For some women, motherhood offers the first opportunity in years, even decades, for a long-held image of the mother to ripen and mature.

The majority of new mothers can discuss these new opinions of their mothers *with* their mothers, or can adjust their behaviors to reflect their new point of view. Motherless daughters, however, lacking that kind of direct contact, have to integrate this new awareness with memory. This can be a particular challenge for women who were younger than twelve when their mothers died, since they hadn't yet reached the teenage years, when a mother usually gets toppled from her pedestal.

"For twenty years I thought of my mother as this strong, larger-than-life character," says twenty-nine-year-old Lauren, who was eight when her mother died. "Now I've got this baby, and I realize how little a mother actually knows at first. You can only learn it by doing it. And I realize how my mother must also have felt this overwhelmed and incompetent once. So, I've had to find a way to fit that in with this other image I've always had of her as this all-powerful and all-knowing woman. It's taken some getting used to, but I actually feel closer to her now."

Women who were adolescents when their mothers died often have a different response, especially when their mother-daughter relationship was halted at a time of conflict or turmoil. Until I became a mother, I had no idea—let me emphasize, *no idea*—what it takes to keep just one child happy and safe, let alone three. When I was single and professional, I thought of my mother as a woman who abandoned her true self when she left teaching to raise her children. Now, with two daughters of my own, I think of her managing a household and a family of five, full-time, without losing her mind, and she's one step short of heroic to me.

That's one thing motherhood does for you. It completely revises your history.

It also knocks your mother down to the level of mortal woman, with hopes and dreams and fears of her own. And once she's down there with you, it's impossible to view the loss just from the position of abandoned daughter anymore.

For thirty-eight-year-old Trudy, this new perspective sparked an additional phase of mourning for a mother she barely knew. Trudy was only three months old when her mother died in a car accident. Afterward, she was raised for several years by her grandparents and a great-aunt, and then by her father and a stepmother who abused her. No one spoke about her mother, perhaps assuming that because Trudy was so young the loss would hardly affect her. As a result, Trudy was never able to grieve for her mother as a child or adolescent.

"I didn't grieve for my mother until I was in my early thirties," Trudy explains. "And then I got married and had my daughter, and I grieved for her all over again as a mother."

This second wave of grief was triggered when Trudy was involved in a near-fatal car accident herself. The car rolled over three times into a ditch on a major highway, and one of the passengers was badly injured. Trudy's daughter, at the time, was just five months old.

"I really feel I was given a second chance to be the mother I never had," she says. "But the accident made me grieve for my mother from the position of a mother. I realized I was getting the opportunity she didn't get, to see my daughter grow up." Trudy suddenly became aware of all her mother had lost when she died, and discovered she needed to mourn for this woman, too—a woman who was now, in her mind, very much like her.

This new, internal relationship with a mother, healing as it may be, is never more than second best to the real thing. When a motherless mother sees her friends interacting on a more adult level with their living mothers, she wishes she could do that herself. At toddlers' birthday parties, she can barely stand to look at grandmas snapping photos or passing around the cake. *Why don't my children have that?* she wonders. *Why don't I?* The long-term mourning process isn't just about mourning for what was actually lost. It's also about mourning for what never got to be.

Replacing Lost Care

I was one of the lucky ones. I had a solid, reliable mother for seventeen years. Then I lost her for the next sixteen. I didn't even realize how lost she was to me until my first child was born. And then my mother quietly reappeared, a constant, silent presence in the nursery. And it calmed me. When I took good care of Maya, it often felt as if my mother were simultaneously taking care of me.

Quite a bit has been written about "the reproduction of mothering," the process by which new mothers subconsciously and automatically replicate the infant-care behaviors they received when they were very young. According to psychoanalysts such as Melanie Klein and Nancy Chodorow, the memory of being lovingly cared for as a newborn—assuming one was lovingly cared for as a newborn— remains encoded inside us all until our own children are born, when it's then summoned up and transferred into action.

This can be particularly comforting to women who were very young when their mothers died or left, and who have no conscious memories of her care. "We remember in so many different ways, not just in words and images," Maxine Harris explains. "We also remember with our bodies. If your child squirms and you lean into her and cuddle her a certain way, that bodily expression is actually a memory. You can feel tremendously comforted by a sensation that really is a connection to a mother you may have only known for a couple of years."

For many motherless women, the experience of caring for one's child also doubles as a form of self-care. When I put antibacterial cream and a Band-Aid on Eden's knee, I'm doing more than administering first aid. Being an attentive, loving mother brings the spirit of an attentive, loving mother into the room, one who simultaneously nurtures the childlike self that had to manage without adequate nurturing in the past.

"It's similar to the kind of reparative work I might have someone who was abused as a child do in my office," J. William Worden says. "The adult goes back and renurtures that little kid inside. The difference is that motherless mothers aren't doing it in an office. They're doing it with their own progeny."

That's what Elsa experienced after her son was born. Elsa, now fifty-nine, was nine when her mother died of cancer. Her childhood ended that day. She was thrust into the role of caretaker for her younger brother and sister, and she never felt protected or cared for in her childhood home again.

"My father was completely damaged by it all," Elsa recalls. "His mother died when he was two. Then he got married and had three kids and his wife died. He was completely *damaged*. So he was not very helpful with our raising. We were sort of like wild children. I would sign my own report cards, and I drove the car for years without a license. He never noticed I didn't have one."

Elsa married at twenty to escape her father's household, and gave birth to her son four years later. Taking care of him as a small child and setting boundaries for him as a teenager, giving him the structure she never had and allowing him to have a full, complete childhood, gratified her enormously, she says. "Looking back, I see that the things I did for him made me feel . . . like nurtured, too, somehow," Elsa explains. "I could be my own mother, in a certain way."

Any mother who looks at her child can't help seeing a younger version of herself, but a motherless mother who looks at her child first sees the version that needed protection, attention, and love. Her parenting is informed by her opinion of what a child needs in order to thrive—which is usually what she lost, or never received from the start—and that's what she prioritizes above all else.

"The mom that I always wanted was the mom I made sure my daughter had," admits fifty-five-year-old Louise, who was six when her mother died. Louise went on school trips, helped with homework, volunteered as her daughter's Girl Scout troop leader, and put a great deal of thought into every parenting decision she made. "Everyone told me I was the model mother, because I was so committed and so devoted and so involved in her life," Louise says. "I think my daughter would beg to differ with that," she adds with a laugh. "In some respects, I think I was the mother my daughter wanted, and in other respects, I probably wasn't. She's said she didn't have enough independence. It's hard for me to sort it all out. I think there's something natural about a daughter wishing her mother had been a different way, but that's something I can't really understand. The only thing I ever wished was that my mother were *alive*."

Thirty-five-year-old Christine was also six when her mother died, but unlike Louise, Christine is at the very beginning of her parenting journey. Her two daughters are just four and one. Christine chose to leave her corporate position and become a full-time mother after her first child was born. Her primary goal as a parent is to be available and attentive, like the mother she remembers, who died of cancer almost thirty years ago.

Christine, the fourth of six children, has vivid early memories of her mother sewing most of their clothing, cooking meals from scratch, and gardening outside. Before her mother's illness became terminal, their family was close and happy, Christine recalls, and the children felt secure. Then their safe world turned upside down.

After their mother died, the children were supervised by a series of housekeepers during the day, and nominally cared for by their father at night. "Dad would get home and the housekeeper would leave," she remembers. "There would be dinner on the table, but it wasn't a nanny situation. It was definitely 'I've done my job, now I'm going home.' And my father would have his dinner. He would be worn out. I think he had a second job on the side. And then he hit the bottle, starting at seven at night. So, I was six years old, putting myself to bed, brushing my teeth and washing up, getting myself up in the morning. The last housekeeper left when I was in third grade and my youngest brother was in school full-time. So, you can imagine, you're in third grade and one day a week now you're responsible for making dinner."

Christine remembers this portion of her childhood as a lonely time, buffered only by her close bond with her younger sister and brother. During high school, she developed a close friendship with a teacher, but no one ever stepped in with the kind of attention to detail and degree of commitment she felt a mother would have provided.

Even when a motherless daughter's basic childhood needs for food and shelter are met, chances are good that no one will notice which vegetables she likes, or whether her underwear still fits. Yet when someone does pay attention to the small details of her welfare, a child absorbs the message that *all* her needs are important and, by extension, that she is valued and that she matters. Christine knows this from experience, because that's the type of emotional security she lost when her mother became gravely ill and died.

In her house now, Christine is the Goddess of Small Things, the one who notices and catalogues tiny details, because those were the ones overlooked when she was a child. "Sometimes I get annoyed with my husband because he'll just slap food on the table," she admits. "And I'll say, 'No. They like this much cream cheese, and no more.' When I pick Kyra up from school, she likes her milk hot in a sippy cup, and when she gets in the van and sees the sippy cup sitting in the holder next to her chair, she gets this huge smile on her face. And I think, 'Oh, *God*, I'm *so glad* that made you happy, that little thing.'

"When I open Kyra's closet and her clothes are all lined up and they're clean, when I know what she had for breakfast and that she has a healthy diet, it makes me feel so good inside," Christine continues. "She's right at that age, four and a half, when things started getting really bad for me. That's when clothes weren't getting washed and I wasn't being taken care of anymore. I tell my husband, 'I do for Kyra and Melanie what wasn't done for me.' If that means I have to sacrifice this or that, well, it's not a sacrifice. Because by giving them what I didn't get, I'm actually giving to myself. That sharp, pointed edge of pain is finally getting worn down and rounded off. The best therapy in the world is to be able to raise a child and give that child what you didn't get."

Revisiting the Past

The images, even more than thirty years later, are so vivid they can still make me cringe. A pair of silver scissors. A young female hairdresser. My mother's tightly compressed lips reflected in the mirror. And a mound of my brown hair suddenly lying in dark contrast against the white tile floor.

It was, to an eight-year-old, the ultimate betrayal. When I wasn't looking, my mother had silently snipped the hair at the base of her own neck. The hairdresser glanced at the tangled mess hanging halfway down my back, saw the small, ragged section where we'd recently cut out a piece of gum, and knew what to do. By the time I started screaming, I was halfway to a pixie cut. When it was over, I looked like a nearsighted elf. I wore a ski hat to school for two weeks.

My older daughter, Maya, has inherited the same kind of hair I had as a child: fine, curly, and prone to truly sensational knots. I know now why my mother gave up. It's a battle every morning to get a brush all the way through.

"Ow!" she cries, trying to swat my hands away.

"I'm almost done," I lie. Every morning she puts her hands on top of her head to block me. Every morning I apologize and offer the same lame excuse about how this hurts me as much as it does her.

Sometimes, to deflect her attention, I tell her the story about how my mother told the hairdresser to cut off all my hair. The subtext, of course, is, *I could, but never would, do that to you.* Which is true. Because as close as I might come to wanting to, I would never unilaterally decide to cut my daughter's hair. First, because she doesn't want it cut. Second, because every morning that Maya boards the school bus with her hair neatly brushed is a small victory for me, one more step toward loosening that knot of anxiety from my past. Every morning, I get to be both the eight-year-old in the salon chair and the mother who—this time—keeps her hands by her side.

Psychoanalyst Therese Benedek was the first to propose that experiences like this are what make parenthood a developmental phase in its own right. It's not just the experience of caring for an infant that matures a parent, she said. It's also the experience of reliving our own childhoods, piece by piece, as we watch our children grow. According to Benedek, a unique type of psychological transaction takes place between mothers and their children, especially when children reach "critical periods" of maturation, such as the first day of school or the onset of puberty. At those moments, the mother's lingering conflicts from parallel moments in her own past are revived, which gives her the opportunity to rework her own emotional knots. This time, however, she gets to do it from an adult perspective, applying all the insights and experiences she accumulated between then and now.

If the mother's feelings from that time in her own childhood are still deeply unresolved, she may be unable to help her child. She may even act out or withdraw when the child reaches those trigger points. But more often, the mother is able to work through her residual feelings of sadness, bitterness, or grief from the same juncture in her past. In this respect, parenthood is more than just an opportunity to rewrite history. It's a chance to revisit and repair it in real time.

"Having a child is the only form of time travel I've ever experienced," says Michael Schwartzman, PhD, a clinical psychologist in New York City who specializes in parent-child relations. "The line I use for this—and it sounds a little spiritual, although I don't mean it that way—is that God gives us children to help us resolve our own issues. That's why adolescence is such a provocative time for parents, because so much of what's unresolved in ourselves goes back to that period."

For a motherless mother, this will mean revisiting times when a mother's presence was missed, such as a first menstruation, a school graduation, or a special birthday. Another critical period occurs when a child, particularly an oldest daughter, reaches the age a woman was when her mother died or left. This type of anniversary event, as it's called, reactivates whatever feelings—shock, anger, sadness, grief—the mother had at that age and may not have been able to express at that time.

Smoothing out these past emotional bumps may not be an easy process. Sometimes a child's developmental crisis opens up a mother's emotional lockbox, and the sensations that fly out are too intense for her to master on her own. That's when therapists, support groups, a compassionate spouse, or close friends are needed. Women who didn't have this support, or didn't feel comfortable calling upon it, have reported stuffing the feelings back into the box until a later date, or sinking into a depression that ultimately led them to seek help.

While both sons and daughters can guide a mother back to unresolved moments in her past, daughters typically give mothers a more direct route to their own childhoods. That's because so many of a child's maturational events are defined by gender. A daughter's puberty, menstruation, the onset of dating and sexual activity, and her transitions to wife and mother can all trigger a mother's engendered memories and lingering emotions from those times.

Forty-two-year-old Alma, who was ten when her mother died of cancer, remembers her teenage years, first spent living with an aunt and uncle, then with her father and stepmother, as a period of self-enforced independence. "My attitude, from the moment I left the hospital after my mother died, was 'No one's going to help me, no one's going to teach me, whatever I need to learn I'll try to figure out myself,'" she recalls. Her first menstruation at age thirteen was a time of bitter pride. She missed her mother desperately, yet she insisted she could handle the rite of passage herself.

Today, Alma is the mother of three daughters, ages fourteen, twelve, and five. She's especially close to her oldest daughter, Chelsea, who recently got her period for the first time. "She was in Florida visiting some relatives, and she must have called me five or six times every day until she got home," Alma says. "And I thought, 'I'm so glad I'm there for her.' Because it was such a terrible time for me. I was so independent, and acting like I didn't need anyone."

Supporting her daughters through their rites of passage has been deeply meaningful for Alma. But it has an unexpected consequence: it's sent her back into the mindset of the stubborn, proud teenager she once was, and the loneliness and confusion from those years started bubbling to the surface again. "From watching my daughters grow up, I'm learning a lot about the kid I was and what that kid missed," Alma says. "It's been good, but it's been hard, too. It makes me very sad. Very sad. I grew up thinking, 'I'm okay. I can handle everything. I can figure out everything.' I realize now what a fight I put up all those years."

At the time we spoke, Alma had recently started seeing a therapist to work through this profound sadness. She had started keeping a journal of her feelings and memories, and was talking more freely about her childhood than she'd been able to before.

"Having children puts you in touch with your childhood in a way that not having children prevents you from ever achieving," Terry Rando says. "It allows you to go back and look at things, to rework them and do them differently this time." Through parenting our children, we revisit the time of loss and the years that followed. Because of them, we get a chance to mourn differently—more maturely and more completely—the second time around.

Stepmothering

Of all women in the Motherless Mothers Survey, 23 percent were either separated, divorced, or in a second or subsequent marriage. For some of these women, stepparenting is, or will become, a reality. And about half of them will have had prior experience with stepmothers of their own, which will play into the background of the stepparenting decisions they make.

Thirty-seven-year-old Petra falls into that category. Petra was eleven and the oldest of three children when her mother died in a commercial airline crash. Three years later, her father married a woman Petra had met only once before. "At first, she made an effort and was pretty pleasant," Petra recalls. "There wasn't anything not to like right off the bat. But pretty quickly, she felt like she had to impose discipline and order on the house. My father had given me a credit card to use when I needed to buy clothes, and that ended right away. And there were lots of chores. We'd kept the housekeeper we hired after my mother died, but my stepmother Xeroxed sheets with chores for us to do that were already being done by the housekeeper. So everything would get done twice. She got very rigid and controlling, and then she got pregnant within a year."

Petra remembers the next four years as full of conflict, anger, and overreactions. Her stepmother would get mad at Petra and her younger brothers and yell at their father for their behavior. He would then turn around and yell at the kids. "We were so afraid [in the house] that we never expressed emotion around them," Petra says. "It was never a safe place to be mad or to get sad. We were just always trying to keep someone from getting angry at us."

When, in her twenties, Petra married a man who had two young children from a previous marriage, she was determined to be a better stepmother than the one she'd had. She transposed what she could remember from her mother's parenting onto her role as step-mother, and used her stepmother as an example of what not to do. She got to know her stepchildren slowly, encouraged her husband to take a more active, involved role in their lives, and never wanted to say anything negative about them.

"A lot of my approach toward them came from what my mom did," she says. "Getting involved in their school, making sure they had good teachers. I was at every parent-teacher conference and back-to-school night. And there were little things I used to do for them that my mom used to do for me. Like the first time we all went on vacation together, I said, 'We should make S'mores!' It was out of my mouth before I really had time to think about it, so I figured it must have been something she used to say to us."

One benefit of becoming a stepmother, as Petra discovered, was that she didn't have to wait two or three years for a baby to become old enough to enjoy the kind of activities she had once shared with her original family. Stepmotherhood gave her instant entry into a family that enjoyed spending time together, although they could do it only a few times a month. "I didn't really experience it as 'This is what it was like when I was little,' but it was an opportunity for me to go back into a positive family situation after so many years of being in a family full of conflict and anger," she says. "So, if I'm really honest about it, my effort wasn't only about helping them have a better relationship with their father, although that definitely was part of it, too."

But one of the drawbacks of stepmothering as a motherless

daughter, Petra admits, was how much she was influenced by the years that followed her father's second marriage. Petra became so focused on being a model stepmother, and thereby proving that her own stepmother had, in fact, been inadequate in the role, that she occasionally lost sight of what her stepchildren actually needed. She'd been trying to be the kind of stepmother she'd needed, and wished she'd had. But her stepchildren hadn't lost a mother to death and had a new woman thrust upon them in her role. They'd been separated from a father by divorce, and now had *two* women in a mothering role—a very different situation, requiring a different set of tactics. Petra also inadvertently created conflict with the children's mother, who bristled at the degree to which Petra wanted to be involved in their lives.

Six years ago, Petra gave birth to a son, and has since found additional healing as a motherless daughter through raising him. Nonetheless, she was able to resolve other parts of her childhood through stepparenting. Becoming a loving, involved stepmother, and experiencing the difficulties inherent in the role, helped her understand that her stepmother had problems of her own, not that she as a teenager had been unworthy of parental love.

Today, she retains close relationships with both her stepchildren, and she tries to be a stable, supportive influence in their lives. "I have a friend who has a stepdaughter," she says, "and she said to me, 'You know, I'm not really that invested in her.' And I couldn't relate to that. It's *really* important to me to be a good stepmother."

Grandmotherhood: Second-chance Mothering

Sixty-nine-year-old Natalie doesn't get prophetic about the healing aspects of motherhood. The thirty years she spent raising two sons and a daughter weren't easy for her. In fact, Natalie found parenting to be a difficult, challenging odyssey.

As a child, Natalie never lived with her own mother, who was in and out of sanitariums before dying of tuberculosis when Natalie was nine. Without any memories of maternal care to draw from, and with no support from family, Natalie often felt lost and unprotected as an adult. As a mother, she was confused and fearful, she says.

"I was so afraid about everything my children did," she recalls. "It was always 'Don't do that!' 'Don't hurt yourself!' 'You can't do that!' I was married to an alcoholic for forty years, and that didn't help the situation, either. My daughter tells me I wasn't a good mother, and that really hurts. That's why I say I've been given another chance with my grandchildren. Even though they don't live with me, I can give them the love of a grandmother. I see them as often as I can. I praise them and let them know how important they are to our lives. And I never criticize them. My children never had a grandmother on either side, but I can be one for my grandchildren."

Natalie's story isn't uncommon. To experience motherhood as healing, a woman needs to have mourned her loss to some degree, and some adult women haven't had the emotional support, the financial means, or the inner security to do this before their children arrive. These motherless daughters begin motherhood still consumed by their own unmet needs, or afraid to become emotionally vulnerable again. For these women, grandmotherhood rather than motherhood may be the maternal experience that allows them to reconnect with the children they once were, and to mourn more fully for the mothers they lost.

Like Natalie, fifty-four-year-old Carolyn describes herself as a loving grandmother. "I'm very loving with my grandkids," she says. "I'm more patient. I'm willing to take more time. I think this is true for all grandmothers, but it's especially true for me."

Carolyn's relationship with her thirty-five-year-old daughter, on the other hand, has been severely compromised by Carolyn's early family experiences. Carolyn was six years old when her mother, a victim of domestic violence, committed suicide, and she was then separated from her siblings and raised in a series of foster homes.

When we first met, Carolyn expressed concern that I was planning to write a book about how glorious motherhood is. It hadn't been glorious for her, she said. It had been difficult from the start.

"With all the violence in my home, I just didn't feel comfortable being a mother," she explains. "I was always anticipating more violence in my life, always thinking someone would be taken away from me. I was the mother who kept going up to the crib to make sure the baby was breathing. Also, I had never seen normal mother-child interaction. I didn't have a single, consistent role model. There wasn't a grandparent. There wasn't a father. So I just flat-out didn't know how to do it. I made it up as I went along and learned from my mistakes. My daughter is very angry with me for that. Even though logically she can say to me now, 'I understand you did the best you could do given the cards you were dealt,' emotionally she can't accept it."

Because Carolyn never had the opportunity as a child or teenager to mourn the loss of her original family, and because her loss was so dramatic and confusing to a child, she entered motherhood without solid emotional resources for parenting. By the time she started therapy and began revisiting those lost years, Carolyn was well into adulthood and her daughter was already grown.

"I think that *when* we finally get a chance to mourn or to express our grief has a lot to do with how we get on," she says. "I think I can have this close relationship with my grandchildren now because they came along after I started a lot of the grief work I've done. My daughter, unfortunately, came along before any of that got started."

I once told groups of women, "It's never too late to start mourning a mother." The number of stories I'd heard from eighty- and ninety-year-old women who'd only recently begun grieving indicated this was true. But in some respects, perhaps it *can* be too late to start mourning. It may, in fact, be too late for Carolyn and her daughter to repair their fractured emotional past. Carolyn's grandchildren, though, came along when she could offer them a nurturing relationship free of the anger and confusion that hijacked her mothering years. As a grandmother, she's able to express the kind of maternal love she couldn't express as a mother because she lost it so young herself.

It's 8:20 P.M. now, and we're getting the kids ready for bed. We're in that unpredictable transition zone between bathtime and tooth brushing, when stalling techniques tend to make themselves known. Any minute now, someone's going to insist on a sliced apple or a cup of water, or to start negotiating for the last ten minutes of *Crocodile Hunter* on TV.

Uzi takes Maya into her room for her pajamas, and I pull Eden's bedtime books from the shelf. When I open her bottom dresser-drawer, she takes off running down the hall. It's like this every night. She hides in my bedroom, I make a big show out of trying to find her, and then I toss her in the middle of my bed and wrestle her pajamas on. Every night she laughs like this is the funniest charade she's ever played.

When we make it to the bathroom, I hand Maya her Shamu toothbrush and the fennel-flavored toothpaste she likes best. Eden gets Care Bears, her special blue toothpaste for kids, and an empty cup she likes to fill and pour while she chews on the toothbrush. I try to sneak a spare toothbrush in to give her teeth one decent pass. Maya takes a mouthful of water, spits it out all over the faucet, and opens her mouth for inspection.

"Good job," I say.

It's back to Eden's room, where we read the same books every night. *Goodnight Moon*, which she calls "Hush and Mush," and *Peeka-boo Bugs* because she likes to lift the flaps.

Two books, one song, and Eden's in her bed with a cup of water on her nighttable. Maya gets two books, too. One she reads to me, and one I read to her. Then the light goes out and I sing her a song—tonight it's all the lines I can remember to "Both Sides Now" by Judy Collins—and she's asleep before I'm done. Then I go back to Eden's room to see if her eyes are closed. On a good night, they're both down by 8:45.

I used to wonder, before I became a mother, how I'd survive the monotony of parenthood, going through the same routine every morning and every night. I thought it would be the death of whatever spontaneity I had, which turned out to be right. But the truth is, I get as much comfort from our routines as my kids do. They need the structure to feel contained and secure, and to have a predictable rhythm to depend on. I need it because structure helps me feel like part of a family that's solid and reliable, a family that works.

I head downstairs for kitchen cleanup, or computer time, or half a magazine, or whatever it is that mothers do in that slim margin between their children's bedtimes and their own. On the way, I check back in Eden's room to make sure her bed's side rail is secured tight. Then I remember to close Maya's window so the coyotes' yipping won't wake her in the middle of the night, and I notice her water cup is empty. It's downstairs for more water, upstairs again, and then I'm back in the hallway, one child sleeping in the room to my left, the other to my right. My little bookends.

They contain *me*.

Do all mothers get this much satisfaction from shepherding their children safely through another day? Probably they do. Do they also catalogue their children's likes and dislikes, eccentricities and idiosyncracies, to such a meticulous degree? Knowing which toothbrush Maya likes best, or exactly what page in *Peekaboo Bugs* always makes Eden smile can fill me with such happiness it almost borders on rapture. It bathes me in relief. Finally, *finally,* someone around here is paying attention to the small details again. The big surprise is that it's me.

2

Pregnancy

TIME TO PREPARE

*I*t was not a made-for-television moment. There were no anxious clock-watching minutes, no spontaneous whoops of joy. No one walked in announcing the rabbit had died. It was just me alone in the living room, staring at the little window on the strip of white plastic in which, against all odds, had just appeared two unequivocally red, parallel lines.

Positive. Positively pregnant.

There was a phone in the room, and from some great distance I remembered that phones were for calling people. I picked up the receiver and pressed TALK. The dial tone buzzed its monotonous drone. I stared at the buttons. Uzi was at work. I couldn't give him this news over the phone. So I dialed my sister. A sister can handle anything over the phone. At least, my sister can.

"Woo-hoo!" Michele shouted. "That's great!"

"What's so 'woo-hoo' about it?" I asked.

"You two wanted to have a baby eventually, right? So. Eventually is just coming sooner than you thought."

She had a point. A baby, in a few years. A baby, in a few months. What was the difference, really, in the grander scheme? I was thirty-two, Uzi thirty-six. A child was something we knew we wanted—just, well, not yet. I felt air seeping back into my lungs. We could do this. Maybe.

At my sister's apartment, where I spent the hours before Uzi returned home, I sat on the upholstered blue couch. She curled up in an Adirondack chair across from me.

"This is a good thing, Hope," she said. "Really, it is," and I started to cry—out of shock (those unexpected red lines) and outrage (that faulty method of birth control) and fear (how would Uzi react?), but mostly out of a deep and nearly overwhelming sense of relief. Motherhood, for the first time since my own mother had died, felt within my reach.

At thirty-two, I'd spent much of the past year crying in the back seats of cabs as they sped me home from uptown baby showers, grieving for the family I was afraid I'd never have. What seemed so effortless to others still felt so unattainable to me. The majority of my high school and college friends had landed in stable marriages that had predictably blossomed into threesomes after three or four years' time, while I was still stumbling around in relationships, trying to figure out what made one last. I could be difficult and moody, I knew, and throughout my twenties, I'd had an inconvenient fascination with men who were similarly inclined. Yet I felt, and always had felt, that I'd be a devoted mother. By the time I met Uzi, I'd begun to think I'd manage fine without a man. But without a child? No. I couldn't imagine a future without one. So, as each month passed, and another friend announced her pregnancy—it felt as if each month brought several of these phone calls, although I knew that couldn't be true—I held on to the hope of motherhood in my future, without any clear idea of how to get there and no real sense of how it might turn out.

And then it just happened. With a man I'd been dating for seven months. Who lived in Los Angeles. In an apartment with a month-to-month lease. With a futon for a bed. For once, I was glad I didn't have to tell my mother the news.

Is there really such thing as a surprise pregnancy? I wonder now. Before I became pregnant, I would have answered, without hesitation, yes. Menstrual cycles can be irregular. Birth control isn't always reliable. And lovers sometimes lie. But since Maya's arrival, I can't answer that question with such certainty anymore. Her conception and birth set into motion a chain of events that became so necessary—and, in retrospect, so inevitable—to my development as a person that it's impossible to label her existence a fluke. She is my child and I am her mother, and the complex and powerful connection I now feel to both her and her sister—that blinding, ferocious, crippling, consuming, transcendent power we call mother love—now makes those New York cab rides feel more cinematic than real, as if an actress who only vaguely resembled me had gone through the day-to-day motions of a life I only distantly remember as my own.

When Uzi came home from work that night, I showed him the pregnancy test and we walked endless circles around his apartment complex in the dark, trying to find the right answers in the comforting, purposeful rhythm of our strides.

"The odds were so completely against it," I told him as we walked. "It makes me think this baby made its own decision to come through."

He nodded. In the moonlight, his profile looked solid and reliable against the backdrop of passing SUVs. "I've been thinking the same thing," he said.

But there was little time during early pregnancy to think about such matters of destiny or spirit. A more dramatic mental upheaval had started to take place within me, a shift from thinking of myself as a daughter to thinking of myself as, possibly, a mother. While I was still trying to adjust to this change, I went off to my first

prenatal appointment, and my journey into the medical model of
pregnancy began.

I didn't yet have an obstetrician in California when I became
pregnant, so I booked an appointment with one who came recommended by a friend. Dr. P. was an energetic, compact man in his
early fifties, with a matter-of-fact demeanor and a tidy, dark beard.
After he performed the perfunctory pelvic exam and confirmed
the results of my urine test, he motioned me into his office, where
he walked behind a massive walnut desk and settled into a leather
swivel chair.

"So," he said.

"So," I repeated.

"According to my calculations, your due date is . . . ," he picked
up a white due-date calculation wheel from his desk and maneu-
vered it half a revolution, ". . . October twelfth." He reached out and
thumbed through his 1997 appointment book, then looked up and
flashed me a brilliant smile. "That'll work."

I raised my right hand in a small, automatic gesture of resistance. "Just a minute," I said. In the examining room, I'd told Dr. P.
that technically I still lived in New York, and that this pregnancy
hadn't been planned. I wasn't yet married, I'd explained, and I was
trying to make an avalanche of decisions, judiciously and fast. But
now it felt as if some of those decisions were being made on the spot,
without my input.

"I have to think about it," I said.

By this I meant "I have to think about whether I'll choose you to
deliver this baby. But first, I have to think about whether I'm having
this baby in California or New York. And I have to think about how
I'm going to put together a wedding before I'll need to wear a maternity wedding gown. I have to think about whether anyone even
makes maternity wedding gowns." The past six days had sent my
plans for the next nine months into a dizzying spin, cluttering my
mind with so many facts about fetal development, marriage license

requirements, and cross-country moving rates that much of what I said was barely coherent to anyone else—which probably explains why my uncertainty came out sounding like an expression of doubt about the pregnancy itself. Which, at some level, I'm sure it was.

The doctor tipped back in his swivel chair. "Uh-huh," he said. His smile didn't falter, but his eyes dimmed just slightly. I had the distinct feeling that I'd just made an unwelcome deviation from the script.

I looked at Dr. P. He looked at me.

Eventually, someone was going to have to speak.

"So," he said finally. "Are you going to have this baby or not?"

Compassion comes in many forms. It was hard to imagine this as one of them. "That's not something I can answer on the spot," I stammered. "There are . . . a couple of things I have to do first."

"Such as?"

"Such as get married, for starters." I bit down hard on the tip of my tongue, an old trick I used to keep myself from crying. "And find a place for us to live." The self-confidence that had buoyed me as I'd walked into his office was gone. Just forty minutes ago, I'd been glamorously bicoastal, in a committed relationship that was evolving toward marriage, and taking the obligatory first step toward responsible motherhood. Now I was homeless, single, and stupid enough to get knocked up without an engagement ring. I looked down at my bare left hand. *Dumb, dumb, dumb.*

"All right," the doctor sighed, when it was clear I had nothing to add. He reached across the desk to flip his appointment book shut. "Let me know when you get it figured out."

I've relived this conversation, word for word, innumerable times over the past eight years, picking at it like a sore that won't heal, and each time I ask myself, "Why do I keep trying to condemn this doctor?" He never pretended to be a psychiatrist. He didn't advertise himself as a life coach. He was an obstetrician, trained to monitor pregnancies and deliver babies, and, according to my friend, he'd done an excellent job with hers. Still, I'd needed just a small amount of kindness that afternoon, and right or wrong, I'd expected it to come from him.

As I wrote my check at the billing desk, the nurse-receptionist asked how my pregnancy was going. I told her fine so far, although I didn't have much appetite, probably a result of stress. "I doubt it could hurt the baby," I said, then added uncertainly, "Could it?"

"Oh, I wouldn't worry about it," she said cheerily, as she handed me the receipt. "It's really hard to mess things up in there. Even women in concentration camps had fat, healthy babies."

Back in the car, I ran through a mental list of things that had been wrong with the past hour. First, the doctor's blunt questions, so dispassionate they'd felt almost like an interrogation. Then, the nurse's idiotic comment about babies born in Nazi camps, which I knew to be untrue. But what bothered me most was that I'd just gone through all that alone.

Why had I been so insistent on going to that appointment by myself? Uzi would have gladly accompanied me, but I'd assured him that a first prenatal visit was only a formality, and not worthy of skipping an afternoon of work. "They'll just make me pee in a cup and take some blood," I'd told him. "It's not a big deal." I'd breezed into the office as if arriving for a routine gynecological exam. Yet as each successive moment had passed—sitting alone in the examination room, squared off with the doctor across his desk, smiling politely at the receptionist before I bolted out the door—I'd felt my disappointment expand. As I'd sat waiting for the doctor in my pink gown, swinging my legs off the edge of the examining table, I'd found myself eager for a nurse to part the curtain with congratulations, or for another pregnant patient to walk by and acknowledge me with a smile and a nod. I'd needed some kind of validating gesture, however small, but I had been just another patient, one of many that day; and in the car that afternoon, I felt foolish for having hoped for anything more.

Halfway back to Uzi's apartment, I pulled my rental car over to the curb and rested my cheek against the steering wheel. Cars raced along Ventura Boulevard beside me at hungry speeds. Everyone talks about the physiological changes of pregnancy, the heartburn and the hemorrhoids and the swollen feet, but no one ever talks about how important maternal support can be at this time. What I really wanted as I sat in the February sun by the curb was a mother to call with the good news, a mother to reassure me that despite the enormous changes that were about to take place, the decision I was making—to have this baby—was the right one. I don't even know if my mother, had she lived until 1997, would have said those things. I knew it was more likely that whatever she would have said wouldn't be enough, that I'd then inevitably have to deal with the disappointment of her giving me less than what I'd hoped for. Still. Not even having her to call made early pregnancy feel much more uncertain and lonely than I knew it was supposed to feel. The sun pressed down against the car hood and my mind spiraled out into a manic free association of images and emotion. I was becoming a mother and I didn't have a mother and how was I going to be a mother and where was my mother and why hadn't anyone told me to expect all *this*?

The Secret Side of Pregnancy:
Psychological, Emotional, and Intense

The focus of pregnancy in Western, industrialized societies is on achieving a safe outcome, and who can reasonably argue with this? Every pregnant couple wants a birth that guarantees smooth passage from womb to delivery room, and most of them will get it. Sterile surgical environments, antibiotics, rigorous prenatal and maternal care, fetal heart monitors, and ultrasounds have brought infant mortality in the United States to an all-time low. There's no question that life-saving advances in medicine and technology, and our willingness to use them, have saved countless infants' and mothers' lives.

In this context, it's not terribly surprising that pregnancy in America is treated mainly as a physiological condition. What *is* surprising is how little attention is paid to the enormous, simultaneous psychological, emotional, and social changes that also occur.

As any woman who's been pregnant knows, the nine months of a first gestation are much more than just a bodily event. They also mark the beginning of the most dramatic social transformation she may experience in her life. Just one generation ago, marriage separated the women from the girls, explains Susan Maushart, PhD, author of *The Mask of Motherhood* and *Wifework*. But now that the boundaries of marriage have become permeable, pregnancy and birth have emerged instead as the major transitional events in most women's lives.

Pregnancy is temporary. Its outcome, however, is irreversible. A pregnant woman will eventually revert back to a nonpregnant state, but a mother can never be a non-mother again. And like most major life changes where the outcome is unknown, this one naturally inspires some anxiety and fear. A typical expectant mother, motherless or not, worries about how she'll adapt to her change in lifestyle; how she and her husband will adjust to parenthood; whether labor will be too painful for her to bear; whether her child will have an uncomplicated birth; and whether she'll be able to handle the round-the-clock demands of new motherhood. *Am I really up for this challenge?* virtually every pregnant woman wonders at some point during pregnancy. *Have I made an irreversible mistake?* Even as a woman recognizes what is to be gained by a birth, she's also aware that fundamental pieces of her identity will soon be lost. It's not unusual for a pregnant woman to feel as if she's mourning the loss of the youthful, carefree life she'll soon leave behind in favor of the complexity and responsibility that motherhood involves.

If she's a motherless daughter, she may also find herself mourning for the mothering she lost or never had, and for all her mother lost by dying or leaving before this grandchild could be born. An expectant motherless mother doesn't just wonder if she'll be as devoted a mother as her own mother was, or if she'll manage to do better. She worries if she'll know how to mother at *all*, if she hasn't had a mother to observe or interact with for so long.

Various studies have found that anywhere between 12 and 20 percent of expectant mothers experience some symptoms of depression, though fewer than half of them receive counseling or medication. Pregnancy was once thought to protect women from depression. Now, for some women, pregnancy is considered a predictable trigger for depression—and potentially a dangerous one, since, left untreated, depression can lead to poor prenatal care, low birth weight, premature birth, and, according to some studies, to secondary infertility. And women who experience depression during pregnancy are at high risk for also being depressed postpartum.

With all this at stake, why aren't psychological and emotional support automatically included in prenatal care? Part of the problem lies with the managed-care model of health care, which affects 93 percent of insured Americans today.[*] When medical fees (which determine the number of appointments a physician books per day) are set by health care companies, most obstetricians can barely allocate enough time per patient to learn about a pregnant woman's psychological or emotional state, let alone do anything about it. "How are you feeling today?" a doctor asks at the beginning of a prenatal appointment, but he's usually expecting to hear about morning sickness or water retention, a symptom that can be fixed with either a prescription or prescriptive advice. The protocol of the typical prenatal visit has evolved in a direction that leaves little room for emotional reassurance. Typically clinical and perfunctory, these visits have time for only a single goal: affirming the health of the pregnancy.

"It isn't that the medical profession ignores the psychological part of pregnancy," explains Gail Peterson, MSW, PhD, a psychotherapist in Berkeley, California, who specializes in prenatal and

---

[*] This figure includes consumers enrolled in HMOs, and also in managed-care hybrids such as PPOs and POS plans.

family development and has written several books on pregnancy and birth. "It's that there isn't an easy place for it." Most birth providers haven't been trained to identify or treat each patient's unique psychological needs, Peterson explains. "You could say it should be worked into childbirth preparation classes, but most childbirth professionals don't have the training to do psychotherapeutic work, either," she says.

Yet for many women, especially motherless ones, the psychological and emotional side of pregnancy is just as significant as its physiological side. In fact, for motherless women, a first pregnancy is *mainly* a psychoemotional experience. She is preparing to assume the role that has previously signified absence and loss, a powerful metaphor for historical repetition and all it implies. *Will I also die young?* she wonders. *Will I leave my child motherless, as my mother left me?*

"Taking on the role of mother requires a branching out in your self-concept, and understanding who you are," explains Gina Mireault. "It's going to be a more complicated process for someone who's lost a mother, because the experience of *being* a mother involves much more." Women naturally review their mothers' behaviors as they prepare to become mothers themselves, she explains. "If a woman who's had early mother loss looks toward her own mother as a model—and it would be hard not to, no matter what kind of mother she was—there's a personal threat about what it means to become a mother: an early death for yourself."

Of all the trigger events a motherless daughter will encounter in her lifelong passage through mourning, a first pregnancy and birth top the list. For all women, these are times of natural uncertainty, often causing an adult to regress to a more childlike, dependent state. When the motherless daughter regresses in this manner, however, she's reminded once again that the one upon whom she depended as a child (or should have been able to depend upon) isn't there. This can send her reeling back into another cycle of sadness or grief that she hadn't known to expect.

Thirty-eight-year-old Trudy was just three months old when her mother died. Because Trudy had no memories of being mothered, she didn't expect such an early loss to affect her pregnancy in any way. But it did, from the very start.

"At my first doctor's appointment, I was sitting in the waiting room, and I saw all these daughters there with their mothers," she recalls. "And there I was, sitting by myself. I sat down in the examination room, and I just burst into tears. The nurse came in and said, 'What's wrong?' But how do you explain this to someone who doesn't know?"

Seeing other women with their mothers was a painful reminder to Trudy of what she had lost, causing her to feel unhinged from a maternal connection at the exact moment her own entry into motherhood was about to be confirmed. It also opened up a grief response that had been kept at a distance for many years. As a child, Trudy never had an opportunity to mourn her mother. Family members had believed she was too young to have been affected by the death, and never allowed or encouraged her to ask questions. As a result, Trudy's early loss remained unresolved until adulthood, when maturational events forced it to the forefront of her emotions.

Pregnancy, like any time of emotional stress, magnifies existing problems in our lives, especially those still unresolved from the past. Grete Bibring, MD, was one of the first medical researchers to call attention to this phenomenon. Back in the 1950s, Bibring, a Boston-area psychiatrist, supervised a study in which a psychiatrist, a social worker, and a psychologist interviewed new patients at the Prenatal Clinic at Beth Israel Hospital in Boston. The specialists intended to act preemptively: they hoped to identify patients with severe emotional disturbances and refer them for psychotherapeutic help during pregnancy, instead of waiting for problems to surface after birth.

The women they interviewed weren't part of a psychiatric population. They were just ordinary pregnant women who happened to be using that clinic for their obstetrical care. That's why Bibring and her colleagues were so surprised by what they found. A disproportionate number of the women at the Beth Israel clinic were at first diagnosed as having "borderline" personality disorders, showing the kind of symptoms—depression; anxiety; magical thinking; and paranoia, frequently surrounding their own mothers— typically seen in severely disturbed patients. But Bibring knew it was almost impossible for such a large percentage of women in a random sample to actually have borderline personalities. Instead, she concluded, the symptoms had to be a function of pregnancy itself.

Pregnancy, Bibring concluded, is a "developmental crisis" that affects all expectant mothers. By "crisis" she meant a turning point in a woman's life that creates psychological and emotional upheaval, leading to a new stage of maturation. Throughout this process, normal psychological defenses loosen, and unsettled or incompletely settled conflicts from the past bubble up to the conscious level. That's a main reason why mother issues come up during pregnancy, for all women, but especially for motherless daughters like Trudy, who've been struggling with unmourned losses for years.

By the time a woman gives birth a second time, her maternal identity has already taken shape. She can superimpose the idea of herself as a mother of two or more children onto the image she has already developed of herself as a mother of one. But first-time mothers don't have that kind of prior personal experience. They turn to memories of their own mothers instead. That's why scant or negative recollections leave a woman feeling as if she has no model to draw from, even when she's surrounded by older female friends and relatives she admires—as the story of forty-four-year-old Stacey reveals.

Stacey loves being a mother. She *loves* it. Her whole demeanor sizzles when she speaks about her two sons. She refers to them as "delicious." A former health-care executive, Stacey spun off as a home-based consultant after her first son was born, and though she remains committed to her career, her children clearly come first. When her sons return home from elementary school during our interview, she excuses herself for fifteen minutes to make them a snack and hear about their days, even with a babysitter hovering nearby, waiting to offer help.

Stacey grew up in an affluent East Coast family with an emotionally distant mother and a full-time nanny who met her day-to-day needs. Because of this, Stacey says, her single most important goal as an adult is to be present and focused with her sons.

"My mom was just not the mothering type at all," Stacey explains. "She was nineteen when my brother was born, twenty-one when she had me, and I think she was just too young. She couldn't take care of our needs. She wasn't awake when we went to school, and I don't think she was there when we came home. My brother and I have no memories of her putting us to bed or reading us bedtime stories. Our nanny did all that. My parents were out socializing much of the night, or they were off traveling."

Stacey's parents divorced when she was thirteen. Four years later, her mother committed suicide. She was thirty-eight. Stacey was seventeen.

For the next decade, Stacey tossed herself into a whirlwind of college, career, and romance. When she married at thirty-one, starting a family wasn't on her mind. "We didn't even really talk about it," she remembers. "My husband had a daughter from a previous marriage, and parenthood wasn't a burning issue for me, probably because I was so scared of it. I thought, *Being a mother? No way.* But then I got to be thirty-six. My husband and I had been married for five years. We felt it was time to start another chapter in our lives. We felt ready for parenthood. So we got pregnant.

"At first, I didn't take it that seriously. I was, like, 'Everything's great, my pregnancy's great.' I didn't yet realize what it all implied, how incredibly committed a mother needs to be, and what responsibility I would have. If I'd really thought long and hard about it beforehand, I might have talked myself out of it. I'm glad I didn't. But then, as the pregnancy went on, I started getting really scared that I wouldn't be able to do it. I had such doubts about my ability to be a mom, because I had such a crummy role model."

Fortunately, there's no evidence that women who were un-mothered or "undermothered" are categorically unable to nurture their own children. Numerous studies on parenting behavior have shown that even women exposed to neglect or abuse as children are able to form close bonds with children of their own, even though their lives as women and as mothers are "made more complex by having missed first-rate care in childhood," explains Kathryn Baker, the author of *Mothering Without a Map*.

Most mothers who abuse their children do come from childhood homes where they experienced abuse or neglect. But the opposite doesn't hold true: the majority of children exposed to abuse or ne-glect do *not* grow into adults who abuse their own children. "One of the best mothers I see in my practice is a woman whose own mother abused her," Therese Rando says. "She's had to do an enormous amount of work on this, for many years. And she's one of the best moms I know. Sometimes people have to be brought up with good parenting to be able to pass it on, and sometimes people can make very good choices by doing the opposite of what they had."

If Stacey had received even short-term psychological support during her pregnancy—assuming she'd been willing to ask for or accept it, a difficult step for many motherless women who are accus-tomed to managing on their own—her months of anxiety and doubt might have been short-circuited. Even a few therapy or support-group sessions seem to benefit pregnant women. That's how Grete Bibring and her colleagues confirmed that most of the women in the Beth Israel study weren't borderline personalities after all.

True borderline patients often require hospitalization or short-term medication to get through a crisis, and need long-term psycho-therapy to manage their distrust and rage. The majority of women in the Beth Israel study, however, improved dramatically after just a few, carefully planned psychotherapy sessions, and went on to have pregnancies free of further emotional distress. In some cases, a social worker only had to express appreciation for the woman's role as expectant mother to have a healing effect. This "positive attitude of a motherly figure toward the patient's pregnancy," as Bibring called it, was a very simple intervention, but led to a dramatic response. When such small amounts of empathy and reassurance inexplicably went such a long way, Bibring and her colleagues were left to wonder, "How did we achieve so much with so little?"

In my eighth week of pregnancy, I walked into another California obstetrician's office. This time, it was to interview a team of female doctors referred by the friend of a friend. After my encounter with Dr. P., I knew I needed a more supportive practice, and I hoped to find that with a woman physician. Preferably one who was a mother and who might—though it felt like too much to hope for—have a little extra maternal energy during office visits to offer some to me.

The office sat in a squat, square high-rise. The waiting room was decorated in soothing shades of lilac and mauve. A stack of parenting magazines rested on a pink cube that doubled as an end table. I sat down carefully and put my purse next to my feet. A pregnant woman sitting across from me looked up and smiled.

Dr. H. was dark-haired and effusive. She looked like a perfect cross between the actress Tyne Daly and my mother's childhood friend Marcy, who'd been a constant in my childhood as well. She put her arm around me as she escorted me to her office, which was decorated with photos of her children. We talked about my pregnancy, my upcoming wedding, my recent move from New York. When she looked at my medical history and saw that my mother had died from breast cancer at forty-two, she made a little wince and gave me a sympathetic murmur.

I liked her and, for reasons I couldn't yet articulate, I trusted her. At the end of our interview, Dr. H. placed both her palms on her desk and smiled at me. "Well," she said. "I'd love to deliver your baby."

"Good," I said, extending my hand to shake hers. "I'd love it, too."

Susan Maushart describes her prenatal visits as "oases of affirmation in the long desert of pregnancy," and over the next seven months, I came to understand this metaphor well. Each time I drove the forty-five minutes to Dr. H.'s office on my monthly, then biweekly, then weekly schedule of appointments, I found myself eager to receive validation that the baby was growing normally and that, by association, I was doing everything right. Pregnancy, it seemed, was already a form of mothering, insofar as the choices I made during those nine months continually took someone else's well-being into account. I told the doctor and her partner about my twice-weekly yoga class, my sudden aversion to broccoli, and my equally sudden loss of interest in sex. They listened to me and gave thoughtful responses, and I felt reassured that I was getting quality medical care.

Still. In the efficient, organized compartment of time allotted to each of my visits, I never felt comfortable sharing the two concerns that plagued me most: the fear that I could die during the birth, if not on the delivery table then sometime soon after, and leave a newborn motherless; and my concern about my husband's interest (or lack thereof) in the pregnancy. He was becoming increasingly less available at a time when his availability mattered a great deal, working every night until nine or ten P.M., even missing two of our six Lamaze classes because of business trips. His behavior wasn't all that different from what the other women in my prenatal yoga class described in their own homes, but they didn't seem to mind it as much. They even seemed grateful for the time alone. But I couldn't handle the solitude. It had me worried, very worried, that I was about to face the most intense phase of motherhood alone.

Alone. How many times had I used that word to describe myself over the past fifteen years? Enough times by now that I'd started wondering if I weren't somehow manipulating events to make this the inevitable outcome. Such a familiar state it was, almost comforting in its predictability. And I knew how to manage it so well. Over the years I'd prided myself on being a survivor, on taking care of myself in times of extreme distress. I was far less adept at letting others take care of me, though that was often what I craved most.

How could I explain such a contradiction to my doctor, or my husband? It didn't even make sense to me.

Uzi later told me he'd wanted to be more excited about the pregnancy, but the baby was just too much of an abstraction to him before she was born. By carrying her and feeling her constant movement, I had a relationship with her, but Uzi, of course, didn't. So, throughout my pregnancy, I was left feeling a little like a celebrant without a party to attend, a cheerleader without a team. Where were the people who understood that a miracle that was taking place beneath my skin, I wondered, the ones who should join me to spend *every waking minute* celebrating the pending birth of this child? My father, sister, and brother—they were excited, but they, too, needed an actual baby on which to focus their enthusiasm. My in-laws were eight thousand miles away, accessible only by e-mail or phone. My friends—happy for me, but busy with jobs and relationships and children of their own.

No, I thought during my first pregnancy, my mother was the one who would have been most interested in this child's development and in my pregnant self, the one who would have called in the middle of a day just to see if I was feeling tired, the one who would have rejoiced, without me having to point it out, that this child would be the third firstborn daughter in a row. *My mother,* I often thought during those nine months. She would have shared stories with me about her own pregnancies. She would have reassured me that whatever emotions I was feeling were normal, or inevitable, or—if nothing else—at least not the ravings of a madwoman. She would have convinced my husband to come home from work in time for dinner, to bring me flowers for the hell of it, and to just sign already for God's sake the life-insurance papers that had been sitting on the kitchen counter for three weeks, not because his wife was insisting that he do it, but because it was something a father-to-be should do.

This mother of my fantasy was all-knowing and constantly available, with encyclopedic information about pregnancy and birth, and with one hand perennially resting on the phone. Pure fantasy? Maybe. Maybe not.

Of all motherless daughters who took part in the Motherless Mothers survey, 88 percent said they missed having emotional support from their mothers during their first pregnancies and post-partum periods. It's easy to label that group "wishful thinkers" until we see that two-thirds of women with mothers in the control group survey report they *did* receive emotional support during pregnancy and after the birth. In fact, this latter group was more likely to receive emotional support from their mothers than any other kind of support from her, including practical help, such as infant care or babysitting, or information, such as details about her pregnancy or about themselves as newborns.

The nature of mother-daughter interaction during pregnancy, it seems, is based more on comfort and emotional support than on handing down information about those nine months. And isn't that what pregnant women need most? It's helpful to have a blueprint for comparison as the trimesters progress, but it's more important to have someone who you know will empathize with your morning sickness, and whose assurances that you'll be a competent, loving mother are the ones that are easiest to believe, because they're coming from the person who's known you the longest, and the best.

It's so easy to idealize. It's so hard to know for certain how the future might have unfolded otherwise. Knowing how badly my mother would have wanted this first grandchild—or is that just part of my fantasy, too?—I imagine she would have eagerly anticipated reports of each prenatal visit, and would have made arrangements to be nearby for the birth. But then I get real. There's a good chance she would have still been living in New York, two thousand eight hundred miles away from my California home. The amount of practical assistance she could have provided over the nine months would have been minimal, at best. The amount of emotional support she might have offered me in person or by phone—well, that, I'll never know.

Taking the Plunge

I've always maintained that "unplanned" isn't synonymous with "unwanted." I wanted my daughters, both of them, quite a bit. But as a mother who was taken by surprise with both pregnancies, I'm always amazed by women who make the decision to get pregnant, and then do. It seems to require way more organization and much better timing than I've ever had.

Yet for more than half of all women who become pregnant in the United States each year, conception is a planned and antici- pated event. For some, it's a decision made without much conflict. For others, it's a stage reached after a great deal of debate. Among motherless daughters, the conscious decision to attempt a preg- nancy may be a complicated one, often made (or decided against) from a position of competing emotion, between the intense desire to create an intact family of one's own and the fears of being a bad mother or dying young and leaving a child behind.

No statistics exist on the percentage of motherless women who remain childless by choice, although therapists whose clienteles in- clude large numbers of motherless daughters report that many of their clients have consciously decided not to have children.* Laurie Lucas, LCSW, a psychotherapist in Irvine, California, who has been leading Motherless Daughters Support Groups since 1996, believes this may be because early mother loss sends the message to some daughters that it's not safe to have a mother. "That may later shift to 'It's not safe to *be* a mother, because if I'm a mother, I place my child in the same potential situation I was in,'" she says.

Lucas, the mother of two adopted children, was eight when her own mother died. While counseling other motherless daughters

---

* This may be because women who have difficulty sustaining adult relationships are less likely to bear children, and are also more likely to seek therapeutic help. Or it may be that this inner conflict is a particularly hard one for some motherless women to resolve.

over the years about the transition to motherhood, she's observed two psychological extremes. "There's either an exaggerated need to have children and a family, which was my personal experience, or there's an avoidance and ambivalence about it," she explains. "Women talk about how overwhelming it is to think about parenting without a mother there to support them, or without a good role model for motherhood."

Thirty-four-year-old Sandy, who lost her mother at age eleven, is trying to work through those feelings right now. Sandy and her husband, who have been married for more than ten years, both work at high-pressure jobs and cherish their free time. These are obvious reasons why a couple might delay parenting, or forgo it altogether, and Sandy's uncertainty does stem in part from the demands she knows a child will make on her time.

"I feel like, 'Oh my God, if I have kids I know I'll be the one who ends up cutting back at work, and I don't want to put pressure on my husband to be the one who has to bring home the money," she says. "So that's part of my ambivalence. And then the whole idea of raising kids, and having a teenager. I say to people, 'Why raise a kid when they'll eventually turn sixteen and look at you and say, 'I hate you. I wish I was never born.' I don't know that much about kids, anyway, and I think, *What if I'm a horrible parent? What if they turn out to be completely bad?* It's a control thing. I want to know in advance what it's going to be like, and how it's going to end up."

Having control is important to Sandy. After her mother died, she was raised by a father who withdrew from the family's emotional life, leaving her to essentially raise herself through adolescence. What little comfort she had at that time came from the orderly, predictable world she created for herself.

As Sandy spoke about motherhood, she wavered back and forth between intellectually rationalizing her decision to remain childless, and questioning whether this was the right decision to make. Several times, she expressed the wish that someone else would tell her what to do. It was almost as if she were hoping for a mother to materialize, to point her in a direction she couldn't commit to on her own. In the meantime, Sandy said, she's placing the decision in the hands of fate. She'll continue taking her birth control, she says, but if it were to fail, she'd let the pregnancy continue.

Sandy struck me as the perfect fusion of the young daughter afraid to make her own decisions and the adult daughter who's capable of parenting if it should come about for reasons beyond her control. Birth control, Sandy admits, gives her a feeling of control over her future, and for the time being, that's a form of security she needs.

It may take Sandy several years—or more—to work through her uncertainty and take a firm stand either way. Some motherless women consciously choose to delay motherhood until well into their thirties or beyond. Sometimes this is for work-related reasons, but often it's because they need time to gather the emotional confidence they need to embark on motherhood.

For Jennifer Lauck, it was both. Lauck, author of the bestselling childhood memoir *Blackbird*, which describes her mother's death when she was seven and the subsequent loss of her father when she was ten, says she was in her early thirties before she could start thinking of herself as a mother. Before then, she was intensely focused on her career as a television reporter, but she soon discovered she also had some heady emotional obstacles she needed to overcome.

"When I started thinking about having a child in earnest, I didn't think I would be a good mother," she explains. "I thought, *I don't think someone like me should have children,* because of my history. I didn't have a mother for most of my childhood. I didn't know anything about mothering, or about being mothered. And that's when I realized how little I knew about my own mother, which inspired me to get to know her better, which inspired me to search for her story. At seven, we're told so little. So I searched for her story, and in searching I discovered a profound love relationship I'd shared with her that I'd been suppressing because it brought up the deep, deep loneliness I'd been carrying around for so many years."

Only when Jennifer was ready to reconnect with the memory of her early years with her mother and to feel the intense pain of having lost that relationship was she able to see herself as a potential mother for the first time. "Once I worked through all this, with therapy and some time, I realized I would make a wonderful mother, because I had been mothered well," she explains. "Then, of course, I was ecstatic. I wanted to have a baby right away, and I got pregnant the first month we tried."

Reuniting with the mother was an essential part of Jennifer's psychological preparation for motherhood. Other motherless women, however, find they need to do exactly the opposite: to let go.

Thirty-one-year-old Michelle, now the mother of fifteen-month-old twins, was twenty-seven and already married when her mother died of cancer. She and her husband wanted to have a child, but her mother's death brought their plans to a halt. Michelle had always expected to have the benefit of her mother's guidance and support when her first child was born, and she couldn't imagine going it alone.

"For the first few years after my mother died, I was, like, 'My mom's not here—how am I going to do this without her?'" Michelle recalls. She knew she needed time to release the idea of her mother in the maternal grandmother role. But mostly what she needed, Michelle soon realized, was time to grieve that as a legitimate loss, too.

"It's like there was another step in the process, another wave of grief I had to go through before I could say, 'Okay, now it's time to have a baby,'" Michelle remembers. "I was almost reluctant to do that grief work, because I didn't want to go through the pain. I didn't want to let go of my mom more, but I had to. I had to go through the experience of fully realizing that she wasn't going to be there as a mother and grandmother, and of being afraid to do it alone.

"I didn't go to therapy," she explains. "I did it in my own way. I cried a lot. Talked to my husband about it. I don't feel that I completely let her go, but I had to reach a sort of acceptance, I guess, that she wouldn't be there."

Yet still other motherless women, who were adults when their mothers died, find that mother loss instead speeds up their plans to have a child. Even when a relationship is ambivalent or troubled, the death of a family member can inspire the desire to reaffirm life by creating a new one. And if the relationship was close, there's often a powerful longing to share that special closeness with another human being again.

Twenty-eight-year-old Samantha, now the mother of two young sons, was twenty-three when her mother died after a twelve-year battle with cancer. Samantha and her husband starting trying to get pregnant soon after the funeral, and within five months she had conceived.

Samantha describes her mother as her best friend, her champion, and her confidante. "I mean, we were very, very, very close," she explains. Despite a geographical distance of two thousand miles between them during her mother's illness, Samantha flew back to her parents' house every two weeks to spend time with her mother and help care for her. The death was a devastating loss, the pain relieved only by news of her positive pregnancy test.

"When I found out I was pregnant, I felt this wave of relief for the first time since my mom had died," she remembers. "Relief, because I so missed the mother-daughter relationship we'd had. Or I should say the 'mother-child' relationship, because I have boys, though at the time I didn't know if the baby was a boy or a girl. But a mother-child relationship was missing in my life. And I thought the only way I was going to get that back was to be on the other side of it. And I thought that once the baby was born, that would fill the void of the relationship I was missing, because I would get to have that bond with someone."

The reasons why motherless women choose to become pregnant or adopt are as unique as their individual loss experiences, and equally colorful and complex. But it was hard not to notice how many women I met who, like Samantha, spoke of the longing to re-capture what was once lost, especially by having a daughter; of the desire to create a long-lasting love relationship; or of the chance to make amends for one's past. I spoke with women who felt the im-pulse to have a child soon after their mothers died, to recreate the maternal bond ("the replacement baby"); motherless and under-mothered daughters who'd always longed to be loved uncondition-ally and hoped a child would fill that unmet need ("the fulfillment baby"); and women who believed that having a child, in some way, would right a wrong from their motherless pasts ("the atonement baby"). But of all the stories I heard, the most poignant one by far came from JoAnn, whose search for atonement after her mother's death led her into the arms of a teenage boyfriend, and into a preg-nancy, when she was just fourteen.

JoAnn, now fifty-one, was the younger of two daughters born to young, emotionally ill-prepared, hard-drinking parents. Her early years were filled with periods of neglect. For most of her childhood, JoAnn and her sister moved back and forth between their paternal grandmother's house and their own. During JoAnn's twelfth year, her mother took a vacation without her father. Before she left, she drove JoAnn to her grandmother's house for the week. Thirty-eight years later, JoAnn vividly remembers the argument that took place between them during that ride.

"I was in the seventh grade, and my face had started breaking out," she says. "I said to my mother, 'I want to go to a dermatolo-gist.' She said, 'What do you think, we're made of money?' And I said, 'Well, *yes*, because you just got that new suede outfit for your-self, and nothing for us.' My mother said, 'Don't talk to me like that,' but it must have been sad for her to hear, because she started crying. When we got to my grandmother's house, I saw an opportunity to show my mother how I felt about her. I wouldn't talk to her. I wouldn't kiss her good-bye. And the pain in her face was so great. You could just see that she knew she needed to make changes. I felt very proud of myself. So then she left on the trip . . . and while she was gone, she got in a car accident and died."

JoAnn was devastated. Nothing could convince her that the anger she'd felt toward her mother hadn't somehow caused the death. The next two years were lonely and disorienting for JoAnn. She kept thinking about the last time she'd seen her mother, and the way she'd behaved. Her life became a routine of going through the motions at school, and trying to survive at home with a grief-stricken father. Then, at fourteen, she met a boy at school. His name was Miguel. "I was so drawn to him," she remembers. "He was a track star, and he had shiny black hair, just like my horse. We became as thick as thieves." A few months later, she discovered she was pregnant.

"Abortions were illegal at the time, but there was a doctor in town, my father's doctor, who did them," she says. "And I knew my dad, because he was such a strong and dynamic figure, would make me have an abortion if it were physically possible for me to get one. I knew that our house was a zoo. I couldn't imagine bringing a baby home to the craziness there. I just knew that I didn't want to have an abortion. I didn't feel I had the right to choose to abort somebody, which was how I perceived it."

A gym teacher at school, who recognized the signs of advancing pregnancy, gave JoAnn an ultimatum: tell your father or I'll tell him myself. So, JoAnn gathered her courage and told him one night.

"He was just, like . . . 'What?' He couldn't fathom it. It was awful. He started crying, he was so upset. Then it took him about six minutes to make a phone call, grab his car keys, grab me, and the next thing I knew we were racing to the doctor's office at a hundred miles an hour."

The doctor conducted a pelvic exam and, realizing the pregnancy was already four months along, exited the room to break the news to JoAnn's father. A heated argument began between the doctor, who refused to perform an abortion, and the father, who insisted a baby would ruin his daughter's life. Yet despite the violent shouting in the next room, as she lay on the examining table, JoAnn felt a deep sense of calm. "I knew I'd just crossed a big border," she explains. "I didn't know whether I could keep the baby, but I knew the baby would be born. And it was just a flooding relief to know, 'Okay, whatever else happens, I'm not *that* bad a person.' Because for two years I'd been suffering through being the 'bad-person-who-doesn't-kiss-her-mother-good-bye-and-then-her-mother-dies.' In some strange way, if you feel that you've caused one death but then you feel that you've saved another life, it equalizes things." *

Infertility:
Another Kind of Loss

In 1995, the last year for which such statistics are available, about one out of every ten U.S. women between the ages of fifteen and forty-four was unable to conceive. About the same proportion of women interviewed for this book said they'd had difficulty getting pregnant the first or subsequent times. Some had been actively trying to conceive for a year or more. Others had undergone fertility treatment that resulted in a pregnancy, or had abandoned treatment and become pregnant naturally, or had chosen to become adoptive parents. Whatever the circumstances, the inability to conceive a child was a heartbreaking dilemma for many women who yearned to create the kind of family they'd lost or had once been denied.

Most infertility cases can be medically explained, such as forty-three-year-old Randi, who was diagnosed with severe endometriosis and later adopted a son; and thirty-eight-year-old Corinne, who had trouble conceiving due to her husband's low sperm count but

---

* JoAnn's story, after thirty years, found its happy ending. At fifteen, when her son was born, she relinquished him for adoption. She and Miguel married, had another son a few years later, and then divorced. Many years later, she was reunited with her older son, who had grown up in a secure and happy family. When we met, she was just about to travel to attend his wedding.

later went on to have two children with him. About 10 to 20 percent of the time, however, standard infertility tests can't isolate a cause, and a couple's infertility is described as "unexplained."

This has been a particularly maddening label for thirty-four-year-old Cecilia, who's been trying to get pregnant for three years. When her mother died a sudden and painful death from colon cancer fourteen years ago, Cecilia had a hard time accepting that some questions—*Why my mother? Why like this?*—would never be answered. She wanted explanations. Justifications. Now, when faced with similar, tough questions—*Why us? Why now?*—she's looking for reasons again.

"After my mother died, my brother and I became really close, and I thought maybe that was the reason it happened," Cecilia says. "So, with being unable to get pregnant, I've started to think, *Am I not supposed to have a baby?* It's like there has to be a *reason* why it's not happening, like something bad is going to happen to me and that's why I can't get pregnant. If they'd found a tubal blockage or something they could go in and fix, I'd feel better about it. But 'unexplained' seems like some kind of cosmic situation I have to figure out or fix."

When Cecilia and I spoke, she and her husband had just decided to try in vitro fertilization (IVF). Adoption, she says, is a possibility, but she's not yet ready to give up the dream of a biological child—not because of its genetic similarity to her or her husband, she explains, but because of the connection it would have to her mother.

I heard this from several motherless daughters: that giving birth was a means of giving a lost mother immortality, ensuring that her genes would continue even if her body could not. Some women, like Cecilia, were hopeful that a child might even resemble the mother in some way—even if just in eye color, or in mannerisms.

The experience is even more difficult for women who have miscarriages, and who know that there was, if only for a brief while, an actual fetus developing inside them. For these women, the end of the pregnancy is the loss of hope and potential, and often evokes strong memories of prior loss. As Linda Gray Sexton wrote of her miscarriage in *Searching for Mercy Street*, "I was overwhelmed with grief for the baby I had lost, angry once again at the echoes: death had taken someone I loved with unpredictable swiftness."

When thirty-one-year-old Ruby first contacted me, she wanted to talk about her anxiety surrounding motherhood and her concern that she wouldn't be a competent mother. Ruby was four when her mother died of breast cancer, and none of the three stepmothers that followed became a close mother figure to her. Now that she and her husband were trying to conceive, she had a vivid mental picture of the kind of mother she wanted to be, but was also afraid of failing a child the way she felt she'd been failed when her mother died.

But by the time we managed to conduct our interview, she had become pregnant and miscarried. The loss of this pregnancy, she says, was devastating.

"I couldn't go to work for a couple of days," she explains. "I was just kind of like in mourning. And I was really surprised by that, because of the horrible fear I'd had when I took the pregnancy test. When I saw it was positive, the first thing I thought was 'Oh my gosh, I can't do this. What did I get myself into? I can't get out of this.' So, after the miscarriage, I was surprised by what a deep sense of loss I felt. The day after the miscarriage, that's all I was thinking about, that there was something we had created. A human. A baby. A child. In a weird way, I thought, 'Look! I failed this baby.' That was my thinking, even though the doctor assured me it was nothing I did.

"As silly as this might sound, I think the miscarriage was kind of a blessing. I'm not saying losing the baby was a blessing—I mean for my peace of mind. For showing me yeah, this is what you want. Because I think somebody who really didn't want a child would feel relieved. So we're going to try again next month."

While a number of women who struggle with infertility or repeated miscarriages eventually will bear a child, others will choose to enter motherhood through adoption. These women face specific issues en route to becoming adoptive parents, including the emotional significance of giving a home to a motherless child; the identification they may feel with the child; and the frustration of handing the transition to motherhood over to bureaucratic red tape. And some motherless women will choose to adopt a child without ever trying to conceive, either because of age or marital status, or because they have a strong desire to parent a motherless child, or because they identify with a vulnerable child who might otherwise grow up in an orphanage or in foster care.

Laurie Lucas, who has been counseling motherless daughters for six years and is herself the mother of two adopted children, says she also identified with both her children's birth mothers. Having become hypersensitive to loss at an early age, when her own mother died, Lucas says the joy of becoming an adoptive mother was made bittersweet by her awareness of the necessary losses involved in such an event.

"My son was an open adoption, so I knew his birth mother, and was very involved in her prenatal care," she recalls. "It was very hard for me to disengage from her when my son was born. It was really a loss, in a way. I find I'm very attuned to people who lose a parent-child relationship."

A Matter of Preference:
Girls or Boys

In a Parenthood.com worldwide survey of 10,648 parents, 79 percent admitted to having a gender preference during their pregnancies. It's the quiet little secret so many mothers carry. We're supposed to want a healthy baby, nothing more. Of *course* that's everyone's first choice. But once a fetus's good health has been confirmed, most women feel free to quietly nurture their preference for a daughter or a son.

In most of the world, particularly in Asia and the Middle East, sons have been preferred over daughters for centuries, because of the privileged status males occupy over females. Not surprisingly, the majority of women who took the Parenthood.com survey said they'd wanted boys—most because their spouses had strong preferences for sons.

Ask a motherless daughter about her gender preference, though, and her answer is likely to be different. A full three-quarters of the women I interviewed face-to-face admitted they'd wanted a daughter during their first pregnancies, usually as a means of re-producing the mother-daughter bond they'd lost.*

"I wanted a daughter, badly," forty-six-year-old Ruth told me during our interview. "I wanted that mother-daughter relationship, because I felt I never had one. I mean, I had one for eleven years, but I felt that I needed to finish something in my life."

This proportion of women who told me they'd hoped for a daughter was too large to ignore. These were women like forty-four-year-old Stacey, the mother of two sons, who—like 68 percent of the Parenthood.com survey respondents—learned her baby's gender during her first pregnancy. When she received the results of her amniocentesis, she was stunned to learn the child was a boy, and she took the news hard.

"I was very depressed for twenty-four hours," she remembers. "Because I had convinced myself that I was having a girl. I had told myself, 'There's just no way it could be a boy. God is going to make this all right. He's turning things around for me. He's going to give me my little girl, so I can have the relationship that I never had.' But sure enough, it was a boy. I cried for about a day. My

---

* Curiously, only one-third of the motherless mothers who took the online survey said they'd hoped for a girl. Sixteen percent reported a preference for a son, and the rest claimed to have no preference. This may reflect the emotional differences between answering a survey question and answering a question in person during a two-hour discussion. Our natural impulse is to present ourselves in writing as we'd like to be or wish we were, whereas one-on-one interviews offer less opportunity for us to hide our true feelings.

husband . . . well, he was thrilled to be having a boy, and he didn't understand my response at all. I tried to explain it to him, that I wanted a girl so badly because of my mother. And that there was also a comfort level, like, 'I'm a girl, so I know what to do with girls.' But a boy? I was like, 'Oh my God! What do I do with a boy?' But after that initial twenty-four hours, I was fine. I thought about it a lot, and I realized there was a plan there for me."

Stacey and Ruth both gave birth a second time, and both again had sons. While Stacey felt her family was then complete, Ruth, at age thirty-four, knew she wanted another baby. "With that pregnancy, I had an amnio, and I was pretty prepared to have a boy," she recalls. "They always say if you have two of the same sex, you have an 80 percent chance of having the same sex the third time. When they called and told me I was having a girl, the world stopped. I called my husband at work, and when he picked up the phone and I heard his voice, I couldn't stop crying."

Whether they found out in an ultrasound exam room, or in their own living room when they called for amnio results, or on the operating-room table, the moment when motherless women learned the child they were carrying was a daughter was often emotional and intense. They repeatedly dramatized the scene in their interviews, choosing to render it in great detail, as if reliving the wonder and the thrill. It was the moment, some of them said, when they consciously recognized that their broken pasts were being repaired.

A notable exception to this majority, however, was the small but articulate group of motherless mothers who expressed strong preferences for sons. These expectant mothers were concerned they didn't have adequate feminine or maternal resources to draw from to raise daughters properly. Most of the women in this category had grown up with difficult or abusive mothers, and felt the emotional damage they'd incurred somehow made them less able to have good relationships with daughters of their own. Other women, who had neutral or even close relationships with their mothers, still felt they were lacking an essential ingredient necessary to raise a daughter to become a knowledgeable, self-assured woman who was comfortable with her femininity—usually because they didn't feel that way themselves.

"I prayed for boys," says fifty-two-year-old Suzanne, the mother of two sons and a daughter. "I thought I'd be a much better mother to a boy than to a girl, partly because I'd raised my younger brothers after my mother died, and partly because I didn't have a lot of the social cues I thought I needed. And I didn't feel confident enough to raise a daughter." She laughs as she admits this, knowing now that her daughter is a strong-willed, ambitious college freshman confident enough to choose a university two thousand miles from home.

The initial twinge of disappointment women described when a baby's gender turned out to be other than they'd hoped for was rarely more than that: a momentary pang of disillusionment. This corresponds with the more than ten thousand parents who participated in the Parenthood.com survey, not one of whom said they felt dissatisfied with their child's gender after the birth. As every mother soon discovers, it is not the sex of the child that closes the circle. It is the force of the connection, the unwavering devotion that flows between mother and child, and the ability to embrace one's child, as a unique and perfect individual, with one's whole heart.

I loved being pregnant, loved the feel of the baby somersaulting and hiccupping inside me, loved the minute-to-minute knowledge that, for these nine months, I held a sliver of the life force within me. Mine was an uncomplicated pregnancy, supported by a good diet, a flexible job schedule, and twice-weekly prenatal yoga. After my Thursday morning yoga class, I used to walk along Montana Avenue in Santa Monica, pausing to gaze at my swelling body in the windows of fashionable boutiques.

The physical part of pregnancy awed me. My thoughts were the part that threatened to get out of control.

Last-minute fears. That was the subject line of a message I posted on my CompuServe pregnancy support group the week before my

1997 due date. In a florid gush of last-minute doubt, I typed: *Will I be able to handle pain in labor? Will I need an epidural? Will the baby cry all the time? Did I buy the right clothes? What if I don't know how to bathe her? What if I chose the wrong pediatrician? What if she doesn't sleep more than two hours at a time? Will a bassinet be good enough at first? Should we have bought a crib from the start? What if I can't breast-feed? What if it hurts? Are those infant car seats really that safe? Did I buy the right stroller? Will I know what to do if she chokes?*

A dozen women at varying stages of pregnancy wrote back to confess similar fears. At least that many tried to give me reassurance and support. But it was the matter-of-fact response from the SysOp, a mother of two who'd been actively overseeing our board for months, that calmed me the most. *Every first-time mother has these doubts,* she wrote. *But look at it this way. You've got breasts, right? And you've got diapers, right? That's all you need. In some cultures, you don't even need the diapers. So you're going to manage fine.*

This was the kind of no-nonsense reassurance I'd been craving, this loving yet firm whack on the head. *Right,* I thought when I read her message. *Breasts. Diapers. Got them. I'll be fine.*

I made it through the last trimester of pregnancy by relying on my online support group; the women in my prenatal yoga class; and a few good friends who'd given birth before me: Elizabeth, who'd had twins earlier that year; Stacey, whose voracious appetite for parenting books had turned her into a de facto encyclopedia on child care; and Lisa, my oldest friend and also the mother of twins, whose mother had grown up with mine. Together, these women made up my unofficial community of elders, each one bringing a different, unique perspective to the table.

And throughout the pregnancy, I hung on to the small bits of information I had about my mother's pregnancy like a lifeline. Lisa's mother told me that the smell of boiling hot dogs made my mother nauseous when she was pregnant with me. It was a small detail, but it gave me confidence that the mild morning sickness I experienced was something that would pass. I also knew that all three of my mother's children were born on their due dates, which made me trust my pregnancy would go full-term, which it did.

The mother-model is powerful, infiltrating a woman's psyche in unexpected ways. For first-time mothers, the mother's experience is the blueprint, the light source, the guide. But its influence diminishes with each successive pregnancy. When I became pregnant with Eden, three years after Maya was born, I had my first pregnancy to refer to for comparison. I'd had morning sickness the first time, so I expected it the second. My first labor had been long and arduous; I figured my second would be shorter, by comparison.

Midway into my second pregnancy, I switched from the obstetrical model of care to the midwifery model. Every time I arrived for a prenatal visit, the midwife and her assistant hugged me hello, and they hugged me good-bye at the end. In between, they asked about what I was eating, how I felt about the pregnancy, and if I was experiencing any emotional stress. They wanted to know about any marital problems, and they talked with me about helping Maya prepare for a sibling. If you ask a midwife why the midwifery model of care boasts such a low cesarean section rate, they'll say, "Because we know our women well." At appointments, my midwives were constantly feeling me out, trying to help me identify and work through whatever emotions might complicate my labor or my transition to second-time motherhood. They asked their questions, and then they listened. It wasn't the same, I knew, as having an interested and involved mother—in some ways it was probably even better—but it was the closest approximation in a birth attendant that I could find.

I am the dominant mother in my life now, every day becoming slightly more confident about relying on my own experience as my guide. But getting from there to here has been an arduous journey, and one that began with an auspicious start. My transition from pregnant woman to first-time mother took fifty-one hours, long enough for me to think about what was happening in great detail. In early labor, when the contractions were still easy to breathe through, I typed a letter to my daughter on the computer. I told her

I'd do my best to be a good mother. Then I told her I wasn't entirely sure that I was ready for her to arrive. Yet.

But doesn't every woman feel that way? After forty weeks of waiting, the final push happens so fast, catapulting us into such unfamiliar territory. Even though my first pregnancy went full term, it still felt too soon to let go. Too soon to lose what I'd been holding close for so long. How little time it takes, when it actually happens, for what has been internal to become external, for all the longing and emptiness and love a motherless daughter has been carrying to finally find its object—not in the mother she has been missing, but in the child she labors to bring forth.

3

🔊

Labor and Delivery

CROSSING THE THRESHOLD

"The special events that take place during and right after
delivery are like the tumblers of a lock falling into place
one by one until the door into motherhood swings open."

—Daniel Stern, *The Birth of a Mother*

*J*ust as pregnancy is an intensely emotional event for motherless women, so, too, can be labor and delivery. As the final,
irreversible step into motherhood, childbirth marks the instantaneous transition from being a woman with neither mother nor child
to being a mother with a child. It's an emotionally loaded eight or
twelve or twenty hours, yet it's barely enough time to process all
the feelings that may arise. When a motherless woman receives
emotional, in addition to physical, support during labor and delivery, however, the birth process can become an enormously healing
experience.

This concept went straight over my head the first time I went
through labor. The purely physical side of it—baby is inside, baby
needs to get outside, nurses and doctor oversee safe passage from

there to here—that part, I got from the start. I was hoping to give birth without pain medication, if I could stand it, but mostly I saw birth as a necessary means to a desirable end. The idea that labor and delivery could be transforming processes? Please. The horror stories that trickled in as pregnant friends gave birth before me made that idea seem naively quaint. ("Brutal," as I recall, was the word Allison used to describe the birth of her daughter a week before my own due date.)

The reports that filtered back from delivery rooms bore little resemblance to the even, sweet tenor with which Judy, the leader of our six-week childbirth-education class, spoke of birth. Nonetheless, the classes were helpful—a lifeline, really, for a first-time mother. On Tuesday evenings, Uzi and I sat on the floor with eight other pregnant couples, educating ourselves with diagrams of concentric circles that represented the cervix at various stages of dilation, and practicing the three types of breathing Judy recommended we rely on as labor progressed.

By the end of six weeks, we could talk in great detail about the three phases of labor, the different effects Demerol and epidurals had on mother and baby, and how to ask for a heparin lock intravenous line. All this would have been enormously useful, if only such knowledge actually made a difference in a real birth situation. One of the hidden secrets of childbirth-preparation classes, as I soon discovered, is their well-intentioned yet impossible task of preparing you for a birth you're unlikely to have. As Susan Maushart has pointed out in *The Mask of Motherhood*, a good deal of childbirth is left up to chance: you either get the right combination of physical endowments, fetal positioning, and timing to easily push the baby out on your own, or you don't. Having control over the event is only an illusion, especially in the hospital system. Of the nine couples in our class, eight had said they planned to give birth without pain medication or medical interventions. Only one actually did, and that was because they arrived at the hospital too far into labor to do anything but deliver. The rest of us wound up with meticulously detailed stories of epidurals and pitocin, one emergency C-section, and several cases of that dreaded "failure to progress." My own birth story, I later found out, became something of a legend—or perhaps more of a cautionary tale—when news got around that I was in labor for fifty-one hours before Maya was born.

That's right. Fifty-one hours. Count 'em. God knows, we did.

For a long time, when anyone asked about Maya's birth, I would say the first forty-two hours weren't that bad. I was at home for much of that time with weak, irregular contractions that were painful but not too difficult to endure. "All you can really do is walk around and wait," said Dr. H.'s partner, who was the one on call that weekend. So Uzi and I walked. We waited. We walked and waited, and walked and waited some more. On the morning of the second day, when the contractions were finally five minutes apart, we checked into the hospital, but the nurse who did my first internal exam removed her gloved hand and frowned. I was "barely a fingertip" dilated, she announced. After all that walking and waiting, this hardly seemed fair.

Women in my family, I've since learned, are prone to long labors. Who knew? I couldn't ask my mother about hers, and it hadn't occurred to me to ask her sisters. If I'd known to expect this, I might have tried to stay home longer than I did. Hospitals, as it happens, are not in the habit of letting women labor on site for several days, particularly on busy maternity weekends. The medical staff gave me six hours of additional walking in their hallways before "speeding things up" became everyone's explicit goal.

In the letter I'd typed to Maya that morning, I'd told her, *You're coming soon, but I don't know if I'm ready yet. Just a few more days—I feel as if I need just a few more days to prepare.* Was I somehow subconsciously holding the baby in, I wondered as I paced the hospital halls, in an attempt to get more time for myself? Every few minutes I would lean against a wall and try to will my body to relax and urge the baby down. "It's okay to come now," I whispered. "I'm ready."

But even as I said them, the words felt clumsy and inauthentic, a facsimile of what I thought I was supposed to say instead of what I really felt.

When I returned to the birthing room, the doctor asked for permission to strip my membranes, a term we'd never heard in Judy's class. When this didn't have the desired effect, two hours later she manually broke my waters. This resulted in a good deal more pain, without any obvious gain, and my stamina started to wilt. It was now Sunday afternoon, and I hadn't slept since eleven P.M. Friday. My endurance had been tested, I sobbed to Uzi, and I just wasn't up to the task. In the forty-second hour, I broke down and asked for an epidural so I could get some rest. I climbed onto the bed to wait for the anesthesiologist, let the nurse hook me up to the fetal monitor, and pretty much stayed there until the end.

Suffice it to say the next nine hours included a violent reaction to the narcotics in the epidural, which only worked on half my body anyway; two intravenous bags of pitocin; a moment of confused panic when Uzi picked up the red phone on the wall by accident, causing a whole NIC-U team to explode through our door in full alert and making our already irritated nurse dislike us even more; a precipitous drop in both my blood pressure and the baby's heart rate; an oxygen mask to keep me from fainting; and, finally, a vacuum extractor to pull Maya out in a single, terrible yank. She arrived at 2:53 A.M. on my third day of labor, nine and a half pounds of her, huge and red-faced and screaming, with a big purple bruise skewing the top of her head to the left, like Gumby.

I thought she was gorgeous.

Once I took that in, I was just grateful to have survived.

In the photos taken after Maya's birth, I'm managing a weak smile, but I'm terribly pale and drawn. My eyes are narrowed into little exhausted slits. Uzi's expression is harder to place. It reminds me of how he looks after he's just watched two animals tear each other apart on Animal Planet and then clicked over to a kitchen renovation on Home and Garden TV. Calm in the middle, but with

residual trauma around the edge. He'd seen Maya's birth from the
doctor's point of view and apparently it was very, very red. It took
almost half an hour and more than forty stitches to put me back
together.

The truth about childbirth preparation is this: the only thing that
can adequately "prepare" someone for labor and delivery is prior
experience with labor and delivery. It's much larger and more painful and more exhilarating, more bloody and more emotional than
any classroom diagram or video can possibly convey. A main reason
why my daughters are four years apart is because it took three of
them for me to work up the courage to face all that again.

For my second birth, I didn't bother with a Lamaze refresher.
I went straight for hypnobirthing. I figured I'd help myself most
by learning to blank out. Also, because we had by now moved to
the other side of Los Angeles, I needed a new obstetrician. Male,
female, young, experienced—I wasn't going to be picky this time.
My only criterion was to find someone willing to use my first birth as
a blueprint for what not to let happen next time.

Because of my intolerance for narcotics, I couldn't chance an
epidural again. I had to find someone who'd let me labor unmedicated, in my own time, without pressure to intervene. That immediately reduced my word-of-mouth referral list to a handful of
physicians on the West Side of L.A. The one I chose was a stunning
ob/gyn about my age, who listened patiently to my concern about
another large baby.

"We'll check the size constantly. If it looks like this one's going to
be a nine-pounder, we can induce you at thirty-eight weeks. We'll
make sure you get a nice eight, eight-and-a-half-pound baby." It
sounded so easy, so neat and precise.

"Can I do it without drugs?" I asked.

"I'll tell you what I tell all my patients: you can do pretty much
anything you want, as long as it doesn't endanger you or the baby,"
she said.

The problem was, I didn't know what I wanted, other than the opposite of what I'd had before. This kind of negative patterning got my project moving, but couldn't take it very far.

"I'm terrified of going through a hospital birth again," I confessed.

"Your baby will be fine," the doctor said, smiling gently.

"I know the baby will be fine," I said. "I'm worried about *me*."

Then we met Anna.

I should tell you from the start that I'm not objective about Anna. When I first met her, I thought she was full of bizarre ideas, but the more I listened to her talk about birth, the more sense she began to make. In Topanga Canyon, the little mountain enclave in Los Angeles county where we both live, a few dozen women call themselves "the cult of Anna." She helped all of us give birth, and I think each of us is a little bit in love with her, in the way you fall in love with a stranger who hoists you out of a swollen, rushing river and deposits you on solid ground—intact but forever changed.

Anna is a Dutch woman, a former labor and delivery nurse who had recently left hospital work to become a birth consultant and birth doula,* or labor coach. A friend had described her as a home-birth advocate who would also do hospital births. I was already midway through the pregnancy by that point, and my fear of the hospital was gathering momentum each day.

Robust and confident, with a waterfall of waist-length brown hair shot through with strands of silver, Anna Verwaal arrived at our house one afternoon during my fifth month of pregnancy toting a small library of books and videos about natural childbirth. One showed women giving birth in large tubs set up in their homes, while their older children swam around. Another included clips of Russian women giving birth in the Black Sea. Uzi thought all this was fascinating. I thought it was plain weird. We'd already

---

* For a full definition of "doula" I defer to *Mothering the Mother* by Marshall Klaus, John H. Kennell, and Phyllis H. Klaus: "an experienced labor companion who provides the woman and her partner both emotional and physical support throughout the entire labor and delivery, and to some extent, afterward."

considered home birth for a good five minutes before I shot down the idea. From our relatively remote canyon road, the nearest hospital is a thirty-minute drive, with all green lights and if there are no other cars on the road. It was pretty clear that in the event of a home birth emergency, either the baby, I, or both of us would need to be helicoptered out.

"But if you have a normal, uncomplicated pregnancy," Anna said, "there shouldn't be an emergency." Also, she told me, because I'd had a vaginal birth before, I was a good candidate for home birthing.

"What if what happened last time happens again? If the baby is too big for me to deliver on my own?"

"I'm not convinced you couldn't deliver that baby," she said. "My guess is that if you'd been allowed to labor upright, and if you hadn't been so sick from the epidural, you could have pushed her out just fine on your own."

It was the kind of statement that sounded radical enough to be fantasy, but also provocative enough to potentially be true. *If Maya's birth had been allowed to progress at its own pace . . . If I'd been able to labor in the bathtub, or sitting down, instead of lying on a bed . . . If the anesthesiologist had checked my chart and seen I couldn't metabolize narcotics, or if I hadn't needed to take the epidural at all . . .* What if the first event in that long chain had never been set into motion? If the doctor hadn't stripped my membranes, would the entire birth have taken a different course?

I'll never know how Maya's birth would have turned out if I'd delivered her in a birthing center or at home. I knew only that I didn't want my next daughter to make the same type of entrance my first daughter had. When I thought about it this way, the decision was made. Three weeks later, I had a midwife who saw clients in a lovely house perched on a hillside, with a dining room filled with birds, and who told me to cut sugar from my diet and walk two miles a day to keep the baby's weight down. And so, this is the story of how I wound up delivering an eight-and-a-half-pound baby that December in the master bedroom of a pink house in the Santa Monica mountains, and learned a couple of useful things about birthing along the way.

Now that Western women no longer have to worry about high rates of maternal and infant mortality, we're free to obsess about the emotional styles of our births. It used to be that a "good birth" was the kind in which both mother and baby survived. Now a "good birth" is more likely to mean the kind of birth the mother hoped for, and one that didn't incur much physical or emotional trauma.

If I'd had a truly obstructed labor, or a postpartum infection without access to antibiotics, I'm sure I'd be writing a very different chapter here, if I'd lived to write it at all. Technology has indisputably improved birth to the point where life-threatening complications to mother or child are tragic aberrations. But the fact remains that modern medicine *has* given women an opportunity to focus on the emotional side of birth, and given the importance this has for motherless daughters, we might as well.

When I started researching how prior loss experiences might affect labor and delivery, information wasn't easy to find. Obstetricians who recognized fear or grief when it surfaced in the birthing room typically tried to comfort women with technical reassurances, reminding them that the medical staff had everything under control. Popular childbirth books weren't terribly useful, either. One of my favorites, *Dr. Miriam Stoppard's New Pregnancy and Birth Book*, was emblematic of most books of this genre. The chapter called "Preparing for the Birth" includes sections on organizing your home and buying the right items for a nursery. "Getting Ready for the Birth" lists all the equipment necessary for a home birth and all the items a woman should pack into a hospital bag. Don't bother looking up "psychology" in the index—it isn't there. And under "emotions" you'll find only a brief reference to pregnancy hormones and their effect on a woman's moods.

Unlike obstetricians, who typically appear at labor's midpoint or beyond, and nurses, who move in and out of birthing rooms to meet the needs of several patients simultaneously, midwives and doulas are more likely to be by a woman's side throughout labor's full course—"continuous observation," it's called. This makes them also more likely to notice subtle psychological and emotional shifts as they occur, and to identify connections between emotional states and physical changes during labor. So it wasn't a tremendous surprise to find that the most vivid and compelling material I uncovered came from birth attendants such as these.

As Ina May Gaskin, the legendary midwife who has attended more than 2,200 deliveries at her birthing center, The Farm, in rural Tennessee; Gayle Peterson, the author of *Birthing Normally*; and others agree, a woman's unique psychological makeup can have profound implications on the way she gives birth. Fear of motherhood, disharmony with a husband or partner, unsupportive home environments, and feelings of personal inadequacy, especially concerning motherhood, have been linked with the interruption or eventual complication of labor. It appears that the stress, fear, and anxiety surrounding these psychological crises cause physiological responses that can slow down uterine contractions, or even make them stop. Whether the exact biological culprit is higher levels of metabolites, adrenalin, or noradrenalin in the bloodstream remains a matter of debate.

Peterson describes labor and delivery as a time of "creative stress" for women who have the inner resources to handle stress creatively. Because, as she also points out, the way a woman deals with stress in her everyday life is an indicator of how she'll deal with it in labor. Is she the kind of person who prefers to face obstacles head on and find a way to grow from them? Or does physical or emotional pain cause her to regress to an earlier emotional state? "A woman who has developed a style during her lifetime of being able to meet and handle stress without creating *dis*tress for herself, will be less likely to create blocks for herself in labor," Peterson explains.

Thirty-six-year-old Gretchen attributes her ability to handle stress in labor to her disciplined and committed Zen practice over the past eight years. Long before she went into labor with her son last year, Gretchen, who lost her mother at age seventeen, began to prepare for the event through meditation and focused thought. In an e-mail she sent me reviewing her labor and delivery, she wrote:

> Most people approach life, and labor, with the belief that pain and death are bad and should be avoided. This isn't in keeping with Zen practice, in which one practices to see that whatever exists simply exists. When I was three months pregnant, I stood by my father's hospital bedside and watched him die, after a completely unexpected car accident. His death, though heart-wrenching and full of grief, seemed at the same time an absolutely integral part of the cycles of life and death I was participating in. Similarly, I went into labor holding the belief that pain was a natural and necessary part of bringing my baby into the world. (Of course, that didn't prevent me from hollering during labor, "I've changed my mind!" or, most melodramatically, "Just kill me!") During my pregnancy I made choices that helped me embody that belief—midwives, yoga, a great birthing class geared toward women who wanted to deliver without medication, but at the same time an open mind to events unfolding as they would.
>
> But entering this space didn't happen automatically. It was a process that continued to unfold during my pregnancy. During the last session of our birthing class, the instructor invited couples to voice their fears about labor. Most common were fears that something would go wrong, the mother or baby would die, or that she wouldn't be able to handle the pain. My fear, though, was that I would not feel supported by my support people. I specifically had my husband in mind—that everything he would do or say would be wrong.
>
> While this might fit the motherless daughter's experience of needing to be cared for, I was able in the course of my pregnancy

to look anew at my needs and fears. Shortly after this birthing class, I gave a talk to my Zen group, in which I spoke of how through my fear of not feeling supported I was able to look at the larger existential truth that, in fact, we are all in this—labor, but also life—alone, and to recognize that my expectations of my partner in labor were the same as in our relationship. ("Why don't you automatically know how to make me feel better, or the right thing to say?") Directly looking at this, meditating on it, helped me to claim responsibility for my own experience during labor, and to foster the intention of gratitude for whatever my support people *did* do right. (I say "intention," because it wasn't 100 percent effective when push came to push and my husband was reading the newspaper, napping, and doing back exercises during my labor, but it was much better than it otherwise would have been.)

Women with a history of mother loss, or a highly complicated mother-daughter relationship, may need extra support throughout labor and delivery if sadness, fear, and grief episodes come and go. One of the most poignant birth stories I heard came from Christine, who was six when her mother died of cancer. Although Christine was eager to become a mother herself, her first pregnancy was marked by long stretches of self-doubt and fear. Like most expectant mothers, she was uncertain about how motherhood would change her life. As a motherless daughter, she was also deeply concerned about her ability to care for a newborn with so few memories of being mothered to draw from, and without any family support at all.

"As I was pushing the baby out, my husband said, 'I'm so excited for her to arrive!'" Christine recalls. "And I said, 'This is going to change our whole lives.' He said, 'I know. It's going to be great!' And I said, 'Someday, Brian, it's going to be really great, but right now it's not. I wish she weren't coming right now.' And he got kind of upset. I just knew in my heart how hard it was going to be for me to do this alone."

When I heard this story, I couldn't help wondering how different Christine's experience during delivery might have been if someone she'd trusted had told her, during labor, that she was doing well, and that she would manage motherhood just fine. What if someone had talked with her, either before or during labor, about her mother's absence and let her talk through her sadness? Would it have made a difference for her emotionally? Would she have stepped into motherhood more confident, or less afraid?

Norma Tracey, PhD, an Australian psychotherapist and founder of the Parent Infant Foundation in Sydney, Australia, believes that childhood trauma resides in a sensory, physical, and primitive area of our psyches. Because of this, she says, the primitive, physical event of birth can unlock previous childhood or adolescent traumas that reside in the same area, particularly those associated with death and catastrophe. In some motherless daughters, labor and delivery can also unlock fears of dying as their mothers did, and of leaving their helpless children motherless. Many women fear death during childbirth, but for a motherless daughter, this fear is grounded in an identification with her mother rather than in general anxiety or medical fact. Fewer than .001 percent of women who give birth each year in the United States die from pregnancy- and birth-related causes, but this means little to a motherless daughter in the throes of what may be the most painful or frightening physical experience she's ever encountered. Double that fear during a second or third birth, when the assurance of having given birth once competes with the anxiety of possibly (no matter how small the chance) leaving motherless not just a newborn but a dependent preschooler as well.

Unfortunately, scientific research on the impact of grief, fear, or sadness on a woman's labor is rare. To collect sufficient data to confirm or refute connections, scientists would need to observe large numbers of natural, uncontrolled births, which are no longer the norm in Western countries. Enough anecdotes, however, begin to create a compelling case. Ina May Gaskin writes of an early birth she attended, in which the laboring woman's cervix remained stuck at seven centimeters for many hours. Gaskin could find no physical cause for the interruption, and her obstetrics texts offered no clues. Finally, a close friend of the laboring woman arrived on the scene. As Gaskin recalls,

> On being invited into the birth room, she asked, "Has Sheila [the laboring woman] told you about her mother yet?" My body tingled all over on hearing those words. I then learned that the woman in labor had been adopted and had confided to her friend that she had grown up afraid that her biological mother had died in childbirth. She was apparently too embarrassed or too far beyond speech to admit that she was afraid of dying if she surrendered to the power of her labor. Once this profound fear was mentioned aloud, her cervix relaxed and displayed abilities it didn't seem to possess earlier. It wasn't long before it was completely open. A healthy baby was born within two hours of the mention of the secret fear.

And then there is this story, from Anna Verwaal's nursing days, about the impact of grieving during labor for a prior, unresolved loss:

> I was working the night shift, and I had just finished a C-section when I was sent to take care of a woman in room 512, who might be ready to push. So I went in there and said, "Hi, I'm Anna, you don't know me, but I'm taking over from your nurse. I'm here to check you to see what's going on, and to see if you're going to have your baby soon." I examined her cervix and she was completely dilated. I said, "I'm going to go to the desk and tell the doctor you're ready to start pushing your baby out, and I'm going to get the supplies and come back in." Ten minutes later, I looked at the monitor and I saw her contractions were completely gone. I thought, *Wow, that's bizarre, what happened to her?* I told her she was ready to have the baby, and her contractions stopped.
>
> I hadn't been given a full report, because it was such a crazy

night, and I thought I'd better have a look at her prenatals to see what her story was. When I read the chart, I saw that two and a half years before she had given birth to a baby who was stillborn. So I instantly felt, *oh my God.* The minute I told her she could have her baby, her body went into the fear of letting go of the baby, because last time she pushed out a dead baby.

Her doctor then told me, "If she's not contracting in the next ten minutes, let's start her on pitocin." And I thought, "No, that's not fair. She doesn't deserve that. We need to go and take her back in time." So I walked back in and said, "I'm going to come in here and sit with you for a little while. I read your prenatal records and I realize you were here two and a half years ago and gave birth to a baby who had died in your womb." I said, "I can imagine how scared you must be to let this baby come through you, out of the fear of losing it. But that's not going to happen. This baby is fine. Why don't I turn the fetal heart monitor on loud enough so you can hear the baby as you're pushing, and know your baby is fine?" Then I said to her and her husband, "I'm going to leave you alone a little bit, because maybe you need to say good-bye to your first baby one more time before saying hello to this baby." And they burst out in tears, held each other and cried, and fifteen minutes later, contractions were back. She never needed any intervention other than just acknowledging what had happened.

The critical point in both these stories is that laboring women heard their fears spoken out loud. I can't overemphasize the importance of this. No one has ever won a medal during labor for martyring her feelings to please or protect others. Acknowledging one's fear and receiving support for it—provided that you're in the company of at least one person who can support you—can dramatically relieve tension during labor, and may even help a stalled labor progress. Ina May Gaskin believes these "true words spoken" relax pelvic muscles by discharging emotions that block progress in labor.

Non-Western cultures have known about this phenomenon for centuries. Women in some African countries who experience a slow or blocked labor, for example, are urged to confess their sins out loud, and the Manus of New Guinea treat blocked labors by encouraging the husband and wife to express any hidden anger they may be harboring toward one another.

My second, unmedicated home birth gave me, too, the chance to see the direct impact of the spoken word. Once again, it was a long labor—thirty-eight hours from first contraction to last. It began around midnight as Friday eased into Saturday, and I waited until late Saturday morning to call the midwife, when I was sure it was true labor.

"Uh-oh," she said, when I told her. "It's my birthday. I've got a bunch of people going out for dinner tonight. I'm going to have to call everyone to cancel."

"I'm sorry," I said. I felt ridiculous apologizing, but what was I supposed to say?

"No, no." She recovered quickly. "Don't worry about it. I'm just thinking out loud. Okay. Call me back in a few hours and let me know what's happening."

I hung up the phone, fighting fury and tears. *Her* birthday? I thought. And then, *But what if she's too busy to come? No,* I told myself. *It's her job. She'll be here. But I'm ruining her birthday,* I thought. And then, *I can't believe I have to think about this now.* I walked around the house to calm down, waiting for the next contraction to grip me. Fifteen minutes. Twenty minutes. Half an hour. Nothing.

I called Anna in a panic. Anna is also a motherless daughter, having lost her adoptive mother at twelve. She completely understands the mindset of someone for whom the threat of abandonment is disastrous.

"Listen to me," she said. "Your baby is coming whenever your baby decides to come, and if it happens to be on someone's birthday, well, too bad. She'll be there. She won't miss the birth. You're going to have a beautiful, perfect baby. Let's focus on that."

Relief poured through my legs. *Yes,* I told myself. *She's right.*

Beautiful baby. Now breathe. I took a deep exhalation, and slowly let out the air. Within minutes, the contractions started up again.

This stop-and-start pattern was to happen several more times throughout the next day and a half: when the midwife and her assistant arrived in a flurry of activity, unloading their duffel bags of equipment in my bedroom and completely changing the energy in the room; and again, when my sister said she wasn't sure she could keep Maya at her house for a second night, and I had to quickly call around to create a backup plan. Each time the contractions slowed down or stopped entirely, and resumed only when I regained emotional calm. I felt like a finely tuned anemometer. Was I so bizarrely sensitive that any cross-eyed glance in my direction could make my body seize? Or was it because I was laboring at home with plenty of time and little else to distract me that I could notice, this time, the exquisite dance that occurs between body and mind during a birth?

And then, finally, it was late Sunday afternoon. I'd reached the critical transition stage of labor, when the cervix begins its final stretch from seven centimeters to ten. This is the point when panic usually sets in, when women lose confidence and shout, "I can't do this!" or "I want to go home!" But I already was at home, which limited my options considerably. Instead, I stumbled out of the bathtub and announced I wanted to take a nap.

"Right," Anna said. "A fine idea. Why don't you just climb up here on the bed and take a nap, then?"

I lay on top of the pale blue flowered sheets. Anna and the midwife looked at me. Then they looked sideways at each other. They knew something. It may or may not have had something to do with the cold, twisted knot lodged between my ribs. I was holding on to something tight. I could feel it.

"Could I be alone with Anna for a minute?" I asked, and we waited for the midwife to leave the room.

"What is it, sweetheart?" Anna asked, brushing my hair off my face. It was such a simple gesture, so gentle and so pure. How long had it been since any woman had touched me that way?

"Anna," I said, and my voice cracked open wide. "I miss my mother so much."

It was not something I'd planned to say, certainly not something I'd been carrying around consciously through the house that day. It hadn't been part of my first labor, and until that moment I hadn't known it was going to be part of my second. Yet there it was.

"I'm so sad she's not here," I said. Tears and snot poured down my face, but I didn't stop to wipe them. "I'm so sad she won't ever get to see this baby." Each time I said that phrase out loud—*I'm so sad*—I felt a tautness in my muscles loosen just a notch. A tightness I'd been holding on to, a protective sort of stinginess, released just a little and made room for more air.

"I know, sweetheart," Anna said. "I know."

And then it was over, and I blew my nose and suddenly I was tired, so tired. I closed my eyes, and I took a nap. Except it wasn't really a nap. It was some other kind of state, a blank, floating place, where neither pain nor emotion could reach me, and when I opened my eyes again, it was half an hour later, and the midwife was at the foot of the bed, telling me it was time to push.

Did this really happen just as I recall it, or has memory collapsed events to better express an emotional truth? I don't have hard proof that grief or sadness caused my labor to slow down. The umbilical cord was wrapped tight twice around Eden's neck, which just as easily could have been the cause. But I know, in a place that exists beyond intellect or science, that letting myself miss my mother and saying it out loud mattered a great deal during Eden's birth. I was in labor with Eden for thirty-seven hours before I missed my mother out loud, and only forty-five minutes after. I might have saved myself some time by getting to it earlier, but it took me a day and a half to figure out I needed it.

If a lost mother can have such an impact on a daughter's labor, what impact might a difficult relationship with a living mother have? I couldn't help wondering about this after Eden's birth. Ina May

Gaskin remembers a number of women in this situation, several of whom had mothers who insisted on being present during their labors. "This isn't so unusual," she explains. "One grandmother-to-be came all the way from Germany to be with her daughter, who couldn't stand her. We managed to keep grandmother busy in another house while her daughter was in labor.

"A recent birth involved something that happens pretty often: the grandmother-to-be phones when her daughter is busy pushing the baby out. In this instance, she called about fifteen minutes after the birth, before the placenta. Usually, moms don't want to talk to anyone on the phone so soon, but in this case the new mother took the phone from me. Unfortunately, her mother regaled her with the story of the postpartum hemorrhage she had when giving birth to her, and our woman promptly began bleeding a lot and fainted. We're much more cautious now about phone calls before the placenta [is delivered]."

Labor and delivery are highly suggestive times, when a woman may find herself absorbing ideas or information that she'd otherwise resist. This was the case with Dina, whose estranged mother resurfaced last year with an unexpected message in the middle of her granddaughter Alexandra's birth.

Dina's mother wasn't much of a presence during her daughter's pregnancy. In fact, she didn't even know about the pregnancy until Dina was six months along. "She was supposed to see me at four months," recalls thirty-five-year-old Dina. "I hadn't seen her in years, and she was finally going to show up. I was expecting her on a Sunday, and thought I'd tell her about the pregnancy then, but she called and canceled. She said she couldn't see me. Just like that. And she went to the beach for the day instead."

Dina tells her story matter-of-factly, without obvious rancor. Still, she rolls her eyes a little when she mentions the part about the beach, the kind of unspoken gesture that conveys, *My mother. Well, what can you expect? That's just her.*

Her mother's lack of interest in the pregnancy was a

disappointment to Dina, but not much of a surprise. Theirs had always been a complicated relationship. Dina's mother was only fourteen, a young French student, when she became pregnant by an American living overseas. She chose to marry him and keep the child, believing that marriage and motherhood were a means to leave Europe for a better life. But she was young and inexperienced, and the responsibility was often more than she could handle.

"Obviously, she was not in any way prepared to be a mother at fifteen, not even prepared to be a woman herself," Dina explains. "I was always told that I was a mistake, and that I prevented her from becoming anything. When I was a teenager, she always introduced me as her sister, because she was embarrassed to be thirty with a fifteen-year-old. She and my father stayed together for fifteen years, in a dysfunctional marriage of addictions and affairs. Many times, my mother wouldn't show up to pick me up from school, and I'd get a ride home and find her passed out in the driveway in an alcoholic stupor."

Dina left home at sixteen—"sooner than I should have"—and barely spoke with her mother over the next two decades. They saw each other twice during Dina's twenties—once, when her mother was participating in Alcoholics Anonymous and was sober for a short time, and again after Dina married. Then they spoke twice during Dina's pregnancy. It was, at best, an erratic relationship, but Dina had long since learned not to expect or hope for more.

As the due date for Alexandra's birth approached, Dina began to prepare for a home birth. Her waters broke one morning, close to her due date. Like many first births, however, hers involved a long, gradual labor—so long, in fact, that the midwife had time to deliver another baby in the twenty-seventh hour and still return in time to deliver Dina's.

"Before the midwife left, she asked me to trust," Dina remembers. "She kept saying to trust that she'd get back in time, and to trust that my body was capable of delivering the baby. She kept using the word 'trust.'" But, as Dina knew, 'trust' can be a tricky

term for a daughter who was never able to rely on a parent, especially when the message "It's not safe to trust" was the anthem of
one's childhood.

The midwife's departure sent Dina into an emotional spin. "I felt
completely abandoned," she recalls. "But I didn't want to deal with
it, so I tried to just be in my body and force and push and make it
all happen. And nothing was happening. For the next eight or nine
hours I stayed totally stuck."

Some birth attendants will say this is how it happens, that a
woman's life story is mirrored in the way she gives birth, with her
labor encountering roadblocks in the same places where she met
with obstacles in her past. In effect, the departure of Dina's midwife
and the feelings of abandonment it fostered forced Dina to confront
and sit with memories of her mother when she was already vulnerable and struggling to stay calm.

And then the phone rang.

"I heard my mother's voice on the answering machine," Dina
recalls, "and I was, like, *Oh no, I can't fucking believe it. Of all the times
for her to call!* I was, like, *Go away, bleh, bleh.* I told my husband not to
return her call."

Five minutes later, the phone rang again.

This time, the birth doula picked up the receiver and handed
the phone to Dina. "I gave her such a look," Dina remembers. "I
told her, 'I don't want to talk to my mother.' But then something just
told me to take the phone."

Just a few minutes earlier, Dina had been gazing at a photo of
her spiritual guide and praying to have whatever obstacle was blocking her labor removed. "So when the phone rang," Dina explains,
"the message I got was 'This is what you need. Face this.' So I took
the phone, and I sat there with my mother. At first I heard only the
desperation I always hear in her voice, that alcoholic *blaaah.* But
then I softened a little, and beneath that I could hear that she did
really love me. You know, when you're in labor you're in this kind
of transcendental phase, so it was all less muddled in me than it

normally is. In her desperate way, my mother was telling me she loved me, which I wouldn't take in at any other time. And I kind of knew that even though she's so messed up, she's still my mother."

After hanging up the phone, Dina lay down with her husband and cried "a big, deep cry, like a tsunami of release," she says. The call had helped her achieve a level of empathy for her mother that she'd never felt before. "I understood how deep the bond of motherhood is, even when clouded by substance abuse," she wrote in the birth story she typed up a few weeks later.

But the phone call wasn't the end of it. Dina still had another emotional task to complete before her labor would progress.

After their shared cry, Dina's husband walked outside for a few minutes and Dina found herself alone. Only she wasn't completely alone, she realized—she was sitting with the baby who would soon, if all went well, be in her arms. But how could she be a good mother, if she'd received such limited mothering herself? It was a question she'd asked herself multiple times throughout her pregnancy. Now, she knew, she had to push past this fear. She rested her hands on her abdomen and started to talk, with a new sense of compassion and forgiveness for both her mother and herself.

"I explained to my daughter that I'd be the best mother I could," Dina recalls. "I told her, 'This is what I come from, and this is what I carry with me, but I'll try not to pass it on to you.' That was the moment I really connected with her, and told her I was ready and prepared to be her mother. And there was a huge contraction and I felt a *whoosh* inside me, and the baby turned around and dropped. Something shifted inside me, and I suddenly felt so much power."

The birth moved quickly from there. The midwife called to say she was on her way back. By the time she arrived, Dina was almost ready to deliver. From start to finish, her labor was thirty-eight hours: thirty-six hours before her mother's phone call, and two hours after.

"I didn't realize it before I went into labor," Dina says, "but I needed to forgive my mother for never being there when I needed her. And I got that she was there for me at that moment, when I most needed her. In the past year since the birth she's tried in her own way to be there for me, but once again it's not working out. Still, right then and there when I needed her, she was there, and that was huge."

And Now There Are Two

Immediately after giving birth, many women feel exhilarated, powerful, and indomitable, flush with the force of life. They've been through what was probably the most physically grueling task they've ever had to face, and prevailed. They may even feel something akin to triumph.

Other women feel a rush of gratitude and relief that they and their babies survived what may have been an urgent or dangerous situation, or, in the case of unmedicated births, are just darn thankful the pain has stopped. Whatever a woman's emotional state at this time, one fact is immutable: a very new, extremely small person is in the room, who was not there before. What was just moments ago a compact bulge of fetus contained inside one's abdomen is now a squirming, wet windmill of arms and legs wiggling on one's chest. After both of my daughters' births, my first reaction was utter astonishment, as if the birth attendant had just pulled a white rabbit out of an unexpectedly magical hat between my legs. "I can't believe *this* came out of *me*," I kept saying, to anyone who walked into the room.

A good deal has been written about birth as a loss experience for a mother, insofar that the fetus she nurtured automatically for ten months is now a separate entity, whose physical survival no longer depends on hers. Given the high degree of sensitivity motherless women have to loss, I'd expected to come across some examples of this in my interviews, but that wasn't the case. Instead, the excitement of knowing that a reciprocal maternal-child relationship had now begun seemed to eclipse any experience of loss the interviewees may have felt.

I did come across, however, some bumpy transitions in delivery rooms, when the focus of attention abruptly swings away from micromanagement of the laboring woman's needs and onto the new baby. At 2:02 A.M., she was the sole object of interest and scrutiny in the room, but by 2:03 A.M., she had already become secondary.

This seemed to be an especially difficult moment for women who had relished the attention lavished upon them during pregnancy. Those ten months may have been the first time since childhood, perhaps the first time ever, that anyone cared so much about what they ate, how well they slept, and their overall level of comfort and contentment. Although they may have known, intellectually, that this attention was in service to a larger, external goal—the safety and health of the infant—this fact became unambiguously clear the moment the baby emerged from the birth canal.

"During labor, I needed so much support that I couldn't handle anyone in the room caring about somebody other than me," remembers thirty-four-year-old MaryJo, the mother of a four-year-old daughter. "Then, when it was all over, everybody was talking about the baby. And I was just sitting there all exhausted and bloody, like, 'Would somebody come along and love me? Love the girl side of me? Let me take a bath, or let me have some nice pretty things to smell?'"

Stepping aside at this moment is a crucial move into motherhood, which allows a child's needs to take precedence over one's own, and the women I interviewed didn't actively resist it. But several, like MaryJo, did acknowledge how disconcerting it was at first, indicating that women who are already sensitive to being left behind may be vulnerable to slight feelings of abandonment at this time.

At the same moment that a fetus becomes a baby, a pregnant woman becomes a mother, yet aside from allowing her to clasp the newborn against her chest—provided she can do so—there is little external recognition of this dramatic internal event. Only after the baby is cleaned, weighed, and removed from the birthing room does attention shift back to the mother, and even then it is most often of a medical nature, to finish delivering the placenta or stitch up a tear.

Women who experience complications after delivery, such as a retained placenta or a postpartum hemorrhage, do remain the center of attention for longer, and women whose newborns are rushed off to intensive care are unlikely to dwell on their own emotions at such a critical time. As with most other aspects of childbirth, this particular emotional issue is likely to surface only for motherless daughters whose birth experiences were relatively straightforward, which gave them the opportunity to reflect on matters other than physical survival.

Why Birth Styles Matter

Hospital birth, home birth, an unexpected, urgent delivery in the back seat of a speeding taxi cab—what difference do the details of a birth make, really, as long as mother and child come through the delivery fine? I'm reminded of a pregnant friend, a highly educated woman in her late thirties, who had gone through years of fertility treatment to conceive, and decided during her second trimester not to bother with a childbirth preparation class. She and her husband were both crazy busy at work; she didn't feel like sitting in a room full of strangers once a week; but mostly, she didn't really see the point of it all. "I mean, a doctor's going to be there," she explained. "No matter how prepared I am, it's her job to get the baby from there to here. She knows what to do."

Some women approach labor and delivery hoping for a personal growth experience; others see it as a necessary state to be endured; and others—most others, I believe—fall somewhere along the wide spectrum in between.

The problem is, most of us don't realize the connection between our birth experiences and our post-birth states of mind until the birth is over, and by then it's too late to make a different choice. A woman's subjective experience of childbirth—meaning, the way she perceives a specific birth to have gone—appears to have a direct impact on her state of mind and her behavior toward her infant during the postpartum period. Women who had poorly controlled pain in labor or during delivery, who felt out of control during the births, who felt that the birth environment was hostile or unsupportive, and who had preexisting depression or histories of sexual abuse were more likely than others to perceive their births in negative terms. And those who perceived their births negatively, in turn, were more likely to suffer from postpartum depression. Women who describe their births as difficult are also more likely to feel disconnected from their infants and to report bonding problems.

"Underlying these feelings are often intense feelings of failure and feelings of inadequacy as mothers," explains Kathleen Kendall-Tackett, PhD, a clinical psychologist at the Family Research Lab at the University of New Hampshire in Durham, New Hampshire, and the author of *The Hidden Feelings of Motherhood*. Confusion or trauma associated with a childbirth experience can be resolved if a woman is encouraged to talk about it, and when her concerns are treated as important, but there's little opportunity for this kind of debriefing in postpartum care. Likewise, few women talk about the impact a difficult or negative birth has had on their self-esteem, especially those who needed C-sections and were left feeling that their bodies somehow failed. "Many women are afraid to 'complain' about their births because they don't want to appear 'ungrateful' for a healthy baby," Kendall-Tackett adds.

This silence can be terribly disconcerting for women who fear their birth experiences validate the concerns they've had about their ability to be good mothers. *If I were truly meant to be a mother,* the logic goes, *wouldn't nature have given me a body that could deliver my own child?*

Of all the motherless women surveyed for this book, 75 percent recalled their first birth experience either as "very positive" or "somewhat positive," with the other 25 percent describing it either as "somewhat negative" or "awful." Women whose mothers are still alive, however, tend to remember their first births slightly more positively—86 percent answered "very" or "somewhat" positive. This raises the question of whether motherless women are somehow predisposed to have objectively difficult birth experiences, or whether they're more likely to subjectively assess their birth experiences as negative. Perhaps motherless daughters, many of whom grew up believing that events happen to them rather than through them, are more likely to perceive labor and delivery as events outside their control. Or perhaps they're less likely to have a support network—or to call upon one—in which they can talk about their births after the fact, process the experience, and receive emotional support for any lingering doubts or distress.

Given how important birth experiences can be to a woman's psychological and emotional transition into motherhood, what can motherless daughters do to create a compassionate, supportive birthing environment for themselves? The following suggestions have been compiled from published research, data, and interviews with motherless mothers.

Consider hiring a birth doula.

Birth doulas, or labor assistants, provide a calming, reassuring element to a laboring woman. According to Phyllis Klaus, MEd, CSW, and Marshall Klaus, MD, who have studied the births of more than 1,500 women, continuous support during delivery results in a major reduction in the length of labor, more than a 50 percent decrease in cesarean sections, and a reduced need for pain medication. The effects extend beyond the birthing room, as well. During the postpartum period, mothers who've had birth doulas show less anxiety, fewer instances of postpartum depression, and higher self-esteem than women who did not have such assistance.

For motherless women, the most critical aspect of birth doulas is *they exist to take care of you.* They'll massage your legs, breathe with you, bring you fresh ice chips—whatever you need. Most important, they'll make sure you're never left alone. For the duration of a woman's labor, they'll mother her, which, depending on her willingness to be mothered, can help her traverse the emotional bridge to motherhood in sync with the physical journey.

Fifty-four-year-old Martha, who lost her mother at age five, went through three deliveries without any female support, and raised two children to adulthood, mostly as a single mother. Six years ago, she saw a news program on birth doulas. The mothering aspect of the profession appealed to her. What better way to give birthing women what she hadn't had? She entered a training program soon after. At the time of our interview, Martha had attended more than 130 births as a doula, including the birth of her granddaughter.

Because of her personal history of mother loss, Martha says, she pays particular attention to her clients' relationships with their mothers. "Last week, I was at a birth for a client whom I just couldn't connect with," she recalls. "I had met her mother, who was very cold and standoffish, and I thought, 'Well, okay, this is probably how she was raised.' We got to the labor, and she was already panicking and crying at two centimeters, saying, 'I can't do this.' I said, 'Give me fifteen minutes. Let's see if we can make you more comfortable and, if not, you can get your pain medication.' And in those fifteen minutes, we got into the groove. I started breathing with her, and I was holding her and rocking her with the contractions. She got into it and just did amazingly well. It was like we were one person, in tune with each other in a way that I don't think she ever connected with her mom. It was one of those rare, really strong bonds. Just before she reached ten centimeters, she said to me, 'Thank you for loving me.' And I was so moved by that. Afterward, she said, 'You must fall in love with every birthing woman you help.' And I said, 'I can't say it's every woman, but it's definitely part of my job to love you like I'm your mother, and to mother you in a way that your own mother can't.'"

Be aware, however, that the doula-client relationship has the potential to go the other way. Women who aren't comfortable being cared for by a woman may not respond well to a doula's care, and women who don't entirely trust other women can wind up projecting and reenacting the abandonment that took place in their pasts onto the doula, and feel abandoned by her as well.

Make sure your obstetrician, midwife, and/or doula knows about your early loss.

If your mother has died, or if you have a difficult or estranged relationship with her, let your practitioner know early in your pregnancy. Don't assume that she'll remember your mother has died just because it was included in your medical history. Because stress associated with fear, anxiety, and self-doubt can affect the progress of labor, and because early bereavement may be a risk factor for pregnancy-related and postpartum depression, doctors and midwives need to be reminded, so they can get you the help you need. Even a few counseling sessions during pregnancy appear to make a difference to mothers' outcomes during labor by reducing the length of labor and the need for cesarean births. Tell your birth attendant that you are a motherless daughter, and that labor and delivery have the potential to bring up strong emotions for you. If he or she acts uncomfortable with this idea, or tries to dismiss it, consider finding another practitioner.

Carefully choose your birth team. Revise as needed.

Pregnant motherless daughters are extremely good at "if only." *If only my mother could be here during my labor. If only she could be in the birthing room, to see this grandchild born.* Yet, in reality, only a minority—16 percent—of women with mothers surveyed for this book had their mothers present during their first births.* Plenty of women I know

---

* Nonetheless, they were still more likely to have a mother present than a mother-in-law, a sister, or a friend.

would say their mother is, in fact, the very *last* person they'd want attending their births.

"When I interview women, I always say, 'I'm there as your mother, your sister, your best friend, all rolled into one,'" explains Martha, the birth doula. "Sometimes I see this look of panic on their faces, and I'll say, 'Wait. Not *your* mother. *A* mother. Your fantasy mother.' And I see them breathe a sigh of relief, because their mother may not be the person they actually want during labor. A lot of women either don't have good relationships with their mothers, or don't want their mothers to see them in pain, or feel that they can't open up in front of their mothers. The *idea* of a mother is what they're looking for in labor, and that's what a doula is. The perfect mother, with whom they have no history."

Yet at the same time, some motherless daughters do know, in fact, that their mothers would have wanted to participate in the birth. As Linda Gray Sexton recalls in *Searching for Mercy Street: My Journey Back to My Mother, Anne Sexton,*

> Mother hadn't really told me much about her own labor, and so her silence conferred upon this travail an aura of indescribable pain. She had promised me that she would be there for my labor, as her mother had been there for hers; she had promised me that she would rub my back to help with the pain, as Mary Gray had rubbed hers. My father had been in the Navy at the time Mother went into labor; John would be by my side for the birth. She had had her mother; I did not. I was scared. *Where the hell are you when I need you?*

Because the birth-room environment can affect the course of labor, it's important to carefully select who'll be in it. From the thousands of births she's witnessed over the past thirty years, Ina May Gaskin has observed that labor can stall when someone who's not intimate with the laboring woman walks into the room, and resumes when that person leaves. Gaskin attributes this to what she calls "Sphincter Law." In simplest terms, Sphincter Law allows a woman's cervix to open up as long as she's comfortable and relaxed. It can begin to close, and contractions can slow down or stop, if she becomes upset, frightened, humiliated, or self-conscious. (It's the same principle that causes shy bladders.) Sphincters function best, Gaskin maintains, in an atmosphere of familiarity and privacy, so it's harder to have a smooth and uneventful birth if someone who irritates or upsets you is in the room.

If you notice that someone's presence is affecting your labor, or even if you're mildly uncomfortable with a certain visitor, you, your husband, or the nurse can perform what Gayle Peterson calls a "parent-ectomy" or a "person-ectomy." That's what thirty-four-year-old MaryJo did during the birth of her daughter four years ago. MaryJo and her husband had originally invited his mother to join them in the birthing room to see her first grandchild born. But the scenario didn't play out quite as warm and fuzzy as MaryJo had envisioned it.

"It was the beginning of labor, and we had just arrived at the hospital," MaryJo recalls. "My mother-in-law was running around, calling all her family members in Italy to tell them her grandchild was coming. She wasn't there for me at all. So, I asked her to leave, which I think deeply hurt her. I had also called my aunt, my mother's sister. I had just gotten to know her a few years earlier, and it wasn't a superclose relationship or anything, but I'd asked her to come. I had back labor, and both she and my husband were pushing on my back to make the pain go away. I asked her if she would mind standing behind the curtain when the time came to push the baby out, because I was embarrassed to have her see my privates. Because I really didn't *know her* know her, but I'd wanted to have a blood relative in the room. I was, like, 'Just be here with me and be my people.' When it came time for me to push, she said, 'Okay, hon, I'm going,' and I told her, 'No, just stay here.' She said, 'Are you sure?' and I said, 'Just stay here!' By then, I was okay with it. She'd been there with me, and we'd bonded."

Self-control? Forget about it.

Different women define "control" during labor and delivery differently—some as control over the birthing process; some as control over their own behavior, and some as control over the pain. Screaming in pain, moaning, crying, swearing, even taking a swing at a husband or a nurse: actions like these, normal as they are within the context of childbirth, may make a woman feel ashamed after the birth, or cause her to apologize, repeatedly, between contractions to everyone in the room. During Maya's birth, I paused from loudly cursing out the anesthesiologist only to beg the doctor to shut the door, because I was horrified by the idea of another laboring woman witnessing my lack of self-control. No one else in the labor ward that night was screaming as I was, which I took to mean that everyone *else* was getting it right.

Loss of self-control has a nasty way of making a motherless woman feel infantilized and needy, sentiments she may have taught herself to stamp out or repress in the past. They don't correspond with the resilient, self-sufficient image she typically tries to project. This creates internal dissonance at a most inconvenient time. To alleviate her distress, she may make hasty decisions about pain medication or birth management to help her regain a sense of control.

During my second labor, I had permission to cry when I needed to, to scream when it hurt, and to punch pillows when I thought I couldn't stand the pain for another minute. Nobody acted as if this were out of the ordinary, or as if anything were wrong with me. And I learned that there was no shame in acting like this. The lack of inhibition, so out of character for me, actually felt kind of good.

For Eden's birth, I was fortunate to be attended by two midwives and a birth doula who believed in the birthing room as a place to loosen psychological knots, who saw it, in fact, as the perfect place for a woman to do so. I was equally fortunate that my knots were neither too complicated nor too formidable to resist the challenge.

At our very first appointment, my midwife told me that whatever birth a woman has is the birth she is meant to have, the birth she most needs to learn from. If we can begin to think of labor and delivery not just as the final sprint into motherhood but as a journey in and of itself, then perhaps we can begin to see how opportunities for healing present themselves by way of even the most unfavorable circumstances.

"I wanted to have a home birth in my own bed, with my husband and a couple of friends there," says forty-four-year-old Wendy, who was fifteen when her mother died of cancer. "I'd been at a friend's home birth, and it was one of the most incredible experiences of my life. But that wasn't the only reason. I was scared of hospitals because, really, the last time I had been in a hospital was when my mother died." But Wendy's home birth plan fell apart when she contracted a strep infection during her ninth month of pregnancy and had to be hospitalized. Her water broke in the hospital, and she gave birth there under emergency circumstances.

"In some ways, it was a blessing that things didn't work out the way I'd wanted them to," she says, "because I ended up having an incredibly wonderful experience at the hospital, and I got to reframe my fear. Now it's easy for me to go to the hospital. I'm not afraid of it. People were good to me in the hospital. It's not all bad."

I once thought Eden's birth in 2001, and my mother's sudden appearance in it, was meant to heal me from Maya's birth in 1997. Instead, I now think both births were essential parts of the same package, and that the first birth was exactly the one I needed to set me on course for the second. In birth, there is joy and pain and gratitude, sometimes human error and even tragedy, but there is never a mistake. Every birth has its own divine little plan.

4

Postpartum

THE FIRST SIX WEEKS

The temperature topped off at 101 degrees the day we brought Maya home from the hospital. It was October 14, 1997, an unexpected autumn heat wave, and the sun was at its midday height. We would have been happy to leave earlier, but the maternity nurse wouldn't let us go until the baby peed. Every ten minutes, I peeled off Maya's tiny diaper to check, hoping she had wet it in the interim. As morning slid into lunchtime, I became more and more anxious. What, exactly, could the problem be? Not enough colostrum? Dehydration? Kidney failure?

My God, that must be it. Something was wrong with her kidneys.

I dispatched Uzi into the hallway to call his father, a nephrologist in Tel Aviv, for a consult. While he was on the phone, the nurse officiously stepped up to the foot of my hospital bed.

"Still nothing," I informed her.

She shrugged, unimpressed. "She'll do it eventually," she said, and lifted the baby from my arms.

Fifteen minutes later, she returned, pushing Maya in a little plastic bassinet on wheels. "She peed!" she announced.

Given that four hours of my obsessive checking had yielded nothing, this was hard for me to believe. "But I didn't *see* it," I said.

The nurse let go of an exasperated sigh. "Just because *you* didn't see it doesn't mean it didn't happen," she said.

I asked to see the diaper. I needed proof my baby was all right. Didn't this nurse understand? Within the hour, Maya would be released from the medical system into the care of a mother who knew nothing about the mysteries that lay beneath a baby's skin. There was so much I now needed to learn, whole textbooks full of warning signs and precautions, and so little time left before they set me loose to figure it out on my own. Right about then, a volunteer breezed in with a complimentary Peter Rabbit diaper bag and started packing up all our free samples and flowers, and then Maya was swaddled and plunked in my arms and I was being wheeled downstairs and out through the sliding glass doors, where Uzi—when had he left the hospital?—already had our red Jeep idling outside.

First hurdle on the new-parents' learning curve: the infant car seat. In the baby-products store, it had looked like such a carefully constructed, cozy little bucket. But in practice, it was a torture device in disguise. Even with the pink terrycloth insert the store owner had insisted I buy, Maya's head kept flopping over at alarming angles. "Pull over! She's going to suffocate!" I kept shouting from the back seat. Finally, I discovered I could press the heel of my right hand gently against her forehead to keep her head upright. This, of course, raised the question of how I would ever drive her anywhere alone, but I wasn't thinking that far ahead yet. It was enough, at the moment, to get her home alive.

Fortunately, we had Lorraine to help us. Lorraine, my father's second cousin, was the closest thing to a mother figure I'd had since my mother died. Orphaned as a teenager, she'd raised four children herself and understood the implications of bringing home a newborn with no grandparents around. When I'd first called her with news of the pregnancy, she'd spontaneously offered to fly from her home in Australia to help me after the birth, and she kept her promise. For those first two postpartum weeks, we sat together in the living room every day while I breast-fed Maya on the white couch. Lorraine curled up in an armchair with her knitting and told stories about my paternal grandparents while I balanced myself on a blue doughnut pillow that had been a baby gift from my friend Irene.

I was feeding on demand, as everyone had advised me, which meant for half-hour intervals every ninety minutes. To pass time when Lorraine was busy, I propped novels against the arm of the couch and devoured stories of heat and passion in distant lands: *The English Patient* by Michael Ondaatje and Arundhati Roy's *The God of Small Things*—an apt title for this strange new role of mine.

These would have been wholly good weeks, recuperative and adaptive, if not for the way Maya cried. It had started in the hospital the night after she was born, although the pediatrician on call who'd examined her there found no obvious cause. "Some babies just cry a lot," he'd explained. But like *this*? She cried all morning, she cried all day, and she cried on and off for most of the night. It was more of a scream, really, a red-faced, foot-kicking, urgent shriek that persisted for hours without pause, grating on my inner ear and shredding my nerves. The screaming echoed inside my head even when it paused, which was only when Maya ate or slept. So I fed her, constantly, until my nipples cracked and bled, and then I fed her more. We were up to thirty minutes out of every hour now. Between feedings, Lorraine patiently bounced Maya on her shoulder with her face twisted into a sympathetic grimace. "Babies cry," she echoed the doctor, trying to console us. But, when pressed, she would concede that none of her four children had cried this often or this hard.

That was motherhood, week one.

At Maya's one-week checkup, the pediatrician said most babies cry between four and six hours a day. When I clocked Maya at fourteen, the doctor diagnosed colic and prescribed patience and plenty of child-care help. The crying would, she promised, start petering off at about twelve weeks. Twelve weeks! Who could survive that long? By the end of week two, Uzi and I were already frantic with worry and exhaustion. We paced a shrieking infant back and forth across our bedroom carpet for most of the night until he would finally give up and hand her over to be fed. And so, I would latch her on to my breast and sit awake in the dark for hours, overcome by helplessness, knowing this was a less than optimal solution but not knowing what else to do.

One of the first major lessons of parenthood is learning how to trust that what exists today will not necessarily exist forever, or next week, or even tomorrow. Acquiring this wisdom, however, requires several years of experience and a good amount of faith, neither of which I possessed at the time. Yes, there were moments when I would gaze down at the baby and spill over with wonder and awe that this was my *child*, that she had come from my body, and that all she needed to thrive was, miraculously, coming from me. But then she would finish sucking, arc away from my body, and start that infernal shrieking again. And I would think: *Oh my God. We've made a tremendous mistake.*

Here was motherhood, as I had once envisioned it: Baby and me, constant companions, moving through a series of uneventful days. We'd drive down to the market, maybe stroll by the beach, and attend Mommy & Me yoga two mornings a week. After lunch, we'd visit a friend with a baby of her own. Maya and the other baby would sleep in their strollers while my friend and I drank tea, swapping cute infant stories. Right on schedule, both babies would wake to be fed, and I'd lift Maya and deftly position her under my shirt without missing a conversational beat.

This illusion of newborn as accessory was demolished almost the moment the genuine article was placed in my hands. What on earth had made me think Maya would mold to my routine, instead of the other way around? Afternoon tea? Um, no. By the second week postpartum, I was spending half my time crying in the upstairs bathroom and the other half snapping at anyone who dared to cross my path. As Lorraine's departure date fast approached, Uzi, quite frankly, started to get scared. So he did what any thirty-six-year-old father with a screaming newborn and a semi-unhinged wife would do: he called his mother for help.

This was slightly complicated by the fact that his mother lived eight thousand miles away, but never mind. My mother-in-law is a former nurse-administrator, practical and straightforward and efficient. If one of her children needs her, geography is not a deterrent. It took her just forty-eight hours to book her flight. The same afternoon we dropped Lorraine off at the airport departure dock, we looped back around to arrivals and met my mother-in-law at the baggage claim.

I was terribly, excessively, profoundly grateful to her for coming on such short notice. God yes, I was grateful. The way she bounced Maya around the house for hours, trying to soothe her cries, filled me with admiration and relief. So, it was hard to understand how such gratitude kept getting mixed up with such hopelessness and anger. Like the way I became just *so mad* when she rearranged my kitchen right after she arrived. Or the fury and despair I felt when she kept pointing out everything I was doing wrong with infant care, instead of complimenting me for doing anything right. "What's the problem?" Uzi kept asking me. "She came here to help." And then I was angry at him, too, for acting as if now that his mother was here he could breathe again, that control had finally been restored in our home and he could go back to work without guilt or fear. I think I even hated him a little during those weeks, for having a mother who would cross oceans to help him when I didn't have one of my own to call.

One afternoon, Orli, an Israeli friend, came by to visit and spent some time speaking in Hebrew with my mother-in-law. Afterward, she told me what they'd discussed. "I told her to go easy on you," Orli said. "I told her, 'Give her a break. This is a hard time for her. She doesn't have a mother.'"

I hated the way that made me sound. So pathetic and weak.

"That's not the problem," I insisted, but, naturally, it was. My mother-in-law was *a* mother, yes, but she wasn't *my* mother. She and Uzi were like their own little team, trying to tow him through this temporary rough spot. And she was Maya's grandmother, of course, and taking excellent care of her. But, understandably, she was under no obligation to also take care of me.

It feels a little embarrassing to write this now, but during those early, chaotic first weeks of motherhood, I wanted nothing more than to be mothered myself, without judgment or fear of retribution. I wanted the license to act badly if I needed to, to cry whenever the tears came, and to share the responsibility for my own care, which felt enormous when added to everything that had to be done for the baby. But even as I write this, I'm hyperconscious of exposing that needy, whiny voice inside me, the one so unbecoming to an adult woman, the voice I worked so hard to stamp down throughout my late teens and twenties and replace with one of controlled competence.

Need. Needy. Just that single letter makes the word leap from a verb of survival to an unflattering adjective. I didn't like needing anything I couldn't provide for myself, but there you have it: after Maya was born, I was needy. I needed my mother.

This was not a completely new feeling for me, only a new set of circumstances around which to shape the desire. All of my uncertainty and exhaustion and self-doubt and fear compressed into a hard little orb of longing. To have someone who would do more than sweep into my house with practical solutions. Someone who would toss an arm around me and say "You're doing fine," even when I felt I wasn't. Who would not just hold the baby when I needed to take a sitz bath, but who would notice that it was time for my sitz bath, and maybe even run the hot water for me. Someone to whom I could admit this new, strange feeling of incompetence without fear of appearing inept or weak. Perhaps the real reason I felt so incompetent as a mother during those first six weeks was because I still needed so much mothering myself.

Other women were getting it. At least some of them were, I knew. Half of the yoga moms had mothers who drove over or flew in to help after the babies arrived, and their daughters seemed to appreciate the support. Research studies have found that even grandmothers whose child-care skills are rusty or outdated none-theless have something valuable to offer after a child is born. When Myra Leifer, PhD, conducted an in-depth study of 19 pregnant women, she found that for most of her subjects, the honeymoon of the hospital stay was prolonged by visits from the new grand-mothers, who came for a week or more after the birth. In most fami-lies, it was the wife's mother, not the husband's, who provided most of the help. The visits weren't entirely stress-free: only a few of the women said their mothers had been helpful in providing instruc-tion about child care, and they often disagreed about infant-care philosophies. Most of the new mothers preferred to care for their babies themselves and have their mothers help with housework and provide companionship and emotional support. Yet, at the same time, most women felt a striking need to be mothered after the birth of their children. Those whose mothers came to help expressed feel-ings of relief at not having to assume total responsibility for child care while recovering physically from the delivery.

Psychiatrists call this type of available, nurturing grandmothers "containing mothers," for their ability to symbolically hold their daughters together through vulnerable times. A containing mother's steady, empathic presence gives her daughter the security to regress, to fall apart emotionally and then come back together, knowing that someone on the outside will remain steady, stable, and integrated. Just knowing such a person exists can give a daughter the courage and self-confidence to pull herself through.

My mother-in-law could serve this function for her three daugh-ters, but she couldn't do the same for me. She wasn't my mother, and I wasn't her daughter. The emotional history just didn't exist. Maya, on the other hand, was her granddaughter, and it was only natural for her to put the baby's needs first. I realized this one afternoon early in her visit, when I was alone in the house with Maya for an hour or two. The beds were unmade, the laundry needed to be done (again), and the baby, as usual, was screaming. So, I did what my friends on the CompuServe pregnancy forum—my only daily connection to the outer world—had been suggesting for the past week: I put Maya in her bassinet for twenty minutes while I took a quick shower and made my bed. They'd assured me it wouldn't hurt her, and that I would feel better after the break.

As luck would have it, just as I finished making the bed, my mother-in-law returned and heard the screaming. When she saw me calmly tucking in the top sheet while the baby lay crying at my side, she snatched the hollering infant from the bassinet and made a dash from the room. She was discreet enough to say nothing about the incident, but her sense of alarm had conveyed to me, *What are you doing to this baby? How can you leave her there to cry?*

If I'd had a clear head that day, I would have followed them downstairs. I would have explained, "It's all right. I wasn't hurting her. I just needed a minute to make the bed." But three hours of broken sleep per day do bad things to your nerves. Instead of going downstairs, I sat on the edge of the tub in the upstairs bathroom and cried. Where, I wondered, was the person who was supposed to ask not "What are you doing to this baby?" but "What is this baby doing to *you*?" Never was the distinction between infant care and mother care more clear to me. I was a mother, now fully responsible for the emotional survival of a child, yet also, it seemed, still emotionally very much on my own.

How much of this longing, I wonder now, is the natural response of a new mother, how much comes from being a motherless daughter, and how much is representative of a woman's individual personality? That's always the question, isn't it? Am I a normal mother, or a normal motherless daughter, or just off-the-charts unique?

For most of us, I suspect, the answer is a bit of all three. The first six weeks of motherhood are a notoriously uneven time for even the most prepared and experienced of women. A major upheaval in one's personal life, a vast and disconcerting new set of responsibilities, physical recuperation, and dramatic hormonal adjustments create a pretty standard recipe for temporary chaos. If I had five dollars for every friend who's called me during her first month of motherhood, wailing, "Why didn't anyone tell me it was going to be like *this*?" (though, of course, we all had; she just hadn't listened) . . . well, I'd have enough funding to open and staff a new-mothers' support center of my own.

The first weeks of motherhood have been described as a phase of intensity and paradoxes, a time that includes both massive increases and plunging deficits in a woman's self-esteem. Infant care awakens in a mother an exquisite sense of power to comfort, protect, and respond to her newborn's needs. Yet moments of confidence and self-pride can be quickly undone when what worked so successfully yesterday has no visible effect today. And then the self-doubt comes rushing back in.

At the same time, these weeks are also a sacred, precious period of intense bonding and intimate seclusion, when the world of regular routines, professional commitments, and household tasks is abandoned in favor of a snug and timeless cocoon perfectly de-signed for two. British pediatrician and renowned child psychiatrist D. W. Winnicott, MD, called these first weeks of motherhood a time of "primary maternal preoccupation," during which the mother sur-renders all else to the service of meeting her newborn's needs. By withdrawing in this manner, and zeroing in on her baby with such intense concentration, she can identify with his most basic needs and determine how to best meet them. For motherless mothers, this is often a time of great satisfaction and gratitude, insofar as they feel able to give a child the kind of intense, focused mothering they once lost. At the same time, it can be a time of great sadness, as they try to adjust not only to new motherhood but also to motherlessness from a different angle.

"Even though I have wonderful in-laws, they live across the country," explains thirty-eight-year-old Felice, who lost her mother at age twenty-one and now has a year-old son. "So, my husband and I did this new-baby thing alone. It was just very scary, very lonely. Doing it without my mother was probably the hardest thing I've ever done since losing her. I've gone through a lot of emotions about it. I went to my doctor after I gave birth and said, 'I feel so sad.' I was actually feeling two emotions at once: happy and blessed that I had my son, but also so sad about not having my mom. I would think, *How can I feel these horrible, sad feelings when I have this beautiful new baby?* I would just sit there and hold him in my arms and cry for the loss of what my mother would never see. More than anything, she wanted to be a grandmother, to see her daughters get married and have kids, and she never got to see that. So I cried for her, for me, for him. Everything. And then there was the guilt that came from feeling so lonely when I had a wonderful husband, and a wonderful new baby, and a wonderful life but still felt scared and lonely, really, about how to do it. I wanted someone I could call and ask, 'What do I do?' but there was nobody there."

Only a handful of studies have been conducted on motherless daughters and their transition to motherhood, but the few that exist offer some evidence that this group adapts to the postpartum period differently than other women do. A British study comparing forty pregnant women who'd lost a parent to death or separation before age eleven with a control group of "non-loss" pregnant women found that the parent-loss group tended to act in a more polarized fashion toward their newborns. They were either overanxious about being perfect mothers, or more neglectful toward their babies than the other women were. They were also twice as likely to be depressed, felt more helpless as new mothers, and reported having more health problems and fatigue. Even though they had prepared for the arrival of their babies more efficiently, when things went wrong with their housing, marriages, or caretaking behaviors, they seemed to go wrong in a more extreme manner. Instead of experiencing marital stress, for example, women in the parent-loss group were more likely to separate or divorce.

Nancy Maguire, PhD, a clinical psychologist in Oakland, California, in her study of forty first-time mothers, found that women who'd experienced early mother loss felt more stress and postpartum depression during their transitions to motherhood than other women did. Another British study, however, found no direct connection between early loss and postpartum depression. Instead, as its authors explained, early loss acts as a "background vulnerability factor," which, when coupled with a stressful event during pregnancy or the postpartum period, such as marital disharmony, loss of another loved one, or lack of social support, is likely to lead to depression.

My survey results didn't find that motherless mothers are more prone to postpartum depression than other women are—20 percent in the motherless group, versus 10 percent in the control group, both within the range considered "normal"—but I did find that some motherless daughters are more vulnerable than others. Those who'd lost a mother before age six, who'd had a negative experience with labor and/or delivery, and who received no outside help from family members or friends after their first baby was born were more likely than other motherless women to be diagnosed with postpartum depression after the birth of a first child.

Lack of support during the postpartum period is a well-known risk factor for depression. Other risk factors include prior episodes of depression; social isolation; low feelings of self-efficacy and self-esteem; a history of victimization or abuse; profound sleep deprivation; marital stress; serious doubts about having this particular child; a complicated emotional relationship with one's own mother; a family history of mental illness or suicide; a baby who cries excessively; and a naturally pessimistic or fatalistic point of view, especially when a woman believes she has no control over external events.

Early bereavement also places women at risk, says Shari Lusskin, MD, the director of Reproductive Psychiatry and a clinical assistant professor at New York University School of Medicine. Any motherless mother who feels sad or weepy for a prolonged period after a birth should alert her physician, Lusskin advises.

Postpartum depression, however, is not to be confused with the more prevalent "baby blues." The blues, characterized by weepiness, sadness, anger, and moodiness, affects between 50 and 80 percent of all new mothers, and typically lasts from twenty-four to forty-eight hours after the birth to up to ten days.

Postpartum depression is a more serious, long-lasting state most commonly seen during the third to ninth month postpartum, although it can start as early as six weeks after the birth and last up to one year. It involves more intense feelings of sadness, anxiety, and despair, and often interferes with a new mother's daily functioning. Postpartum depression affects up to 20 percent of new mothers. An even more serious condition is postpartum psychosis, which generally occurs in women who have a personal or family history of mental imbalance. Postpartum psychosis is an extremely dangerous condition, in which the mother may feel the urge to hurt the baby. It's quite rare, affecting fewer than 1 percent of all new mothers, and requires immediate treatment.

With motherless mothers, it's possible that baby blues and postpartum depression are complicated by—and even sometimes confused with—the kind of fresh mourning cycle often experienced by a motherless daughter undergoing a major, transitional life event. Clinical depression and grief reactions share similar characteristics, such as sleep disturbances, irritability, sadness, hopelessness, weepiness, and despair, and it's important for clinicians to distinguish between the two. While traditional methods for dealing with depression can improve these women's ability to cope, grief counseling should also be considered as part of their treatment protocol.

Because obstetricians tend not to ask patients about their psychiatric history or their current psychiatric state, it's important for motherless mothers to be proactive about getting help, Lusskin explains. "They need to ask their obstetrician to refer them to somebody," she says. "And they should ask their o.b.s to keep an eye on them. If an o.b. isn't interested, they should find a new o.b. And if they're seeing a therapist already, they should alert their psychiatrist that this is likely to be an issue for them. This is a whole subgroup of women who are at risk."

Don't minimize—or let anyone else minimize—the extent of your distress. "Anybody who thinks they're depressed postpartum is depressed until proven otherwise," Lusskin adds. "Because very few new mothers will volunteer that they're feeling depressed. Whereas someone with garden-variety depression might just call up when they're feeling bad, postpartum women systematically defer care out of shame, guilt, or embarrassment. They feel that they should be grateful for their child, and to not feel bonded to that child is very scary."

Thirty-six-year-old Christine, whose daughters are now four and one, remembers the period just after the birth of her first daughter as a time of wildly mixed emotions. Christine was four when her mother was bedridden with cancer, and six when she died, and has few memories of being mothered herself. "I never saw anyone take care of a child," she explains. "My father was a full-blown alcoholic, so after my mother died, it was fend for yourself." This lack of role modeling meant that Christine would have to find her confidence as a mother through the act of mothering itself. It's not an uncommon situation for a motherless daughter to be in, but this kind of acquisition, as Christine soon learned, takes time.

"I was terrified when Kyra was first born," Christine recalls, "but then, six or eight hours later, she was lying in her little bassinet in the hospital and she opened her eyes and looked right at me, and this feeling came over me about what I would do to take care of her. I was, like, 'You are my cub and I will *kill* anyone who tries to hurt you.' From that point of view, we were connected, but I was always scared. There are so many videotapes, when she was an infant, where I have this look on my face, like I have no idea, this deer-in-the-headlights, I-don't-know-if-I'm-doing-this-right look. I was following the books, I was talking to my friends, but I still felt completely lost. So completely lonesome for my mother. I woke up every day scared, and I went to bed every night scared. I remember her sleeping in the bassinet next to my bed, and I was terrified. I used to always say to myself in my head, *God, don't let me screw this up. Please, don't let me screw this up.*"

Repeatedly during our interviews, women described their first month or two of motherhood as joyful and exhilarating, but also colored by a sort of existential loneliness, as if giving birth to a blood relation served as a painful reminder of being untethered from a similar relationship in their past. Taking on the identity of mother had a way of further reminding them of their motherlessness, which was often the very opposite of what these women had expected. Motherhood, they had hoped, would restore the mother-child bond, not call more attention to the one that was severed.

The lack of practical and emotional support motherless women have—or perceive themselves to have—relative to other mothers during the postpartum period is the most obvious and most common reason why motherless mothers describe these weeks as a particularly challenging time. But I've found that the postpartum experience for most motherless mothers involves additional factors specific to this group. Defined broadly, they fit into the following categories:

Hyper Self-reliance

"Being pregnant [the first time] brought up a lot of stuff for me: I'm alone, I'm going to have to do this alone, I'm scared to do it alone," recalls Jennifer Lauck. "But also, because I'm such a self-sufficient person, it brought up how I was more alone by my own competency. I'd been mothering myself for so long, in this very willful way, that when it came to breaking down and needing help, needing a mom, I didn't know how to start to ask. I wouldn't ask my husband for help. He was actually really ready to help me, but I wanted to project this image that I thought he needed to have of me, that I was this all-competent, totally pulled-together woman. When, instead, I was literally sleep-deprived and hormonal and totally overwhelmed, which led to kind of a breakdown. I went into therapy again, and my therapist said, 'You're sleep-deprived. You need help. Ask for help.' It sounded so easy to do, but for me it was really hard. But I got a nanny, and I started doing trades with other moms. It was a great experience for me. Because I really don't like being alone anyway. I don't like not asking for help. It had just become a conditioned behavior."

Motherless women are, for the most part, highly practiced at the art of self-reliance. Many of us were given a good deal of control over our own lives at an early age, and by adulthood, we've become accustomed to molding situations (and avoiding situations) to meet our own emotional needs. Most of us learned long ago that we couldn't trust others to act in our best interest—too often, they'd let us down. Relying on ourselves, on the other hand, worked as a pretty good hedge against disappointment.

As motherless women, we're also hyperconscious of asking for too much, especially from older women, worried about exceeding the boundaries of propriety or facing a polite refusal that so often contains the unspoken addendum, *because you're not my daughter*. So, we train ourselves not to ask. And, as a result, we grow into women with self-images that leave little room for neediness. I suspect this stoic self-reliance, so crucial to a motherless daughter's emotional survival, is a significant reason why motherless mothers report having so little outside assistance after their first children are born*—not necessarily because no one exists who would help them, but because they don't ask. Even worse, they've lost faith that help asked for will be forthcoming.

Self-sufficiency, as Harriet Lerner, PhD, author of *The Mother Dance*, explains, is the archenemy of the newly minted mom.

---

* Fifty-two percent of the motherless group reported having help from "no one" other than a husband or partner after their first child was born, compared to only 15 percent of women in the control group.

Sooner or later, she's going to have to pick up the phone. For some motherless women, the postpartum period may be the first time since a mother's death that willful self-reliance alone is not enough. Meeting an infant's needs twenty-four hours a day leaves little, if any, time to meet one's own needs. It may not take a whole village to shepherd mother and child through their first six weeks, but it surely takes more than one frazzled woman, operating alone.

Yet the United States is one of the few cultures on the globe where new mothers are expected to take full responsibility for a newborn immediately after birth, when its needs and her needs are most intense. It's no coincidence that in non-Western cultures, where highly elaborate, structured postpartum rituals and female support for a new mother is prevalent after a birth, postpartum depressions are rare. The high degree of ceremony, ritual, and personal attention given to new mothers after births in Nigeria, Nepal, China, and Southeast Asia, for example, is believed to contribute to the comparatively low rates of postnatal depression and baby blues in those countries.

As motherless daughters, many of us had to be thorough and resourceful to survive. We're accustomed to doing things well, and doing things right. We became perfectionists by circumstance, if not always by nature. But these can be particularly unhelpful character traits during the postpartum weeks.

"Someone who's a perfectionist is at high risk for getting into trouble postpartum," Shari Lusskin explains. "Because babies are not born with an instruction manual. You can't master infant care. If you're used to getting an A in everything, you'll want to get an A in mothering, but it doesn't work the same way. A woman who is used to doing things well and doesn't immediately feel a sense of mastery as a mom feels bad. This is a good time for a woman to let go of obsessive, perfectionist tendencies. And the ones who can't let go, we treat, because those tendencies interfere. The tenser a woman is about all this, the tenser her baby will be."

Some researchers believe that a new mother's ability to find confidence and autonomy relies on having good practical and emotional support in the home, but mothers need contact with experienced mothers, too. The first stage of motherhood is a vulnerable, suggestible time. A network of like-minded others becomes essential for advice, support, and reality checks. Female relatives and friends, pediatricians, support group leaders, older neighbors, even the woman who owns the pharmacy on the next block all can act as vital resources for a woman who's trying to find diapers that don't leak, or is having trouble finding the right position for burping, or is wondering if her mother-in-law's aversion to pacifiers is an opinion shared by more than one.

For a new mother, such women constitute what psychiatrist Daniel Stern calls an "affirming matrix," a psychological environment of sorts, which helps her feel secure enough to explore her parental abilities and trust her instincts. Of particular importance to this matrix is one or more models or guides—sort of "master craftswomen," as Stern explains it, who've already passed through the new-mother phase. For some women, this is the biological mother, but, obviously, not for all.

"The affirming matrix often has at its center the wish for a benign mother figure or idealized grandmother who can perform the positive roles of a mother without the inevitable bad parts," Stern writes. "This is a dream solution that is rarely realized. The new mother's mother may be too far away, or no longer living, or the relationship with her too problematic, but even so, most new mothers seek elements of it whenever they can. Mothers have a profound need, whether conscious or not, for psychological support that expresses itself in the urge to swap information and observe other mothers in action. Wherever mothers find each other, whether in the park or in play groups or at the pediatrician's office, an exchange of information and perception takes place on many levels. These interactions satisfy the need for assurance (I am taking care of my baby adequately), learning tricks of the trade (so that's how you keep the pacifier from getting lost), measuring how you are doing (I figured out how to quickly collapse the stroller to get on the bus), and belonging to the new domain of motherhood (I am not alone in this new land)."

My first instinct when feeling overwhelmed is to retreat into a small, tidy space and try to think my way out of the dilemma. This kind of behavior—need I even say it?—couldn't sustain me for long after Maya was born. I *had* to ask for help. So, even though it was hard, terribly hard, for me to make some of those phone calls, and to admit to select individuals that this person who'd previously had such visibly high levels of competence didn't have any idea what to do, I had to willingly put myself in a position where I might hear a woman say, "I don't have time for this," or even a simple, "No." Such refusals always felt like rejection, and I was terribly afraid to come across as needy or whiny. Still, when I couldn't handle the isolation or the confusion anymore, I picked up the phone. And I found that other mothers, for the most part, were glad to give me advice.

I called the yoga moms, friends with older children, and a maternal aunt in Florida. My husband called his parents in Israel when we had medical questions. We asked our neighbor, a nurse, if we could call her in case of emergency. When Maya was ten weeks old, and the crying finally stopped, I joined a new-mothers' support group that met once a week. And with this patchwork quilt of support, I got by.

Members of the affirming matrix, as other motherless mothers have discovered, often come from unexpected places. That's what thirty-eight-year-old Corinne, who was eight when her mother died, learned after her son was born. Corinne and her husband had help from Corinne's childhood friend for their first week home from the hospital. After her friend left, Corinne had to immediately return to work, planning an event for one of her clients. Her husband went back to work, and she was spending daytime hours home alone with her newborn son, making phone calls during his naps. She remembers those as chaotic, isolating days.

"I was working from home, not taking showers for days in a row, stressing, trying to pull it all off," she says. "I wasn't sure how much of what I was feeling was normal postpartum stuff, and how much of it was just overwhelming. It's hard for me to ask for help, so I had to literally force myself to pick up the phone and anticipate who might be a safe, potential resource for all my new-mom questions. I had to force myself to create a support system. That was a little out of the box for me, but I made myself do it.

"You have to swallow your pride to not be too self-sufficient," she continues. "If you've never been a mom before, you don't know this stuff. It's not innate. Most of it is very much learned. When I called the doctor's office for the first time, the nurse-practitioner got on the phone. I said, 'I know this is an obvious question, but I have to ask. I'm a new mom.' And she was so nice and patient. There was never that hesitation or that tone of voice I was so afraid of, that would say, 'You're an idiot.' I just bonded with her on the phone, and she called back the next day to see how my son and I were doing. Between two of my girlfriends who already had kids and the fact that I could pick up the phone at any time and call this nurse-practitioner and she would call me back, I managed to get through the first month or two. At some point, I even told the nurse, 'I don't have a mom,' just to be upfront, as a way of saying, 'I need some extra help here.' It was just the greatest gift that she came along."

Is there a foolproof way to ask for help, when years of practice have taught a woman to get by without it? "Just do it," Harriet Lerner says. "Avoid self-sufficiency at any cost. You're not the only person who's feeling vulnerable and terrified and worried that you're getting it all wrong. You need to connect with all the functional family members you have, and with friends who will tell you the truth. You don't want to seek solace with mothers who tell you they're getting along swimmingly. You want mothers who are going to tell you how hard it is for them, too."

Persisting Loyalty to the Lost Mother

For many women, accepting the help that's offered can be just as hard as asking for it—especially when it comes from someone other than the person who, in most cultures, is designated to step forward and provide assistance after her daughter's child is born.

Mothers-in-law, stepmothers, older sisters, or other family members and friends may all offer help with newborn care, but a subconscious loyalty to one's own mother, and the fantasy of the care she'd provide at this time, have a way of making anyone else's assistance seem inadequate and incomplete. This is the stubborn insistence of the child, born from a lingering, fierce attachment to the lost mother and a resistance to letting anyone else fill her role.

Motherless women, Daniel Stern theorizes, may feel a "guilty inhibition" about accepting help from other women. "These women have a feeling when their mother dies of 'I'll never forget you. I'll always love you. No one will ever displace you,'" Stern says. When coupled with a lifelong pattern of saying, "I've got to do it all myself," a deep ambivalence about accepting postpartum help from others can emerge.

That's how new mothers wind up in the confusing position of feeling both grateful and resentful for the help they do receive: grateful that someone answered their request for help and provided it, yet resentful toward anyone who tries to fill the mother's role. When thirty-one-year-old Michelle and her husband brought their premature twin daughters home from the NIC-U, they had round-the-clock help with feedings and diaper changes from Michelle's aunt, her best friend's mother, and several close friends. They couldn't have managed otherwise, she says, which is why she worries about sounding ungrateful when she admits that the support they received wasn't the kind of support she needed most.

"At first, having the help wasn't helpful," she explains. "I don't know if it was the personalities of the people who were there, or what. I remember feeling resentful toward them, thinking, *What are you doing here? My mom should be here.* I was the first one of my friends to have children, and I had them in a big way. People did the best they could. But now I look back and wonder, *Gosh, why didn't they just make a meal? Or why didn't they watch the babies so I could have slept?* Because I was on bed rest for five weeks, I didn't have much muscle strength, but I did inherit my mom's strong will, and I think that's what got me through. There was a day when I just didn't eat all day long, because I was in that really busy time, changing diapers, feeding them, and no one noticed. It was just crazy."

What Michelle really wanted was someone who would recognize what she needed and take the initiative to provide it. Better yet, she wanted someone who would intuitively know what she needed, and automatically know how to fill those needs, without having to be asked. This is the extended fantasy of the motherless child, yearning for the person who can magically heal and fix and realign, who acts from a place of identification and empathy rather than from altruism or duty. Just as the young, egocentric child expects a mother to read her mind, to know exactly which needs to meet and when, a motherless daughter imagines her mother, as a grandmother, would be able to do the same.

The "Other Grandmothers"

Relationships with stepmothers and mothers-in-law can be particularly tricky at this time, since these family members are in the most obvious position to fill an absent mother's place. Sometimes they'll step forward with offers of help and advice. Sometimes they won't. I've heard stories from women whose stepmothers kept a wide berth during their stepdaughters' postpartum periods, silently reemphasizing the lack of blood ties, while giving preferential treatment to their biological daughters after a birth. I've also heard from women who did accept help from stepmothers and mothers-in-law, with varying degrees of success. But most frequently, I heard stories from women who pushed away their mothers-in-law and stepmothers, treating them like interlopers trying to intrude on someone else's rightful place.

"At the beginning, I didn't want my in-laws to be anywhere near my son, because I was so angry that *I* didn't have anybody for him," remembers sixty-eight-year-old Marty, who was twenty-two when her mother died and twenty-five when she lost her father. "I tried to keep them away. I hated it when they came over. And it was their *grandchild*. They had every right to be there. I wrote a letter to my friend about how I felt, and she pointed out, 'You know, those are the only grandparents he has.' And I thought, *You know, she's right*. Looking at it that way started to turn everything around for me."

Her friend's direct statement, so simple yet so obscured by Marty's feelings of loss, helped Marty cross a critical line during her postpartum period. She went from thinking as a daughter without a mother to thinking as a mother with a child, and put his interests before her own. Her in-laws *were* the only grandparents her son had. Did she want to deprive him of that relationship because she was grieving for what she didn't have? When she thought about it honestly, the answer was no.

Marty was fortunate: she had in-laws who were eager to see their grandson, and were enthusiastic in their offers of help. But other women have objectively difficult or rejecting mothers-in-law and stepmothers, from whom assistance has rarely been forthcoming, and to whom they're unlikely to turn for support. Still other stepmothers and mothers-in-law live too far away to offer practical help, or are too elderly to lend a hand when a new baby arrives.

Whatever the individual situation, few motherless mothers wind up relying on these women, or receiving support from them at this time. Although a mother-in-law was the most likely person to help a motherless mother during her first postpartum period (other than a husband or partner), only 16 percent of the women surveyed said they'd relied on her (7 percent had help from a sister; 11 percent from another family member, such as a grand-mother or aunt; and 7 percent relied on friends). Even more strik-ing, however, is that although 52 percent of the women surveyed had stepmothers, only 3 percent of them reported receiving help from her after a first child was born. Perhaps this is because the re-lationship between motherless daughters and stepmothers is rarely an easy one. Only 6 percent of the women who have stepmothers reported being "very close" to her, and 65 percent reported being "not close at all." For these women, "stepmother" may feel like a generous term. "My father's wife" is how many of them choose to describe her.

It may be emotionally easier for motherless women to accept help from a compassionate stranger for hire, such as a baby nurse or postpartum doula. With a skilled professional, there will be no hurt feelings, no crushing disappointments, no family dramas if the ar-rangement doesn't work out. Most important, a baby nurse or doula is less likely to be perceived as a substitute for the mother, and if any confusion or awkwardness does develop, the relationship is a busi-ness transaction and can be stopped at any time.

When twenty-eight-year-old Samantha, who was twenty-three when her mother died, gave birth to her first son, her father wanted to provide her with support he knew he couldn't give. So, he offered to pay for two weeks' services from a baby nurse. It was a generous gift, Samantha says, since she and her husband would never have spent their own money on one. Having an experienced woman in the house was important to Samantha, and she was re-lieved it turned out to be someone with whom she had no history. "Because who otherwise would have been there for me when the baby came home from the hospital?" she asks. "My mom. If my dad had asked my mom's sister, or my mother-in-law, or even my best girlfriend to come live with us for a week and help me take care of my baby, they wouldn't have measured up, because they wouldn't have been my mother. And so, having a stranger there was easier than having my aunt, or anybody else. There was no personal relationship, there was no disappointment. The baby nurse came, and it was great."

The Myth of Instantaneous Bonding

Five days after Maya's birth, I was nursing her on the white couch when the phone rang. "Julie!" I shouted. It was a yoga mom whose due date had been two days after mine, and her call could mean only one thing. Another yoga baby had been born.

I could hear the newborn cooing from the hospital bed as Julie related the details of her birth. "I'm completely in love," she confessed. Her voice was dreamy and ethereal, as if she were in the first flushes of romance.

I looked down at the black-haired infant sucking furiously at my right breast. On good days, we called her "Baby Mo." On bad days, which were becoming most days, Uzi referred to her as "our vicious little screaming thing."

Responsibility, yes. Attachment, I suppose. But love? No, I couldn't say that's what I was feeling. Not yet.

Fortunately, a friend who'd given birth to twins ten months earlier had warned me about this. "Don't worry if you don't love the baby right away," she'd said. "For the first couple of months, I was just going through the motions, but somewhere during the third month, I looked at them one day and it just hit me that I loved them *so much*."

Birth folklore strongly suggests that women feel an immediate, powerful bond upon first glance of their newborn, as if identification were the only prerequisite for love. But in truth, hours or days of grueling labor and anesthetics that numb body or mind hardly leave women in optimal physical or mental condition for what Susan Maushart calls "the soft-focus swoon" of postbirth. If a woman can manage a weak smile after all that, she's doing pretty well, but we're led to expect more from ourselves. Much more. Immediate and instantaneous love, to be exact. And the result? Too many women feeling guilty, ashamed, upset, or scared by what they think is an alarming deviation from the norm.

As Andi Buchanan so succinctly writes in *Mother Shock*, we're given nine months of preparation to become a mother, and only about thirty seconds to snap into being one. What on earth makes us think the transition can happen that fast? For many new mothers, the "falling" part of "falling in love" is gradual rather than instantaneous, a process that evolves rather than one that's unconscious and swift. The taking-hold time of the postpartum period is, in many couples, delayed at least until parents bring their infants home from the hospital and start feeling comfortable in their new roles. The shock of new parenthood takes at least that long to wear off, often longer. Some women, like my friend, don't feel completely attached to their infants until the end of the third postpartum month, which, in most cases, isn't reason for alarm.

Motherless mothers who expected a sudden rush of love that never arrived, however, may perceive this absence as validation of their self-doubt. Some women may have spent the last nine months (or longer) questioning their ability to mother. *Oh no,* they think when they don't feel instantly bonded. *Maybe this means I really don't have what it takes to be a mother, after all.* They may also identify with what they interpret as their infant's loss, perceiving him as an unloved child and feeling sorrow and pity for him.

"When my son was born, I expected all this flood of emotion, like, 'Oh, I'm a *mother*,' and "Oh, I *love* this wonderful baby,'" recalls forty-one-year-old Penny, who was seven when her mother died. "But I didn't feel that. I mean, I was maternal, I took care of him, but I didn't feel a strong bond to him. And I thought there was something wrong with me, because we'd done the Lamaze class and heard all about bonding with the baby right away and how important it was. I was actually a little worried. I wasn't abusive toward him at all, but I was afraid that because I didn't feel the way I was supposed to feel that something like that could happen. So, I was kind of afraid to be alone with him at first.

"He had to have hernia surgery when he was six weeks old, and that was very hard," she continues. "Because I felt, like, 'Here's this little boy, this baby. He's just a newborn and he's going under the knife. Does he even know that his mother doesn't quite love him? Can he feel that?' I was terrified that something would happen to him, and he would never know that. When he came out from the surgery, I just kind of attacked him. I grabbed him up and told him how much I loved him. I still wasn't feeling it quite yet. But that was the point when I started to open up. I'd say it probably took about three years to really feel connected to him."

Penny's son is now twenty and they share a very warm mother-son relationship. She also has a fourteen-year-old daughter, with whom she feels solidly bonded. Her second postpartum experience was easier, she says, partly because she knew what to expect from a newborn. But partly it was easier because having already opened her heart fully to her son, she was no longer afraid to let a child in. Fear of loving so completely, of loving a child as fiercely and intensely as a mother does, may also cause motherless mothers to bond slowly with their newborns. Such love, to someone who's lost it before, opens up the possibility of another devastating loss. But warming slowly to a child feels safer, like wading into a deep ocean step by step, testing the sensation a few inches at a time.

Postpartum feelings of attachment can also be delayed by the stress of a premature or difficult birth; problems connecting with the fetus during pregnancy; the workload following the birth of twins or triplets; and by the baby's temperament. Mothers of colicky infants and babies who cry excessively, for example, report lower feelings of attachment toward their infants until the crying stops. Maternal attachment also appears to be related to the quality of a woman's marriage or partnership, and the extent to which her husband contributes to child care. There is absolutely no evidence, however—I repeat: *no evidence*—that a slow and gradual attachment means a woman is unqualified as a mother. While women who didn't receive adequate mothering may be at statistically higher risk for bonding problems with their infants, this is by no means their destiny. The equation just isn't that simple.

Feelings of attachment may grow slowly, but in the vast majority of cases, they do arrive. And there's no question about recognizing them when they do. "It took me a while to really connect with my boys," explains thirty-one-year-old Paula, the mother of one-year-old twin sons, who was twelve when her own mother died. "And I felt guilty about that for a while. Now I feel that bonding is more of an evolving process. Every day I get closer with them. Every day it's a little bit harder to leave them when I'm heading out, even for an errand. I kind of look at them a little differently, or appreciate them a little more every day. I was surprised by that. Because I think that what I'd read, what I had in my head, was that I was going to have this immediate, overwhelming love for them. Yes, I loved them, but it wasn't quite that intense at first."

Motherless daughters who expect motherhood to be a magical transformation from the start are bound to be disappointed. Expecting a newborn to rouse an awesome maternal power from within places quite a burden on a week-old baby. A baby is not meant to be a catalyst for enormous inner change, nor a means to instantaneous healing. A baby, by design, is a baby. Soft and smooth, lovely to cuddle and heavenly to smell, but a baby nonetheless.

The primal, fierce connection we crave with a child of our own eventually does come. It just may not be during the first few weeks of motherhood. These are days of adjustment and accommodation, of watching and responding and learning how to recognize cues. The most startling aspect of new motherhood, for me, was not the dramatic internal shift I felt in the first few postpartum days, but the lack of one. During pregnancy, I'd imagined that delivery would somehow erase the self that had existed before and instantaneously usher in a higher, more fully rendered version, someone who had flung off the cape of immaturity and now stood confident and proud. Instead, sitting in the hospital bed and at home on the white couch, I basically felt like myself with a baby. Everything had changed. Yet not all that much had changed. Each time I looked in the mirror, I was surprised to see the same old face looking back. Same old eyebrows. Same old lips. Same me. That's one of the biggest mysteries of the postpartum period: how the emotional bonds of motherhood, when they finally come, can transform a woman *so much*, yet how she can nonetheless remain, fundamentally, so much the same.

5

Getting Attached

MOTHER-CHILD BONDING

We turned a dramatic corner as a family when Maya was ten weeks old. I was preparing dinner in the kitchen while she sat in her blue bouncy chair on the floor near my feet. Every so often I looked up at the wall clock above the pantry door. Ten minutes. Fifteen minutes. Could it really be? At twenty minutes, I couldn't stand it anymore. I called Uzi at work. He answered the phone at his desk.

"Guess what!" I shouted. "Maya's been in the bouncy seat for *twenty whole minutes* without crying!"

"Really?!" His enthusiasm soared to meet mine, then quickly retreated a notch. "Damn. I wish I were there to see it," he said.

It was a measure, perhaps, of exactly how awful ten weeks of colic had been, that twenty minutes of silence could produce such an exhilarating effect. Maya started crying just after I hung up the phone, but no matter. We'd made it twenty minutes without

screaming, and those twenty minutes of peace were our first brilliant indicator of hope.

It's laughable now, but before Maya was born, my vague idea
of parenting a newborn involved pretty much everything I'd
done before—grocery shopping, dinner parties, even Friday-night
movies with friends—except with a baby in tow. The concepts of
sleep schedules and crying jags were utterly foreign to me. The one
time we tried to take Maya to a movie, she screamed so long and so
loud that I spent the entire second half nursing her in an otherwise
empty lobby. Ditto for dinner parties. I became so accustomed to
breastfeeding on family-room couches while the other adults clinked
glasses in the dining room that eventually I didn't see the point in
going out at night anymore.

Motherhood was not what I had expected in this regard, and I
was resentful about this at first. But after three months, we'd developed something of a truce. I thought a little less about everything
I'd given up, and when the crying stopped, I began to recognize
what had been gained. At the end of January, we bought Maya a
polar-fleece snowsuit and took her on an airplane to New York to
see my family, our first trip as a threesome. It seemed we had made
it through the hardest phase. At night, Uzi and I lay in each other's
arms while Maya slept peacefully in the bassinet beside us, and did
breathing exercises together, believing that nothing we could encounter in the course of parenthood—not belligerence, not failing
grades, neither drugs nor early sex, *nothing*—could be as emotionally taxing as those first three months had been.

And once the colic had passed, Maya was *happy*. Excessively
happy, almost embarrassingly so. She sat in the stroller and played
with her bare feet, gazing up at strangers with a huge, gummy
smile. People stopped on sidewalks to ogle her and remark, "What
a happy baby you have!" From three months onward, she charmed
everyone, not least of all her parents, who were damn relieved to
finally discover what all the fuss over babies was about.

For ten weeks, I'd felt horribly incompetent as a mother,

hopelessly inept at calming my baby's cries. She wanted me, but nothing I did seemed to matter, which was frustrating and confusing, at best. But at three months, and four months, and six, a more reciprocal relationship developed. Maya smiled at me, I smiled back, and she laughed and stuck her foot in her mouth. When she cried, I cuddled her, and she stopped. A logical form of cause and effect had filtered into our household, and figuring it out considerably boosted my morale.

Studies have shown that first-time mothers of easygoing babies report high levels of confidence in their own abilities, and that mothers of fussy or hard-to-please babies feel less competent in their new role. Mothers who feel socially isolated also reported feeling less confident as mothers, a good argument for hauling oneself and one's child to morning or weekend new-mothers' groups. "In the beginning, motherhood is so lonely," says forty-six-year-old Sarah, a mother of three, who was eleven when her own mother died of cancer. "When my first son was born, I had one group of friends, the people I worked with, and they didn't have kids. I stopped working when he was born, so I tried to establish new relationships with other mothers. Support groups, play groups, whatever. Because I'm pretty shy, it was really hard for me."

Early mother loss often resonates in mothers as feelings of inferiority, lack of self-esteem, and self-doubt, and during her son's first year, Sarah remembers, she was eager to do everything right. "I was always afraid I would screw it up," she recalls. She bought all of the best baby items and read all the recommended books, hoping that products and information would somehow compensate for what she felt she lacked. "My sister used to look at my baby bag and say to me, 'You know, if you got stuck somewhere, that child would not be hungry, tired, or bored for six weeks.' Because I always had six diapers, three changes of clothes, formula, books, toys. I used to call it my roadie bag. It was part of the feeling of 'What if I don't have what I need? What if I make a mistake?' In the beginning, what motivated me most was that anxiety, that fear of doing something wrong."

The Tuesday-morning class I attended with Maya was useful, insofar as when I looked around the circle, I saw that I appeared no more and no less competent than most of the other mothers in the room. Sure, some of them had live-in nannies, and others dressed their children in spotless starched dresses with white tights and matching hair ribbons, but for the most part, we were all consumed by radical mother shock, struggling to figure out the rules and expectations of this new terrain. Several women were decidedly more frantic about this than I was, and though I don't like to profit from another's misfortune, recognizing this comforted me a great deal.

And there were also the yoga moms, who met at a different house every Friday morning for almost two years, providing me with my first real sense of a mothering community. We called each other with parenting questions early in the morning and late at night, got together on the weekends with our husbands, and celebrated each child's first birthday with joyous parties and elaborate party favors for everyone in the group. There was even talk, for a while, of starting our own preschool.

Still, all this concerned the minutiae of child care, not the real stuff, not the stuff about how substantially motherhood had changed us or what thoughts and fears sped through our minds the moment we closed our eyes each night. Why, I often wondered as Maya advanced into toddlerhood, do I love my child with a passion beyond all reason, yet sometimes, nonetheless, have such a panicked, urgent need to escape her demands? Why does she adore me most of the time, yet painfully, even embarrassingly so, reject me in public on some occasions? Why do I struggle so hard, so much harder than other women, it seems, when she shouts "I hate you!" or "Go away!"? I knew that at least some of the answers related to the way I responded to stress in general, but I didn't know exactly how.

The answers would start arriving years later, after I began research for this book. They would come when I began reading about attachment theory and its relationship to early loss. And then my early years of motherhood began to make more sense.

A Brief Summary of Attachment and Loss

The smiling, cooing, and babbling that Maya did as an infant were exactly what a baby is programmed to do. These instinctual infant responses, along with crying, clinging, sucking and, later, following a mother around, are all attachment behaviors that create an emotionally charged connection between the baby and his mother, bringing her into close proximity when he feels distress. Crying, for example, calls his mother to his side when he's hungry or tired, and clinging keeps her close when he's scared.

Seminal attachment-theorist John Bowlby believed a mother's responsiveness to her baby's cues creates a form of attachment between them, which sets the stage for the child's ability to form bonds with others later in life. Fathers are important, grandmothers can serve as secondary havens, but the mother, Bowlby maintained, is the dominant attachment figure of a child's early years.

The nature of a mother-infant bond depends on a number of variables, including the child's individual temperament, the values of the surrounding culture, and the child-rearing practices of that particular family. Most important, however, is whether the mother responds sensitively and appropriately to her baby's cues in her everyday behavior. Does she come to him when he cries, or does she ignore or resist his call? Does his clinging make her want to comfort him, or does it trigger fear or panic in her, causing her to act frightened or push him away?

A very young child needs to be physically close to a responsive caregiver to feel secure and comforted. From this closeness, she forms a mental image of the experience of being loved and cared for. As she gets older and ventures out on her own, she carries the mental image of a loving mother with her, and the security she draws from this relationship sustains her during their short separations.

Some children can tolerate separations from their mothers with less distress than others. The reason for this, Bowlby believed, was because they had different types of attachments to their mothers. In 1978, Mary Ainsworth, a developmental psychologist at Johns Hopkins University and a colleague of Bowlby's, came up with a way to classify different attachment patterns between mothers and their young children. She called it the "strange situation," which operates like this: a mother and her child (who must be old enough to crawl or walk, usually twelve to eighteen months) are brought into a room full of toys. The child is allowed to play and freely explore. After a few minutes, a stranger enters the room, talks to the mother, and moves toward the child. The mother then leaves the room for three minutes, and returns. After a while, she walks out and comes back again. Researchers watch how the child reacts to the stranger's arrival, to his mother's departures, and to his mother's returns.

From observing infants in the "strange situation," Ainsworth identified three distinct attachment patterns. The first, *secure* children (70 percent of her sample), explored the room as long as their mothers stayed nearby, and showed signs of missing them when they left. They greeted the mothers eagerly when they returned, accepted their gestures of comfort, and were calmed by their embraces. After a few moments of "refueling," they would resume their play, keeping their mothers in slightly closer proximity than before. When these mothers were observed and rated for their sensitivity, acceptance, and cooperation with regard to their children, they ranked high in every category. They were emotionally accessible to their children, and responded quickly to their signals. They were fast to pick them up when they cried, and held them longer than the other mothers, with more apparent pleasure.

The rest of the children were classified as insecurely attached. Of those, 20 percent were found to be *avoidant*. These kids ignored and avoided their mothers upon reunion. Instead of seeking comfort

from their mothers, they shifted their attention to exploration.*
They seemed emotionally cut off, as if they were trying to cope with
stress by disengaging from anger and hurt, into what psychologist Robert Karen calls a "protective state of indifference." Their
mothers ranked lower in sensitivity, cooperation, and emotional accessibility, appeared hostile or rejecting, and showed less emotional
expression, as if they were fighting to hold in their anger or irrita-
tion. They held their babies just as much as the other mothers, but
they behaved less affectionately when doing so, and they sometimes
spoke of their dislike of physical contact.

The remaining 10 percent of children were categorized as *ambivalent* (sometimes called *anxious-resistant*). These kids appeared anxious and highly focused on their mothers from the start, even before
the separation occurred. They were very distressed when their
mothers left the room, and, upon reunion, they actively sought close
contact while simultaneously showing anger, resisting the mothers'
efforts to comfort them, or both. They gave the impression of wanting comfort and connection, but ruined their chances of getting it
because of their anger. Their mothers also ranked low in sensitivity,
cooperation, and emotional accessibility, but unlike the mothers of
avoidant children, who acted rejecting, these moms appeared frus-
tratingly inconsistent and unpredictable.

Yet mothers with avoidant or ambivalent kids didn't behave in
a consistently negative fashion. In his 1994 book, *Becoming Attached*,
Robert Karen describes them as ranging from "mean-spirited
to merely cool, from chaotic to pleasantly competent." Many of
them were affable and well-meaning; some were good playmates
and teachers. "But what they all had in common was difficulty responding to the baby's attachment needs in a loving, attuned, and

---

* It's not unusual for toddlers to act angry or to ignore a mother when she returns
after a prolonged separation, usually a day or more, that has stressed their coping
resources. They try to control their feelings of abandonment by creating a temporary, emotional distance from the mother, which can last for as long as a few hours.
Children categorized as "avoidant" in "strange situation" experiments, however,
acted this way after the mother had been gone for only a few minutes.

consistent way," Karen explains. "Inevitably, this problem was compounded as the babies became more demanding and distressed, the mothers more irritated and overwhelmed. The power struggles that resulted inevitably brought out a more hostile and rejecting side of the mother's personality."

Secure, avoidant, or ambivalent: most kids that Ainsworth observed could be described in one of these three ways. A certain proportion of kids, however, didn't fit neatly into any of the categories. Their behaviors looked inconsistent to researchers. They'd initiate an attachment, then almost immediately undermine it. For example, they'd rush to the mother for comfort when she returned, but then stop short, turn around, and avoid her. Or they'd get up to greet her, and then throw themselves prone on the floor. Sometimes they'd sit on her lap for a few moments and, without warning, suddenly freeze all movement. These children were acting as if they were frightened to complete the actions they'd started. It's not unusual for a child to act this way under stress when a parent isn't present, but researchers weren't accustomed to seeing such behaviors, at such high levels of intensity, when the parent was around.

These kids kept psychologists stumped for years. Then, in 1986, Mary Main, a psychologist at the University of California at Berkeley (and a former student of Ainsworth's) looked at the behavior of these unclassifiable kids in greater detail. She noticed a variety of attachment behaviors that could be described as "disorganized" or "disoriented," such as those above. From her "strange situation" observations, Main created a fourth attachment group for children, which she called the "D" group.

Why were these kids acting in such a scattered fashion when they needed comfort from their mothers? Main didn't know, but she suspected the answer might lie in the parents' attachment pasts. So, five years later, when she did a follow-up study on the same Berkeley pairs, she interviewed the parents, too. She wanted to get a sense of how they perceived the childhood relationships they'd had with their caregivers, to see if this had any bearing on the kind of attachments they formed with their own kids.

What happened next made attachment history. Adults, Main found, could also be categorized in three ways, based on how they remembered their relationships with their parents. The ones who talked about their parents (or other primary caregivers) in a coherent, relevant, and reasonably succinct fashion, even when the relationships were difficult or traumatic, and who acknowledged both good and bad aspects of care they'd received, were classified as *secure-autonomous*. A second group, identified as *dismissing* of attachment, either claimed to be unable to remember their early relationships or described their parents in glowing terms that didn't match up with the stories they told. (For example, "My parents were perfect parents," followed by "I hid outside when my father was mad, to avoid getting hit.") These adults also spoke about their relationships with their parents in a distanced or detached manner, and minimized their long-term importance.

The third group spoke about their histories with their parents and caregivers in excessive detail. They seemed to be still confused or angry about the early relationships, appeared to be still entangled in them, and gave long and convoluted answers to the interviewers' questions. These adults were classified as *preoccupied* with early attachments.

Then Main compared each mother's category with her child's "strange situation" category during infancy. As she expected, secure mothers tended to have children who were identified as secure; mothers described as dismissive were most likely to have infants seen as avoidant; and preoccupied mothers tended to have children who'd been classified as ambivalent. Most important for our purposes, however, was that when Main looked at the mothers of infants in that perplexing D group, the ones whose behavior appeared disoriented, she found those mothers tended to have experienced the death of a close family member before the age of eighteen.

Not all of the mothers who'd experienced early loss had disorganized infants, though. Quite a few of them had infants who appeared perfectly secure. When Main pressed further, she noticed that some of the early-loss mothers acted disoriented themselves when they talked about the loss. They had trouble completing thoughts, expressed disbelief that the loved one was truly gone, and paid unusual attention to detail. (For example, "My mother was forty-six years and three months old when she died, on the eleventh of December 1989, a Tuesday afternoon, at 4:46 P.M.") On other topics, they came across as perfectly intact, but on this particular subject, they seemed distressed and confused.

Main believed these lapses occurred when a parent's early loss had never been processed. When he or she was asked to talk about the loss, fear and anxiety would bubble up. These parents, she concluded, were struggling with *unresolved* losses, and when she looked at her data again—bingo. The parents with unresolved losses, and not with early losses per se, were the ones most likely to have infants in the disorganized group.

But what, exactly, was making these women's children act disorganized when they needed maternal comfort? Main believed the mother's unresolved mourning was key. Mothers who hadn't mourned their losses, she said, were still frightened by their loss experiences, which resulted in anxious behavior that could, in turn, be frightening to an infant. A mother who had lost a loved one in an auto accident, for example, and who had never resolved the loss, might panic and grab her child roughly before crossing a street, even when no cars can be seen. Or a mother who felt consistently rejected as a child might be extremely sensitive to any perceived rejection from her own child, focusing on the infant with a desperate, pleading look when he turns his back on her or doesn't want to play. Main also identified unusual vocal patterns (including a marked dip in pitch and intonation at the end of words) among these mothers; unusual movements (such as getting right up in a child's face, or handling the child with extreme timidity); and unusual speech content (such as implying that a child's actions could have disastrous results—"You're going to suffocate that doll if you keep doing that!"—or making a frightened intake of breath and a loud "Uhh!" sound when no objective danger is present).

"Frightened," overreactive behaviors such as these don't pose a physical threat to a child but they can nonetheless scare him. Because they come from a mother's personal history rather than from the child's direct experience, the child can't identify their source. Even when a mother knows why she's acting this way, to a child her behaviors are puzzling, unpredictable, and inexplicable, and they make a child feel and act scared. That's why the children exhibited stop-and-start behavior in the "strange situation," Main believed: because when reunited with their mothers after an episode of stress, they were faced with an irresolvable paradox. The person to whom they needed to turn for comfort was also their source of alarm.

So, what does all this mean to motherless mothers in real life?

1) It emphasizes the importance of predictable, consistent parenting behaviors.

The key word here is *predictable*. Most mothers who exhibited frightening behavior—as well as those who were avoidant and preoccupied—didn't act this way all the time. Usually, they displayed sensitive and affectionate behavior, and none of them were abusive. Whatever they were doing to scare the infants was subtle, but it was interfering with attachment nonetheless. A child needs to be able to anticipate a mother's response and to understand the context of that response in order to form a secure representation of "mother" in her mind. A mother who yells at her child in a panic because her anxiety has been triggered by an unseen force, or a mother who "loses it" whenever she doesn't feel in control creates an environment in which her child has trouble gauging her mother's behavior and predicting its outcome.

Patrice, now thirty-three, was ten when her mother died of breast cancer, and afterward, she developed an intense fear of losing her father. Now the mother of two daughters, ages one and three, she describes herself as "living in fear" of another devastating loss. She's an attentive, loving mother to her daughters, but also admits, "I'm a big overreacter. If I see my child choke a little bit, I'll scream and lunge at her. And I feel like I'm terrifying my children, making them afraid, too. I see it even with my little one. If a truck drives by outside and makes a loud noise, she'll jump and then look at me and study my face. 'Is it okay, Mom? Is it okay?' Because she's used to seeing a panicked look on my face. I'll say, 'It's okay. It's okay.' But still, when I'm feeling scared or threatened, it's hard for me to hide it."

2) It underscores the long-term impact of early mother-infant interaction.

When the Berkeley researchers revisited the children from their "strange situation" study five years later, they found that more than three-quarters of the time, a child's classification at age six was the same as it had been at age one. Children in the "secure" group, whose mothers had been the most responsive five years earlier, were now secure six-year-olds, with few behavior problems in kindergarten and good conflict-management skills with peers. They were receiving a mother's support, acceptance, and active encouragement of learning and competence at home.

Children classified as ambivalent at age six, however, tended to have mothers who were overinvolved and indulgent, and who discouraged their children's independence. Avoidant children were likely to have mothers who were critical and hostile.

Children who had fallen into the D category at age one—the ones with parents whose early losses were unresolved—seemed to be acting more consistently and predictably toward their mothers at age six. They also appeared to be more controlling. They tried to either direct their mothers' behaviors through commands, or to lift and guide their mothers' moods in a semiparental manner. Main speculated that these children might be receiving subtle messages from their mothers to act as the caregivers, instead of expecting to receive care from the mothers.

Other studies have found that at age three and a half, secure children appear more advanced in social relationships, being almost twice as likely to initiate activities, show sympathy for a peer, or be sought out by other children. At ages four and a half to five, they showed evidence of higher resilience, self-esteem, and independence. Ambivalent children, on the other hand, often seemed too preoccupied with their own needs to focus much on other children, and avoidant children were more likely to ridicule other children, take pleasure in their unhappiness, or withdraw from social situations altogether. The ambivalent children, who had trouble tolerating acts of aggression, were often the target of bullies, while avoidant children were typically the aggressors. Secure children, on the other hand, were more likely to turn an encounter with an aggressive child into something positive, withdraw from it, or shrug off aggressive advances with the observation "They're mean."

Other studies tracking kids up to age eighteen have found that those who received sensitive care during their first year and a half were more likely to form secure attachments in late adolescence. But secure attachment in early childhood is not a guaranteed route to healthy emotional development. Adverse events that disrupt the mother-child relationship, such as parental divorce, physical or sexual abuse, foster care, or parental death, have the power to make secure kids preoccupied and insecure in their attachments, regardless of the quality of maternal care they received as babies.

3) It creates a convincing argument for doing grief work.

When a mother dies and takes a daughter's secure base with her, especially when surviving caregivers cannot provide her with the emotional support she needs, the daughter is at risk for becoming insecurely attached to others. To survive with a rejecting or disinterested caregiver, she may withdraw from her emotions, or she may become ambivalent about other loved ones, longing for connection but always guarding herself against unwanted results.

When a daughter's loss is sudden or traumatic, she may put up defenses to keep her at a safe remove from emotional pain. That's what fifty-five-year-old Charlotte, the mother of a twenty-eight-year-old daughter and a twenty-four-year-old son, believes happened to her at age twelve, when both her parents died within the same year.

"Even though we had aunts and uncles who took us in, I always felt like I was an intruder," recalls Charlotte, the third of seven children. "There were so many of us, and I always felt that we were interrupting their lives. We were told not to talk about our family situation because people would pity us as orphans. So, when other children asked why I lived with my aunt and uncle, I would just say, 'Because we do.' I never made waves. A child in that situation just learns to cope."

Charlotte got through adolescence by pushing her loneliness and sadness aside. She became a quiet, sweet child who tried not to think about her early years and who didn't dare talk about the parents she had lost. But by detaching from her grief, she inadvertently disconnected herself from having any strong emotions at all.

"I closed down my heart," she explains. "When I got married, I didn't feel like I really loved my husband. I didn't want children at first. After my daughter was born, my husband kept saying, 'A little human being! Look! It's a little human being!' And I looked at her face and said, 'Oh.' I literally didn't feel anything."

When raising her children, Charlotte constantly told them she loved them, but she never felt the deep connection she knew other mothers felt. "When my son was little, we used to lie on the couch together, and he liked to lie on my chest," she recalls. "I asked him once, 'Why are you always doing that?' and he said, 'Mom, because it feels good.' I didn't know what he meant. You see, I didn't have that feeling back then. I was so disconnected."

Five years ago, Charlotte started working with a therapist who began helping her mourn for the parents she lost nearly forty years earlier. With help, she's become able to feel truly connected to others for the first time. "I *do* love my husband, and I *do* love my children, but it's only been in the past five years that I can really feel it," she says. "Now I realize that when you lose two parents so close together, it feels too risky to ever truly love again."

By the time Charlotte began mourning her loss, her children were already out on their own. Mothers who can be helped to mourn much earlier, however—when their children are infants or toddlers—have the chance to alter their behaviors when small adjustments can still yield big results. Children seem most able to change attachment styles during their early years, before behavior patterns become solidified during adolescence.

The psychoanalytic work of Selma Fraiberg offers compelling evidence that unfreezing emotions related to a loss can change attachment styles for the better. The most striking example she and her colleagues provide is of the woman they call Mrs. March. Mrs. March had been abandoned by her mother during a psychotic episode, shortly after birth, and was raised in poverty by an aunt and, later, by a maternal grandmother. She married in her late teens and gave birth to a child, a daughter named Jane. As a mother, Mrs. March was disconnected and consistently unresponsive to her baby's cries. When she talked about her past, she did so in a distant manner, rotely recounting the facts, while her child lay on a nearby blanket or on her mother's lap, without moving or showing expression.

From the start, Fraiberg believed Mrs. March could not hear her baby's cries because her own cries had never been heard. Through a series of home visits, Mrs. March's private therapist, Mrs. Adelson, encouraged the new mother to tell the story of her childhood again. This time, she tried to openly empathize and put into words what the young child must have felt. *This must have been so hard for you . . . Of course you needed your mother . . . There was no one to hear you.*

The therapist gave Mrs. March permission to remember her feelings and to experience them. Within just a few sessions, the younger woman started to access grief, sadness, and anguish for herself as a child. As Fraiberg and her colleagues explained,

> And now, with each session, Mrs. Adelson witnessed something almost unbelievable happening between mother and baby . . . as Mrs. March began to take the permission to remember her feelings, to cry, and to feel the comfort and sympathy of Mrs. Adelson, we saw her make approaches to her baby in the midst of her own outpourings. She would pick up Jane and hold her, at first distant and self-absorbed, but holding her. And then one day, still within the first month of treatment, Mrs. March, in the midst of an outpouring of grief, picked up Jane, held her very close, and crooned to her in a heartbroken voice. And then it happened again, and several times in the next sessions. An outpouring of old griefs and a gathering of the baby into her arms.

It would take four months of psychotherapy before Fraiberg felt convinced that Mrs. March was adequately responding to her baby's cues, and another year before she had resolved more of her inner conflicts. By the end of two years, however, Jane was judged to be an attractive, bright, verbal, sociable child. She would momentarily stop her play when her mother became uncomfortable, such as when she was discussing painful memories, but otherwise showed no evidence of developmental or attachment problems.

Mrs. Adelson acted as a containing mother (see page 100) for Mrs. March, a stable female figure whose steady, empathic, reassuring presence grounded the younger woman enough to help her feel safe to revisit her past. Because Mrs. March trusted that the therapist would remain composed and "together," Mrs. March could risk temporarily coming apart as she grieved.

Alicia Lieberman, PhD, a former student of both Ainsworth and Fraiberg, who is now with the Infant-Parent Program at San Francisco General Hospital, reported similar results in 1991, when she was working with a mother of an eighteen-month-old son. Lieberman also supervised a one-year program with one hundred mother-infant pairs that had been categorized as anxiously attached in the "strange situation." By offering preventive treatment to both parents and children when the children were still young, she found, the anxious pairs could be helped to become more secure.

As children get older, it may be harder to expect such fast results. Kids who've been acting hostile, defiant, manipulative, or withdrawn for years may be caught up in behavior that makes it impossible for them to get the love they seek. As Robert Karen points out, "Even a mother who has sought therapy, who's found a stable mate, who's overcome distracting financial distress—who has in one way or another become ready or able to take a more responsible, consistent, nurturant role toward the child—may find it hard getting through to the child who has adopted such survival strategies . . . the mother or father whose own emotional problems were responsible for the anxious pattern to begin with finds both ends of this task difficult. To keep loving in the face of rejection is contrary to the parent's own internal model. To want to hug a distressed toddler only to have him squirm away, to speak lovingly to the six-year-old only to see him look at the ground and fidget impatiently, seems beyond endurance. By the same token, to be respectful and to steadfastly demand respect, to discipline a child in a moderate way, to neither indulge, seduce, manipulate, nor explode—all this is contrary to emotional habits built up over a lifetime."

Resolving loss may also affect the way we think about parenting in general. A 2004 study that followed 109 women from late pregnancy until their children were two years old found that those who'd resolved an early loss were more sensitive caregivers than those who had an unresolved loss in their pasts. In fact, women in the resolved-loss group were just as responsive to their infants as the women who'd never experienced loss at all. The researchers had expected to find this. What they hadn't expected to find was that women who'd resolved their early losses spoke more negatively about their transition to parenthood than any of the other women did. They reported having higher levels of depression, isolation, and lack of competence during their children's first two years.

Is this necessarily a bad thing? Could resolving a loss actually lead to increased depression, or lower self-esteem? The researchers thought not. It's more likely, they said, that mothers who'd resolved their losses are more adept at recognizing and reporting the emotional problems they experience. It may not be that mothers in the "resolved" group are more depressed or isolated than other women, only that they're better at expressing it.

4) We should take all this seriously, but within reason.

Most mothers have lapses in otherwise exemplary behavior; many of us act inconsistently in the course of a given week; and quite a few of us raise our voices from time to time. None of this indicates we're insecurely attached to our children, or they to us. Attachment theory is relevant insofar as it offers scientific validity for what motherless mothers intuitively know: that the experience of past loss affects the way we respond to our kids. The exact nature of this cause-and-effect relationship, however, will vary considerably from woman to woman, and from child to child.

Mothers of young children may wonder, at this point, if they should hurry to the nearest university psychology departments to enroll their child in a "strange situation" experiment. That's unnecessary, Robert Karen says. Parents need only make an effort to be more sensitive to their children's attachment issues, and to consult an experienced therapist if they're truly concerned about their behaviors and the impact on their children. To that I would add that a motherless daughter who knows she has not yet mourned her early loss should begin to confide in a safe other—a loving partner or a compassionate therapist, or even a good friend—with both her and her children's best interest in mind.

Fortunately, there's good evidence that grief work can help a mother who's preoccupied or dismissive in her attachment slowly become more secure. When a mother's attachment style changes, so can her infant's. Babies are beautifully adaptable in that regard. If continuing to resolve our losses can have such an effect on our children's long-term attachment styles, let us commit to doing it, all of us, starting right now.

6

⚘

Zero to Four

RAISING BABIES, TODDLERS, AND PRESCHOOLERS

*M*aya started preschool on a Tuesday morning in early December, when she was two years and two months old. Left to my own machinations, I would have kept her home with me until the following fall, but marriage is a democracy, and Uzi comes from a culture and an era where children were enrolled in neighborhood day-care centers starting at six months of age. The idea of Maya spending most of the week in the company of a single adult seemed strange and unnatural to him. I held firm for more than a year, whipping out data on one-on-one care and mother-child bonding, until other evidence landed indisputably in his favor. From about eighteen months onward, Maya easily integrated herself into other children's play at the park, and she would lift her arms and plaintively cry, "Kidz! Kidz!" every time we walked or drove past groups of children. It seemed pretty clear that I'd either have to enroll her in preschool, or give birth to a twenty-month-old sibling for her. Biology having the limitations it does, I started making phone calls that fall.

The school we chose—or, this being Los Angeles, the one that chose *us*—was a homey, laid-back enterprise in a residential neighborhood in our canyon, located inside a brown wooden house that reminded me of my old summer camp's bunks. The director was a soft-spoken woman in her forties who wore peasant skirts and Birkenstocks. She looked like the kind of woman who said "no problem" and meant it. After watching her interact with the children on several preliminary visits, I knew she was someone in whose care I could safely leave Maya.

That was, if I could bring myself to leave her, which wasn't nearly as easy as I had envisioned. For weeks before the big day, I'd visualized walking her into the classroom, engaging her in play with a toy or another child, and then slowly backing out the door. We'd visited the school in advance so she'd be familiar with the layout. She'd spent some time interacting with the teacher. She seemed eager to start. But on the big day, as soon as we walked into the classroom, she grabbed hold of my leg and wouldn't let go. To walk out of the door, I would have had to physically peel her off and leave her crying for me, something I flat-out refused to do.

Perhaps she sensed my ambivalence? I suspect the teacher may have. "I'm going to need to stay awhile," I told her. She invited me to join the class that morning, and the next morning, too. That first day, I helped hang artwork and serve snacks. The second day, I sat on a couch reading while Maya brought each classmate over to meet me. On the third morning, I sat on the same couch doing not much of anything while Maya played with the other kids. The director approached me then. Warmly yet firmly, she said, "It's time to go."

I'd understood from the start that she'd let me stay until she thought Maya could tolerate me leaving. But this teacher was smarter than I'd realized. Only in hindsight do I see she was waiting to see signs that I could tolerate it, too.

My behavior, as I later learned, wasn't terribly unusual for a mother with a history of separation in her past. Women like me, Selma Fraiberg said, are frequently influenced by "ghosts in the nursery"—invisible visitors from the mothers' pasts whose presence directs the mothers' present-day behavior—when our children are young. Even in new families where love bonds are stable and enduring, intruders from the mother's past can break through at moments of stress or vulnerability, and mother and child may find themselves reenacting a moment or a scene from another time.

Fraiberg believed that nursery ghosts take up residence on a selective basis, depending on what areas of vulnerability a mother has in her past. During early motherhood, she said, they often appear around issues of feeding, sleep, toilet training, or discipline. In my case, they pretty reliably surface around issues of separation. Nursery ghosts can make mothers feel helpless or anxious, Fraiberg said, but I've found they can inspire mothers to act compassionately and responsively toward their young children, too. Because I identified with Maya's fear of being left, I refused to leave her abruptly, which helped her make a more secure transition to preschool, I believe, than she might have made otherwise.

The first four years of a child's life are a period of rapid physical and cognitive growth. They're a time of enormous change for mothers, too. We go from being novices on the job to experienced parents, capable of navigating a landscape dotted with innumerable peaks, valleys, and unexpected speed bumps we call "phases." How we handle the journey is, as always, influenced by our unexpected visitors from the past. One-on-one interviews with seventy-eight motherless mothers revealed that nursery ghosts were most likely to surface during a child's first four years when the following issues came up:

Mother Shock

Motherless mothers with a history of caretaking experience, usually for sick mothers or younger siblings when they were still children

themselves, said that the round-the-clock nature of infant and toddler care sometimes brought up familiar emotions from the past.
"Early child care? Ugh! I hated it," confesses fifty-nine-year-old Elsa,
who was nine when her mother died of cancer and immediately had
to assume a caretaking role for her younger siblings, ages six and
three. "I mean, I did a good job and I was a nice, loving mom to my
son, but I felt completely intruded upon as far as space and time,
probably because I'd been so intruded upon in my early years. And
you know, babies are such a lot of work! When Bobby was two, I separated from my husband, and then he spent half the time with his
dad and half the time with me. So I mothered and took care of him
half of the time, and had my own, independent life the other half.
That worked well for me, having the level of resentment that I did. I
looked forward to him coming, and I looked forward to him going."

Fifty-two-year-old Shira, the mother of two teenage sons, spent
much of her childhood as her mentally ill mother's watchdog, trying
to prevent her from harming herself. After several failed suicide
attempts, her mother fatally overdosed when Shira was fifteen.
Twenty years later, Shira found the experience of raising an active
toddler to be emotionally similar to her adolescence with a mother
whose behavior she also couldn't control.

"It put me right back into where I was before, when I really
couldn't cope," she says. "My son was a handful, with all his energy,
and I could feel myself becoming resentful. I realized it was like
having to take care of my mother, and it felt terrible, sometimes, to
be with him. It wasn't just resentment. It was a kind of panic that set
in, this feeling like, 'I can't do it. It's too overwhelming. I can't go
back in there and take care of somebody else again.'"

When early child care feels so all-encompassing, it's important
for a motherless mother to remember that the coping strategies she
had as a seven-year-old overwhelmed by child care and household
tasks, or as a fifteen-year-old who felt responsible for keeping her
mother alive, were fewer and less developed than the ones available to her today. The out-of-control, trapped feeling so common to

mothers of young children may feel emotionally similar, but practically, the situations have far less in common.

Naomi, thirty-eight, is discovering this right now, as she mothers her three-month-old daughter. Naomi was thirty-three when her mother died after a long struggle with emphysema. As the only child of a single mother, Naomi was her mother's primary caretaker. She shuttled back and forth between her apartment and her mother's house, slept in hospital rooms, administered oxygen and medication—putting most aspects of her own life on hold for six years to tend to her mother's urgent needs.

When we met at Naomi's house on a sunny afternoon, her daughter, Rose, was napping for most of the interview, and Naomi sat curled up in an upholstered armchair, relaxed and centered. She claimed to be exhausted after a difficult night with the baby, but it wasn't evident. In fact, she came across as one of the calmest and most patient new mothers I'd seen in a while. Utterly devoted to caring for her child, she was already talking about trying to have another.

To Naomi, taking care of a child and taking care of a sick parent have been two very different experiences. The time and effort she puts into child care are an investment in someone's future, she explains. When taking care of her mother, in contrast, she was always aware that her efforts were in the service of a different, inevitable outcome.

"The child will eventually grow up, whether you like it or not, and won't need you to take care of them," she says. "With a parent, you don't know when the responsibility might end. I have a very different emotional response to taking care of Rose. With my mother, I felt helpless all the time. Sometimes I feel helpless as a mother, but I know it'll pass. And this time, there are things I can do to make it better. For example, Rose cries whenever I put her in the stroller, but once I start pushing the stroller, she's happy. I remind myself that crying is her way of expressing herself, because she can't speak, whereas my mom cried because she felt pain, and I didn't know how to make it stop."

Thoughts of One's Own Demise

We put so much love and effort into taking care of young children, believing that every moment together counts. Yet in the backs of our minds lurk these nagging questions: If we were to die tomorrow, would our toddlers even remember us? Would our preschoolers soon forget all that we've done?

"My little sister was five when our mother died, and she remembers nothing," says thirty-three-year-old Patrice. "Nothing. That makes me so sad. Especially because I have a three-year-old, and to think that if I died—twenty years from now, she wouldn't even know who I was. All these three years of investment. I'm her *world* now. And to know that I'd be zero, no memories."

A child may be left with no conscious memories of her mother if she loses her before age three, but many theorists believe that the maternal care we receive during those crucial early years sticks with us nonetheless. In *The Reproduction of Mothering*, Nancy Chodorow maintains that women internalize the mother love they receive, and draw upon it years later, when they have children of their own. Some studies have found that mothers also feed and hold their infants in a manner similar to the way they were once fed and held, even though they were too young to have committed such events to retrievable memory.

For motherless mothers, this issue is twofold: they want their children to know they are loved and cared for, and they want to be remembered as the good mothers they are. Those who have few memories of mother love themselves are especially concerned about leaving a lasting legacy. Thinking about everything their children won't remember brings up fresh mourning for all the memories they lost themselves.

Brenda, a forty-three-year-old mother of a young son, lost her mother to an asthma attack when she was seven. Even though Brenda doesn't have the same disease her mother had, she often thinks about what would happen if she, too, were to die young: "I think, *Who would raise him? Would my husband be okay without me? Would my son remember me?*" she says. "This is the big one that goes through my mind. I'm with him so much, and we have so many experiences together. I feel so close to him. But he's only four, and I realize that if I die now, he probably won't remember me. And I think, wow, I was seven, so I had three more years' experience of being close and being held by my mother, and I have so few memories of her. I just get really sad thinking about that, and knowing that if I die, he won't remember me, either."

Sleep Training

To a child, falling asleep is another form of separation from a parent. The world he's in, the one that contains his mother, disappears. It can be a vulnerable time of day for parents, too, since it can bring up issues of separating from the child and causing the child distress. At some level, a parent may experience the child's descent into sleep as a small abandonment, a leave-taking of their intimate time together.

Many of the women in this book followed a similar sleep-training protocol: letting a child cry at night at steadily increasing intervals until he eventually learned to fall and stay asleep. A number of interviewees, though, found listening to a child cry for comfort or companionship to be so difficult they either couldn't participate in sleep training, or abandoned it altogether.

"My husband had to kick me out of the house," says forty-two-year-old Sarah, who was seven when her mother committed suicide. "Otherwise, the back-and-forth would go on for hours. He felt that I was hampering the process. So he said, 'There's the door.' And I went. And that's when my son finally learned how to sleep through the night.

"I've noticed that sometimes I won't give validity to my husband's point of view because it's so contrary to what I feel a mother-child relationship should be," she continues. "Whereas sometimes he has enough emotional detachment, maybe as a man or maybe as a father, to see things differently. This was one of those times. He said, 'Honey, he's got to cry, because he needs to get sleep, and so do we.' But I just couldn't see it that way, because to me everything begins and ends with the emotional connection."

Rebecca, a fifty-year-old mother of four, remembers the emotional havoc that months of trying to teach her first child to fall asleep caused her. "She would cry for me, and my heart would ache," she explains. "I couldn't stand it. Once I came in and there was vomit all over the crib. I thought, *To hell with everyone else. I'm going to follow my heart.* She came into bed with us, and we threw the crib away. It worked for us. Some of them stayed in our bed for a long time. Jordan, my youngest, will still climb in with us sometimes, even though he's fourteen. He would die of embarrassment knowing I'm saying this, but I love it. I know I'm going to blink my eyes and he'll be gone. These are precious few moments. I think motherless daughters have really strong instincts of what children need, maybe an overabundance of them, from being left motherless. Children don't need the Gucci rooms. They need two arms. They need comfort. When my mother died, we had lots of money. We had a Cadillac, we had a swimming pool, we had lots of things the other kids didn't have, but I didn't have my mom."

Unfortunately, kids who don't fall asleep on their own also can't put themselves back to sleep when they wake in the middle of the night, which quickly leads to very tired parents. The nighttime scenario in these homes goes something like this: the child wakes at night and calls out for the mother or comes into her room. The mother, wanting to spare him anxiety or loneliness, either brings him into her bed or climbs into his. Every parent does this from time to time, but when it's a regular occurrence, a mother's sleep is chronically disrupted, and the child gets the message that nighttime anxieties can't be conquered without the mother's help.

Night waking in toddlers has been found to be related to a mother's fears of separation, to neglect or inadequate caregiving during a mother's childhood, and also to maternal depression. A British study of first-time mothers found that those who'd experienced a separation from one or both parents before age eleven had infants with significantly more sleep problems than infants of mothers who didn't have a separation in their pasts. The "separated" mothers also reported feeling more anxious, depressed, and irritable than the other mothers. When their infants' sleep problems were resolved, however, mothers' depression improved considerably, indicating a strong link between sleep deprivation and a new mother's mood.

I've often said that if it weren't for the first few months of sleep deprivation, I would have had four kids by now. I'm only half joking. My mother liked to tell the story of how as a newborn I slept through the night at six weeks. I was moderately interested in this as a teenager, but it became a considerably more amazing fact when Maya was six weeks old. *How on earth did my mother accomplish that?* I wondered nightly. Did she sit outside the nursery door with clenched fists while I cried it out in my crib? Did my father send her out grocery shopping and do the dirty deed himself? Or was I just some kind of super precocious, glee-inducing, power-sleeping newborn? I was obsessed with wanting the details, but my father claimed he didn't remember. At seventeen, I hadn't thought to ask about her method, but damn, at thirty-three, I badly wanted to know.

Sleep training emerged as an area in which motherless women strongly felt the lack of a mother's guidance and experience. Perhaps that's because chronic sleep deprivation (sleep desperation, we called it in our house) has a way of catapulting a mother into such despair. Or because there's so much pressure and competition between mothers to get infants on a workable schedule that when you can't, it's easy to feel you're failing, and to long for reassurance. Notice how thirty-six-year-old Nadia's story of putting her boys to

sleep naturally leads to thoughts of her mother, who committed suicide when Nadia was fourteen:

> Everyone tells you to put the baby to sleep awake so they can
> learn to sleep by themselves. Well, I just loved holding Ethan's
> warm little body *so* much I couldn't bear the thought of letting
> go. It didn't matter that he ate every hour and forty minutes. I
> still loved holding him. At night, when all was quiet, it was just
> the two of us.
>
> My husband and I wanted our children close in age, so, when
> Ethan was six months old, we were elated to know Number Two
> was on the way. When Jack was born, he was a great little sleeper.
> He took long naps and fell asleep in his crib right away. He was
> terrific. But by the time the boys were two and one, we were still
> lying in bed with Ethan, waiting for him to fall asleep. And let
> me tell you, those Little Tykes car beds are not very comfortable
> for adults. After he fell asleep, we would have to slide down the
> trunk and crawl our way out the door.
>
> I wondered if I was doing not what the book said but what
> felt truly right. I wanted to know if my mother had to do that
> with us and if she wondered whether we would turn out all
> right. I wanted to know that my son would still love me in the
> morning. I knew he would, but I just wanted to *know*. You know,
> you want your mother to tell you that she did the same thing
> with you and look, you still love her, don't you?

Physical Separations

Of all the women surveyed for this book, 58 percent work outside
the home. For them, day care and nannies are a necessity of early
parenthood. Full-time mothers also need breaks from child care,
and couples need time without children. When a mother-in-law

or sister isn't available to watch the baby, leaving him with a baby-sitter may be the only option. Yet to leave your child in the care of someone you don't know well, even for a few hours, requires trust, faith, and the knowledge—or at least the belief—that the child can manage in one's absence. It's especially hard to leave one's child when the idea of separation kicks you back in memory to times when you, as a child, were left behind.

"I couldn't leave my children when they were little," admits Rebecca, who lost her mother to cancer at age ten. "When my oldest was born, my husband and I said we'd wait until she was six weeks old and then take a class we wanted to take. But at six weeks, I leaned over the crib to look at her, and I could not leave her. I bawled. I thought, *This baby is going to cry. She's going to wake up wanting me, and I won't be there.* I was absolutely identifying with her. So we didn't leave our kids. We found creative ways of having fun with them. We started an organization at our church, where the parents could dance and bring their little ones. People used to say to me, 'Don't you feel you need to get away from your kids?' I would say, 'Yes, I do need to get away. But not at their expense.' That was my battle cry when they were little."

Rebecca's response to her baby's cries was heartfelt, but not necessarily an accurate assessment of a six-week-old's capacities. At that age, Rebecca's daughter couldn't yet differentiate between her mother and herself, which meant she didn't yet have the capacity to miss someone. That doesn't develop until about eight months of age. Before then, a baby may show preference for her mother, but in moments of distress, another's arms will do. That's why visiting aunts and uncles can calm down a four-month-old by cuddling and cooing to her, but can't get a nine-month-old to come into their arms without crying. By this point, babies have started to develop "stranger anxiety," a heightened fear and aversion to people they don't know well. From about eight or nine months onward, the mother is strongly preferred, and missed when she's gone.

But Rebecca was right about how her daughter would experience separation as she grew older. For very young children, who have no concept of time, being apart from the mother *is* the emotional equivalent of being left by her. They can't distinguish between "a couple of hours" and eternity. When the mother walks out the door, she's gone. When she returns, her child is doubly relieved: he's happy to see her, and also thrilled to discover he hasn't been left for good.

Children have a natural anxiety about separation, Michael Schwartzman explains. Anxiety *over* separation, on the other hand, is a parent's plight. Some parents have legitimate concerns about their child's ability to function without them, but others have unconscious fears that come from their own histories of being left. Telltale signs of this are blaming a child for being too young, "badly behaved," or "hypersensitive" to be left with anyone else; the inability to *ever* find an adequate substitute caregiver; and chronically canceling engagements because of fatigue or the possible onset of illness. When a mother begins with the premise that her child will suffer without her, necessary separations such as doctor's appointments and returning to work become much more difficult for her than they might otherwise be.

Thirty-nine-year-old Susannah, who lost her mother at seventeen, remembers how her anxiety about separating from her daughter colored her first year of motherhood. "I couldn't bear it when I left her," she says. "If I went out when my husband was there, I would think about her constantly. I was absolutely afraid of the separation. I went back to work when she was seven months, and I put her in a day-care nursery. I would go back at lunchtime to breast-feed her, and that was what kept me going. Because the thought of leaving her somewhere else—and it wasn't even that far away—created a physical ache for her. My relationship with my husband suffered greatly that year, partly because I was so isolated as a new mother but also because I became so obsessed with my daughter. I transferred all of my love onto her. I could *not* leave her. It was that mother-daughter relationship—I wanted it back, to the exclusion of everyone else."

At the other end of the scale are mothers for whom past separations were so traumatic that they disconnect when separating from their own babies. Norma Tracey, PhD, and her colleagues at the Parent Infant Foundation of Australia described these mothers as emotionally "switched off" from distress of any kind. They "separated from their babies with no thinking to either planning or directing the dose or the timing of the separation, sometimes creating a trauma in their infant similar to the one they themselves had previously suffered, either in infancy, childhood, or adolescence," Tracey explains. Instead of overidentifying with their children's distress, these women—who may have had histories of avoidant attachments—seemed removed from it altogether. As a result, they kept reenacting the drama of their own past abandonments with their children.

We need to remember that "separation" and "abandonment" are sufficiently different concepts. To a motherless mother, they may feel similar, but that doesn't mean her child must experience them that way. A child can be helped to tolerate the former without feeling the latter. Many times, I've had to hug a tearful child good-bye in the morning when I left for work and then cried the entire four miles down the hill, consumed by grief and guilt for her pain—only to call home as soon as cell phone reception kicked in to hear her playing happily in the background while the nanny said, "It's the weirdest thing. Two minutes after you drove away, she was fine." Still, it requires inner steel for me to walk out the door sometimes. I tell myself I have to be tough for their sake, but really, it's for mine as well. The way a mother handles separation teaches her child how to accept it, and seeing that my daughters can manage it helps me learn how to tolerate it, too.

The First Day of Preschool

When a child stays with a babysitter, it's because the mother has taken the initiative to leave. The first day of school, by contrast, usually marks the first time a child goes off on an age-appropriate task himself. Instead of the mother departing through the front door, the child is the one crossing the threshold into new experience without her.

Children's separation from mothers gets most of the attention on this day, but mothers often need help separating, too. The paradox of the day is that even as a mother walks away from the school, she, too, has to struggle with the pain of being left.

"A mother's job is to be there to be left," Anna Freud once said. By "be there" she meant to be empathetic, engaged, and sensitive to a child's needs. By "to be left" she meant just that. When a child goes off to explore, even if it's only to toddle a few feet away, he leaves his mother behind. Mothers first experience this during a child's first year, when he begins back-and-forth explorations, walking a few steps away from her, then returning for reassurance and comfort, then toddling a few steps further the next time. "He's not a baby anymore," parents say at this time, both celebrating and mourning their child's ability to venture forth without them.

By the time preschool begins a year or two later, the child is ready to tolerate longer separations from his mother. But he must have her help to do this. For a child to master the developmental task of starting school, psychoanalyst Erna Furman believed, he needs a mother who can allow herself to miss him, who can tolerate feeling not needed, and who will remain lovingly available at the end of each day when he returns.

Furman observed two behavior patterns among mothers who could not bear to be left when their children went off to school. The first group acted angry and anxious, often clinging to their children emotionally when school began, and making it impossible for the children to enjoy their new adventure. The other group avoided the opening-day drop-off, or scheduled an appointment or trip so they wouldn't have to participate in the separation—and therefore not have to bear the pain. Most of us fall somewhere between these two extremes, treating preschool as a momentous occasion, dressing a child in fresh, new clothing and loading the cameras with film, yet struggling to maintain composure as they bravely sit on the little blue chairs alone. "I don't know what's happening to me," mothers say through their tears, while plucking tissues from the school receptionist's desk, or lingering on the sidewalk with other parents before heading to work or home.

I imagine the first day of preschool is pretty much the same everywhere. One or two children will be dropped off by a babysitter and deposited directly in the teacher's care. A few children will make the separation easily, quickly hugging their mothers good-bye or even trying to push her from the room. Others will start crying when they realize their mothers are ready to leave. Some teachers will encourage parents to stay that first day. Others will steer them out the door. A handful of mothers will always try to find reasons to linger in the classrooms for five minutes more.

I keep hoping that preschools will offer first-day support groups for mothers. We could adjourn into an adjacent building for coffee and bagels, where we'd sit in circle time while a group leader explains that our tears are perfectly normal, that they're not just for our child's distress, but for ours, too—for all the times we felt left behind, and for the bittersweet knowledge that our children now need us, during daytime hours, just a little less.

This last concept can be a difficult one for a motherless mother to accept. She's cared for her child with such intensity and determination for two or three years, every day or close to it, comforting his hurts, planning his meals, micromanaging his schedule for optimal learning and fun. Now he's in an environment for two or four or six hours a day that the mother can neither supervise nor control. Someone else is going to soothe his hurts, witness his milestones, and interpret his cues. *What if he can't adequately express his needs?* she wonders. *What if he wants me during the day, and I'm not there?*

Some motherless mothers say their sensitivity to separation has made them highly empathetic to their children's distress on this day. They try hard to make the transition as smooth as possible for a child, remembering what it felt like to be powerless to adults' decisions.

"My father never told my mother she had cancer," says fifty-five-year-old Louise. "And when she died, he used euphemisms. I was six, and I didn't get it. He said she 'went to another place.' And I spent months opening closet doors and thinking she was going to jump out and tell me the whole thing was a game. Consequently, being honest and telling the whole story has always been important to me. And it was really important to me as a mother. When my daughter was about to go to preschool, I took her there in advance and let her see where she'd be going. I was very adamant about preparing her for things, and not throwing her into anything and making her have to figure out how to cope."

I've loved *all* of the preschool experience with my daughters, from the first day of every school year until the last. Bringing them to a place where I knew they were well cared for, where they had fun activities and orderly cubbies and good friends, has given me a sense of accomplishment as a mother, a firm feeling that I'm getting this part right. When I pick up Eden now in the afternoons, and she looks up from the snack table, smiles her huge smile, and rushes over to hug me hello, I'm always awed by the simple knowledge that she's a child, and I'm her mother, and we're doing exactly what children and mothers do. I'm bringing her to school. I'm picking her up. She's happy to see me. She has a mother. It's me. Sometimes the gratitude and reverence for such facts can nearly overwhelm me. We hardly have any photos of our kids performing in preschool concerts, because I'm the parent who's always crying too hard to take them. Not because they're so adorable, or so innocent and vulnerable, although all of that is true—but because I'm just so happy to *be* there to see it.

Anger and Rejection

It seems that as soon as a toddler can form opinions of his own, he forcefully makes them known. The fourteen-month-old's arched back when it's time to get in the car seat evolves into the twenty-month-old's adamant and persistent *"No!"* that becomes the two-year-old's tantrum and the three-year-old's insistence on doing everything her own way. Most mothers recognize these as natural acts of emerging autonomy, and accommodate them as best they can.

No one eagerly signs up for the part of motherhood, though, where the three-year-old shouts "I hate you!" or "Get away from me!" *How can you* hate *me?* a motherless mother thinks. *I'm your* mother. *How can you tell me to get away? Don't you realize what you're saying?*

"When my daughter gets humiliated or scared about something, she'll take it out on me," says thirty-four-year-old Jasmin, a mother of three. "She'll say, 'I don't like you!' And I'll be so sad. Because I won't have done anything. Once a man said to her, 'You'd better get off that railing, because you might get hurt.' He wasn't being mean, but she felt so hurt by that. She got off the railing and glared at me and said, 'I don't like you.'"

As hard as it can be to tolerate such outbursts, verbal assaults from toddlers and preschoolers shouldn't be taken personally. They're not an indication of how your child feels about you. A child this age is still learning how to manage her emotions, and she doesn't waffle about them in the meantime. When she's happy, she's almost uncontrollably happy. "But when things don't go her way, she feels that life is bad, that you're bad—and that she hates you," explains developmental psychologist Becky Bailey, PhD. She might want to stomp away from you, or send you away, but at the same time she doesn't want you to leave *her*. That's why a three-year-old who angrily shouts "Get away from me!" will cry when you walk away, and why she'll struggle with a difficult Lego project, then look up and shout, "I hate you!" when your only crime was to enter the room.

Just the other morning, Eden spilled her cereal all over the dining-area rug, and when I handed her a towel and asked her to clean it up, she clenched her fists and gritted her teeth at me. "Ooooh-*ooh!*" she roared. "I *hate* you!"

This wasn't anything new. Last week, she hated me when she couldn't open her lip gloss. And just last night she shouted "I hate you!" when I reminded her it was time to brush her teeth. I've been trying to take it in stride.

"That's okay," I said. "But you still have to clean up the cereal."

She narrowed her eyes and stamped her foot. "I *hate* you!" she shouted again, with emphasis. Then she added, "I'm not your girl! *Any! More!*"

I've called Eden "my girl" since she was six months old. "Good night, my girl," I tell her when I kiss her to sleep at night. "I love you, my girl," I tell her every morning when I drop her off at school. So, this actually hurt. In that instant, before rational thought kicked in, emotion surged forth, and the first one I caught hold of was rejection. *She doesn't love me anymore,* I thought. And the panic I then felt was almost—almost—strong enough to make me rush over and mop up the cereal myself, to wipe both the milk and the bad feelings away.

Fortunately, intellect did arrive. It reminded me that "I hate you!" meant "I hate it when you want me to do something I don't want to do!" and "I'm not your girl anymore" meant "I'm feeling really angry at you right now." And I knew that all this anger meant she was feeling powerless, and probably also guilty for making such a mess.

"It's okay to be angry," I said. "But it's not okay to . . ." I was about to say "shout at me like that," but before I could finish the sentence, Eden's face had collapsed into her hand and she was crying, a pitiful ragged sound, as if the strength of her anger had been too much for her to bear.

Suddenly, she was so little, too little for the timbre of such anger, too small and helpless to have the power to hurt me so bad. "Do you need a hug?" I asked her. She nodded without lifting her head. I scooped her up and sat on a kitchen chair, kissing her wet cheek. "I want to be your girl again," she sobbed.

Children Eden's age are learning how to handle ambivalence. They can't quite grasp how to love someone and be angry at that person at the same time—they're only capable of feeling one emotion at a time. When Eden was angry, she was wholly angry, and for that moment, it was true: she no longer felt love for me. But she probably couldn't handle the strong surge of anxiety that followed such a statement, because she also can't yet understand that someone else can be feeling anything different than what she does. When she was so angry at me, at some level she experienced it as if I were equally angry at her, and the possibility of that and, by extension, of losing my love, was intolerable to her.

It's useful to understand Eden's behavior, but it's equally helpful to understand mine. That instantaneous regression to the place where "I hate you!" makes me feel like a child still terrified of losing someone's love isn't a place I frequently visit. I was surprised to find it that day. I was doubly surprised to discover how quickly a child could send me there.

Colleen Russell, MFT, a therapist in Mill Valley, California, who frequently counsels motherless women, believes that some motherless daughters' reactions to anger and rejection from their children may be related to post-traumatic stress from their childhoods, especially in families where abuse took place. "Certain things a child says can trigger flashbacks to other events in a mother's life, and the mother at that moment could have feelings associated with that time," she explains. It's an automatic emotional process, not a rational one. The mind doesn't have time to process *this is a three-year-old talking* before the feelings associated with the earlier trauma come flooding in, she says.

The ones we love most are always the ones whose words cut deepest, even when that person is a toddler. But that's an awareness for adults to reconcile, not for children to witness. If I'd said what I'd felt in the kitchen the other morning—"Oh my God, Eden, it makes me so sad when you say that"—I might have given her a terrifying feeling of power over my emotions. If I'd run over to mop up the cereal, I would have sent the message that she could manipulate me with anger (and get out of doing the task herself). No, what was important was for me to stay steady and balanced, to remind myself that I was the adult, and to be the lightning rod for her surging emotions. To bear the pain and anger of these inevitable rejections—because, however ephemeral, they are, after all, rejections—because this is what a child needs from a mother in order to grow.

Developing Autonomy

Self-care such as feeding, dressing, hand-washing, and tooth-brushing allows toddlers and preschoolers to claim ownership of their bodies and to develop competence and self-esteem. Mastering self-care, Erna Furman believed, more than any other development during these years, makes the toddler feel that he is a somebody.

Women who lost mothers at a very early age may find themselves feeling uncertain about guidelines for a toddler's or preschooler's self-care. A mother who took on partial responsibility for herself at age four, for example, may find herself torn between wanting to foster competence in her child, wanting to offer him the security of a mother's care, and hoping to find self-healing by doing for him what was not done for her.

"My daughter wanted to start dressing herself just after she turned three, and it just tore me up inside," says Arlie, who was five when her mother died of cancer. "It actually felt like a loss. I don't want to squash her independence, but I *like* helping her get dressed every day. I had to start picking out my own clothes and dressing myself when I was in nursery school, because my mother was usually too sick to get out of bed in the morning. My father had already left for work, and there was nobody else to help me. I would go to school with my clothing inside out, dirty, mismatched. Nobody at home really noticed. So I was really looking forward to dressing my daughter every morning, and knowing that it was getting done properly and with love.

"On the other hand, I know if she wants to do it herself, I should let her. I don't want to interfere with whatever's normal for her age. The thing is, I don't *know* what's normal for her age. Should I let her pick out her own clothes? Can I start letting her brush her own teeth? I think about letting her help unload the dishwasher, and I worry that I'm turning her into a tiny servant, the way my father had me doing kitchen chores after my mother died."

Early loss has confused Arlie's understanding of what's age-appropriate for her daughter and what's not. She remembers how much self-care she was capable of at age four, but also believes that such premature independence cost her part of her childhood. Now, as a mother, she seeks to find a comfortable balance for her own child.

For thirty-six-year-old Christine, the issue is household chores. The mother of two young daughters, ages four and one, Christine lost her mother at age six and was left with an alcoholic father and several younger siblings to help care for. Her husband also has a history of neglect. Because both adults had to meet their own needs so young, Christine says, they made the decision when their first daughter was born to "let children be children," she explains. "They should be taken care of. Now, Kyra will scrape her plate and put it in the sink. She has little chores. But I don't have her getting a stool and washing the dishes. I don't even have her unload groceries with me unless she really wants to help. Because she's *only four and a half*. At four and a half, I was almost an adult. I swear, by the time I was eight, I could grocery shop, balance a checkbook, run the house. I was doing all that in the third grade."

Most child-development experts agree that children as young as eighteen months are capable of some self-care and small chores, and that parents should encourage them to do both. Interest in self-care is a natural urge, and mastery of these skills is a developmental marker of normal progress. As parents, we should perhaps not ask ourselves "Should I let her brush her own teeth or dress herself?" but "Does she want to do it?" In most cases, her urge is a natural one, and her insistence "By myself!" a sign of readiness.

Chores are important, because they help a toddler develop self-reliance, responsibility, and a sense of teamwork. Toddlers are eager to help—"Like Mommy!" Eden used to say, muscling her way over to the dishwasher as I loaded dishes—and love receiving praise. Because toddlers are interested in helping and imitating, simple chores, such as working side by side with you to pick up blocks or stack laundry, work well for children two and younger. By about age three, a child can hold two ideas in her mind at once, allowing her to tackle more complex, two-step instructions, such as "Please clear your plate and put it on the counter." By age four, most kids are capable of feeding a pet, weeding the garden, setting the table (minus the knives), sorting laundry, washing plastic dishes and cups, sweeping up the floor, and cleaning up their own spills and messes.

Every morning, I let my kids pick out their own clothes for the day. Sometimes I help them get dressed; sometimes they dress themselves. They're eight and four now, and we divide and conquer the mornings. Maya brings me the hairbrushes. I braid their hair. Uzi gives them breakfast. Eden feeds the cat. Everyone puts on their own socks and shoes. For me, it's a constant dance between wanting to do for them and knowing they need to do for themselves. What is a mother, if not the one who makes her child's life easier? But what is a mother, if not the one who helps them learn how to take care of themselves?

Their independence, I know, is their most important survival tool. I am all too aware they will eventually have to manage without me one day. Every morning, I try to grant them an infinitesimally larger slice of free will. Which is how I wind up one morning with a preschooler who marches triumphantly into her classroom wearing a blue-and-white gingham Wizard of Oz dress, sparkling ruby slippers, and brown socks decorated with miniature Scooby Doos.

Second and Subsequent Children

Some women interviewed for this book spoke openly about the conscious decision to have just one child, for reasons of age, fertility, or the presence of stepchildren from a husband's previous marriage. But the majority of women surveyed—65 percent—had given birth to two or more children. And because the average interval between first and second births in the United States is about thirty months, talk of a second child is likely to begin when the first one is of baby or toddler age.

It's a relief during a second (and third and fourth) pregnancy, to be free of the "Will I know how to be a mother?" anxiety that plagues the first one. Instead of testing whether you've got the resources to be a mother, a second child gives you the opportunity to witness how much you've learned. The questions that arise when one is considering subsequent children are typically about whether a woman can expand her existing resources. *Will I be able to love a second child as much as I love the first?* a mother of one wonders. *Will my first child suffer when I have to divert some of my attention to another? Do I truly want another child, or do I mainly want my first one to have a sibling?*

Most second-time mothers worry that having another child will mean depriving the existing ones of love and attention, and many even go through a sort of grieving—especially during the third trimester of pregnancy—over what author and mother Katie Tamony calls the first child's "dethronement."

Motherless mothers have all these second-child questions, too, yet theirs often include parenthetical additions related to early loss. "Will I be able to love a second child as much as I love the first *(when the first one brought the mother-child relationship back to me)*?" she might wonder. "Will my first child suffer when I have to divert my attention *(as I suffered when I lost my mother's love)*?"

To some extent, a first child always claims a special spot in a mother's heart. The wonder of pregnancy and childbirth, the joy and relief of discovering such a strong emotional connection, and, for motherless mothers, the bittersweet joy of becoming a mother without a mother—all this is inevitably felt most strongly when it occurs for the first time.

Thirty-nine-year-old Susannah, who spoke earlier in this chapter about her early difficulty separating from her infant daughter, is now the mother of two daughters, ages five and one. When thinking about a second child, she wasn't concerned about her ability to love the next one at all. She was concerned about her ability to love it as much.

"I just could not contemplate the idea of anyone other than Brooke having so much of my love," she says. "Also, my marriage wasn't great because of that first year of motherhood, so we certainly didn't leap into having another. In the back of my mind, I was thinking, *Oh, three years would be an ideal gap.* And then three years passed and I hadn't done anything about it. I thought, *If I'm going to do it, I've got to do it soon,* and that's when I realized yes, I did want to have another one. I got pregnant very quickly, so I was lucky."

When her second daughter was born, Susannah was pleased and relieved to feel a rush of love and connection right away. What was unexpected, she says, was how the urgent, all-encompassing investment she'd felt toward her first daughter lessened after her second one arrived, and by the depth of guilt she felt for taking attention away from Brooke.

"I felt almost as if I were betraying her in some way," she admits. "There were so many complicated emotions that went on at that time. I still loved her, of course, but the intensity had slightly decreased. It happened almost overnight. Zoe arrived, and I was worried about Brooke, obviously, and about how she was going to react to it, and took a lot of time getting her prepared for a sibling. She responded to it well initially, but after the first few weeks, she became quite difficult to handle. We really went up and down. My relationship with her now is fine, but during the first few months, I would think, *Oh dear, what's happened?*"

I've heard similar stories from other motherless women, and experienced it myself as well. Before Eden was born, I would sometimes look at Maya while she slept and feel such a rush of love for her that . . . well, that I knew with a solemn certainty that I would not be able to live if she were to die. I would watch her in her crib, both arms flung over her head, holdup-style, so innocent and sweet, and that's where my mind swiveled: to the possibility of loss. I had no idea if such thoughts were normal for a mother to have. Did women without a history of early loss, I often wondered, think this way about their children dying? Did they automatically assume, as I did, that their lives would end at that moment, too? Or was I involved in a kind of creepy and pathological overidentification that would ultimately stunt my daughter? I would often think about having a second child to spread the intensity around—to keep myself from loving the first one so much, and stop myself from having such desperate thoughts about my inability to survive.

Of course, the way to stop having these thoughts is not to have another child (and is, in fact, a very bad reason to have another child), but to figure out why one is having such thoughts in the first place. Which, fortunately, I went into therapy and did before Eden was conceived. After her birth, however, I'd be lying if I said the feelings of emotional risk didn't level off. Having a second child did make me feel less vulnerable, and also made me less anxiously focused on Maya, which I can only interpret as a good thing. In the postpartum hormonal funk after Eden's birth, I remember feeling enormous relief first that she was healthy, and then from knowing her birth was insurance that would keep me safe. I knew now that if one child were to die I would need to keep on going for the other.

For a motherless daughter, any experience of abundance has a way of being trailed by nagging thoughts of potential loss. "Many of the women I see are healed, in a sense, by motherhood," says Irene Rubaum-Keller, MFT, who counsels motherless daughters in Los Angeles. "They now have all this love in their life. Some of them want to have six kids so they'll be surrounded by love. Yet, at the same time, they have this idea, 'Okay, if one dies, I still have five others.'"

Thirty-three-year-old Nina, the mother of a four-year-old son and a two-year-old daughter, was thirteen when her mother died of cancer. She was then raised by her father, along with an older sister and a younger brother with whom she remains close today. Her experience of early loss and the relationship she shared with her siblings, she says, has factored dominantly into her family-planning decisions.

"I have a lot of anxiety about losing my kids," she says. "So much so that I think maybe I should have a third child, so that if I lose one I'll still have two. Crazy thinking like that. And also thinking that since I have a daughter now, I really want her to have a sister, because the sister bond is just huge. Having a sister has really helped me in that I have another female role model in my life, even if I don't have a mother."

Uzi and I stopped at two children, because it was the largest number we felt we could handle in a home with two working parents. It was a purely practical decision, and the right one for us. But if I weren't a working mother, or if I'd started having children younger—would we have had a third? With enough resources, who knows? Perhaps I would have. And would that have felt like enough? Is there ever enough? There is no magic, healing number of children a motherless daughter can have before all threat of loss disappears. Every child is precious, every one of them irreplaceable. There is also no magic number beyond which a mother's love stops multiplying. Every mother of one child wonders if she'll be able to love a second just as much. Those who have a second soon discover the remarkable elasticity of mother love. A mother's attention may get split in two when a second comes along, but not her love. That doubles.

7

The Absent Grandmother

FILLING THE VOID

"After my kids were born, I was so sad for my mother, that
she wouldn't get to see them and know them. And I was sad
that when they did something cute, I couldn't pick up the
phone and tell her, 'Oh my goodness! Jake just smiled for
the first time!' It's amazing how long that was my main concern, what *she* was going to miss out on. But now, I sort of
feel that it's really *them* who are missing out the most. They
would have been so lucky to have had her in their lives."

—28-year-old Samantha, the mother of two young sons,
who was 22 when her mother died

$\mathscr{I}$t's Grandparents Day at the preschool again. Technically,
it's "Grandpals Day," a title created for families with grandparents who can't attend, or who don't have grandparents to invite.
Those of us in the no-grandparents category appreciate the gesture,
but we know better. No matter what it's called, to us it's Grandparents Day, all the same.

My sister, Michele, cheerfully steps in for this occasion each year,
and we're grateful for it. Because of her, Eden has someone special

to play with and perform for today. Otherwise, she'd be like the kids sitting on the carpet alone, impervious to the teacher's attempts to engage them. Every time I look at one of those kids, my throat starts to constrict. If Michele hadn't been able to make it today, I think, I would have just kept Eden at home.

Around the classroom, gray-haired grandmothers bend over art projects and admire the wall displays, murmuring their approval over watercolor paintings and macaroni art. Some of the mothers have come today, too. They cede the miniature chairs and the bare spots on the carpet to their parents and in-laws, but Michele and I get down cross-legged on the floor. Eden works a Montessori project, and we tell her how good she is at the wooden rods, how smart she is to know exactly where each piece goes. "Great job!" we tell her. "You're so good at this! Look at you—you got them all!"

We're overdoing it, but that's the point. It's like an unspoken agreement between us. If Eden doesn't have a grandmother to invite today, damn it, we'll make up for it big-time. We'll give her two adults to show off for, *two* adults to tell her how perfect and special she is.

The truth is, of the eighteen kids in Eden's Montessori class, only about half have grandmothers present. The rest of the grandmas live too far away, or aren't able to travel, or, like my mother, are no longer alive. Some kids have a grandfather present, and I notice a few older women who could be godmothers or family friends. But the maternal grandmothers are the ones I can't stop watching, because that's the one kind of grandpal my daughter doesn't have.

From the moment Maya was born, there's been a hole in our family where a maternal grandmother should be. That might sound obvious, but it was a hole I'd never noticed until I became a mother myself. Before then, I never really thought of my mother as a grandmother. She'd been so irrevocably removed from that role by dying young that trying to imagine her as a grandmother felt preposterous, anachronistic, even somehow lewd, like one of those photos of a six-year-old all coiffed and made up to look like a beauty queen.

For at least a decade after my mother died, I was focused on what I had lost, then on what she had lost as well. Motherhood added a whole new twist to this line of thought. Now I constantly think about what my daughters have lost, too. No adoring older woman to dote on them. No home away from home. No opportunity to witness a woman age. My husband's mother is in her seventies, still active and energetic, but we see her, at best, only every other year. As a result, my daughters are cut off from an entire generation of women in our family. This messes with their perspective. I'm forty-one, and they think I'm old.

I don't mean, in any way, to minimize my mother-in-law's importance. When we're together, she's a loving grandmother, and I know she'd like to be as involved with my daughters as she is with her own daughters' kids. I wish it, too. But I know, even if we lived closer, it wouldn't be the same. She's my daughters' paternal grandmother, and that makes her an entirely different force in their lives. Women are almost always closer to their daughters' children than they are to their sons'.* And if their daughters have daughters, the deal is cinched. Those girls are the ones who'll get most of that grandmother's interest and the largest chunks of her grandmothering time.

My daughters, of course, don't worry about any of this. They're perfectly happy to have my sister show up on Grandparents Day. She's fun, she's pretty, and she showers them with attention. That's good enough for them. Having never had a maternal grandmother, they don't have any idea what they're missing. But I do. My mother's mother lived to be ninety, long enough to see me well into adulthood, though not long enough to see my first child. She was a complicated woman, but a steady, reliable presence during my childhood, showing up at our front door several times a week with sweet smiles and small gifts for everyone. Because of my grandmother, the world of my childhood was a far more expansive place than it would have been otherwise. Her house was a place of unlimited discovery,

---

* A notable exception to this occurs in some non-Western cultures, where older women live in their sons' homes and help raise their children.

with glass bowls of candy perched on end tables and treasures lurk-
ing behind teetering piles of five-year-old magazines. Her car was
a wide, wondrous vehicle capable of transporting me to tidy, colorful worlds. Bloomingdale's. Howard Johnson's. The kosher market
near her house. Sometimes she hugged me so hard I couldn't
breathe. She loved me with a purity and a ferocity I still miss.

What, exactly, do children miss out on when they don't have a
maternal grandmother? I often wonder this, mostly to assess what
my daughters lack so I can compensate for it in some way. I look for
consistent, loving babysitters who'll open up their homes. I try to
cultivate friendships with older women who'll spend quiet time with
them. Lately, I've been scheduling our library trips for Wednesdays
between three and five, to coincide with the hours that "Grandmother Judy" volunteers in the children's section. Both girls sit with
such quiet reverence when she reads to them. But I can't watch it.
There's too much space between them at the table. Shouldn't they
be touching? Shouldn't my daughters be snuggled into the crook of
a grandmother's arm?

That's when I think I'm foolish to believe I can make up for what
my daughters have missed. Reading is more than just reading with a
grandmother. Dinnertime is more than just food on a plate.

Thirty-nine-year-old Renee, who was twenty-two when her mother
died, also misses that special synergy between grandparents and
grandchildren. Renee spent large amounts of time with her maternal grandmother as a child. Now the mother of two school-age
children, Renee can barely stand listening to friends who talk about
dropping their children off at the grandparents' for a weekend or—
even worse—who complain their parents and their in-laws are fighting over who'll get to take the grandchildren that Saturday night.

"I feel like I'm talking about my mother as a nursemaid," Renee
says. "But it's not just about that. It's about my kids having the opportunity to spend a large amount of time with my mother to really
find out what kind of person she was. And to let them hear crazy
stories about me. To let them know that I'm not just a mom. I almost

got killed three or four times when I was a kid, fell off a railing, hit my head, that kind of thing, you know. I was just a maniac. I want them to know that I was fun when I was young like them, and that I used to do crazy things with my sisters and get into trouble. I'd like them to hear it, the same way I heard things like that from my grandmother when I went to her house. She used to say, 'Oh, your mother. She was a stickler. What a temper.' And so I knew I'd gotten my temper from my mother. But when I say the same thing to my daughter, who has the same exact personality that I do, she doesn't know what I'm talking about. She can't see where it's coming from. And I want her to be able to see."

Although a great deal has been written about the relationship between children and their maternal grandmothers, very little has been written about children who don't have one. Like so many questions about loss, this one must be answered through a back door: first, by looking at what children with maternal grandmothers *do* receive, and then by extrapolating the inverse from there.

Maternal grandmothers are important influences in the lives of grandchildren, this much is known. In virtually every survey conducted with grandchildren who have four living grandparents, the maternal grandmother ranks highest in their affections. Mothers' mothers tend to be the grandparents most likely to make grandchildren feel good about themselves, to help in emergencies, to act as intermediaries between children and their parents, and to share secrets with grandchildren. This is mainly because of the relationship a mother shares with her mother. Married adult women tend to live closer to their parents than men do, receive more child-care assistance from mothers than they receive from mothers-in-law, have more frequent contact with their parents than husbands do, and be more involved in their mothers' lives. Maternal grandmothers thus become the grandparents with whom grandchildren have the most contact, and the ones on whom a family typically relies the most.*

---

* This is especially true in families where the mothers are divorced.

From these studies and others, it appears that a warm, loving relationship with a maternal grandmother offers a child—especially a granddaughter—one or more of the following:

A less stressful, less complicated, less emotionally invested relationship with an older woman in the family

Mothers, immersed in the minutiae of day-to-day child care, parent with an inevitable anxiety. They see their actions and decisions as critical determinants of their children's happiness, and perceive their childrens' behavior as an indicator of their own failure or success. Parenting is a high-speed adventure, with schedules to stick to, activities to plan, expectations to meet, and unexpected setbacks possible at any turn. Grandparents, on the other hand, are freed from the heavy responsibility of full-time socialization and instruction. They, like grandchildren, also have more time to enjoy each other than parents do, and time spent together can move at a slower pace. Children recognize this, appreciate it, and oftentimes need it to balance out the intensity of the nuclear family.

In addition, the mirroring that goes on between mother and daughter rarely exists between grandmother and granddaughter. Mothers often see daughters as extensions of themselves and may therefore react to a daughter's behavior with envy, self-pride, or fear. A grandmother is far less likely to perceive a granddaughter this way, or to confuse the child's behavior or feelings with her own. Her relationship with her granddaughter usually has less emotional charge, and her presence can soften the mother-daughter relationship. As a result, grandchildren are often willing to tell a grandmother about a problem before they'll confide in a parent, knowing that the reaction and the outcome will be different. And because family characteristics tend to be transmitted mostly from the mother's side of the family, children gain an additional female role model for socialization.

An alternate maternal viewpoint in the family

Sometimes a grandmother reinforces the mother's attitudes and methods, giving the child an influential double dose of the same behavior. Sometimes she offers a benign, corrective influence instead, counteracting a mother's rigidity or permissiveness. Either way, the child is exposed to another way of being, and learns that what may pass as "normal" inside her household may not be the only way to live. This is particularly important in families where mothers are harshly critical, self-absorbed, distracted, or preoccupied. In these cases, the impact of a mother's harsh personality can be tempered by simultaneous exposure to a grandmother's softer approach.

Grandmothers can also act as mediators or interpreters for the generations, smoothing out and defusing conflict, especially during a granddaughter's teen years. The unspoken knowledge that she and her daughter weathered the daughter's adolescence and emerged with their relationship intact—assuming they have—provides assurance to the younger generations that they, too, will make it through the storm.

A sense of extended family

Women in their fifties and sixties are typically the "kinkeepers" of their families, bringing aunts, uncles, cousins, and in-laws together for special events. Their homes become the hubs for holidays and family celebrations. The rituals that take place there are often the ones that granddaughters remember, years later, as the ones that gave them ethnic, religious, or cultural identity as a child. Even grandmothers who don't handle the logistics of family events are often the focus of family contact, the "excuse" for family members to congregate.

When a grandmother acts as a family kinkeeper, her grandchildren receive security and continuity from knowing they are part of a large, extensive system with its own internal structure. They come to understand the general rights and obligations that come from being part of a kin network, and learn how to abide by the unique rights and obligations associated with their families. Their individual psychological needs for safety, predictability, structure, and containment can be fulfilled. Put most simply, an extended family can assure a child that he belongs to something larger than the nuclear unit, and is even more widely appreciated and loved.

Insight into long-term mother-daughter relationships

Watching a grandmother interact with a mother gives a child a glimpse into the world of adult female interactions. Does the mother dote on the grandmother? Or does she become childlike in her presence? Does the grandmother treat her daughter as an equal, as a superior, or as an inferior adult? The behavioral cues that children pick up on in a grandmother's backyard or in a mother's kitchen introduce them to the complexity of intergenerational relationships.

Mothers and daughters disagree, mothers and daughters shout at each other, but ultimately mothers and daughters love each other without condition: this is what many girls learn from observing mothers and grandmothers interacting over time, and what they can later remind themselves when raising daughters of their own.

A less-stressed, warmer, and more confident mother

The presence of an empathic maternal grandmother can act as an emotional "stabilizer" for mothers, helping them handle the maternal role with more competence, patience, and warmth. When grandmothers are available to offer comfort and support to their adult daughters at stressful times, such as illness, divorce, or post-partum periods, or anytime the mother needs to be mothered, the whole family benefits, but no one more so than the mother herself.

Mothers who have contact with their own mothers also appear to feel more confident about themselves as mothers. Of all the women with mothers surveyed for this book, 53 percent said they never worried about their ability to be a good mother, compared to only 23 percent of motherless mothers who were asked the same question.

Social, cultural, biological, anthropological—no matter which discipline informs us, the answer is always the same. Maternal grandmothers matter. But it's also important not to over-romanticize the role of a grandmother in the family, or to sugarcoat all grandmother-granddaughter relationships. Like any human bond, when this one is good it can be very good, but when it's bad it can be devastating. Children who grow up under the influence of autocratic or mentally imbalanced grandmothers, or even with grandmothers who are mildly yet consistently critical, may emerge from those relationships with a diminished sense of self-worth, an excessive desire to please others, or a tendency toward self-blame. Living in the same house as such a grandmother can teach a child from an early age to fear or resent female authority.

When a difficult grandmother is a secondary figure in the family, however, conflicted feelings toward her are less likely to evolve into disastrous results. Even when a grandmother is a negative force, a child can gain a sense of who she is in relation to her. Granddaughters will often push against grandmothers who are harsh, judgmental, or critical—as long as the mother or father does, as well—and become their own person as a result of that distancing. Maternal grandmothers matter a great deal to these granddaughters, too, though for very different reasons.

The Unknown Quantity

What kind of grandmother would my mother have been? Active? Devoted? Distant? Is it even possible to know? If her younger sister's grandmothering offers hints, then she'd be loving, patient, and proud. If my father's behavior toward my daughters offered clues, then she would have been endlessly charmed by their exploits, and called often to hear amusing stories.

Indulge me for a moment, please. It's last month, or last week, or next week. The timing doesn't really matter. I'm standing in the kitchen, rinsing ketchup off the dinner dishes. The kids are playing in the TV room off to my right. They're sailing off the back of the couch and landing loudly on the gray carpet, ignoring my pleas to be careful. The dishwasher door is pulled open, and I'm mindlessly stacking dinner plates inside.

The black cordless phone is trapped between my left shoulder and my ear. I'm talking to my mother, long-distance in New York. She asks if Uzi's home. I glance at the clock—6:50 P.M.—and tell her I'm expecting him soon. "How did Dad manage to make it home every evening by 5:30?" I ask her. She laughs. "Because he caught a 6:00 train to work every morning," she says. "Don't you remember, he was never there to help get you ready for school?" She's right, and I know I've got it easier. I'd rather have Uzi with us in the morning than for the extra hour at night. I tell her I have no idea how she handled three of us. She says it wasn't always easy. Somehow, that makes me feel better. Then she asks about the girls. I tell her Maya's building a fairy-tale castle for school, and Eden's new best friend at preschool is Alexandra DuManoir, but you have to pronounce the name correctly, or she'll make you try again. "Can I talk to them?" she asks. I hold the phone in the air. "Who wants to talk to Grandma!" I call in the general direction of the TV room. Maya flies through the air and lands on the floor like a crouched frog. "Do I have to right now?" she says. Eden pauses midway up the back of the couch. "Later!" she shouts, and resumes her climb.

"They don't want to come to the phone," I say into the receiver.

"Hm," my mother says, and in that tiny exhalation I hear just the slightest edge. It could be impatience, or even disappointment, but it sounds like judgment to me. My mother has always been able to convey paragraphs in just a single word. *What's wrong with your kids?* this one says. *Why haven't you raised them to come to the phone when they're asked?* And it makes me a little crazy. Because they *are* acting impolite. And I don't know why. We'll talk about it as soon as I get off the phone. In the meantime, though, doesn't she realize I'm doing the best I can?

"Can't you bring the phone to them?" she asks.

"No," I tell her. I'm in a pissy mood now. "I *can't.*"

I'll end this dreamscape now, before it slides further downhill. You get the idea. She'd probably be a terrific grandmother, but it wouldn't be a constant holiday. No adult mother-daughter relationship is. That much I do know to be true.

Since becoming a mother, I've been closely watching my girlfriends with kids. Most of them are grateful to receive their mothers' help, but only when they want it. They'll take their mothers' advice, but only when they ask for it. Their behavior toward their mothers ranges, in my observations, from mildly appreciative to barely tolerant.

Do I often want to grab hold of a girlfriend who complains about her mother as a grandmother and shake her, shouting, "You don't know how lucky you are to have a mother?" Of course. But would I treat my mother any differently if she were alive? Well, probably not. I'm no saint, that's for sure. Like many motherless daughters, I suspect I see the enormous value of a mother's presence because I live every day with its absence. It's not hard to appreciate the grandmother who never got to be one, or to exalt the wisdom of the sage who's not there.

When a mother was abusive, neglectful, or mentally ill, however, projecting her into a grandmothering role can be a more troubling exercise. It means imagining one's children under her influence or her care, and that's enough to make some motherless daughters balk. *My mother? With my kids? Not a chance.*

At the same time, daughters of troubled mothers who've died often acknowledge that these mothers, if they'd lived, might have fared differently in the grandmother role. A woman's performance as a mother doesn't necessarily determine the kind of grandmother she'll be. In fact, many women who've had poor relationships with their daughters nonetheless manage to have close and loving relationships with granddaughters, especially those who became mothers when very young, or had many children close in age, and found the maternal role overwhelming, suffocating, or too intense.

When speculating about what kind of grandmothers these difficult or neglectful mothers might have become—and most motherless mothers can't help doing this—their daughters often bounce back and forth between images of distant and unhelpful women and warm and nurturing characters. They seem torn between their upsetting memories of childhood and their adult desire to speak fairly about the deceased.

"If my mom were alive . . . I don't know if she would have been any help to me," admits thirty-five-year-old Rachel, the daughter of a neglectful mother who died when Rachel was nineteen. "I think she might have been a good grandmother. She loved little kids, everyone tells me that. They say, 'Oh, when your mom would come over she'd play with my kids and she was so good with the babies.' So, I do think she would have been a good grandmother. But I don't know if she would really have offered much support when my kids were born. I mean, she might have. But just knowing that she was gone and that I didn't even have anyone to ask was hard, even though she might not have been any help."

Forty-year-old Pamela, the daughter of a distant, critical mother who died when she was twenty-three, also has difficulty imagining her mother in the grandmother role. "One of the hardest things for me is that I never saw my mother with babies," says Pamela, whose daughters are now three and one. "So I have no *idea* what she would have been like as a grandparent. And that's hard for me. Because I think, *As a grandmother, she wouldn't be so critical.* But I think she would be. Then I kind of think to myself, *What if she were just loving and nurturing and grandma-ish, and I got to see that?*"

Pamela's story raises an important point: seeing her mother as a loving grandmother might have had an impact on her feelings toward her mother, and her perception of their relationship. In families where a difficult mother later becomes a loving grandmother, a daughter's response depends largely on how she feels about her mother today. If she's angry or resentful about the way she was treated as a child, she may become envious when she sees her children receive the warmth and affection she believes she was denied. But if she has come to a place of forgiveness and peace with her mother, she's more likely to place the past in the past and allow her children to have a relationship with their maternal grandmother.

The Not-so-absent Grandmother

How is it possible that my daughters don't know my mother? The answer is obvious, yet the unreality of the situation still catches me off guard. She was my *mother*. A daily influence on me at their age. The hand that guides my parenting. And yet they have so little idea of who she was. How remarkable this is, and how very, very bizarre.

In her memoir *Searching for Mercy Street*, Linda Gray Sexton, the daughter of poet Anne Sexton, recalls visiting a local bookstore with her ten-year-old son and seeing a paperback edition of her mother's biography, with a photo of her mother prominently displayed on the cover.

"Look," he said. "There's Grandma Anne."

I put my arm around him. "Isn't it strange to see your grandmother here like this?"

"It's stranger never to have met her."

We stood in silence for a moment more, then turned and walked toward the door.

"I miss her," I said then.

"I'm sorry, Mom," he answered, and then, overcoming his burgeoning distaste of physical contact with his mother in public, he took my hand and squeezed it. A gift. "I wish I could have known her."

I squeezed back. "Me, too."

Sexton's sons grew up acquainted with their grandmother's legacy and her writing. When it was their turn to be "person of the week" in school, they would bring their grandmother's books—along with their parents'—for display. Sexton writes about this with a bittersweet pride, grateful for her sons' connection to her mother yet aware of how much her mother would have enjoyed watching her grandsons grow.

Most motherless mothers hope to create some kind of emotional or historical connection between their children and their mothers. More than three-quarters of the motherless mothers surveyed said they now keep photographs of their mothers on display in their homes, and 79 percent said they've talked about their mothers with their kids.[*] One woman plays tapes of her mother's favorite lullabies as her children fall asleep each night. Another used a photo of her mother as a calming, focal point during labor, ensuring that her mother's image was present in the room when her child was born. Most motherless women try to make their mothers a part of their new families—a task that takes on additional emotional purpose when fathers or stepmothers tried hard in the past to shut that door.

Thirty-one-year-old Paula, who was twelve when her mother died, vividly remembers cooking side by side with her as a child. "This is something your grandmother made," her mother would say as they chopped walnuts or rolled dough. "I remember making these with her, and they'd take all day to make." Now the mother of eleven-month-old twin boys, with a third child on the way, Paula worries that her children won't have any sense of who her mother was, and this pains her. So she plans to retrieve her mother's recipe

---

[*] Some of the women in the other 21 percent had children who were still infants or toddlers, and may just not have talked with them yet.

box from her father's house as soon as her children are old enough
to join her in the kitchen.

"It's a way we can remember her together," Paula says. "And
I'll be able to say, 'Oh, I remember making these with my mom as
a girl.' I think that'll help them get in touch with her a little bit. I
hate going to the gravesite—it never brought me any comfort as a
kid—so I don't think that will be something I'll do with them. I'd
rather do something I feel compelled to do, some kind of ritual. My
mother's birthday was on Christmas Eve, and every year my family
would do fondue that night so she wouldn't have to cook. I still do it
with my father and my siblings, actually. So, I think that's something
I'll try to continue with my kids, too."

As Gina Mireault explains, "For some women, the idea of keeping the eternal line going can be one of the motivators for entering
motherhood, whether it's conscious or not. I also think one of the
joys for motherless women is that they have an opportunity to preserve the mother and to pass along her memory to their children.
Obviously, as motherless women, we have a great interest in our histories. And we expect that our children will have a similar interest,
at some point."

I'm reminded of a conversation I had with Rebecca, the mother
of four children ages fourteen to twenty-seven. For many years,
Rebecca did not speak to her children of the mother who died when
she was ten.

"The kids didn't ask about her, and I thought, *I don't want to burden
everybody with it—my mom is gone,*" Rebecca explains. "And I didn't want
to be hurt that they wouldn't care. So I never brought her up, until
about three or four years ago, when I reached my mother's death
age. A lot of anxiety and depression hit me then, and I went into
therapy. The therapist helped me get started. She said, 'Why don't
you take your mother's nursing uniform out and put it on a form?'
It inspired me to bring out pictures of my mom and make her part
of my family. I started talking to my kids about things she'd done."

As Rebecca's children were introduced to aspects of their grandmother's life, they began to develop independent relationships with her. "We're Catholic, and we have a sort of spiritual basis for praying for the dead," Rebecca says. "My father died when my oldest daughter was in the second grade, and she knew him. She's always felt close to him. And strangely enough, she says she also feels close to my mom, and that she talks to her all the time. I love that. I *love* that. Now, with all the children, if they've lost something or they're going to have a test at school, I say, 'Do you want to ask my mom and dad for help?' and they'll say, 'I already did.' It's become habit for them."

Every night at bedtime for the past year now, Maya has asked for a story from my childhood. A year's worth of stories is a lot of stories. I've started to run out of new ones.

"Can it be from when I was older, like when I first met Dad?" I ask, as I arrange the down comforter around us.

"No," she says firmly. "I want it from when you were a kid. Like the time you broke your toe or got paint all over your bedspread. Something like that." She wants the real stuff, the dirt. The bloody noses. The head-lice inspections. The bullies I'd rather forget.

She's looking for guidance as she navigates her own girlhood, I realize, and I'm supposed to provide her with clues. So I try to come up with good examples. Sometimes she murmurs, "That was good thinking, Mom," at the end of a story. Sometimes she'll snort into her pillow, roll over, and say, "God, Mom, you were so *dumb*."

I *was* so dumb. And yet it's remarkable how all those mistakes have turned out to be such useful examples for my daughter of what not to do.

My mother told me stories about her childhood, too. About the summer her cousin saved her from drowning, and about her patience with a boyfriend who stuttered. They were helpful stories, good rudders for a developing female mind. So, when I start running out of stories about myself for Maya, I think, *why not?*

To Maya, these bedtime stories are learning opportunities. To me, they've become a way to bring my mother into the room.

I tell her about going to visit my mother's childhood country house as a child, how the piano seemed so tremendous to me and the yard so much smaller than I'd imagined. I tell her about the summer my mother almost drowned in the nearby lake and was saved by an older cousin.

Whose stories are these now, hers or mine? Does it matter?

Lately, Eden's been listening, too. I tell them both about the day my mother and I got our ears pierced together, when she was thirty-six and I was ten. I went first, and my mother couldn't watch the jeweler punch holes in my ears without feeling sick. As I remember it, she stumbled backward from the kiosk in the mall with her eyes averted, sending me little, encouraging good-bye waves with her right hand as she retreated into a candle store, and came rushing back over as soon as he was done. I didn't mind her leaving. I liked feeling that I was old enough to have this experience on my own.

"Why did she walk away?" Maya asks. Eden doesn't say anything, but she gently takes hold of my ear lobe and won't let go.

"I don't know. Maybe she was afraid if she watched, she'd chicken out when it was her turn," I say. "Or maybe it was just too hard for her to watch the jeweler do something that might hurt me."

"Like when the dentist had to give me a shot and you cried?" she asks.

"Yeah," I tell her. "Like that."

By day, my mother is an enigma to my daughters, but at night she comes to three-dimensional life. Through story, I give them a grandmother who's wise and friendly and funny, highly creative and rarely strict. It's not that far from the truth, although I'm leaving some parts out for now. The nervousness, the self-doubt, the occasional lack of self-esteem. What's the point of including all that now? For now, my mother can be perfect. And I love that. I *love* that. It's the one fine thing I can still offer her, my lasting, final gift—this life after death in which she can become, in the minds of her grand-daughters, the kind of woman she always aspired to be.

8

⁂

The Grandma in Heaven

EXPLAINING DEATH TO KIDS

*I*t begins with a question from a three- or four-year-old, so sweetly innocent yet so piercingly blunt: "Where's *your* mommy?"

"There's nothing more terrifying for a parent with a deceased parent to hear," says Dan Schaefer, PhD, the author of *How Do We Tell the Children?*, "because this is when discussions about death start."

In our house, it began one afternoon when Maya was three. We were sitting on the floor of my office, sifting through a bag of photos from my childhood. I was sorting pictures from the 1960s, 1970s, and 1980s into separate stacks when she withdrew one from the center pile.

"Who's that?" she asked. She pressed the tip of her chubby index finger into the center of a foggy Instamatic square.

I angled my neck to see the photo in her hand. It was a slightly out-of-focus shot of my mother, from the shoulders up. She was wearing a pink-and-green striped sweater, and the camera had caught her midsentence. A pair of brown construction-paper rabbit ears rested on top of her short, frosted hair.

I remembered the afternoon that photo was taken. We were standing in the carpool lane of my elementary school after my sister's third-grade play, and my mother was warning me not to take a picture of her with rabbit ears on her head. After I'd snapped the shot anyway, she'd just shrugged and smiled and said, "Well, *that*'ll be a winner."

I flipped the picture over. On the back, my mother had written "March 1977."

"That's my mommy," I said.

My mommy. The words sounded both odd and comforting in my own voice after all those years.

Maya's little face scrunched up in confusion. I could almost see the tiny mental gears straining to click into place. *Daddy has a mommy . . . and I know who she is . . . but Mommy has a mommy, too?*

"Why can't I see her?" she asked.

"Because," I said, and then I stopped short.

This was the conversation I'd been waiting to have, the one I'd been rehearsing since before her birth. I wanted my child to know about my mother, to know what she'd represented and believed in, and I didn't want to obfuscate the truth about her absence, no matter how scary or painful it might be. I'd decided long ago to wait for Maya to ask, and then to gently and informatively explain. But in the movie version of my life, we were curled up together on the couch in a shared moment of reverence, not sprawled across the mauve carpet surrounded by random, misfiled scraps of my past. In the big-screen version, Maya would ask, "What happened to your mother?" and my answer would spill forth like a clear, sparkling stream released from its source. Instead, at the critical moment of response, I couldn't find any words at all.

Why can't I see her? There were so many ways to answer this question, all of them suddenly clunky, inadequate, and flawed.

I could default into physiology: *Because she died of breast cancer.* Or into a spiritual explanation: *Because she's gone to heaven.* I could even blame it on geography: *Because she's buried far away, in a cemetery in New York.*

I opted for the factual. I'd once read that children respond to the idea of death with the same emotional intensity with which the concept is first presented to them, so I tried to keep my voice matter-of-fact.

"She died," I said. "A long time ago. When I was seventeen."

But seventeen had no meaning to a three-year-old. Neither, apparently, did "died."

"But why can't I *see* her?" Maya insisted.

Then I remembered Otto. Poor, doomed Otto. Such a Petco bargain at only $1.29. We'd placed him in a plastic countertop aquarium with a smaller goldfish named Tallulah. Otto lasted only two weeks. The hardy Tallulah, on the other hand, had been enjoying her private real estate for the past six months.

"Remember what happened to Otto?" I asked her.

"You flushed him in the toilet," she said.

"Not that part. The part before that, when he stopped moving and I said, 'Oh no—Otto died!' Died is like that, when your body stops moving and breathing, and the rest of you goes away to another place and doesn't come back."

"Oh."

She seemed content with the explanation, and I congratulated myself for handling the moment so well. My self-satisfaction, however, was short-lived. A half-hour later, as we descended the stairs to the kitchen, Maya grabbed hold of my hand. "Your mother died!" she sang out cheerfully, swinging my arm. For the rest of the afternoon and into the evening, she kept blurting out the phrase without warning, as if checking to make sure the words still worked. When Uzi came home from work that evening and heard it, he looked at me quizzically.

"We learned a new word today," I explained weakly.

Well, I'd introduced the idea of my mother. That was something,

I reasoned. What my daughter had grasped beyond that was impossible to know. It would take several more years of intellectual maturation and increasingly pointed questions and answers before I knew that Maya had gained a full understanding of death, knew how it applied to a grandmother she'd never met, and realized how, in turn, it would apply to other members of our family one day.

Death is a scary enough concept for adults to grasp. It's equally, if not more, confusing for kids to understand. Such an abstract concept can't find easy purchase in their concrete little minds. To truly "get" what death means, kids need fairly sophisticated cognitive tools that typically start developing at age three or four and don't finish until nine or ten. By then, most kids can understand what psychologists call "the four components of death"—that it's irreversible, it's inevitable, it causes all life functions to cease, and it always has an internal or external cause.

Kids with high verbal abilities and those who have some first-hand experience with death—such as the loss of an extended family member or a pet—tend to grasp these concepts earlier. Children who have a low tolerance for anxiety, however, and those who've experienced the death of an immediate family member usually take a little longer.* Religious beliefs in an afterlife may also complicate a child's scientific understanding of death, and the specific cause of a death—such as homicide, suicide, or natural disaster—may also affect how much kids can understand and when.

Let's look back to my three-year-old for a moment, and try to understand what "died" may have meant to her. Like most kids her age, she'd barely begun to understand the four components of death. To fully grasp them, she'd first need to understand the vast difference between herself and others, and most three-year-olds

---

* It seems that the closer a child is to the person who died, the greater the distortion in the child's mind. This may be because separation from a close relative creates an anxiety that interferes with the cognitive process. Or it may be that losing a close family member causes kids to build up defenses against the idea of death in general.

haven't mastered that yet. They're still likely to believe everyone else thinks and feels the same way they do. She'd also need to understand the difference between animate and inanimate objects, another distinction most three-year-olds can't yet make. To them, stuffed animals are capable of emotion, rocks can roll themselves down hillsides, and trees can breathe.

To fully understand "died," my daughter also would have needed to comprehend time and constancy, have a fairly high verbal ability, and understand cause-and-effect relationships. That's a lot for a three-year-old to master, even a lot for a four-year-old, though not impossible for a bright five-year-old. A child's age is just a general guideline for acquiring death concepts. Her cognitive level is a better predictor, which explains why some three-year-olds will show surprise or pity when an insect or animal dies, while others appear not to understand what happened at all.

At age three, Maya had a very limited understanding of death. Most likely, the word "died" signified some kind of altered state to her, one that happened to other, distant people or objects, certainly not to those she depended upon. Blurting out "Your mother died!" on the stairs didn't mean she understood what the term meant, but that she may have been trying to figure it out.

Three years later, however, her perception of death had matured considerably. By then, we'd lost our family cat, and she'd seen enough Disney movies to understand that mothers can die (and, in inimitable Disney fashion, almost always do). As I was writing this chapter, she was seven, and her second-grade class just happened to be studying the difference between animate and inanimate objects. On impulse, I asked her if she thought rocks could breathe or move on their own, and she gave me a look of such urgent concern for my sanity that the verdict was clear: she had the difference between animate and inanimate objects down, and Mom didn't have a clue.

All children need to achieve a certain level of cognition to understand the full implications of death. Children of motherless mothers, however, have a slightly more complicated task. They need to understand not just what the death of a grandparent means, but also that it happened to a grandmother they never met, before they were born. For them, one abstraction gets layered right on top of another.

To grasp this additional concept, a child first needs to understand that parents can have parents. "It's tough to pin an age on this awareness, but there are cognitive milestones that would be associated with it," says Gina Mireault. "The child would have to be relying less on static reasoning, which is the idea that things will always be and have always been as they are now. She would also have to be relying less on appearance-based judgments, such as 'a child is a little kid, and since my mom isn't a little kid, she can't be someone's child.' She'd have to be able to go forward and backward in her thinking, and to be able to understand relationships between objects. All of these cognitive qualities are characteristic of the concrete operations stage [of cognitive development], so certainly by age six children should understand basic relationships between family members, and more complex ones, like cousins and in-laws, by age nine or ten. A four-year-old might at least be able to identify her grandmother as her 'mother's mother' and have a pretty superficial understanding of that. Kids younger than that, though, may scoff or giggle at the idea, refuse to believe it, or think a parent is mistaken."

Thirty-five-year-old Christine, who was six when her mother died, now has a four-and-a-half-year-old daughter who just recently realized her maternal grandmother was missing from the family. "Not long ago, Kyra put together: 'Daddy has a mommy and a daddy, but you only have a daddy,'" Christine recalls. "It had taken her a while to figure out that Grandpa Jim was a daddy, though. It was like, 'Wait a minute—I get this now! That man is your father!' It was like the lightbulb went on. And that was when she started to say, 'Okay . . . then where is Grandma Frances?'" And then the conversations about death in Christine's house began.

Learning about a maternal grandmother who died in the past may or may not upset a child, depending on her degree of sensitivity. "It's a step removed from the child, so it's not as frightening as losing someone they know," explains Phyllis Silverman. "It's actually a wonderful way for children, little ones especially, to learn about death, because it doesn't affect their daily lives."

It does introduce, however, the unsettling idea that mothers can die when children are young. This can heighten a child's feelings of vulnerability to loss and affect her sense of safety in the world—the main reasons why some motherless women choose not to tell their children too many details about their mothers, or not tell them about her at all.

"We call my mother their grandma in Heaven," says thirty-three-year-old Patrice, who has two daughters, ages three and one. "I have a picture of her out. But my three-year-old's already putting two and two together: 'Grandma's in Heaven, and God's in Heaven . . . so is Grandma with God? Did your mother *die*?' I never said, 'Your grandmother died' or 'My mom died.' She just put it together. And I told her yes, and we talked about it a little. I told her my mother died when I was ten, and then she immediately said, 'I'm almost ten.' And that scared me. I don't want her to put herself in my spot, and she was kind of doing that. We're having to introduce our little children to the possibility of losing their mother, and I don't want to worry about that. I want to tell her the truth. I want to be honest and say, 'Yes, I was sad.' I don't want to hide things from her, but I also don't want to scare her. So, finding that balance is hard."

All children, especially young children, are egocentric by nature. It's hard for them to interpret new information without wondering how it will affect their own lives. *If my mother lost her mother when she was six, or ten, or twelve,* a child wonders, *could the same thing happen to me?*

A child who hasn't accounted for the possibility of a mother's death before now may have to modify her way of thinking to integrate this new information. She might engage in a sort of inner conversation with herself as she tries to fit the new information into an existing category of thought and, failing that, has to create a new category to include it. Reassurance is critical at these times to help calm any anxiety that might come up about the possibility of your own death.

"It's important to realize that kids fear all kinds of things, including things that we know to be completely safe," Mireault points out. "Especially preschoolers. They're afraid of going down the drain in the bathtub, they're afraid of the bogeyman, they're afraid of the neighbor's Pekingese. These are all situations that we know to be safe, and we reassure them about those things. It should be the same with our deceased mothers. The fear that we're going to die is another unreasonable fear. So we can say, 'This is just an odd thing that happened to me. It can happen, but the chances that it will happen to you are really unlikely.' It can be self-reassuring, too, for us to have that mantra that we're not like our mothers, that we won't meet the same premature end."

Because children tend to interpret information so literally, the reassurances a parent offers should be as specific and concrete as possible. "You have to explain, 'Grandma got very, very, very sick,'" advises Dan Schaefer, who assisted more than three thousand children after deaths in the family when he worked as a funeral home director. "You can tell them, 'Sometimes, very seldom but sometimes, people get sick when they're young. But most people live a very, very, very long time. Sometimes it only takes a lot of 'verys' to make the difference to a child."

Of course, we can't always predict what a child will do with the information we provide. Children's inner reality has a logic and consistency of its own. They tend to connect events that don't have anything to do with each other, which is why saying "Grandma got a very bad pain in her stomach and died" can cause wholesale panic in a child the next time you have bad menstrual cramps. General explanations, such as "Grandma got sick and died," also should be avoided, since other family members may fall ill several times in the course of an average year.

I learned this lesson two years ago, when I came down with a particularly virulent flu on a Friday night. It was the first time ever that I was too sick to get out of bed. Maya climbed under the comforter with me and wouldn't leave. On Monday morning, she refused to go to school. It took me another day to realize what was really going on—that she was afraid I was going to die, and believed she could prevent anything bad from happening to me if she stayed vigilantly by my side.

I let her stay home for the day. It was only the first grade, I reasoned, and it was more important for her to see that a sick mother could heal. But underneath my rationalization lay the thought that maybe I'd badly messed up the conversations we'd had about my mother, that I'd somehow, without realizing it, turned the story of my mother's life into a parable about the possibility of my own demise.

The detailed story of my mother's illness goes something like this: an ob/gyn felt a lump in her left breast in 1979, but assured her it was only a cyst. My mother knew she should have it drained or removed, but didn't think there was a reason to rush. Or maybe she was scared. That's the part I don't know. What's certain is that by the time another ob/gyn felt the same lump a year later and sent her straight to a radiologist, the tumor was three centimeters wide and had spread beyond the breast. She had a radical mastectomy, followed by chemotherapy, but there was never any chance for a cure. Years later, her oncologist told me that from the start, the hope was only to extend her life for as long as possible. He managed to keep her alive for sixteen months. By then, the cancer had spread throughout her body. When it reached her liver she ran out of time.

The abridged version I tell my daughters goes more like this: My mom got sick, but she didn't go to the doctor right away. Then she

went to the doctor and found out she had something called breast
cancer. And then she got very, very sick, and she died. But that
won't happen to me, because whenever I get sick I go straight to
the doctor. So if I ever get what she had, the doctor will find it right
away, and I'll get it fixed and, hopefully, I'll be able to live for a very
long time.

It's a good start, Dan Schaefer says, but it could use some work.
"You can also say, 'When my mother was alive, they didn't have the
medicine they have today. Now, they have the right medicine,'" he
suggests. "Also, 'a long time' for children is confusing. Say, 'I don't
expect to die until you're old and married and have children.' It
puts it in better perspective for them."

Where is the proper balancing point here, that perfect sweet spot
between hope and truth? I don't want to tell my daughters fables de-
signed only to reassure them, but I don't want to overwhelm them,
either, with frightening details. Is my loyalty to their emotional
security, or to historical fact? Most mothers would say the former, I
imagine, but it's not so clear-cut to me. My assurances need to feel
authentic to me, too. Promising my children that I'll live a long life
might calm their anxiety for the moment, but it's not a guarantee
I can offer in good conscience, knowing firsthand how hard it can
be for a mother to honor. I'm reluctant to tell my daughters that
I'll live to see their children—not because I expect to die before
then, but because an even greater betrayal than dying when they're
young, I believe, would be for me to make such a promise and then
fail to keep it.

So I hedge. I sidestep. I offer other certainties. I say, "I know it
happened to Grandma, but I'll do everything I can to make sure
I live till you're grown." And although I know it sounds less than
definitive, probably less than satisfactory, it's the most authentic
statement I can offer. It allows me to acknowledge possibility yet still
plant my flag in optimism. And when I still wonder if I'm making
the right choice, I try to remind myself of what Phyllis Silverman the
author of *Never Too Young to Know*, says: when reassuring children,

what matters most is for children to believe the parent is strong and in charge, and is working hard to make sure adverse events won't occur.

Jennifer Lauck's son was six when he first learned her mother died when she was seven. His first question was "How did she die?" Then he wanted to know where her mother's body was. In her essay "Naked Trees," Lauck writes about what happened next, when Spencer's third question, asked through trembling lips, was "Are you going to die?"

> I move back from him and his question hits me hard. I put my hands on his arms and squeeze down to feel his bones.
>
> "No," I say, shaking my head, "no way."
>
> I talk fast then about how strong I am, how I take good care of my body, and how I'm in perfect health. I say it wasn't that way with my mother, that she was very sick, but then I know I'm lying to him. Healthy or not, my life could end in a heartbeat.
>
> I stop talking and just look into his dark eyes.
>
> When Spencer was born, I made a pact with God by asking if the pain and losses of my life could buy Spencer a life free from pain and loss. It's probably not that different of a pact that all mothers make with some divine force, and in our hearts a part of us wants to believe we struck a real deal. The truth is, God never made any promises to me.
>
> I let go of Spencer's arms and stand up. I brush leaves off my knees and pull my bag over my shoulder. I reach for his hand and he weaves his fingers into mine.
>
> "You know what?" I say.
>
> "What," he says.
>
> "I'm going to do my best not to die, Spencer," I say, "that's all I can do."

What to tell children, and what to leave out: it's an issue that most motherless mothers eventually face. Seventy-nine percent of the women surveyed for this book have explained their mothers' absence to their children.* About half of them began the conversations when their kids were between two and six years old. Another 20 percent began when their children were ages six to twelve.

How much should we tell them, and when should we start? The answer depends in large part on a child's ability to understand and process the information, which varies from child to child. Whenever you first broach the subject, the following age-related guidelines may help.

Toddlers: Eighteen Months to Age Three

"Death" has little meaning to children of this age. They have no words to explain it, other than the word itself. A two-and-a-half-year-old may notice pictures of your mother, but she may not know what to say about them, or how to say it. Still, she may be curious about the face in the photo album or the word "Mom" that keeps coming up between you and your siblings, and she might ask a blunt question, like "Who's that?" or "Where is she?"

It's fine to explain that she was your mother, that she died or is otherwise inaccessible, and that it happened a long time ago. Offer a specific name for the child to grasp onto, if you'd like. (In our house, it's "Grandma," since my husband's mother is "Savta.") Be as clear and honest as possible, without going into too much detail. There's no need to elaborate, but try to answer the question, even if it's painful for you to do so. A child whose questions about a grandmother are avoided or dismissed can too easily grow into a child who learns not to ask again.

"The important issue is to use the real words," says Phyllis Silverman. "And don't tell the very young child more than he needs to know. Say, 'That was my mommy. She had a bad disease,' or 'She

---

* Some of the remaining 21 percent are mothers of infants, whose children are still too young to ask about or understand the topic.

was in an accident, and she died.' If the child just says, 'Oh,' that's fine. You can leave it at that. If he says, 'What's that?' then you have to start the conversation about what death is about."

Children in this age range can't yet distinguish between a death and a departure. They don't understand that death is permanent, and they expect someone who died to return. When Eden was two and a half, she and my husband saw a dead cat lying by the side of the street. Uzi explained to her that the cat's body had died but that its soul had gone up to the sky. "The part inside its head," I explained, trying to be helpful. This didn't seem to confuse her. In fact, she treated it like an extraordinarily wonderful piece of news. For the next hour, she kept going up to strangers, to tell them about the cat with its body on the pavement but its head in the sky. Realizing we'd beheaded the cat in her imagination, Uzi then tried a different tactic: the cat's body had died, but its *spirit* went up into the sky. Eden seemed to accept this version, too. But when they were walking back to the car and passed the cat again, she struggled to get out of his arms. "We have to go back and wake up the kitty!" she cried.

Just a few months later, we spent the last two weeks of my father's life by his bedside. He was at home with hospice care, and Eden frequently came into his bedroom to watch cartoons with him or entertain him with animal sounds. After he died, we explained to her what had happened, and she attended the first part of the funeral. Two months later, on his birthday, we wrote a message to him on a balloon and released it into the sky. But now, five months after his death, she kept asking when we could go back to his house. "We can't," I explained to her each time. "Grandpa died when we were in New York. Do you remember?"

"Grandpa didn't *die*," she said, with a look of disbelief. "He's in New York."

While kids this age can't understand that death is irreversible, they can understand the concept of "lost" or "missing." Even if they can't talk about the abstract phenomenon of grandparents who died long ago, they might be able to understand that someone who was once there is now gone. When you tell your two-year-old that your mother has died, she may well understand that something dear to you is no longer present, and that this made you upset or sad. And that might be enough for now. Conversations about death inevitably become more complex over the years, as a child's emotional and intellectual development progresses. There'll be plenty of time to fill in the details later.

Preschoolers

Most three- to five-year-olds still have an incomplete, though emerging, understanding of death. They're generally aware that it can happen to a living thing, and that death is something that makes an animate object die. On the other hand, they're also likely to think death somehow involves the act of lying down, and that a wish or desire can cause someone to die. They're starting to acquire an understanding of death, but they've still got a ways to go.

Because "magical thinking"—the belief that internal events, such as thoughts, can cause external outcomes—is prevalent at this age, a preschooler may believe that death can be caused by someone's bad behavior, or simply by wishing that person gone. Don't be alarmed if your four-year-old asks, "Did you tell your mother to die?" or "Did you want her to go away?" It says far less about your child's perception of your relationship with your mother than it does about his own attempt to figure out how death occurs.

By ages four and five, kids start becoming interested in where the dead go ("in the trees," children in one study said, and "under the ground"). Because children this age think so literally, though, they may conceptualize "heaven" as an actual place individuals can enter and exit at will, and they'll take what you say at face value.

Forty-two-year-old Veronica remembers taking her children to the funeral home after a distant relative died. "My daughter, who wasn't even two years old, was very hesitant to go up to the coffin," she recalls. "But Jackson, who was about four at the time, was very curious about the whole thing. He asked us what happened, and we told him that Aunt Eileen was very sick and, well, she died. He said, 'Why? Did she eat too many chocolate-covered raisins?' And I thought, *Where did he get* that *from?* Then I remembered that a few weeks before, he'd been with my in-laws, and my father-in-law kept feeding him chocolate-covered raisins before bedtime. I'd said, 'Jackson, stop eating those raisins before you get sick.' I was amazed that he put those two things together. So then we had to explain that all kinds of sick are not the same."

It's important to be as clear and honest as possible with preschoolers to avoid confusion or distress. At the same time, take care that the language you use won't frighten a child. Gina Mireault remembers an incident that took place when her daughter was four and had a nightmare in the middle of the night. Mireault went into the bedroom to sit with her and calm her down. "I said, 'You really don't need to worry, because I'm right in the next room and Dad's nearby, and the dogs are alert to anything,'" she recalls. "And then I told her something that had been comforting to me as a kid. I said, 'I always think of Grandma Carolyn when I'm scared, and of how Grandma Carolyn is nearby and watching over me.' And my daughter was just *horrified*. She said, 'I don't want that strange woman in my room!' And I thought, *Oh my God*. My heart broke for a second, but it was a kind of humorous moment, too, where I realized, oh my gosh, what a fool I've been to think that would be comforting to her. Of course it wouldn't be. She doesn't know my mother. So I backpedaled on it quickly and said, 'Well, you know, she's not *really* in your room. You don't have to worry about that. But if you ever feel you need a guardian angel, she would be a good person.' But she assured me that she didn't want a guardian angel; she just wanted *me*."

The preschool years are the time when children start to understand the dangers of being left alone and uncared for. That's why talking about a deceased mother with a child of this age might cause him to fear a similar loss. Children of this age will wonder if they, too, will lose their mothers, and if so, what will happen to them? Where will they live? Who will pack their lunchboxes and give them their baths? Because they're often unable to see a situation beyond its immediate impact on them, don't worry or feel slighted if a conversation about missing your mother turns into a conversation about what would happen to your child if you die instead.

"It's not that kids are selfish," Phyllis Silverman explains. "It's just that they're beginning to understand there's a relationship between what happens in the world and what happens to them."

Specific answers to questions like "Where would I live?" tend to be the most reassuring, and leave a child with less doubt and less room to fill in the blanks with their own ideas. For example, if your four-year-old wants to know who'd care for her if you were to die, explain the most likely scenario—and then reassure her that such an event is very, very unlikely to happen.

If this explanation satisfies her, that's great, but remember that sometimes distress can surface later, and in unexpected ways. "We have pictures of my mother around the house, and Kyra knows Grandma Frances is in heaven," says Christine, whose oldest daughter is four. "She'll ask me: 'Do you miss Grandma Frances?' And I'll say, 'Yes.' 'Do you think about her?' she asks. I say, 'Yes, sometimes I think about her every minute of every day, some days I won't think about her at all, but yeah, I think about her a lot. She was always on my mind when I was growing up. She's in heaven and Mommy misses her very much.' Kyra will usually leave it at that. But when they had a section on death in her preschool classroom, she came home very sad and said, 'Boy, Mommy, if you were ever to go to heaven like Grandma Frances, I would really miss you.' So, she finally made the connection that if I go to heaven, I'm not coming back.' And that's about where I've chosen to leave it for now—that Grandma Frances died when Mommy was little and that Mommy missed her a great deal and still does, but that I have no plans to go anywhere soon."

School-age Kids

Child development theorist Jean Piaget maintained that the greatest leaps in a child's cognitive development occur at around age seven or eight, with the advent of concrete operational thought, and this does seem to be the most critical stage for acquiring a complete comprehension of death. Most six-year-olds have started to figure out that death is permanent and irreversible; that it can occur as the result of external or internal events; that it causes bodily functions to cease; and that everyone, including themselves, will die one day. By age eight, they know that the dead can't dream, think, or feel, and by age twelve, they know that someone who died will look physically different from someone still alive.

All this comes about because during the school-age years, children are developing the ability to think both generally (such as, "all people die") and logically (such as, "lung cancer makes the lungs stop breathing.") They can put sequential events together in their minds, and can conceptualize cause-and-effect relationships. This may make them more curious about death in a matter-of-fact way, causing their questions and reactions to become more practical than emotional. They want more precise answers, and won't accept vague information.

This helps me understand why just a few months ago, when we were driving home from the bus stop, Maya blurted from the back seat, "So, how *exactly* did your mother die, anyway?" We hadn't been talking about my mother—we hadn't actually been talking about anything at all just then—so who knows what caused a question like that to come up? It was almost as if whatever story Maya had been holding in her head to explain "breast cancer" had satisfied her until that moment, when—*click*—the light bulb went on and told her it didn't make sense anymore.

"Well, she had breast cancer," I explained.

"I *know* that," Maya said. "But how did that make her whole body die?" And suddenly there we were, driving home along the S-curves on Topanga Canyon Boulevard at four P.M. on a Thursday, trying to understand together how a cancer that started in a breast could cause an entire body to fail.

Whereas younger children mostly think death is caused by external events, like car accidents or something you catch from another person, children of grade-school age have begun to recognize illness as an internal process. Their newly developed reasoning skills make it possible for discussions about the cause of a grandmother's death to progress beyond a simple "She got very, very sick and died" and include more precise explanations of heart failure, cancer, blood clots, and other internal causes of death.

School-age kids are likely to still think in very concrete terms, though, since the capacity for abstract thought usually doesn't start developing until about age eleven, and isn't used consistently until closer to fifteen. Veronica was reminded of this several years ago, while on vacation with her husband and three school-age kids. Veronica had always talked freely with her children about her mother, who died of pancreatic cancer eighteen years ago. "When they asked me how she died, I would say, 'Well, she smoked a lot. And she got sick and died,'" she recalls. She never bargained for how literally her oldest son would interpret that. "We were in Florida when my son was about six or seven, and he saw a man smoking outside a café," she remembers. "He marched right up to him and said, 'What's the matter with you?! Do you want to die?' And I was like, 'Well, maybe we need to rethink this approach.' Because in truth, it was coffee, it was stress, it was divorce, it was a lot of things thrown in there that contributed to my mother's disease."

As children move through the grade-school years, their attention, interest, and questions about death increase, while their anxiety over suffering a similar loss starts to diminish. They become slightly less egocentric and can now recognize others' points of view, which helps them understand that early loss is not only an important part of our personal histories, but of our present selves, including how we mother them. A statement like "One reason I'm so emotional at your school plays is because my mother never got to come to mine, and that makes me feel happy and sad at the same time" isn't beyond the scope of their understanding, but remember that a child in this age range still may not be able to experience more than one emotion at a time. When you explain to your daughter that you're capable of feeling happy and sad simultaneously, she may accept this explanation without being entirely sure how it's possible. "It's also okay to say, 'You know, this isn't something I can talk about right now. Let's talk about it later,'" Silverman adds. "Kids this age can understand that parents have feelings, too."

School-age children may become more curious about their missing grandmother, and wonder about the type of relationship they might have shared. "You may also get, 'My friend has a grandma and I don't,'" Dan Schaefer says. "Then you can say, 'What do your friends tell their grandmas about? Can you tell your grandma the same things? Let's write her a letter.' They might say, 'I never met her.' That's when having photographs around comes in handy. You can say, 'You don't have to. We have a photo of her. You can write her a letter, or draw her a picture.' Or if you talk to your mother in your head, you can tell your child, 'I talk to Grandma all the time. I imagine she's here and I ask her for advice, and sometimes I get an answer.' If a lot of this information is made very matter-of-fact instead of woo-woo, kids will take it matter-of-factly."

Children also may become more curious as a result of school assignments, especially the ubiquitous Family Tree project of the grade-school years. Not much can jump-start the conversation about a missing grandmother better than the need to know her name and parentage for inclusion on the appropriate maternal branch.

By age ten, most children have mastered the four components of death, and above age ten, can begin hypothesizing about it. Children in this older-age range may now bring speculation into conversations about death, such as guessing what it feels like to die or wondering whether cancer hurts. They're also capable of organizing and assessing information in a more orderly, logical fashion. Veronica's son who charged up to the man smoking outside the café when he was a second-grader is now twelve, and "he'd probably sit down with the guy and try to get him to quit smoking by having a debate with him about all the pros and cons," Veronica says.

When talking with older school-age kids, aim for what Carol Irizarry, PhD, a social scientist at Flinders University in South Australia, calls "respectful engagement." Instead of just offering answers, try to engage children in the subject with questions like "What do you think?" and "What makes sense to you?" Help them search out and explore their own questions, she suggests. Don't be afraid to share your insecurities or hesitancies on the subject, or to acknowledge the complexity of the concept. And remember that it's all right not to have all the answers. Recognizing children's inquiries into death as complicated spiritual concerns, and treating them that way in discussion, helps them begin to ask the kind of important questions and formulating the kind of comforting answers that will guide them for the rest of their lives.

Adolescence and Beyond

Abstract, "adult" thought usually starts developing around age eleven or twelve. From this point forward, kids start formulating theoretical and philosophical questions about what happens when someone dies. As they develop a greater understanding of the emotional, social, and spiritual dimensions, they may start to revise their earlier ideas about irreversibility in favor of the belief that the soul persists after the body dies. It seems, in fact, that kids are continually revising and reformulating their ideas about death throughout childhood, as they accumulate more experience, more education, and a more sophisticated intellect.

An important task of the teen years is to construct a personal history, which involves looking backward and forward in one's life.

This can inspire some teenagers to learn more about ancestors who've died, including those they never knew. They may even start to hold up our mothers as role models or feel connected to them through personal qualities, interests, habits, or talents.

On the other hand, don't be surprised if your teen shows even less interest in your mother now than before. Teenagers can get caught up in their own worlds to an extent where they're much more interested in how a historical event affects them personally than in what it means to others. "It's not that they're indifferent to our experiences, it's that they're learning to live in a way that deals with the outside world," Phyllis Silverman explains. As mini-psychoanalysts, they may be most curious about how early mother loss affects the way we're raising them, and much more interested in letting us know about their conclusions.

But just because a teenager doesn't talk about your mother doesn't mean she's not on her mind. "A couple of years ago, when my daughter was in high school, I happened to read one of her papers," remembers Rebecca, who was ten when her mother died. "The topic was 'What Are You Most Afraid Of?' And I was shocked to see that of all the things in the world she could have chosen, she'd written, 'My mom's mom died when she was in her forties, and this is my fear, of losing my mom.' Before then, I'd never thought my mother's death had even registered with my kids."

Even teenagers who slack off in algebra are capable of doing family math to perfection. I've heard stories of teenage girls who've acted out dramatically when their mothers reached their grandmother's age at time of death, or when they themselves reached the age their mothers were when the grandmother died—usually because they didn't know how to handle the fear that the same thing might happen to them. I've also heard of daughters who've deliberately distanced themselves from their mothers during those years, as if an abrupt separation would somehow be easier to bear if they brought it on themselves.

These kinds of identifications with both the mother and the

grandmother can persist throughout the teen years and even beyond, when the internal calculator becomes even more adept. "This past year, my daughter turned thirty-one, the age my mother was when she died," recalls fifty-five-year-old Louise, who was six when she lost her mother. "It brought up feelings for me that I didn't expect. I decided not to tell my daughter about it. But about three or four months after she turned thirty-one, she said, 'You know, I'm the same age your mother was when she died.' I said I knew but hadn't wanted to mention it. She went on to say, 'She's been visiting me,' and shared their conversations with me. It was amazing. The day she turned thirty-two, all my female relatives went out and celebrated another woman in our family making it to thirty-two."

During adolescence, children become increasingly sophisticated at imagining other people's points of view. When a teenager hears your story about mother loss, for example, the naturally egocentric "What if this happened to me?" may now expand to include "It must have been terrible when that happened to *you*." Nonetheless, don't expect this sentiment to always be accompanied by a rush of empathy. As an intellectual concept worth examining from different angles, death loses much of its emotion to teenagers. And that's how it needs to be, for them to gain the critical distance they need to formulate their own points of view.

Talking About the Hard Stuff: Accidental and Intentional Death

I've yet to meet a motherless mother who refused to speak with her children about her mother's death or departure. I've met several, however, who opted for silence because they just didn't know what to say. These women tended to have tragic stories of mother loss, stories they feared would upset, disturb, or confuse their children beyond acceptable limits. This was often the case when mother loss occurred as a result of suicide, murder, accidental death (especially if the daughter witnessed it), mental illness, or a drug overdose.

It's true that a child who doesn't ask for facts may be a child who's not interested in learning them, but more often a child who doesn't ask is a child who's learned not to. She's picked up subtle clues over the years indicating the topic isn't a safe one to discuss. So, she'll try to fill in the gaps on her own, and very often the answers she comes up with will be wrong.

When children feel confused about a grandmother's death, it's often the result of their parent's confusion, not their own. Dan Schafer recommends framing discussions of these losses in terms that kids can understand, based on your assessment of what your child can process at his or her current age and on what you believe to be true. When explaining a suicide to younger children, for example, you can say, "Sometimes a person is so sad that she feels she'll never be happy again. She doesn't see any other option in life, and she doesn't know how to ask for help, so she chooses to end her life." To explain a drug overdose, Schaefer suggests, "You know how sometimes we take pills to feel better when we're sick? Well, sometimes a person takes pills and doesn't feel better, so they take more, and then they wind up taking too many. That's why Mom and Dad tell you not to take medicine yourself."

It can also be helpful to ask children to share their perceptions of a death. "What do *you* think happened to Grandma?" can give you insight into exactly what information your child has, and how he's processed it. "Sometimes you only need to tweak the story a little bit, and sometimes the kid is way off the charts and you have to pull him back," Schaefer explains.

Above all, make sure the story remains consistent among family members. My friend Beatrice, who lost her mother in a car accident fifteen years ago, has carefully chosen what she wants to tell her four young children up to this point. She's shared stories about her mother's life, and has explained that she died, but has wanted to wait longer before telling them the exact details of the death.

Then, a few months ago, Beatrice's sister mentioned to the kids that their grandmother had died in a car accident. "I can't even begin to tell you the fallout that resulted from that," Beatrice told me. A few weeks later, she was driving in the car with her kids when her six-year-old son made a comment about all of them dying in an accident—exactly the kind of scenario she'd been hoping to delay.

Kids who receive different or contradictory stories about a grandmother's death are bound to be confused. You can minimize this by impressing upon family members the importance of sticking to the same story, even if their take on events doesn't correspond with yours.

"If your father comes to babysit," Schaefer advises, "say, 'We're into the grandparent-death phase, and here's what we want you to say so we're all giving the same story. And if you don't want to say this, then please don't say anything.'"

Explanations that satisfy a six-year-old may no longer appease a ten-year-old, so it's important to pay close attention to your child's development and to keep reassessing her at different stages. "Every few years, I look at my kids and think, 'Oh! They're older than I thought! They don't need a car seat anymore!' or 'Oh! It *is* okay for them to swim in the pool while I run to the bathroom!'" says Gina Mireault. "I have these moments every once in a while, when I realize they're growing, and they're ready for a little more. And I think it's like that when we're talking about sensitive topics. We have to reassess their growth every once in a while, and ask, 'What are they ready for now, when we have this conversation again?' I sense that if kids are really asking and pressing for more information, it's a signal to parents that they may be ready for more than we think."

9

Protective Parenting

KEEPING EVERYONE SAFE

*T*he temperature was cold. The rain was steady. The wind was strong. And for reasons I could not entirely understand, my husband decided this was a good night to be dropped off at the bottom of a twisting, deserted canyon road to walk six miles home. Uphill. In the dark. Alone.

"I *really* don't want you to do this," I said, trying to keep my voice steady when he called to convey his plans. But I couldn't convince him otherwise. It's not that he's deliberately insensitive to my wishes. It's that—like many husbands I know—once he gets his idea of a good idea in his head, an industrial-strength iron crowbar can't pry it out.

"Come on," he said. "I'll be fine."

"What if you get cold? Or hurt? Hardly anyone travels that road at night."

"Exactly. That's why it's safe."

Need I even say this? My husband's perception of risk differs dramatically from mine. Maybe that's what happens when you live through two wars by the age of fourteen, and then spend five years in the military during a third. When my brother called from New York at six-thirty A.M. local time on September 11, 2001, Uzi wrote the message on a sheet of computer paper. *Your brother called. Terrorist attack in New York. Family is fine.* He left it in the middle of our bedroom floor, careful not to wake me, and drove to work as usual. Granted, he didn't yet know the magnitude of the event. Even so, this is not a man who worries about dying young.

To him, a six-mile walk up a canyon road in wind and rain is a stroll in the dark. To me, it's the precursor to the apocalypse.

"I'll see you in about two hours," he said.

"If you're not here in two and a half, I'm calling the police."

"I'll see you in two hours," he said.

Well, maybe he *would* be fine. Just because I'd never make that walk didn't mean it couldn't be done safely. On the other hand, the road was full of sixty-foot dropoffs, most of them without guardrails. When you peered over the edge, you could see the rusted shells of cars on the canyon floor. *He's a seasoned hiker,* I told myself. *But he's walking the wrong way on a one-way road,* I remembered. "He'll be home in two hours," I told the girls. *We'll never see him again,* I thought. Oh, God. Did we remember to pay the life-insurance bill?

That's what the threat of loss does to me: it makes me lose all concept of scale. Before long, I start ping-ponging back and forth between extremes. The new babysitter is a closet kidnapper. Or maybe she's just a sweet, honest woman in need of a job. No. She secretly covets my kids. The coyotes that cross our yard nightly are scared of humans. No—they're furry, rabid little child-snatchers, and we need to start setting traps! Or sell the house! Now!

Even I know that my hysteria can get grossly out of proportion to the matter at hand. So, when my husband set out for his hike, I decided to give the kids their regular bath. In the face of looming disaster, I reasoned, faking normalcy wasn't a bad idea.

I was soaping Eden's shoulders when the phone rang. It was

Kate from next door. "What's wrong?" she said, when she heard my voice. I burst into tears.

". . . and he's walking up in the dark and the rain without a flashlight and no cell phone reception and I'm here by myself with the kids and *what if he gets hurt?*" I sobbed.

I adore Kate. She's irresistibly friendly. She's hysterically funny. But most of all, she's willing to jump into all of my little dramas with both feet. Excellent friend that she is, Kate came up with a plan. She would ask her husband to drive down the canyon road, act surprised when he saw Uzi, and then call us from the bottom, immediately, with a full report.

Fifteen minutes later, Kate called back.

"He's completely fine," she said. "He's charging up the mountain with his arms pumping, getting good exercise, having a great time. He'll be home in half an hour."

Relief filled my body like euphoric helium as I lifted the kids from the tub. Fine! He was fine! Then the self-doubt crept in. Had I been too dramatic? Had there really been that much risk, after all?

I've got lots of stories like that one. There's the one about the first afternoon the nanny took Maya out in her car, and how I stationed myself by the front window a half-hour before their scheduled return, panicking when they were five minutes late. And the one about the first time Maya rode the school bus, how I drove behind it all the way to school—twice—to make sure the driver took it slow. And the way I'm scared to let Uzi take both kids on an airplane without me, or even take them camping overnight—as if a bear would attack a tent when the mother's not present, but bypass it when she's there.

Ask any random person on the street how likely she is to experience a negative life event—such as a health crisis, a natural disaster, or the death of a loved one—in the next year, and chances are she'll say, "Not very." As a general rule, most people tend toward optimism, and assess their personal risk as low. If the person you happen to ask is a motherless daughter, however, she'll probably tell you otherwise. She'll probably say she's been expecting it for years. That's because firsthand experience with tragedy imparts a simple yet important lesson: A bad thing happened once. A bad thing could happen again.

This is the phenomenon of perceived vulnerability, broadly defined as *the degree to which persons believe they are likely to experience a threatening event.* It's not always based on logic, or a bad attitude. In fact, it rarely is. Perceived vulnerability is a psychological state that grows out of personal experience. It's the deep, nagging certainty that something else is going to go wrong. Very wrong. And probably soon.

Perceived vulnerability is a close cousin to—but shouldn't be confused with—perceived *susceptibility*, which focuses on a single disease or problem. A woman whose mother died of ovarian cancer at age thirty-five, for example, might perceive herself as highly susceptible to reproductive cancer at an early age. She might expend a great deal of energy worrying about that specific area of her body, and on making sure she gets regular CA-125 tests and annual gynecological exams. Perceived *vulnerability* is a more generalized type of anxiety, extending beyond a specific disease or event to include any kind of potentially dangerous situation that might affect oneself or a loved one. It's why that woman who lost her mother to ovarian cancer would be adamant not only about getting her annual exams but also about her husband wearing his seat belt and about her teenage son always calling the moment he arrives safely at his friend's house. It's why she worries more than other mothers about her children playing outside without supervision in a private, fenced-in backyard.

Perceived vulnerability is a common response among survivors of sudden, unanticipated loss, for whom tragedy did once arrive without warning. When someone you love is yanked from you through suicide, accident, or homicide, the world starts to feel like an inherently unsafe place, where everyday landscapes are masking hidden landmines. But a heightened sense of perceived vulnerability can appear in anyone who's lost a loved one, regardless of the cause. It's especially common when the time between a mother's diagnosis and death is very short, and family members don't have adequate time to adjust to the news. It's also a common long-term response among children who were too young to understand disease, and therefore experienced an anticipated death as a sudden loss. Without therapeutic help—and sometimes even with it—these daughters grow into adults constantly scanning the horizon, watching and waiting for the next storm to arrive.

"It's like one-trial learning," explains Therese Rando. "You've had this one horrendous experience that has devastated your life, and essentially your alarm system is telling you that another experience like this is coming."

Statistically speaking, the opposite is more likely to occur. An individual's risk of being involved in a negative event drops dramatically after she experiences that event. Someone who's just been mugged, for example, is highly unlikely to be mugged again anytime soon. But statistical arguments fly straight out the window when personal experience enters the room. Because people rely on past experience to predict their futures, experiencing a negative event actually makes people think more about the possibility of it happening again instead of making them feel immune to repetition.

"Remember that scene in *The World According to Garp*, where a plane flies into the house and Garp says, 'Great! We'll take it! Because what are the chances of *that* ever happening again?'" says Gina Mireault. "When you lose someone close to you, it's not the Garp Effect. It's the opposite, which is, 'Oh my gosh. This happened once. It could definitely happen again. And it could happen to *any* significant relationship in my life.'"

Most studies of perceived vulnerability have focused on anxiety about accidents or diseases, but Mireault was one of the first social scientists to connect the dots between perceived vulnerability and the threat of future loss. Her interest grew out of personal experience: every time her husband was late coming home from work, her mind leaped to worst-case scenarios, and she suspected these thoughts stemmed from losing her mother at age three. She also thought she might find a connection between perceived vulnerability and depression or anxiety in adults who'd lost a parent during childhood.

Mireault's 1992 survey of 379 bereaved and nonbereaved college students confirmed what she'd suspected. Students who'd lost parents during childhood or adolescence were much more likely to see themselves as vulnerable to future abandonment and loss than the nonbereaved students were. The students who scored highest for perceived vulnerability were also the ones who scored highest for anxiety and depression. Perceived vulnerability, she concluded, may be an important link between early bereavement and anxiety later in life.

Motherless women who feel vulnerable to loss as adults—though not all do—may also be the ones who had anxious tendencies from the start, Mireault says. This may have been the case for thirty-three-year-old Patrice, a mother of two young daughters who lost her own mother to breast cancer when she was ten. Patrice describes herself as "living in fear" as a mother, constantly afraid that she, her husband, or one of their daughters will die. "I was this way before I had kids, even before my mother died," she admits. "I grew up terrified of losing my father. He was a police officer, and I would worry constantly, crying myself to sleep at night, praying that he would come home."

Most people use the words "fear" and "anxiety" interchangeably, but they're actually two very different concepts. Fear is the reaction to a real-life situation as it occurs. Anxiety is the response to a threatened danger that has not yet taken place. Perceived vulnerability appears to be a dimension of anxiety, partly because it's a response to the possibility of future distress rather than to something that's actually happening. When a motherless mother says, "I'm afraid of dying young," what she's really saying is, "I'm anxious about the chance that it could happen."

As far as anxieties go, perceived vulnerability is a fairly harmless one. "It doesn't always interfere with someone's functioning or require medication or psychotherapy," Gina Mireault explains. "It's more of a mild anxiety, almost like a mild phobia that's specific to loss." Some psychologists even argue that perceived vulnerability is a form of "healthy" anxiety, since it often makes people more vigilant about their own health and safety, as well as the health and safety of their loved ones. A few studies have even shown it gets people to stop harmful behaviors such as smoking, and to engage in healthy or self-protective behaviors such as wearing seat belts or using contraception.

In moderation, anxiety may even be good for us. Developmental psychologist Erik Erickson believed that learning how to master anxiety is an essential component of emotional maturity. Being able to recognize and tolerate an inner sense of danger may have a prophylactic benefit, too. Managing anxiety once may help you manage it better the next time a similar threat presents itself.

Most parenting experts agree that a moderate amount of anxiety is a normal and important element of parenting. Parents need to have some degree of concern for their children's well-being: that's what ensures their offspring's survival. They need to be responsive to signals that aren't evident to others around them, the unique signs that their child is in distress. Daniel Stern calls these a parent's "vigilant responses." They're similar to the type of actions a lioness might take when her cub is in danger, although human threats today are more likely to be staircases and swimming pools than predators in the wild.

Still, it's possible to have too much of a good thing, especially if a mother becomes hypervigilant to the point where she's overly restrictive with her child, or if her worrying starts to interfere with her or her family's daily functioning.

"Basically, what you're talking about is the bubbling up of anxiety, which is unavoidable if you've lost a parent early," says Harriet Lerner. "It's unavoidable anyway, but motherless mothers have this extra rock in their backpacks. And when parents are anxious, they push the extremes."

Typically, anxiety creates two responses: First, the individual regresses to an earlier psychological state where emotion supersedes rational behavior, and the logical, thinking part of her brain shuts down. Then, as her anxiety increases, her ability to assess danger from an adult perspective disappears. She can no longer distinguish between an external threat (such as, "this could hurt my child") and an internal threat ("I could lose another loved one"). To reduce her anxiety, she'll often do whatever she can to avoid future loss, even if it's out of proportion to the actual, external threat.

As Lerner has pointed out in *The Mother Dance*, mothers who worry the most about an issue become least effective at solving problems around that issue. "The toughest emotional challenge of motherhood is to get a grip on our anxiety—or on any form of emotional intensity—so that we can use the thinking part of our brain to sort out the real problems and what we can do about them," she writes.

For motherless mothers, the "real" problems often aren't situations faced in the present. They're what the mother feels or believes to be true, based on her past experience with loss. When Maya first started walking, I had a habit of following two feet behind her at the playground, always ready to help her up the slide, always prepared to catch her if she began to fall. My worry wasn't that she'd tumble a few feet and land painfully on the sand. No, my worry was that she'd fall down and hit her head, get knocked unconscious, the ambulance wouldn't be able to find the park, she'd need to be transferred to a hospital, we'd get there too late to save her, and I would once again lose a primal, irreplaceable relationship. Chasing after Maya with outstretched hands wasn't just about protecting her. (In retrospect, letting her fall once or twice onto the sand probably would have been *good* for her.) It was about protecting myself from the possibility of another devastating loss.

It doesn't take much for me to imagine an afternoon at the playground turning into a screeching race to the hospital. Or for me to turn a pleasant bathtime into a frantic episode involving emergency-response teams. And yet, when faced with my children's high fevers, or mysterious viruses, or deep gashes, I find that I'm surprisingly in control. When Eden once choked in a restaurant, I quickly grabbed her, flipped her over, pounded her three times between the shoulder blades to dislodge the piece of food, calmed her down, and then sat down and finished my meal. It's the *possibility* of crisis, the uncertainty of the unknown, that unnerves me. When faced with an actual emergency, I usually respond fine.

"It's funny," says twenty-eight-year-old Samantha, the mother of two young sons, whose own mother died five years ago after a decadelong battle with cancer, "because I'm not the kind of mom who runs to the doctor every time my kids sneeze. They practically have to be bleeding before I think anything's wrong. Which doesn't coincide at all with the sort of weird, deranged thoughts I have about them getting something serious."

Samantha's thoughts aren't quite as unusual as she thinks. I've met hundreds of women who think the same way she—and I—do. "Every time my children walk out of the door together, I think about what it would be like if they never came back," admits fifty-five-year-old Rebecca, a mother of four, who was ten when her mother died. "If my husband is late or if he's going on a trip—he travels a couple of times a month—I'll go from planning the funeral to 'Where's the life insurance?' to 'What will it be like for me? Will I heal the way other people heal?' I can get very profound very quickly."

Because Rebecca was caught off-guard by a loss in the past, she doesn't want to be caught off-guard again. Letting her mind spiral outward into all the possible outcomes allows her to feel as if she's mastering the next adverse event in advance. "The idea is that if you think about future loss, and plan for it, and are prepared for it, then in some ways you're controlling it," Gina Mireault explains. "I tend to do that myself. I think, *Okay, when I lose my husband*—not *if*, but *when*—*what do I know about his life insurance policy? Would I stay in the house?* Being prepared, thinking about it, talking about it, is a way of controlling it. It means I can almost pregrieve. If I'm ready,

I won't be so emotionally distraught when it happens, because I will have been prepared."

Paula, now thirty-one, was twelve years old when her mother died from an overdose of chemotherapy drugs. As the oldest of four children, Paula immediately started preparing a mental list to follow in the event that her father also died.

"He would go off on business trips, and I would think, *All right, if something should happen, here's who I would call first. Here's the action plan I would put in place,*" she recalls. "And now, as an adult, I do it, too. I don't dwell on thoughts of disaster, but I think, well, this could happen. And if it does, here's a very practical approach to help things fall into place." In Paula's marriage, that translates to having a grasp of the family finances and knowing where all the bank records are kept. "My husband takes care of our money and keeps track of it on the computer," she says. "He's in finance, so that's his thing. But I'm constantly saying, 'All right, tell me again where I can find everything in the event that I need access to it.' And I often think, *If something happened to Robert, I think I'd have to stay in this area because of my support network, but I'm not going to try to support this size house. So how long would I stay in the house for?* I mean, it's almost disgusting, some of the things that come into my head, but it's like my system of practical checkmarks, because I'm so aware that loss is possible in life."

This tendency to catastrophize everyday experience is a common theme among motherless mothers. "Mental-health clinicians have a really hard time with it," Therese Rando says. "Because if you look at the criteria for posttraumatic stress sequelae, this kind of repeated flashback would kind of be a tick in the column for 'Hmm, you've got a disorder here.' And yet for these women, it's just a reality. It's something that's in their filter as they contend with the world."

Rando, who lost both parents in her teens, says thoughts of death and loss flit in and out of her mind with a similar regularity. "If I had my druthers, my kids wouldn't go out of the yard until they're forty-two," she laughs. "Obviously, I know that's not good for them, and that I can't protect them from everything in the world. But it is an ongoing struggle for me, to moderate my desire to protect. Every day. And when I say every day, I mean every day. Motherless mothers need to understand that this is a pull, and to find the way they can best learn to live with it. I try to talk myself through it, being the good social scientist that I am, and say, 'Okay, Terri, just realize that statistically they're going to come home. The odds are with them.' But sometimes I can't talk myself out of it. It just doesn't seem right. So, on those occasions, I might pick them up myself rather than let someone else drive them."

For a motherless mother, the awareness of potential loss is woven seamlessly into the fabric of everyday life. It's the insistence on kissing husbands or partners as they walk out the door every morning, just in case that's the final good-bye. It's the little catch in the throat when the children board the school bus each morning, and the little exhalation of relief every afternoon when they step off.

It's not morbid. It's not obsessive. It just is. As Rebecca explains, "Death is just part of my life. It was a big part of my little life, so I guess it's not surprising that it's part of my big life, too."

The "Overprotective" Parent

Fifty-one-year-old Rosemary recalls a recent wedding she attended with her husband and son. The band was excellent. The food was delicious. The other guests were . . . well, Rosemary didn't get to talk much to other people that night. She spent almost the entire five hours trailing her thirteen-year-old son from room to room.

"There had recently been a picture in the paper of someone who'd molested a child at a McDonald's, and one of the waiters at the wedding looked like the man in that photo," she says. "I spent the whole wedding making sure this guy never went anywhere near my son."

She laughs about it now, acknowledging that at some level she must have known her fears were unfounded. But the memory of that night, and of her fear for her son's safety, remains vivid. No one, real or imagined, was going to threaten her child. She would make sure of that, whatever it involved.

Eighty-six percent of the motherless mothers surveyed for this book described themselves as either a "somewhat overprotective" or "very overprotective" parent. I thought that proportion was astounding, until I discovered that 82 percent of nonmotherless mothers refer to themselves the same way. Surely, so many women can't all occupy such a behavioral extreme. Which raises the question: What, exactly, does it mean to be an "overprotective mother"? Has "vigilant" become synonymous with "overprotective," and has that now become some kind of perceived norm?

The classically overprotective mother is one who smothers a child with her anxiety and good intentions, hovering over him and inadvertently preventing him from ever building confidence or competence on his own. She's well-meaning and doting, believing she's acting in the best interest of her child, but she's overly preoccupied with the perceived hazards of daily life. At her most comical, she's Aurora Greenway in *Terms of Endearment*. At her most frightening, she's the *Psycho* mom.

Eighty-five percent of all mothers can't possibly fit this description. "Cautious," perhaps. "Concerned," okay. "Overprotective," no. *Truly* overprotective mothers aren't even aware they're being overprotective. To them, their behaviors are a necessary response to real and immediate dangers. That's why I encourage women to use the term "protective mother" instead. It's more accurate for women whose vigilance is within reasonable limits, whatever its origin may be.

Motherless mothers who label themselves "overprotective" usually think they're more concerned with their children's physical and emotional safety than a situation rationally warrants. It's often related to a common, unconscious belief that motherless daughters share: *If I couldn't control my mother's death as a child or teenager, I should be able to prevent disaster for my children or spouse as an adult.* Left unchecked, this belief can lead to a highly anxious parenting style, where children are never left alone with relatives or babysitters, and where preteens are never allowed to go to the mall without an adult chaperone.

When a mother dies, a daughter's world spins out of control. Much of her life that follows involves trying to create order and control over external events again. But that approach is in direct opposition to a very basic objective of parenting, which calls for the acknowledgment, at some point, that parents don't *really* have control over their children. They may have a certain amount of control, for a limited amount of time, but every child is a separate individual with desires and agendas of her own. That's often difficult for a motherless mother to accept, especially when it conflicts with her deep and enduring desire to keep her children within her orbit, where she can feel certain they're safe from physical danger and emotional harm.

This was an ongoing struggle for many years for forty-two-year-old Marisol, who was eight when her mother committed suicide. As a child, Marisol was part of a family that effectively shut the door on her mother's death, and she never had the opportunity to mourn. Losing her mother in such a devastating and sudden manner, and without any emotional support, turned her into an adult who feared sudden loss in any form.

"Disaster: that was the key word when my kids were growing up," explains Marisol, who's now the mother of a twenty-four-year-old daughter and a twenty-year-old son. "I was so afraid that they were going to die. They would stay out until midnight as teenagers, and every time I heard a siren, I would get heart palpitations. I gave myself an ulcer." To feel confident about their safety, she even accompanied them on social outings with their friends. "It wasn't terrible, because it was out of love," she says, "but I think my kids had a hard time in the sense that I couldn't detach from them as they would have liked me to. Now that they're young adults, they're happy I was always there for them, but during their growing-up years, I was always struggling internally: *I have to protect my kids, I have to prevent them from suffering.* I guess I didn't let them breathe."

Marisol raised her two children in a large, urban environment where real dangers did exist. The issue for her, she realizes, was not that she felt anxious about their safety—what mother wouldn't, in that situation?—but that the intensity of her anxiety, and how she chose to act upon it, became problematic for her and her family. Her regret now comes from believing she didn't give her children the freedom they needed as teenagers to explore on their own, and that she herself spent so many years living in anxiety about their safety instead of enjoying their newfound independence.

Where is the line between being a reasonably watchful, alert parent and smothering your child? "That's an important question," Michael Schwartzman says. "And the answer doesn't just have to do with the neighborhood you live in, so to speak. It relates to what and who your child is, and what he or she needs, wherever you live." A particularly active and adventurous toddler needs a high degree of supervision on a busy playground, not just for navigating her physical environment but also to test and discover her own limits safely. At the same time, she can't yet reliably assess or anticipate danger and protect herself. She needs a watchful mother. A highly responsible fourteen-year-old in a low-crime suburb, however, usually doesn't need such rigorous supervision when spending a few hours with friends at a local shopping mall.

"There's something wonderful for a child about a parent, over-protective or not, showing a certain faith in the child's ability to handle something that is not a given," Dr. Schwartzman explains. "Being able to let go and offer that to your child can often lead to a change in your own state, where you now feel more in control because you recognize that you've raised a child who's more in control."

Letting go. In theory, it sounds so easy. In practice, it's so hard. How do we learn to let go of our children slowly and appropriately, when our own separation was so abrupt? And even then, how can we bear to do it, knowing what tragedies can befall them beyond our reach?

"When my daughter was a teenager, I would say to her, 'I'm not afraid of your judgment or your choices. I'm afraid of the world, and of the things that could happen to you out there,'" Louise recalls. "That was very bothersome to her, and there was a point in her twenties when she said, 'Mom, I just can't carry your fear anymore. I can't do that for you.' It was scary for me to hear that, because I thought for some reason that if I could transfer my fear to her, she would be more cautious and not put herself at risk."

Louise's daughter saw her mother's fear as an entity separate from her, and had the maturity and the strength to resist it. Younger children, however, are often unable to make that distinction. They're more likely to absorb a parent's anxiety about danger and loss, in much the same way a child might adopt a mother's phobia of spiders or the dark.

"Anxiety is catchy," Gina Mireault explains. "That's true for any kind of anxiety, any kind of fear. If you know someone who's really phobic of snakes, or who's afraid to fly, and you spend any time with them, you can catch that. Because you can easily rationalize how dangerous it is to fly on a plane or pick up a snake." Parents who feel particularly vulnerable to loss, or who worry excessively about danger, can transmit that worry to their children through their actions and behaviors. "When a parent says to a child, 'Be careful, be careful, be careful,' eventually the child gets the message loud and clear that something's dangerous and they should watch out for it," Mireault says. Children who start hearing this from a very young age then experience an inner conflict between their natural impulse to explore and their parent's message that exploration is inherently dangerous.

"A parent who screams 'No!' when she sees her child about to burn herself . . . is reacting out of panic to an emergency," Michael Schwartzman explains in *The Anxious Parent*. "The parent who yells

'No!' when she sees her precious daughter dangling by her knees upside down from a playground gym, however, is creating an emergency where one doesn't really exist. This mother needs to be in control all the time, where she can anticipate everything that's going to happen to her child. But what she's doing is affecting her daughter's sense of how safe she is by constantly questioning it. She's also creating a terrible conflict in her child. The girl is curious and able, but her mother tells her she isn't, that she's going to be hurt. If enough of these problematic events occur, she'll begin to doubt her own abilities and may eventually become fearful of anything new, that is, anything that would displease her mother."

Likewise, children who observe their parents overreacting to minor episodes themselves learn to react in the extreme. Children look to their parents to determine what kind of response a situation warrants. That's why a toddler who falls down will search a mother's face before reacting. If the mother shows panic or concern, the toddler is likely to cry out in fear or pain. If the mother's face remains calm, the toddler is much more likely to stand up and continue on his way without an emotional display.

Mothers need to respond with concern when a situation calls for it. The trick is getting an objective grasp on exactly which situations deserve a visible or audible response, and which ones don't.

Sharon, a thirty-five-year-old mother of a ten-year-old daughter and a six-year-old son, recalls the summer that her daughter took swimming lessons with a blend of amusement and dread. "Every time she'd go under, I'd go, 'Uhh-uhh-*uhh*!' I would just freak out," she says. "Then, one time, another child in the group went under, and his mother brought him back up and said, 'Wasn't that fun?!' I was really impressed by that confidence, by her assurance that the child was fine. It was like a revelation for me: how did she react like that? But then I realized, I just have to practice it. I just have to practice it."

And to do that sometimes means letting a child fall—both figuratively and literally. Not down a flight of stairs, of course, but within safe enough parameters to let her learn how to master her own environment without parental interference. How can a child learn what's she's capable of if she's never permitted to explore on her own?

My older daughter had the kind of mother who ran after her on the playground with hands extended, always ready to steady her if she wobbled, always prepared to catch her if she fell. Perhaps, as a result of this, she was never the type of child who took physical risks. I remember how she used to sit on the second step of our living-room staircase, just below where the safety gate anchors and locks, wanting to leap down to the floor below but too afraid to try without my permission or my help. Maya's gross motor skills lagged behind those of her peers for several years, and I always had the nagging feeling that my protective behaviors had something to do with it. I swore that if I had another child, I wouldn't inhibit the next one the same way.

So, when Eden was learning how to walk, I stood at a reasonable distance and watched her crawl up to the second step of that same staircase and pull herself upright by the safety-gate rails. The first time I saw her wobble, instead of rushing forward to protect her, I stayed back and let her tumble. She rolled awkwardly down the step and tapped her head lightly against the floor. "Oops!" I said as I scooped her up. "You bumped your head!" She cried for a few seconds while I held her, and when she was done, I put her down. Without looking back, she crawled up the step to try again, and this time she didn't fall.

There's no quick fix for perceived vulnerability. You can't get rid of it by flipping a switch, or by cognitively programming it away. It appears to be a personality characteristic, part of a person's central, primitive belief system that stays stable over time, meaning it's probably easier to modify during childhood than during adulthood or even adolescence, when anxiety naturally increases and beliefs take on a heavy emotional component. Still, repeated exposure to harmless events as an adult goes a long way toward unraveling its hold. Only by living a full life year to year, without facing disaster, can you begin to completely trust that what happened once won't happen again.

"All through my sons' childhoods I had such concern that something might happen to them," says fifty-two-year-old Phyllis, who was fifteen when her mother committed suicide, and whose sons are now in their teens. "Whenever they left the house, I would make a point of hugging them and telling them I loved them. That's still always there in my consciousness, but in the last few years, I've released a lot of it. Because I see that they have survived. There have been no great catastrophes in our family. No one has been killed. I really have inside now what I didn't have for many years, which is a feeling of self-trust and inner security. It took me quite a while to get there, but I'm finally there."

When the Unthinkable Happens

For a small minority of motherless mothers, disaster does strike twice. Or three times. Or even four. About 10 percent of the women I interviewed in person for this book had faced the premature loss of a loved one as an adult or had been diagnosed with a serious illness themselves—two women had lost a spouse before age fifty; two had lost children (one as a result of premature birth); three had been diagnosed with breast cancer before age fifty-five; and one had undergone major surgery for a benign brain tumor.

Statistically, this is about what we'd expect to find in a group of seventy-eight American women between the ages of twenty-eight and seventy. Motherless mothers don't appear to be significantly more vulnerable to loss than other women are, despite their belief that disaster is bound to visit them again. Shakespeare got it wrong in this regard: thinking *doesn't* make it so.

At the same time, motherless mothers clearly aren't immune to adversity, either. The women mentioned above are testimony to the fact that subsequent, devastating loss sometimes does occur and, even more important, that it can be survived.

A child who loses a parent is dependent on adults to reduce her feelings of helplessness. An adult who loses a spouse or child is capable—at least in theory—of getting herself the help she needs. But sometimes the magnitude of loss is so overwhelming that a mourner has to put her grief on the back burner, just to be able to make it through each day.

That's what happened to Maureen after her husband died. Maureen, now forty-one, is youthful and quick to smile. Her straight, shiny brown hair swings playfully each time she turns her head. But despite her cheerful demeanor—or, perhaps, in spite of it—Maureen has experienced more loss in the past sixteen years than most people have to face in two lifetimes.

Maureen was twenty-five and newly married when her mother—with whom she'd always been very close—was diagnosed with terminal esophageal cancer. Maureen and her husband moved into her mother's house to help throughout the final months, and they were by her mother's side when she died. Three years later, Maureen gave birth to a daughter, but what should have been a joyous event was soon clouded by tragedy. A few weeks after the birth, Maureen's husband, Bruce, who'd lived with asymptomatic cystic fibrosis since birth, came down with a flu that wouldn't go away. The eventual diagnosis was a virus he contracted on an overseas job. At first, it seemed as if he could recover, but his lungs weren't strong enough to hold out. When his daughter, Robin, was only seven weeks old, Bruce died.

"For the first few months afterward, I thought the ache in my stomach would never go away," Maureen recalls. "I thought I'd never be happy again. I didn't have my mom to share everything with, I didn't have my husband to share it with. I really thought the best days of my life were over at twenty-eight. I was alone in the house every night by myself trying to figure out a baby and my grief."

As Maureen discovered, one of the hardest parts of facing loss after her mother died was having to face loss without her mother's support. "My dad was wonderful, but it wasn't like having my mom there," she explains. "When I got home from the hospital after Bruce died, the garage door went up and the light clicked on, and my dad was already standing there. I don't know how long he'd been waiting there for me. But then he was like, 'Okay, it's been three days. You've got a baby. You've got a career. How long are you going to be like this?' Sort of like, chop-chop, let's pick up. My mom would have felt sorry for me for a little longer. She'd have given me a little more time to grieve."

With the help of her sister and her close-knit group of friends, Maureen slowly began to move forward again. A year and a half later, she remarried, and the following year she gave birth to her second daughter, Lucy. Tragedy, it seemed, was now firmly in her past. But when Lucy was twelve months old, she was badly burned on her hands and legs, an injury that brought her close to death and put her in a children's hospital burn unit for more than a month.

Maureen went through the full gamut of emotions during and after Lucy's surgeries—grief, fear, sadness, guilt. The injuries slowly healed after multiple surgeries, eventually allowing Lucy to regain full mobility. Once again, Maureen was given a respite from crisis. But not for long. Three years ago, she was hit with bad news again. Colon cancer. Her husband, Peter, this time.

That's when she really got mad.

"First of all, I didn't want Robin to lose another father," she explains. "And also I felt, *I didn't sign up for this again*. I just really didn't. I was so *angry* that it was happening again. I was trying to find logic in this, and I couldn't. There's no logic to be found."

Maureen's husband went through surgery and chemotherapy, and now is in remission. Lucy still needs surgery every eighteen months, but otherwise looks and acts like any other child her age. Yet Maureen *still* isn't in the clear. As we spoke, she was waiting for biopsy results on tissue taken from her breast the previous week.

"How do I do it?" she asks. "I wonder sometimes. I don't handle it now as well as I used to. The anger I felt when Peter was diagnosed was not my usual reaction. I've gotten harder. Now, the way I look at it is, 'I lose a mom, I lose a husband, maybe I even lose another husband, but nobody better screw with my kids.' That's where I draw the line. With this biopsy, fine. Give it to me. Just don't mess with my children anymore."

When I wrote *Motherless Daughters*, I believed that the early loss of a mother was the most devastating loss an individual could experience. Certainly, for some women, this is true. But since I've become a mother, I see the potential for a much—*much*—greater loss out there, one I'm not sure I could survive, the absence of which inspires continual gratitude, the possibility of which is something to constantly guard against.

Losing a child. It's every mother's deepest fear.

Leslie, now forty-four, cries when she speaks of her first child, Jeremy, who died fourteen years ago. Jeremy was diagnosed with a rare form of leukemia when he was just three months old, and for the next twelve months, Leslie cared for him at home, administering his medications through a catheter and acting as donor for his bone marrow transplant. She did everything she had to do, surprising herself with her stamina. But despite Leslie's loving efforts, Jeremy died when he was fifteen months old.

"It was the hardest thing that ever happened in my life," she recalls. "It totally changed who I was and who I could become. I realize that, and I'm kind of bitter about it."

"How did you get through those months?" I ask her. Just the thought of my child suffering makes me want to race screaming down the middle of a busy street. "How did you find the strength to get out of bed every morning after Jeremy died, to take step after step throughout the day?"

Leslie shifts in her chair, her shoulder-length red hair obscuring her face for a moment. She clutches a tissue tightly in her hand. "You don't have a choice," she says.

"When does it start to hurt less?" I ask.

"It always hurts," she says. "It's always there. Here's how I describe it. When my mom died, it hurt. There was a huge hole in my heart. When my son died, it was like he took a leg and an arm, or half of my body away. The difference is *huge*. When it's the second time, you really feel like you got handed the sword. It's like total disbelief. Like, How could that *happen*? How could it *possibly* happen? But then I knew that I wanted more kids, and the doctors said the possibility of that disease showing up again was slim. They said, 'Don't worry. Have another one.' A lot of people told me that would help me the most, and I think they were right. Four years later, I had my daughter. I looked at her every minute of the day to make sure she was okay, until she passed the age of my son's death. After she passed fifteen months and everything was fine, and she was walking normally, only then could I breathe."

I saw a card in a gift store the other day with a photo of a toddler on the cover. She was standing in her playdress and little sneakers on a country road, holding her hands open to catch the driving rain. The inscription underneath read "Then, when it seems we will never smile again, life comes back." Crisis management does, over time, revert to living. Slowly, eventually, a new form of equilibrium emerges.

I think often of a woman named Sarah, who has an eight-year-old daughter and a ten-year-old son. Sarah was nine when her mother committed suicide, and she has struggled with depression for much of her adult life. A few months after her son was born, Sarah lost her mother-in-law to suicide, too, and in 2000, she was diagnosed with breast cancer. She went through a year of medical treatment. Yet, despite all these losses, and the hardships that followed, during our interview Sarah was upbeat and optimistic, and more pragmatic about life than most people I know.

"I'm deathly afraid of leaving my children motherless," she says, "but I'll tell you, I've lived through several suicides, my father's death, miscarriages, and breast cancer, and you know what? After everything, I got up and went on with life. And it saved my life and it made my life. I trust that God will be merciful and that I will do everything I can to stay alive. When my times comes, I just hope that I've given my kids enough of who I am and what I stand for. I can't worry too much about it. I don't fear my own death in the way that I used to. If anything, all that I've been through just makes me live my life with more purpose."

Every night, before I go to sleep, I say a prayer of thanks for getting my daughters safely through another day in this crazy world, and then I ask for one more. Just one more day. It doesn't feel like too much to request. One plus one plus one plus one eventually adds up to a lifetime. At least, that's what I'm hoping for.

"Never die," my older daughter demanded of me the other night. She'd just finished watching *Lilo and Stitch*, and she wanted reassurance that what happened to the orphaned Lilo wouldn't ever happen to her. What does a mother say to this? I can't promise either of my daughters, with any certainty, that I'll see their children one day, or dance at their weddings, or even attend their grade-school graduations. They can't promise me they'll make it to those events, either. What we have is today. Life as we are living it. And the commitment to do so to its fullest.

10

✥

Five to Twelve

THE SCHOOL-AGE YEARS

⟋

*T*he day Maya started kindergarten, it seemed that I transitioned from being her protector to her advocate, and from her playmate to her role model and guide. Suddenly, what I did and said started to matter more, not just in terms of shaping her unconscious behaviors but in helping her consciously decide how to act and respond outside the family. In the classroom, on the recess field, at afterschool activities, and in summer camp, the security and instruction she received at home was being transferred into practice in a more sophisticated way.

The way I acted had an effect on her before this, of course, but now it seemed that the socialization factor had amped up several degrees. She observed me very closely, even when it appeared that she was not looking. And she listened, even when she pretended not to hear. An offhand comment I made in the kitchen about how the girls who were meanest were usually the girls who needed friends the most could resurface a week later, when Maya told me she extended herself to the class provocateur when she saw her standing alone.

The way I dress, the way she sees me talk to strangers and friends, the times when I step forth as her advocate—and the times I encourage her to stand up for herself—are already starting to shape the choices she makes for herself. Uzi gets all the questions about science, mechanics, and the natural world, like, "Does a bee sting another bee?" I get the emotional and the existential, like, "How can I make myself stop crying?" and "Where was I before you were born?" She no longer wants definitive instructions. She now wants suggestions, hypotheses, and opinions. How should she wear her hair today? Which summer camp program do I think will be more fun? Ellie is developing a bad attitude with the other girls, and what should she do? "But what do you *think*?" she prods me, if I say, "I don't know." And I find all this both thrilling and terrifying as a parent, because what I try so hard to outwardly model for my school-age daughter—conviction, compassion, decisiveness—is so often at odds with the uncertainty I feel inside.

For me, much of motherhood during the school-age years is a guessing game, trying to piece together strategies based on memories and an intuition I usually—but not always—trust. I keep thinking that if only I can line up my chess pieces in exactly the right pattern, I'll create the perfect playing board for her to navigate her way safely and responsibly through the coming years. And I'm hard on myself as a parent. My standards for motherhood, and for what I tell myself a mother should do and be, are so high that most of the time my fingers barely brush the bar. Alone with Maya I have confidence, but out in the world as her representative and role model I feel that I'm on shakier ground. Each time a conflict is successfully resolved, I feel a flood of relief and exhilaration, because from a dizzying array of possibilities I've managed to choose a good one, and, for a short while, that fundamental insecurity I carry within me—of being a mother who doesn't quite know how to mother, and a woman who lost her role model for being a woman—disappears.

Sandwiched between the rapid developmental years of toddlerhood and the upheaval of adolescence, the elementary-school years are often perceived as a welcome break between twenty-four-hour care-giving and the process of launching a teenager into the world. The mother's focus shifts from a predominantly protective mode to one that emphasizes teaching through instruction and example, and activities become more reciprocal and more fun. A mother learns about her young child through careful observation; she learns about her school-age child also through interaction. The constant "Don't!" of the toddler and preschool years is replaced by the "Let's!" of elementary school. Up until about age eleven, the majority of children will still seek their parents' company and enjoy their attention. "In some ways, you get the best of parenting from ages two to twelve," Maxine Harris says with a laugh. "And then again probably from twenty-two and on."

Yet, as any mother who's raised a child up to age twelve knows, the school-age years call for extreme adaptability and flexibility from parents. While a child's underlying temperament is fairly consistent by this point, his year-to-year (and sometimes hour-to-hour) behavior is anything but. The typical school-age child alternates between outward displays of affection and rejection, and introspective periods of self-confidence and self-doubt. He's still very much a child, dependent on parents for guidance and support. At the same time, he's slowly testing the waters of self-reliance. In the course of a single evening, my eight-year-old daughter will walk down from the stage after a school performance and pretend to ignore her parents in the audience (because we're so embarrassing!) and then scramble to hold my hand an hour later, as we leave the school to walk to the car (because she's so happy I was there!). Your ten-year-old son may choose to spend all afternoon tending to his stamp collection alone in his bedroom, and then want to do his homework at the kitchen table, surrounded by the family's postdinner action. A year later, at eleven, he may want to spend most evenings with his neighborhood friends.

The only reliable predictor of a child's behavior during the school-age years is that just when you get accustomed to a certain pattern, it's about to change. For motherless mothers, this kind of volatility can be particularly disconcerting. It's unpredictable, often defies reason, and ignores our attempts at control.

Yet, at the same time, we understand how critically important the tenor and pitch of a mother's involvement is during the school-age years. She is the one to whom a school-age child is most likely to turn for information; the one he is most likely to push against when asserting his free will; and the one he rushes back to when he needs the security of home.* "Of all the interpersonal relationships the young child experiences through the first ten years of life, that between his mother and himself is probably the most important and intense," maintains Louise Bates Ames, PhD, a cofounder of the Gesell Institute for Human Development in New Haven, Connecticut. The mother is the one most likely to instill feelings of competence in the child, and whose secure base he internalizes and carries forth into the world when they are apart.

This period is also a time when a motherless mother is likely to feel both more and less confident in the maternal role. She has made it through the most physically demanding phase of motherhood, and her child is no longer wholly dependent on her to meet his needs. His ability to perform well in school, to make friends, to engage in self-care, and to complete his daily tasks— all of this is proof that she had what it took to bring him this far. Nonetheless, her past experience with loss continues to inform her parenting choices. A child's development is dynamic, but a mother's

---

* More than half of all American children will spend at least part of their childhoods in a single-parent family, the vast majority of these headed by mothers. The mother-child relationship in these families takes on even more intensity if there is no ongoing father-child relationship to balance it out.

past remains static. What happened to her, happened. Only the way she perceives it and integrates it into her parenting can change.

Some motherless mothers become compassionate guides for their children, adopting a chummy "Let's figure this out together" point of view. Others become staunch advocates for sons and daughters in school and on the playground. Some become highly protective, determined to keep the child physically and emotionally safe (see chapter 9). Some choose to focus on instruction to prepare the child to manage on his own. Most incorporate elements of all of the above.

If a mother lost her mother between the ages of five and twelve, she may feel she lacks an understanding of what's "normal" for this age. The kind of natural time-travel all parents do, rocking back and forth between their children's experiences and their own experiences at similar ages, may yield memories for a motherless mother that depart so dramatically from her children's present-day reality as to feel useless as comparison. A woman who was six when her mother died and was left in the care of a depressed or alcoholic father, for example, may have no context in which to interpret her seven-year-old's natural ambivalence toward her, or her ten-year-old daughter's playfulness toward her father.

Women who were adolescents or older when their mothers died may also find elements of their loss filtering into their parenting during these years. They cherish time with their children, yet they want to make sure the child is prepared to cope without them. They constantly strive to create for their child not just the relationship they lost but the ideal family they never had. All of this comes to the forefront as they assist their school-age children through the developmental tasks that children ages five to twelve typically face at home, at school, and out in the larger world.

Domestic Matters

Instilling early independence, for better or worse

During the grade-school years, kids depend on parents to teach them the life skills they need for future autonomy. Yet they still need to be cared for physically and emotionally as the children they still are. Most mothers recognize a school-age child's burgeoning need for independence and grant it in successively larger doses year by year. When Maya was six, for example, I began letting her go to the bathroom in restaurants by herself, provided that I could see the door from our table. When she was seven and we went to a community Earth Day festival, I let her visit the booths around the baseball field with her friend—keeping her in line of sight from our blanket the whole time. Lately, she's like the toddler who wants to venture farther from me on each small exploration, except now she's wearing size 4 shoes and wants to wander off for half an hour or more. Eden, at four, will panic after five minutes if she turns around and can't see Uzi or me, but Maya follows her inner compass, trusts we're watching her from afar, and—blessed with Uzi's orienteering skills—likes to find her own way back.

A lot of mothers wouldn't allow this kind of independent exploration, I know. Accidents and abductions, and all of that. But this is an area in which I loosen the reins. I want Maya to have the confidence to venture forth alone, and the feelings of competence that come from exploring, discovering, and returning when she's ready. Still, every time I watch the back of her head recede into the distance, I can't help wondering: Am I granting her this autonomy at the right time, because she needs it to build self-esteem at this age, or am I granting it too soon, because I want her to learn in small doses year by year how to manage in my absence, just in case I die?

It's a thought that feels too morbid to be having in a crowded restaurant, or at an outdoor community fair, but it's a legitimate one, says Laurie Lucas, LCSW, who was eight when her mother died. "Most motherless daughters put tremendous pressure on themselves to be very attuned and attached in their kids' lives, because, number one, they enjoy it, and, number two, they want to be there for their children as their mothers were not there for them," she explains. "At the same time, there always is the sense of 'What can I do to keep them from experiencing what I did?'" Emotional distress would be inevitable if we were to die, we know, but wouldn't the loss be just slightly easier on a child who already knows how to pack her school lunches, or shampoo her own hair?

Such details may sound trivial, but to a motherless mother, they're important. She remembers how she struggled after her mother died, scrambling to perform daily tasks for herself or her younger siblings. Or she may recall how, sometimes, these tasks simply went undone. If her father wasn't able to take over the mother's domestic role, or if he transferred household responsibilities onto young children, she may not trust her spouse to pick up where she left off. No, better to teach the child how to do these things herself.

"One of the issues here is the lack of trust in fathers," says Colleen Russell, MFT, a therapist in Mill Valley, California, who has been counseling motherless women for fifteen years. "Because women's fathers often weren't there for them after their mothers died, they feel they can't count on the father to be there, and now they tend to devalue or dismiss their own husbands as fathers."

The issue of preparation may also be influenced by the mother's marital status, Laurie Lucas adds. "I was a single parent, so I really worried all the time that if something happened to me, my kids would not be in a good situation with their father, who was an alcoholic," she explains.

But even women who have and accept the support of a stable husband or partner may find themselves "gently toughening up" their children, as one mother put it, for the improbable yet possible event of early mother loss. Maya's at a stage now where she wants help choosing her school clothes in the morning, and, as we pick out the day's outfits, I try to work in little lessons about what to wear with what. "If you want stripes on top, choose a solid for the bottom," I tell her. "Probably it's not a good idea to mix light purple with dark pink." She's developing an interest in how she looks, and this is her way of asking for guidance, I know. For me, it's also a chance to stuff the information in. These are the years when she most needs me (and will still accept me) as a gendered role model. Does an eight-year-old really need to know not to wear white party shoes with black tights? Maybe. Maybe not. But if our time together winds up being shorter than I hope, there will be no such thing as too much too soon.

At the same time, a motherless mother's parenting philosophy may also include a commitment to do for her child what wasn't done for her, leading her to overcompensate for her child in certain specific areas. A woman who was expected to keep house for her father and siblings at age ten, for example, may find it deeply healing to make her children's beds and pick up their rooms throughout elementary school, rather than teach them to do it themselves. This creates a true inner paradox: How can we be engaged, caretaking mothers who do for our children, while also training them to care for themselves in our absence?

"I worry that I send mixed messages sometimes," admits forty-six-year-old Dierdre, who was fourteen when her mother died, and has tried to instill autonomy in her children from an early age. "Like with breakfast. My twelve-year-old daughter is perfectly capable of making it on her own. I want her to be able to do that, but I also relish being able to nurture her at the beginning of each day by making her a piece of toast. I used to go work out in the morning to get it over with before the day got under way, but as my kids grow, they're with me less, and I feel like the morning is one of the few times I can grab a few moments. So my 'independence training' is a little fuzzy in the mornings."

Motherless mothers who connect their present-day resourceful-ness with the early self-determination they had to develop as chil-dren may be the ones most likely to encourage their children to do more for themselves in and out of the house. "I require incredible responsibility," says forty-one-year-old Melissa, the mother of three school-age children who remembers having to "manage my own life" after her mother died when she was nine. "The amazing part is that they can do it. I have my kids load their plates and dishes into the dishwasher, not just bring them to the sink. My eleven-year-old cleans the kitchen two days a week. My five-year-old sets the table on her own. My boys do the trash and recyling, and feed the dog. We have laundry-folding parties on my bed, where we spread out all the clothes and fold them together. My husband coddles the children more than I do. About every six months, I sit down with him and say, 'We need to reassess. They're older now, and they can do more.' My eleven-year-old actually rejoices that he knows how to clean a kitchen. We live in an area where none of the other kids are doing real-life stuff, so my kids are profoundly unique in their peer groups."

Forty-five-year-old Cynthia, who was six when her mother died, and then helped care for her younger siblings, raised her son and daughter, now in their twenties, with well-defined boundaries and very clear ideas of right and wrong. She wanted them to have good manners and a solid moral foundation. As a single mother, Cynthia also wanted her children to be able to care for themselves at an early age. The thought of her children having to grow up in someone else's home was never far from her mind, and she had verbal agree-ments with several close friends and relatives who would care for them if she died.

"I was extremely strict, and harder than a lot of other parents were," she explains, "because in the back of my head I was always thinking, 'If something happened to me, if you, my best friend, have to raise my children, I'm going to make it as easy for you as possible while I'm still here, so that basically all you'll have to handle is discipline, to some degree, and the finances.' That was in my mind, the entire time I raised them. My kids were ironing their own play clothes when they were seven or eight."

Cynthia would often look at her children and think, *Well, if I'm not here this week, this is how much they know.* From there, it was just a short distance to *How much more do they need?* The problem with this, Cynthia realizes now, is that she was basing her parenting decisions on future possibility rather than on present reality. With her children now grown and out of the house, Cynthia looks back at the way she chose to raise them with some regret.

"I didn't get to live my own childhood, to some degree," she explains. "And then I almost tried to push theirs away by growing them up too fast. Just in case. I always had that in mind: *Just in case.* It was a horrible way to live. My advice to anybody in the same situation would be not to do that."

Some children welcome a great deal of responsibility at just six or seven, but others aren't ready for another few years. A motherless mother may run into conflict when her expectations are too high for her child's developmental stage—which causes frustration for a child—or when her "independence training" starts including emotional autonomy, too.

I've heard stories from women who say that as their children progress in elementary school, they deliberately try to let them handle more social and emotional problems themselves. It's often an altruistic act, committed out of love and concern. A child dependent on a mother, they know, is a child vulnerable to devastating loss. Such emotional withdrawal, however, is a response to a past relationship rather than the one mother and child share in the present, and can lead to feelings of rejection or unworthiness in a child.

I've received at least a dozen e-mails in the past year from daughters of motherless daughters, asking me to write a book about their experiences. Some of them say they were raised by mothers who always seemed a step removed, emotionally, as if an invisible barrier remained lodged between them and their children. Like their mothers, these daughters also had to take a hand in raising themselves. What they perceive as maternal disinterest, however, may have instead been an attempt to protect both of them—to prevent the daughter from becoming too dependent on her mother, and to shield the mother from the pain of losing a beloved daughter—by not getting too close.

Certainly, emotional resilience and self-reliance helped us survive after mother loss occurred. But our children have mothers. Raising them to function without us when we're still here, at its most basic level, doesn't make sense. It denies both of us the warm, involved mother-child relationship we want and our children deserve. When we live with one eye on the future and one on the past, what happens to now?

Coping with Anger, Rejection, and Discipline

A mother is typically the recipient of a child's best behaviors, and also of his worst. In most families, she is the parent against whom he pushes hardest when asserting his autonomy. Feelings toward a father are rarely as intense, mixed-up, or volatile. As a result, the mother is showered with more instances of loving behavior, and also targeted with more episodes of anger and defiance.

It's hard to stay centered when a child misbehaves, and sometimes even harder to maintain self-control. A six-year-old's "I wish you weren't my mother!" or an eight-year-old's "Leave me alone!" can send a motherless mother to a troubled state.

This is a common reaction for mothers to have, Michael Schwartzman explains. "Feeling that you've lost your child's love is one of the most devastating emotional experiences a parent can go through," he says. It can complicate a mother's need to set limits and enforce consequences for impudence or disrespect. A child's anger is the opposite of a warm, loving connection, even if just for a few moments, and motherless mothers who are sensitive to emotional rejection may find the situation difficult to bear. Some parents will "actually bend over backward *not* to discipline," Schwartzman says, because they need their child's affection for them to remain unbroken.

Forty-two-year-old Sarah, the mother of an eight-year-old daughter and a ten-year-old son, says that until recently she was one of those mothers. When her daughter would shout at her or speak rudely, Sarah would silently tolerate the verbal blows. Then, instead of disciplining her daughter, she would try harder to please her. Her reaction, Sarah believes, was related to the abrupt and violent suicide of her mother when Sarah was seven years old, and the subsequent years in which she had no place to express feelings of anger, sadness, or distress.

"I made a huge breakthrough the day I realized, with the help of my therapist, that when my daughter rejects me or says she hates me, my impulse is to overcompensate," she explains. "And that the reason why I keep doing that is because I'm afraid I'll lose her. She'll have had enough of me, like my mother. And I realized I had to risk that in order for our relationship to evolve, and that risking it won't end the relationship the way it did with my mother. It's distorted thinking, to believe that I gave my mother trouble and she shot herself. So now, when my daughter is playing on my emotions, I say, 'If you're going to hate me right now, fine. If you're going to run into your room and be angry, that's okay. I'm not going to worry about losing you. I'm your mother, and I know you love me.'"

Sarah is using what Michael Schwartzman calls a "grounding statement," a calm, reasonable message to herself that diffuses her emotions and gives her a more mature perspective. Instead of succumbing to *You're angry at me, and that must mean you're going to leave*, she calmly thinks, *I'm not going to worry about losing you. I know you still love me*. It's a form of cognitive reprogramming that replaces the motherless daughter's fearful voice with the more experienced, confident voice of the adult.

Children are uniquely sensitive to their mothers' areas of vulnerability, and may learn how to use anger or rejection as manipulation, to achieve a desired effect. Colleen Russell, who was fifteen when her mother died of a drug overdose, remembers driving in the car with her older son when he was five or six. "He was angry at me, and he shouted, 'I'm going to kill myself!'" she recalls. "And it *freaked me out*. I immediately stopped the car, and I said something like 'Why would you say such a thing?' He didn't know about my mother at that point, but he's a very intuitive person, and obviously he'd figured out this was a vulnerability of mine. I think that kids, on a collective level, *know* things, and are pushed to act on them."

For a motherless mother, this can easily lead to a moment when the response "You're lucky to have a mother who cares about you!" or just "You're lucky to have a mother!" comes flying out. Easily half of the women I interviewed could remember a time when they'd shouted this at a child, in exasperation or anger or frustration. Virtually every woman could recall a time when she'd thought it.

For forty-six-year-old Simone, the mother of an eight-year-old son, the memory is a very recent one. "I'm starting to say things that embarrass him now," she says. "I never used to embarrass him before. The other day, we ordered a milkshake, and we were sitting waiting for it. There were three empty seats in a row. I sat down next to him, and he got up and moved to the other chair. And it made me feel really sad. He didn't say anything, but he had that brooding look on his face. I feel very mixed about it. I understand he's supposed to be doing this right now. But the thought *You're lucky to have a mother now*, because he's just past the age I was when my mother died, did flow in and out of my mind. Sometimes, I'm almost jealous that he has me, and I didn't have a mom at his age."

This type of "mother envy" is understandable, especially among women whose children have passed the age they were when their mothers died, says Benjamin Garber, MD, the director of the Barr-Harris Children's Grief Center in Chicago. "Here the child has something that the mother never had at the same age, that she missed out on," he explains. "So there is some envy that the child is better off than she was." Mother-envy isn't a new experience for motherless daughters, many of whom grew up longingly watching other girls their age rely on, argue with, fall back on, telephone, visit, go shopping with, and have lunch with their mothers, but it's a little unsettling when the object of envy is one's own child.

I remember a day when Maya was acting impossible, truly impossible, toward me—belligerent and angry and off-the-charts uncooperative. She was six at the time, and furious at me for no reason I could discern. She hollered at me to get out of her room, and then she added, "You *big fat!*"

If I hadn't been worked up into such a state of exasperation at that moment, I probably would have burst into a giggle. "A big fat *what?*" I might have asked. "Come on, kiddo. We need a noun." Maybe I would have even managed to pull a smile from her, too. But, instead, her anger sent me straight to an angry place myself, the place that says, *What's wrong with this kid? How dare she treat a mother this way? Doesn't she realize how lucky she is to have one?*

I had to get a grip. I walked out of her room. I walked back in. I closed the door behind me, and strode up to where she stood in front of the closet door. Right next to me, she was shorter than I'd expected. So vulnerable and small. "I'm only going to say this one time in your whole life," I told her. My voice was coming out even and steady, though not angrily, which relieved me greatly. "Because I know it's not a nice thing to say. But I want you to think about how you're treating me. I've met a lot of kids your age who don't even have mothers. You're lucky you have one. So you might think about that before you talk to me like this again. You got that?"

She looked at me solemnly. She was listening hard. "Okay," she said.

I cringe now when I remember this. A six-year-old shouldn't be made responsible for her mother's feelings. Maya was having a legitimate outburst, even if I didn't understand it, and, to make her stop, I pulled out my trusty motherless trump card. *Feel sorry for me* was the unspoken message of my comment. *And then, when you do, treat me better.* I wanted her, just for a moment, to have a sense of what it felt like to be me. Was I really that desperate for compassion? Oh, God. If I hadn't already been in therapy, I would have signed up right then.

There's nothing wrong with occasionally reminding a child of her good fortune when she needs comfort or reassurance, such as "Always remember you have a mother who loves you." We get into slippery territory, however, when we ask children to imagine our pain as a behavior-modification technique, or as a means of getting what we want from them. That's manipulation. In younger children, whatever emotions they're trying to express are replaced with confusion, compassion, or pity. In older children, who may understand the nuances of the situation, we may prompt anger or resentment instead.

"I used to tell my daughter how she had it so much better than I did as a child," says fifty-four-year-old Carolyn, who was six when her mother committed suicide, and was raised in a series of foster homes. "I remember, at one point, my daughter said to me, 'Oh, are we going to do competing pain today?' And I thought, *I guess I'll never say that again.* I realized it was almost as if I were putting guilt on her, and it wasn't her guilt to bear. It wasn't my guilt to bear, either, but it certainly wasn't hers."

If compassion is what we need, our school-age children aren't the place to look for it. If appreciation or validation is what we crave, we need to find it elsewhere—from husbands, partners, therapists, or female friends who are generous enough to tell us when they think we're doing a good job. One day, perhaps not until they become parents themselves, our children may recognize the effort we put into raising them. Then, they might tell us how much they appreciate us. Or not.

When a child shouts "Get out of here!" "You don't care about me!" or, worst of all, "I hate you!" we have to remember this: maturity comes about through resistance. It involves struggle. It involves, even at age six, telling a mother that she understands zero. It involves all the angry comments so terribly hard for a motherless mother to hear, the ones that tear into her and make her feel mistreated and misunderstood and underappreciated by a child whom she has put blood and tears and guts into raising. We appreciate our mothers because we know what it's like to no longer have them. It's unrealistic to expect our children to appreciate us the same way.

Understanding when and why children are most likely to act out in defiance or anger can help parents gauge what's developmentally normal and what's not. Individual temperament, the nature of a specific mother-child relationship, and family disruptions such as divorce or death can stress a child's coping resources and lead to frustration or rage at any age. Nonetheless, there are several developmental points that seem more likely than others to produce such behaviors during the school-age years.

Ages six to six and a half: Kids this age are often highly emotional and take out those emotions on whomever is closest to them. For that reason, this is rarely a period of perfect mother-child harmony. When things are going well for the child, he loves his mother; when the slightest thing goes wrong, she's to blame. "I love you Mommy!" in the morning can make a mother feel she's doing the job well, until that evening, when "I hate you! I wish you were dead!" is hurled at her from across the room. Six-year-olds can be especially defiant and resistant to a mother's requests. "No! Try and make me!" is a common refrain during this year. It's fairly typical for mothers of six-year-olds to vow each morning that this will be a better day than yesterday, only to lose that promise to themselves before the end of breakfast.

"Right after my son turned six, he went through what I soon realized was a pretty natural developmental stage," recalls forty-three-year-old Dierdre, who was fourteen when her mother committed suicide. "He had been really easy up until that point, but then he went into 'I hate you! I wish you were dead!' and he'd throw toys around in his room. This went on for a few months. That was actually the first time I went into therapy."

Age eight: Second- and third-grade kids usually have an intense need for closeness with their mothers. They may become angry or upset when they don't receive it. Children this age prefer arguing to being left out, and bickering with parents is common. In the past year, Maya and I have started arguing back and forth to the point where we wind up negotiating and discussing a request for longer than necessary. But I never cut the exchanges off abruptly. There's something too comforting about them. My mother died at a point in our relationship where she and I were stuck in an adolescent ping-pong match. When Maya starts questioning my authority, it's comfortable for me to slip into the space where I have a daughter, she has a mother, and this is how such pairs relate.

Age eleven: Right around this time, a more distant and critical attitude may begin to emerge. Parents who were previously sought out as companions no longer play the starring role in their children's lives. They've been replaced by one or two good friends. What's more, they've suddenly become a source of embarrassment to their preadolescent kids. This new attitude is due partly to hormones, partly to preteen early rebellion, and partly to maturation. "For the parent, it is part confusion, part frustration, and part wanting to throw your precious child out the window," laments Donna Corwin, author of *The Tween Years*, a book for parents of ten- to fourteen-year-olds.

When Laurence Steinberg, PhD, a psychology professor at Temple University in Philadelphia, studied 204 Midwestern families with firstborn children between the ages of ten and fourteen, he found that the majority of mothers in his sample went through difficult patches with their preadolescent kids. What would begin as spats over chores, homework, and back talk would often spiral out of control, leaving parents feeling disrespected and misunderstood, and sons and daughters feeling micromanaged and unfairly accused. Because puberty, which triggers the psychological changes of adolescence, occurs earlier in girls than in boys, these preadolescent conflicts usually appear in daughters before they surface in sons—typically between ages ten and twelve for girls, and ages eleven to thirteen for boys.

Karen Stabiner, author of the memoir *My Girl: Adventures of a Teen in Training*, however, says the tween years don't have to be contentious. Ages ten to thirteen, as she describes them, are a "wonderfully wobbly period." One day, your child is still your little girl, and the next day, she wants to try being a grown-up. Parents still have tremendous access during these years, Stabiner says, and research backs this up: between ages ten and twelve, children say they get just as much information from their mothers as they take in from television and movies, but by age thirteen, 64 percent cite "friends" as their primary source, followed by television, teachers, the Internet, and mothers, in that order. Most children make up their minds about important issues, such as drugs, between ages twelve and thirteen, when they're still open to a parent's influence, making this period a good time to build a foundation for the more unpredictable teen years.

School Days

Empathy for the underdog

We recently attended an eight-year-old's birthday party, where one guest was being systematically left out of the backyard fun. She was a cousin of the birthday girl, and she had Down syndrome. The other girls could sense that she was different, although the word they were using was "weird." The child's mother was trying to take it in stride. "She's going to have to deal with it all her life, so she might as well get used to it," she shrugged, but anyone sitting at the table with her could see she was distressed. "I'll go talk to my daughter," I said. So, I walked over to the inflatable water slide, waited for Maya to come flying down, and stopped her before she started climbing up again.

"That girl over there—she's Lily's cousin Chloe. Can you try to be nice to her? She's feeling left out," I told her.

"Okay," Maya said, eyeing the ladder. "Can I go now?"

Trying to get an eight-year-old to embrace an unconventional child, I knew, was a guaranteed exercise in futility, but I'd felt compelled to do *something*. Watching a child stand alone on the sidelines is a situation I just can't tolerate.

Motherless mothers can be exquisitely sensitive to real or perceived instances of rejection, exclusion, or neglect that involve any child, not just their own. "My daughter's class was making turkeys out of potatoes the other day," says forty-two-year-old Alma, who was ten when her mother died and was raised by a series of relatives afterward. "Each child was supposed to bring a potato. I sent two. I always do that. The teachers say to me, 'Why do you always bring two?' You know why? Because there will always be a kid who doesn't have one. And I always worry about that, because I was always that kid." Placing an extra potato in her daughter's backpack is a small but meaningful gesture for Alma. It allows her to nurture the child she once was while helping an unknown, yet possibly equally unfortunate, child in the present.

Empathy for the underdog leads some motherless women into more complicated territory. In one ongoing motherless-daughters therapy group, participants have been talking about the large parties and play dates they organize for their sons and daughters. Some women invite all the children in a class or neighborhood, to make sure no one feels left out. Lately, group members have been discussing why they do this: because they're driven to create "perfect" childhoods for their children, and to fashion a system in which they feel they belong.

"I was always looking for a family," says fifty-two-year-old Annette, the mother of two teenage sons, who was fourteen when her mother died, "and I tried to create an extended family within our community by having block parties and huge celebrations for Easter and Christmas. For Halloween, I would organize trick-or-treating from house to house, and I would often have thirty kids over and make a huge, wonderful party for them. For me it was like heaven. Yet, ultimately, I didn't get back what I had hoped from it, for my family. We didn't get invitations back. People were involved with their own families instead."

Women who go to extremes to create an idealized childhood for their children—and, by extension, for themselves—often wind up feeling disappointed, Colleen Russell says. "The truth is, you can never get it all back," she explains. "Women realize that all of their busy work is to cover up their intense feelings of loss, and it's almost self-abuse to do all this, in a way, because they wind up so exhausted and depleted." Identifying with the vulnerable kids at school, for some women, is really an attempt to heal the vulnerable child within oneself.

What other mothers know

The kind of "outsider status" a woman once felt as a girl without a mother can be reactivated when her children start school. This time, instead of comparing herself to the other children and coming up short, she zeroes in on the differences between herself and the other mothers, who, in her estimation, possess the experience and training she lacks.

Some of this is just her perception, born from the fundamental feelings of inferiority many motherless women feel, and the crippling self-consciousness they can impose on themselves. Yet some of it may be grounded in fact, especially for women who were quite young when their mothers died, and who never learned to do or to value the kinds of activities other mothers seem to know effortlessly. A mother who never learned the "womanly arts" of cooking, housekeeping, or handicrafts, who grew up in a home where such pursuits were abandoned or ignored, or who had a childhood or adolescence in which hobbies took a far back seat to matters of survival, often feels she can't compete with women who hold frequent-buyer cards at JoAnn's Fabrics. And, in subtle ways, we *are* asked to compete, or at least to measure up, particularly when school projects and parties come around.

"I have total brain freeze on crafts and cutesy homemade snacks, as well as cooking in general," says forty-two-year-old Caren, the mother of a first-grade son, who was eight when her mother died. "So, when it's time to sign up to help with a class party, I have to get myself psyched up to do it. I make sure to tell the other coplanner that I'm a domestic zero, so she's prepared when there are normal mom things I should know how to do but don't. It's the same thing with soccer. I have to study what the other moms bring, so I can figure out what to do when it's my turn to be the snack mom. Some moms cut up oranges for halftime. I don't do this, because I don't think I can cut the oranges the right way—pitiful but true!"

I laughed out loud when Caren sent me this e-mail, not out of ridicule but out of pure identification. When Maya played soccer, I was always worried about how to slice the watermelon so I wouldn't look inept. It's not that I think the other mothers on the soccer field or in Maya's class are better than me, exactly, just that they seem to, well, *know* things that I don't. For years, I've stood on the sidelines of class parties, staring at the elaborately decorated homemade cookies or pots of ethnic food, wondering, *How do they* do *that? Do you have to make that bright blue icing from scratch, or can you buy it in a store?* My attempts to replicate such projects at home have been disastrous more often than not, and I've embarrassed myself countless times in the company of other mothers by admitting that I don't know what whipping cream is, or that I'd sooner buy my daughter new socks than try to figure out how to bleach the stains out of the ones she's got.

I'm not even sure that my mother, had she lived, would have passed this kind of knowledge down to me, or if passing it down from mother to daughter is even how the process works. I just know that I can't seem to do the kinds of things many other mothers can do. When did that point of departure occur? I remember going to needlepoint class when I was eleven, and knitting with my mother at twelve. And then all of those extras disappeared. After she died,

I abruptly swung toward a more practical, masculine side of the spectrum, focused on doing and producing and staying in control. It was as if the wide-angle lens of my childhood closed in on a much narrower field, accompanied by a booming background soundtrack of "survive, survive, survive."

By the time I discovered I hadn't picked up the traditionally female skills most other mothers had, I was already in my mid-thirties, and it felt like too late to change. Energy that might have been put into actually learning how to cook or sew went instead into obscuring evidence that I couldn't do these things, so as not to make my deficiencies known. And, by then, it was hard to value traditional feminine activities, anyway. They'd been missing from my family for so long, replaced by the individualistic work ethic my father had been modeling for all the intervening years. As a mother now, I'd rather focus on my kids' emotional lives, but at the same time, it's becoming clear to them that I don't act like the other mothers. "Why can't you be a normal mother?" Maya once cried out in frustration. How was I supposed to answer that one? Because I never learned how to be one? Or because I refuse to learn?

Because really, how hard is it for me to learn how to bake a cherry pie? Or for Caren to figure out how to slice an orange a certain way? Are we really so afraid of revealing our "difference" that we've become too afraid to take even small risks?

I suspect what scares us most, underneath it all, is giving up the evidence of what makes us unique. When a woman's self-perception, and her identity, has been wrapped up for so long in being a woman who's not like the others, who won't ever be like the others, it's hard to let this go. Being "different," after enough years, becomes its own badge of honor—especially when it potentially means "stronger," more resourceful, and more resilient. I may never have learned how to take pride in keeping a tidy house, a motherless woman can tell herself, but I know what really matters in life. And from there, it's easy to devalue what other women know, while envying them for knowing it at the same time.

We may be afraid of being different from other mothers, but we stubbornly insist on perpetuating those differences, too. It seems to me that this insistence may be just a tough way of defending ourselves against painful feelings of loss. I could easily ask a friend to teach me how to knit, or go ahead and bake a pie for the school bake sale. I could put my perfectionist tendencies on hold for an afternoon. But it's hard to imagine taking even those small steps, when doing so, at a very deep level, reinforces the knowledge that my mother is gone, that she's not ever coming back to teach me. And that I really do have to figure all this out on my own.

Thirty-eight-year-old Trudi, who lost her mother as an infant, has coped with this by coming together with two other motherless women in her neighborhood. They're not ashamed to admit to each other that they don't know what they don't know. "We support each other, and we teach each other how to cook and sew and scrapbook," Trudi says. "A lot of this we learned from our grandmothers, because we didn't have the opportunity with our mothers."

Other motherless mothers may wind up being our most compassionate and most willing guides. They're the ones I seek out now as role models, under the pretense that if they've managed to surmount such a major obstacle and become engaged and knowledgeable mothers, then perhaps so can I. "An important function of the groups we lead is that motherless women can acknowledge that others in the room are doing a good job as mothers," says Judith Zabin, LICSW, who has been leading Motherless Daughters groups in the Boston area for eight years. And I think maybe *that's* what I've been looking for. Not the talents or the skills that other women have, but the reassurance that I can still be a good mother without them.

Activists and advocates

"I don't compare myself with other women," Trudi explains. "I just try to be a good mother, because I didn't have a good mother. My measuring stick is not other people, but what I didn't have."

Trudi's daughter is in kindergarten, and has recently been diagnosed with an unspecified developmental delay. Until the parameters of her daughter's disability become clear, Trudi has been a continuous presence in the kindergarten class, making sure her daughter gets the extra support she needs. "At her school, I'm known as the Good Parent," Trudi says, "because I advocate for my daughter. I work in her classroom. I'm doing everything in my power to try to help her, because I didn't have that. I didn't have a mother to advocate for me."

Dissect any school population, and you'll find plenty of parents who serve as vocal champions of their kids. Now dissect that group, and you'll find the parents who advocate for a very specific reason: because when they were young and vulnerable at school, no parent stepped forth to defend them. They either learned how to feel helpless and powerless to authority figures, or had to learn to speak out for themselves. Now they're determined that their children won't have to stand alone—not as long as their mothers can stand beside them.

For some motherless daughters, assertiveness and advocacy are the natural adult outgrowths of skills they had to develop during childhood. "Many motherless women have experienced abuse and neglect, often by fathers," Colleen Russell says. "No one protected them as children, and they were in the role of the protector for their siblings before they were emotionally ready for it. And, in many families, the daughter had to step in and fill the mother's role after she died. These women are so familiar with being totally in charge and being responsible that they carry that over into their relationships with their husbands and their kids, and even onto the playground."

Forty-one-year-old Melissa, who was nine when her mother died, says that spending the rest of her childhood with an unreliable father meant she had to find practical ways to make things happen for herself. "If I wanted to be a cheerleader, I had to sign myself up and make a friend on the squad whose mother could drive me to practice, so that's what I did," she recalls. Now, as the mother of three school-age kids, she's an adept problem-solver on their behalf. Controversy and conflict don't scare her, she says.

This past year, when Melissa noticed that kindergarteners at her children's school were allowed to buy junk food for lunch, without any supervision, she campaigned to have the school lunch program overhauled. As the result of her efforts, twenty-five "extra" food items, such as fruit rolls and ice cream sandwiches, sold for profit on the cafeteria line, were replaced with healthier choices, including more fruits and vegetables. Her school is now a pilot program for the whole district. "So many people have asked me, 'How did you *do* that?'" Melissa says. "To me, it was such a natural response to speak up for our kids." Now other parents call her for advice when their children need help at school.

At the same time, Melissa says, she recognizes the importance of teaching her children how to speak up for themselves. "I think self-esteem is the key to our children's character and success," she explains. "I don't think that any situation is mine to bulldoze through. When to step in and when to step back will forever be a question for me, and it's a crucial parenting question."

Motherless women need to find a balance between solving current problems and righting past wrongs, Colleen Russell advises, and between empowering their children and rushing in to rescue them. Because this group is highly sensitive to perceived rejection, they may find themselves getting overinvolved when they see their children being excluded or snubbed, she says. "They really struggle with that, because it's so difficult for them to know how much to be there and how much not to be there if they didn't have mothers themselves," she explains.

At moments when you're uncertain of your motivation, or when your response feels out of proportion to the situation at hand, it can be helpful to slow down and take the following steps:

Become aware of your feelings. Ask, "What, exactly, am I feeling?" Is it fear? Disappointment? Outrage? Grief? Articulating those

feelings by journaling, talking to a compassionate and nonjudg-
mental spouse or friend, or consulting with a therapist can help.

Try to see the scene from your child's point of view. Sometimes this new
perspective can help us see that a situation isn't as large or overwhelming as it feels. And sometimes it can alert us to the fact that it's
even larger than we thought, and worthy of immediate action.

Finally, *Imagine what you'd like to happen.* If you can suspend reality for long enough to think about the optimal outcome, you can
better decide whether a situation requires parental action. Sometimes a goal is better achieved by empowering the child in a developmentally appropriate way. By the end of the process, your initial
impulse to charge into the principal's office or confront another
child's mother on the phone may not feel like the right approach
anymore. Or it may feel like an even more appropriate solution
than it did before.

As I finish this chapter, it's the very last day of the school year, and
Maya is stepping from second grade into third. She began in September doing single-digit addition and spelling "very" with two *r*'s.
Now it's June, and she's doing triple-digit subtraction and memo-
rizing her multiplication tables. On her last spelling test, she got
"imagination" and "magical" right. I wrote a note to her teacher
thanking her for being not just an excellent educator but also an
outstanding person. Under her watchful care, Maya blossomed this
year from a child into a girl. Knowing that she spent six hours each
day supervised by someone I respect and trust gave me just that
much more faith that there's a larger system supporting us, and
that even without help from family, Uzi and I aren't raising these
children alone.

None of the other mothers wrapping up the school year in
the classroom today can tell my story is any different from theirs.
On the surface, motherless mothers look a lot like everyone else.
Ninety-seven percent of us describe ourselves as fun parents,
98 percent describe ourselves as loving mothers, and 98 percent say

we're attentive and affectionate with our kids. But spend more time with us, and the disparities start to show. We're less likely than other women to describe ourselves as flexible, more likely to say we're overprotective, and more of us say we're easily overwhelmed.

There's a mother at Maya's bus stop who's been on my mind a lot as I write these final chapters. I first saw her in the middle of the school year, and she was always pleasant and cheerful as she waited for the bus to arrive. She and her son consistently showed up at the corner two or three minutes ahead of the bus, a kind of Swiss timing I admired. I'd seen her son around school, a fourth-grader who seemed the very picture of a lovely, thoughtful, well-adjusted kid. The perfect child, I imagined, raised by a highly competent, confident mother. But then, one day, Maya ran from our car across the empty street to the bus stop without looking both ways, and this mother shouted at her in a panic. Then she yelled at me, too, telling me that Maya had to learn how to cross a street.

What's up with that? I thought. "Thank you," I told her firmly. "I'll take care of it from here."

I kept a respectful distance from this mother for weeks after the incident, until the morning when she walked up and introduced herself to me. She'd read *Motherless Daughters*, she said, and it had left a lasting impact on her. Her mother had been killed in an accident when she was a child, she said, and now, as a mother, she's constantly worried about keeping her kids safe. "That's why I'm so adamant about looking both ways before crossing the street," she explained, and in that moment, I felt the safe distance I'd erected between us collapse. I think I may have hugged her then. I hope I did.

Because in that moment, she revealed to me what lies at the very heart of this book. Motherless mothers: as parents, we are efficient, and resourceful, and engaged, and maybe even a little bit crazy about keeping our kids safe. As Gina Mireault has explained, we're constantly afraid we're not doing the good job that we're doing. Yet, when our children kiss us good-bye every morning and climb onto the school bus happy and well-fed, filled with the simple expectation of having just another good day, we can take it as proof that we've overcome whatever obstacles a difficult childhood planted in our way.

"For me, it's a personal triumph to have such a friendly, outgoing, confident child," says thirty-eight-year-old Corinne, the mother of a six-year-old son, who was eight when she lost her mother and ten when her father died. "He couldn't wait to start kindergarten. He wanted to meet the principal on the first day to say 'hi.' All of these are things that would have described me before my mother died, and, to me, describe an unconditionally loved, happy, healthy child."

Some mothers take pride in their parenting when children score well on tests, or make friends easily, or ask to do volunteer work after school. And while all this is undoubtedly important, motherless mothers aspire to a different set of goals. A smile in the morning, and a smile at night. A day without sadness. Clean clothing and neatly brushed hair. "To me, successful parenting means raising my child to not have the struggles and insecurities that I did after my parents died," Corinne explains. *Sister,* I tell her, *very well said.*

11

✑

The Drive to Survive

KEEPING YOURSELF SAFE

We call our garage the Bermuda Triangle of our house, the vortex in which random discarded and outgrown items mysteriously disappear. The space is an organizer's nightmare, a veritable swamp of camping equipment and Costco bulk items and broken electronics that date back, as my mother would have said, to the Year One. We have long since given up hope of parking both cars inside. I've been planning to clean it out next weekend for the past six years.

My single nod to order is a three-tiered shelf on the south wall. It's packed tight with boxes of children's clothing, mostly hand-me-downs from Maya that Eden will wear one day. The boxes are labeled and lined up in size order: 4T, 5, 6, 6X, 7. Maya wears size 8 now, so you might expect the boxes to stop there. But nothing is conventional in my garage. On the very top shelf are two more boxes, labeled 10 and 12. Those are filled with the dresses, skirts, and pajamas I buy from discount racks at the end of each season, the clothing I've purchased for Maya to wear in two or three years, in case I'm not around to buy her school clothes then.

I once had a writing student named Natalie, who'd been diagnosed with cancer. Her impulse upon hearing the news, she wrote in an essay, was to run out and buy her four-year-old daughter a coat for every winter they wouldn't spend together. When she read those lines out loud in class, I thought of the boxes in my garage. They're my version of Natalie's winter coats, the tangible assurance that my daughters will be lovingly and appropriately dressed in the event I die before they're grown.

As it is, there's not a shred of evidence that I'm going to die young. I eat well. I exercise. I get annual mammograms. In fact, I'm healthier at forty-one than I've ever been before. But who's talking about medical probability here? Accidents happen. Freak diseases appear. In my version of the world, unexpected news has a way of parachuting straight down from a cloudless sky. The way I see it, you can never be too prepared.

I'm not alone here. More than half of the motherless women surveyed said they worried "often" about dying young, compared to only 15 percent of the women whose mothers were still alive.

When you lose a mother during childhood or adolescence, whatever feelings of personal invulnerability you once had disappear. John Bowlby, the noted attachment theorist, described this as "a natural enough type of reasoning, even if mistaken." He believed that children who lose same-sex parents are most vulnerable to this form of distress, because they naturally identify with those parents and unconsciously believe that what happens to a same-sex parent will inevitably happen to them.

"Death anxiety" (the fear of death) and its fraternal twin, "survival anxiety" (the fear for one's own health or physical safety), are familiar to most motherless women, especially those whose mothers died of hereditary diseases. *Will I repeat my mother's fate?* these women wonder. *Will her illness show up in me?*

"Understandably and realistically, you're going to have more anxiety if your mother and your two aunts died very young of a very aggressive breast cancer than if your mother died scaling a glacier, which is something you can then avoid doing," Harriet Lerner explains. But survival anxiety also shows up in women whose mothers died in car accidents or in random acts of violence, situations that are unpredictable and harder to avoid, and death anxiety can show up in anyone who lost a parent young.

"I've always had the feeling that I'm not going to have a long life," says fifty-one-year-old Rosemary, who was seven when her mother died from brain cancer and who herself survived a benign brain tumor at age thirty-nine—the same age her mother was when she died. "I don't worry about it so much that I don't live my life, but I always have the fear that this is not a guaranteed gig. And it's what sets me apart from the other parents I know. I want to give as much as I can to my kids while I'm here."

Contrary to what most of us have been taught about the deleterious effect of anxiety, some researchers now say that a modest level of death anxiety may contribute to good psychological health, because it helps us value human life and relationships more. People who believe their time here may be short are often driven to live full lives, and to make the most of their time with others.

"I think about my mortality, and I think, 'Goddammit, I'm going to be here until I'm a hundred for these kids,'" says forty-four-year-old Stacey, the mother of two young sons, who was seventeen when her mother committed suicide. "I feel like I got gypped out of having a mom for my adult years, and there's no way that's going to happen to my kids. And I just feel this incredible commitment to give my kids 100 percent of me. I look at them when they're happy and playing, and I think, 'Oh God, look at these kids. They're so innocent. They're so vulnerable. They're so loving and precious and delicious.' And I'm thinking, 'This is what it's all about. It's about seeing them grow up.' And I feel like I just have to do whatever I have to do to make that happen."

The downside to death anxiety, however, is that if you're not careful, any potentially risky situation can start looking like a vehicle for one's dcmise. "My boyfriend had a motorcycle when my son was young," recalls fifty-six-year-old Elsa, who was nine when her mother died. "I took a couple of rides with him, and the whole time I was thinking, *What if I die? What if I die?* I stopped riding with him, because I didn't want to die on the back of a motorcycle when I had a six-year-old."

Are these the words of a pragmatist? Or of an overly cautious mom? Elsa knew all too well what could happen to her child if he were left motherless. Why should she take an unnecessary chance? On the other hand, if you follow this form of logic to its inevitable conclusion, virtually any activity—crossing the street, eating in a restaurant, even taking a shower—contains some small element of risk. So, where do you draw the line? I've met motherless mothers who've stopped eating meat, who won't fly over oceans, and who've sold their houses to move to more environmentally friendly zones, all part of the conscious effort to safeguard their lives. While none of these alone spell out an overly restricted lifestyle, piled one on top of another, they can become psychically suffocating. The most immediate danger for a motherless mother may come not from anything on the outside but, instead, from limiting her own behaviors too much in an attempt to stay safe.

Parenthood inevitably kicks up death anxiety for new mothers and fathers. The stakes skyrocket overnight when a child's welfare becomes part of the equation. "Before I had children I had no particular fear of dying, because I had no particular notion of the consequences of my death," the writer Michael Lewis has said. My husband, a former scuba guide, cut back on diving when Maya was born. To him, that's part of responsible parenthood. But for a motherless mother, self-preservation is more than just a responsibility. It's a mission. To give a child the mother you didn't have, it's imperative to stay alive.

Grace, who was eight when her mother died and now has a sixteen-year-old daughter, says, "It's amazing how many things I pull back on because I think, *What if something happened to me?* My daughter had a friend who recently died of cancer, and we were talking the other day about bone marrow transplants. Alice said, 'Mom, I don't know if I could sign up for that. Would you?' And I said, 'I don't know.' I mean, would I donate a kidney to somebody who needed it? I really don't know. Because then I'd only have one left. And there's always this feeling of *I've got to make sure I'm here for her.*"

Because really, that's the dominant issue when we think of our potential demise. Not *Will I be sad to die?* or *Will I see my mother again?* or even *Will it hurt?* When my husband gave up diving, he did it with an imagined notion of the consequences his untimely death would have on us. I, on the other hand, have very explicit knowledge of what my death would mean to our girls. It would be the end of life as they know it. When a motherless mother worries about dying young, she's not just thinking about her life coming to an end. She's thinking, *What would happen to my kids?* And the answer to that question, usually, is *The same thing that happened to me.*

Never mind that she's chosen a partner who would raise their children lovingly in her absence, or that she's made sure her children could manage better in her absence than she managed when her mother died. In her mind, what would happen to her children becomes synonymous with scenes from her own past. She had no one to go to when she was hurt or scared? They'd have no one to go to, either. She had to go to school with her hair unbrushed? They would have to do the same.

"When I'm not blocking those thoughts out of my head—and I try to block them out a lot, I think—I look at my daughter, Ally, who's almost ten, and I get scared for her more than I get scared for me," says forty-year-old Lisa, who was ten when her mother died, and then suffered a lonely childhood in the home of an uncle and aunt, and then with her maternal grandparents. "I don't care about myself dying, but I'm afraid for her to have any of the sad or lonely feelings that I had."

The Neon Number

It's not surprising that Lisa is concerned about her daughter's well-being right now. Both of them are passing through a historically vulnerable zone in Lisa's family. Her mother was forty when she died, the same age Lisa is now. And Lisa's daughter, Ally, is about to turn ten, the same age Lisa was when her mother died.

Reaching and passing the mother's age at time of death is one of the most significant transitions a motherless woman will make. It's a bittersweet achievement, laced with feelings of triumph, sadness, and guilt. It's a key mile marker on her personal journey, a year in which both death anxiety and survival anxiety often bubble up at both conscious and unconscious levels. Many motherless women have strong emotional reactions—often called "anniversary reactions"—as they approach this particularly loaded age.

"I went through terrible spells of anxiety and depression for about two years," recalls fifty-year-old Rebecca, whose mother died of colon cancer at age forty-nine. "If I had tingling in my hand, it was Lou Gehrig's disease. If I had a colonoscopy and the doctor found a little something there, I couldn't sleep for two weeks until the biopsy came back. I just did not take anything remotely connected to cancer well. My second daughter had an ulcer. I didn't take that well, either. And my third daughter had a migraine and went numb on one side. They did an MRI and waited to diagnose her, because they wanted another doctor to look at the results. I was a basket case. Just waiting for a tragedy. I've just leveled off in the past year, and I attribute that to reaching my mom's death age and passing it. My anxiety was really focused on me, but it also overflowed to the kids."

Many motherless mothers experience this year as an emotional crucible in which unresolved grief heats up. It's not unusual for women to overfocus on their health or on their children's well-being at this time, trying to micromanage their safety or getting overly involved in their personal lives. It doesn't typically make for a smooth ride, especially with teens.

"Kids develop an allergy to even the most loving intensity," Harriet Lerner warns. "It can help a lot to move toward what I call 'benign neglect.' Obviously, you're not going to neglect your children's safety, but you're lightening up and giving them more space, and trying to work on your own grief and anxiety so that it doesn't all land on your children with a big thud. If you're all revved up about the anniversary date, your intensity will land on them, not always in an anxious, worried way but sometimes in an angry, blaming way. The challenge for the mother is to get focused on her own self so that she can address the emotional issues of her mother's death and not dump all the anxiety on her kids."

We can speculate about how a child who grows up under such intense circumstances might turn out—that she might develop a persistent fear of losing her mother, or that she might rebel against her mother's anxious impulses—but it's almost impossible to know for sure. Children, fortunately, are exposed to many different influences as they mature. Although the mother's behaviors are critically important, the actions of fathers, grandparents, teachers, and good friends often provide balance by modeling different perspectives. As Maxine Harris reminds us, "The child whose mother is nervous about her own mortality may grow up to do something incredibly creative with that anxiety, or she may become a chronic nail biter. It's one of the variables that shapes who a child will become, but it is only one."

Reaching a mother's death age is a significant milestone for a motherless mother. Living beyond it is another experience entirely. Without a maternal role model paving the way into middle age and beyond, a daughter who lives beyond her mother's age may feel disoriented and insecure. She's entering the years she unconsciously didn't expect to see, and may not have consciously planned for.

Yet at the same time, living beyond the mother can be an enormously freeing experience. "It was just a breather," says forty-four-year-old Leslie, who was seventeen when her mother died at the age of forty-two. "It was, like, 'Okay, this is what it's like to be forty-two.' And then, when I turned forty-three, it was, like, 'Whew. Okay. I made it.'"

Life feels expansive, often for the first time. Elsa, who was nine when her thirty-three-year-old mother died of cancer, never thought she'd make it beyond that point. "Well, now I'm fifty-six and I still look around, thinking, *You know, I might just have the opportunity to grow old,*" she says. "It's kind of an amazing feeling."

Released from the psychological grip of history, a woman may even be willing to take risks or make plans that the fear of death prevented her from doing before. I've spoken with women who've changed careers, filed for divorces, even taken up race-car driving at this time. Yet they're still aware of an odd and disconcerting anachronism. By middle age (or sometimes even earlier), they've grown older than their mothers and collected more cumulative life experience, getting to become, by the most basic definition, the women their own mothers never got to be.

What will it be like to go through menopause? To help a daughter plan a wedding? To turn fifty, or to retire? These are among life's big mysteries to me. My mother died at forty-two, too young to have experienced much of what I still have ahead. And yet, at forty-one, I am almost upon her age at time of death. Soon, I will no longer have her as a model against whom I can measure my progress as a woman or as a mother.

My mother. She has always been just that—my mother. Older, smarter, more experienced, and more mature than I. But she is a static icon, frozen at forty-two. I'm the one who's growing older, and who will soon pass her by. Already she is the age of my peers. Before long, she will be the age of my younger sister, and eventually the age of my daughters. The one who gave birth to me will one day be younger than the ones I've birthed. Thinking about that one for too long can really pretzel up my mind.

Forty-two. It seemed so old when I was seventeen. Because my mother's days looked so boring and repetitive to me, I thought of middle age as little more than a precursor to life's final stage. I believed my mother's most colorful and vibrant years were already far behind her. Granted, forty-two in 1981 was different from forty-two today. Now, my friends in their early forties are doing yoga and having babies with the kind of energy and enthusiasm my mother once put into mah-jongg and the PTA. Still, I look at friends who are forty-five and fifty—or at my husband, who's forty-five—and I get it, I really get it, how much my mother lost. It's difficult to believe that the boyish man I married is already older than my mother ever got to be. Was my mother ever this young? Or was I just always too young to realize it?

For my fortieth birthday, my sister and my husband threw a surprise party for me in a nearby state park. We had sixty guests, field games for the kids, and the most extraordinary three-tiered birthday cake I've ever seen. Still, this was minor in comparison to what I've got in mind for forty-three. Marimba players, belly dancers, the backyard tent—I've already got the whole thing planned. It'll be a joyous celebration of life, the birthday I've never taken for granted, the one my mother never got to have. When the time comes for a toast, I'll raise my champagne glass high. To her. To me. To this life. And to the part of me that always felt I wouldn't make it this far, the part I'll be so relieved to leave behind.

The Other Neon Number

Anticipating and reaching one anniversary date is emotional enough, but motherless mothers also have a second one to face: when a child reaches the age the mother was when her own mother died. Whether she was six, or twelve, or even twenty-one when she lost her mother, the adult mother looks at her own child at that age and thinks, *Oh my God. Look at how much he still needs me.* Then her mind does a quick flip-flop into the past. *Look at how much I still needed my mother at that age. Look at how much I lost.*

How old does a child need to be to manage without a mother? At what age can she survive without maternal guidance and protection? These are questions most motherless mothers turn over and over in their minds. *Is it the age* I *was when my mother died?* they wonder. *Or is it that age, plus the few more years I felt I needed?* Every few months, I look at my daughters and wonder, *If I died now, would they be able to brush their own hair? Would they be able to skin a knee and not cry for me to bandage it?* And every few months, the answer is still a resounding no, filling me with an even stronger commitment to make sure I stick around.

Forty-two-year-old Alma says she knows exactly what I mean. For her first twelve years as a mother, she had a very specific goal: to live long enough to raise each of her three daughters to the age of ten. That's how old she was when her mother died of cancer, and if she could only get her own girls to that finish line, Alma believed, they'd have some good memories of her and some solid survival tools, as she had at that age.

Alma's oldest daughter is independent and resourceful by nature, and although she and Alma are very close, her tenth birthday came and went without much fanfare. But Alma has always identified more with her second daughter, Daisy, who looks a great deal like her. When Daisy turned ten, Alma, in her own words, "took it hard."

It happened the same year that Alma turned forty, the exact age Alma's mother was when she died, and the dual anniversary—what Harriet Lerner calls "a double whammy"—provoked a swell of emotion and grief. "I looked at Daisy and thought, *She's still a tiny little girl*," Alma recalls. "And I realized, at that age, I was already having to deal with so much."

Seeing how young Daisy still was at age ten prompted Alma to extend the concept of a "finish line" a few more years in her mind. "When my oldest daughter was about to turn fourteen, I thought, *Okay. She can handle this. She knows what she wants. I'm done with her*," Alma says. "But now she's fourteen, and not a day goes by when she doesn't look for my approval, or ask for my opinion. Every year, she reaches the age that I think she'll be okay without me, and every year I realize: there *is* no finish line." Having managed without a mother after age ten, Alma had no concept of the integral role a mother continues to play in a teenager's life. She's realizing now that, in one respect or another, her daughters will need her forever.

"Part of the notion of a finish line comes from your belief that you really didn't need your own mother for that long, that what you lost wasn't that much, as if 'Oh, I just lost a couple of years. I would have been fine if she had just been there until I turned eighteen,'" Maxine Harris says. "And then, when you realize that you would have needed her for always, there's a renewed sadness."

Alma's intense focus on the anniversary ages in her family is actually a good sign, indicating she recognizes a link between her past experience and her present sadness. "You're far ahead of most people if you can think about that consciously," Harriet Lerner explains. "What I see clinically is that often the unconscious takes over, so the woman may have no awareness that she's reached an anniversary date, and the anxiety may manifest in all kinds of indirect ways, like having an affair, or becoming anxiously riveted on some aspect of her child's functioning, like the child isn't fitting in at school. It's a much more troubling dynamic when the person doesn't make the connection. Often, mothers are very relieved when I point out the family tree and say, 'Your daughter has just reached the age you were when you lost your mom, and you're around the same age your mother was when she died. Do you think that could have something to do with the fact that the two of you are having screaming fights all the time?'"

Usually, the mother is the one whose anxiety surges around anniversary ages, but sometimes the child acts out, too. That may be what's happening now with Lisa and her daughter, Ally, who's ten. In the past year or so, Ally has been experiencing extreme separation anxiety when Lisa is out of her sight. "I have to be right there to pick her up at the end of school," Lisa explains. "I can't drive up. I have to be standing at the blue door. It seems to go in cycles. Sometimes she'll go to her friend's house and sleep over, and sometimes she won't leave our house." Lisa and Ally have always had a close relationship, but Ally's recent anxiety is a new development, and Lisa and her husband are deeply concerned. "We've talked about my mother's death, and about how I'm not going anywhere, but she still has big issues of abandonment," Lisa says. "We've never given her cause to feel insecure or alone or abandoned, but my therapist said it could be something that's innate, something you pass on to your child not just emotionally but also physiologically. Because these were issues that were so ingrained in me." She recently started taking Ally to a behaviorist who specializes in childhood anxiety, to help them with the issue.

Because this year is the year Ally turns ten and Lisa turns forty—the same ages Lisa and her mother were when Lisa's mother died—it's possible that Ally may be frightened of losing her own mother and is having an unconscious anniversary reaction of her own. It's also possible that she could be picking up on Lisa's unexpressed anxiety about reaching her mother's death age. As Harriet Lerner reminds us, children don't suddenly get anxious in a calm emotional field. A ten-year-old is cognitively mature enough to understand that she and her mother have both reached these loaded ages, but doesn't yet have the emotional maturity to cope with the anxiety this awareness can provoke. She needs the mother's calming presence and reassurance to help her through the year. That usually means, though, that the mother has to get a handle on her own anxiety first.

The potential for problems is highest in families where the grandmother's death hasn't been openly discussed. "Whatever is stigmatized or secret causes more anxiety," Harriet Lerner explains. "Many mothers feel it would burden the child to bring up the grandmother's death. They'll say, 'I don't want to bring it up because then my daughter will think I'll die,' but, in fact, it's a great relief to the child if the mother can open it up. I, for example, help the mother say to her child, 'I know I've been a very difficult mom these past few months and that we've been having a lot of fights, and I think it has something to do with the fact that when I was your age I lost my mom, and I think I'm having a hard time with that. And, I think, that sometimes comes out as me getting overly worried about you when, in fact, you're a very competent person and you *can* walk home from school with your friends.' Whenever facts can be presented calmly, even if they're very difficult facts, children do better. They don't do well with the emotional intensity surrounding the facts."

The Best-laid Plans

In the hard drive of Christine's laptop sits a file with the name "When I Am Gone." She also keeps a copy saved to disk. Her husband, Brian, knows where to find it, if the need arises.

The file is Christine's version of a written will. "I've written down everything about Kyra and Melanie, what they like and don't like, and how to run the house," she explains, "because I am so afraid of dying. Not as much as I once was, because I've gone through an intensive university study that actually said my probability of dying from breast or ovarian cancer was lower than I'd thought. So that made me ease up. And I haven't been teaching our children to take care of themselves, because I believe I'll be there for them. On the other hand, I keep all these little things documented, like 'Kyra likes her milk hot. You fill it up to the second line of the sippy cup, microwave it for 56 seconds exactly, swirl it around, and then put the top on.' And 'Melanie likes to sleep with her waffle blanket. There are six of them. I wash them once a week, alternating three per week. She must have at least one in her bed, possibly two.' Favorite movies, movies they've outgrown, books they like best. It's written, like, 'Okay, here's what you need to know to get them to bed.' I even wrote, 'Okay, Brian, you're going to need to clean their private parts, so let me explain how to do it properly. You go from front to back.'"

At this point, Christine stops and laughs, recognizing how over-the-top this sounds. But, as she keeps talking, it's clear that her attention to detail isn't meant to be funny. To her, it's a serious matter.

"After Melanie was born, I would be up late at night holding her and typing away, writing instructions about how to give a baby bath," she recalls. "When to get their hair cut. When to switch from Velcro shoes to shoes with laces. The little rhyme you teach them when they learn to tie shoes. With Melanie, when do you get her new shoes? 'When you notice she starts falling down or her toes are curled inside the shoes, honey, that means she needs new ones. That's why she's falling down, because her toes are curled and she's not balancing.' Brian doesn't know that. But if I were to die, when would he know how to get her new shoes?"

Christine's voice starts to tremble here. The idea of her baby— any baby—wearing shoes that don't fit because a mother is gone is hard for her to imagine. "Isn't that ridiculous?" she asks, her voice cracking into a sob. "I worry that if I died, he wouldn't know when to get her new shoes." The image of a preverbal child in too-tight shoes evokes the memory of a time in her own childhood, when Christine felt abandoned and uncared for, and the thought of the same thing happening to her own child is almost more than she can bear.

Written instructions. "If I Die Tomorrow" conversations. "I Love You" letters. Meticulously detailed wills. They're all part of the motherless mother's attempt to ensure the family she created will better manage a mother's departure than her birth family once did.

"I know my husband is a wonderful parent, and that he'd do his very best," says thirty-three-year-old Patrice, who lost her mother when she was ten, "but, in fact, just the other day I told him, 'If something happens to me'—I say this a lot—'If something ever happens to me, when you take the kids out, have their faces washed, please. Have their hair brushed. Make sure their clothes are clean. Please. Can you promise me that?'"

How do husbands handle this? Some have trouble taking the concern seriously, especially those who haven't experienced early loss. Constant references to a death that's unlikely to happen can be weary for even the most supportive and well-meaning spouse. Alma recalls a recent conversation with her husband about her life insurance policy: "I wanted to take out this big policy, and my husband said, 'Why? You don't even earn that much in five years.' I said, 'Well, because if I die . . .' and he went, 'Oh, here we go again.'"

It's a maddening experience to have your deepest fears minimized, yet that's often what happens in a household where one spouse's family history differs so much from the other's, and the gulf in understanding between them can feel deep and wide.

"I find myself quizzing my husband, 'If I weren't here, would you be able to do such-and-such? If I fell off a cliff and you were left with two kids, what would you do?'" admits thirty-eight-year-old Corinne. "Initially, he was afraid to give our son a bath. He wouldn't do it for the first year. And that bugged the hell out of me. I'd say, 'What if I were to die tomorrow?' and he'd say, 'Oh, hon, I'd figure it out. How tough is it?'"

Other husbands become accustomed to these conversations over time. Gina Mireault's husband, also a psychologist, barely even blinks anymore when she brings up the topic, she says with a laugh. "Not long ago, I told him, 'If I go first, I want you to have me cremated,'" she says. "He said, 'Okay.' He didn't even look at me like I was nuts. He said, 'What do you want me to do with the ashes?' I said, 'Scatter them at my favorite beach where we go every summer.' He said, 'There are two sections to that beach—Long Sands or Short Sands?' So, he's sort of gotten used to these types of conversations."

And still other husbands—like mine—just quietly accept these concerns as part of the marital package. My husband is gracious enough to say nothing about boxes 10 and 12 in our garage—that is, if he even notices they're there. He walks past the shelf twice a day, but children's clothing has always been my domain. As are shoes. And haircuts. And homework. And most dinners. And most baths.

The uneven distribution of domestic labor in our household is nothing extraordinary: in the vast majority of American families, the mother provides more child care than the father, even when she holds a full-time job. But when she's a motherless mother, her reasons for shouldering the majority of domestic work often have more to do with emotional history than social demographics. Her relentless self-sufficiency; her strong desire to be an available, competent mother; the pure pleasure she derives from taking good care of her children; and the security she gets from having control over family matters—all of this means that she's much more likely to create a family in which she takes on most of the domestic work.* And therein lies one of the central paradoxes in a motherless mother's family life: the more she does for her family, the more essential she becomes. Yet the more essential she becomes, the harder it would be for them to manage without her if she died.

"I told a girlfriend, 'Gosh, David doesn't even know what time the girls were born,'" Alma says. "'If I die, he won't be able to tell them that.' And my friend said, 'If you die, you've got bigger problems than that. He doesn't even know what time they go to *school*.'"

The truth is, if a motherless mother were truly trying to prepare her family to manage without her, she would share more responsibility from the start. Creating written instructions for husbands and planning one's own funeral aren't really about preparing for the future. They're about trying to gain a feeling of control over a situation that feels frightening and huge right now.

Anxiety and control tend to travel together in a perfectly choreographed dance. Anxiety goes up when an individual feels she

---

* Forty-eight percent of women in the control-group study said they provide more than 50 percent of the child care in their households, relative to their partners. Nearly 60 percent of the motherless mothers said the same.

can't control her environment. Anxiety goes down when she can take steps that help her feel in control. Whatever sense of control we have is only illusory—we don't have the power to ensure our complete safety—but it gets us from day to day. Letting go of the idea of control and accepting that bad things happen, some of them randomly, is a seriously difficult step to take. It means accepting that what one fears most could potentially happen.

When a motherless mother realizes she can't control her heredity, or her daily environment, or the driver of the other car heading her way, she heads to her computer or her notebook. And it calms her, for a while. By creating instructions that can be followed in her absence, she gives herself the temporary assurance that she can control the outcome this time. If. When. Just in case.

Photographs and Memories

When Maya was three and a half, I took her to Paris. We had plans to meet my in-laws for a week in Prague, and I hatched the idea to lay over in France for five days on the way. It seemed like an opportunity for a short vacation in Europe, and a chance to get jet lag out of the way before seeing the grandparents. But my husband couldn't take that much time off work, so I recruited my sister and her friend to join me. Paris with a preschooler. Three adults on the case. How hard could it be?

My memories of Paris, by then more than ten years old, were of quaint apartments and sidewalk cafés. Murmured conversations with French men over hand-rolled cigarettes, and steaming cups of café au lait. If you've ever taken a three-year-old to Paris, you know what's coming next. There were no innocent flirtations. There were no cafés. Definitely no café au lait. There was, instead, a ridiculous number of carousels. My sister and her friend spent the first three days sleeping off their jet lag while I spent hours chasing after the back of Maya's head, shouting, "Wait for Mommy!" down countless

Parisian streets. On our final day in France, I took her on a bus tour to Fontainebleau, thinking she'd like to see a real-life palace, but the royal meltdown she had in the gardens there was enough to make me renounce Napoleon, motherhood, and all of France, in history and perpetuity.

And yet, when we returned home and had our film developed, I looked at photos of both of us on the carousel at the Hôtel de Ville, and of Maya eating a cheese baguette on the Champs d'Elysée, and of her running along a garden wall at Fontainebleau just before her tantrum began, and in that moment I knew the trip was worth it. Maya will always have the story of traveling to Paris with her mother, and the photos to prove I took her there.

I carefully inserted the photos in a special travel album. Then I opened Maya's baby book to the page marked "Travels" and added "March 28 to April 2, 2001—Paris with Mom" to the official record.

Look inside the home of a motherless mother, and you're likely to find a shelf of carefully organized photo albums, a sequential row of home videos, or a stack of baby books packed two inches thick with notations and memorabilia. Sometimes you'll find all three. The impulse toward compulsive record-keeping is a strong one, especially among women who have few photos or home movies of their mothers, or scant happy memories of time in an intact family.

"I have a camera at every event," laughs Rebecca, a mother of four. "It's, like, 'Oh, look! A first poop! Isn't it cute!' On the back of every photo I've ever taken, I write when and what it was. I want it all recorded, because if I'm not there one day to tell the story to my kids, at least they'll have a pictorial record."

Forty-six-year-old Dierdre, who was fourteen when her mother died, says she documents everything about her two children and herself, "because I feel like there are so many black holes in my past, no mother to tell me the stories, and an extended family with good intentions but no willingness to talk about my momma or the past, good or bad. So, I want truths to be available for my kids if

something were to happen to me and I could not be there for them
or be there to talk to them."

Husbands can't be relied upon to remember the details of a
pregnancy, or the age when a first tooth appeared, or a child's
first word, twenty years after the fact. Most of us know this from
frustrating conversations with our own fathers when we've tried to
extract this information. The responsibility for cataloguing a childhood history, as we know, belongs to the mother. Making sure the
mother is photographed and videotaped—we know the importance
of that, too. And so, we become the endless chroniclers of our own
existence, every video we take and every scrapbook page we create
affirming, *I was here. You mattered. I cared.*

"Whenever I go on an overnight trip, I write a several-page
letter to my kids, which talks about what's going on in their lives at
that point in time," Therese Rando says. "I don't have the discipline
or the time to keep a daily journal, but they have scores of these letters they can put together to essentially form a chronology of our
family's life. I can't tell you how many rolls of film we have that
aren't even developed. It's *ludicrous*. But I just keep taking photos.
It's the notion of trying to create something permanent. The other
day, my son was at the keyboard, singing with my husband, and I
was sitting there enjoying it, and then I said, 'But I should really get
the videocamera and put this down for posterity.' I don't want to
miss the moment as it's happening, but I'm so concerned that I'll
want to have the video at some future point.

"I think the impulse to chronicle comes from two directions,"
she continues. "One is we don't want to leave our children without
this stuff, because we have our own feelings about wishing we'd had
more. I don't know anyone who says, 'I have enough memories,
enough pictures, enough artifacts from my mother.' And it's also
about not wanting to be forgotten, and wanting to make sure there's
a permanent record of some kind."

These moments with our children are precious, we know. They
might need proof of their existence one day. So, we run for the

cameras and the camcorders, determined to preserve it all, every memorable moment of it, even if being the videographer means standing on the sidelines as the experience unfolds.

"You're trying to enjoy the moment, you don't want to forget it because of what you know from the past, and you want to make sure it'll be in the future," Therese Rando says. "These are complex demands, basically, and they're contradictory."

My family photos from the 1960s and 1970s are a haphazard collection, a bulging shopping bag stuffed with hundreds of Polaroid and Instamatic shots. My parents never kept photo albums or scrapbooks, but in an act of almost eerie prescience, my mother kept painstakingly detailed baby books for all her children. Mine is page after page of information recorded in her careful, beautiful script about my early behaviors, hospital visitors, favorite foods, favorite toys, dental records, vaccination records, even a congratulatory form letter from the White House in response to the birth announcement my mother mailed to Lyndon Johnson.

I keep my baby book in a cabinet in our living room now, along with the book my grandmother kept for my mother in 1938, and the ones I created for my daughters in 1997 and 2001. Every winter, when we pack our evacuation boxes in case of a sudden wildfire, these books go right on top. When I share this with Rebecca, she nods steadily in agreement. "I have my baby book, too," she says. "I constantly referred to it as my children started to grow. If I wondered, 'When did I start solid foods?' I'd look it up. At six weeks?! 'Mother! What were you *thinking*?' I looked up everything. Booster shots. Polio shots. I relied on my baby book to reflect about my choices and to see what my mother had done. I really felt connected to her, as a mother, because of it."

Comparing the pages my mother wrote to the pages I've kept for my daughters, that back-and-forth motion, is as close as I ever get to a parenting dialogue with my mother. I can imagine her pleasure at seeing how closely Maya's early development mirrored mine, or her surprise—and my defensive explanation—upon seeing

Eden's empty vaccination page. Yet, at the same time, seeing written proof that I was formula-fed from the start, and that I started sleeping through the night at six weeks, reminds me that my mother wouldn't have been able to advise me about breast-feeding, or about how to sleep-train a ten-month-old child without letting her cry it out. The mother of my fantasy collapses into a mother of probable reality when I read the record she kept of our first year together, and in many ways, that's a relief. It reminds me that my mother wouldn't have had all the answers, as I so often imagine she would.

Of course, before you can carefully record memories for a child, you first need to have them. Unforgettable birthday parties, exotic family vacations, elaborate holiday celebrations—in a motherless mother's quest to create happy, lasting memories for her children, she's not above orchestrating events with posterity in mind.

For several years, I volunteered to host our neighborhood Halloween party, spending days decorating the house and planning the menu. Yet, as much as I enjoyed the festivities, a part of me always felt urgent and overdetermined as I hung the handmade paper ghosts and bats, as if they were a way of proclaiming, *I'm an involved mom! I'm a fun mom! You'll remember me this way, right?* My husband recently pointed out that last year's party for seventy friends and neighbors—including close to thirty shrieking children running circles through our house until nearly ten P.M.—was too noisy and chaotic for anyone's enjoyment, least of all our own kids. So, this year, I said nothing when a neighbor offered to take over the Halloween helm.

A motherless mother needs to be especially clear about whom the party, so to speak, is actually for. Is it with her child's best interest in mind? Or is it intended to nurture the lost and needy child she once was, after her mother died? If the answer is the latter, she then needs to ask: Is this something my children actually enjoy? And if not, what other (easier, cheaper, more collaborative) method exists for me to get my own need met?

When I look back now on those five days I spent in France with

Maya, the whole thing is almost comical. Two thousand dollars and five years later, her only memory of that trip is riding the Ferris wheel by the Louvre. Maybe one day the photos will interest her. In the meantime, the next time I want to make a lasting impression on a preschooler, I'm going to remember two words: Sea and World. It's only two hours away, and my husband can share the drive.

12

It's About the Child

KEEPING THE FOCUS CLEAR

*B*efore Maya was born, before she was even conceived, I knew what kind of mother I wanted to be: the kind who would plan elaborate birthday parties, lug oversize coolers of Gatorade to soccer games, and tweeze every splinter myself. I'd cook banana chocolate-chip pancakes for breakfast; I'd play marathon rounds of Sorry and Operation, if that was how she wanted to spend an afternoon. She, in turn, would have idyllic early years filled with lawn cartwheels and summer camp; clothing that was clean, pretty, and always matched; and a mother-daughter relationship that extended far beyond seventeen years. The plan was to give her all the finer aspects of my own childhood while neatly sidestepping the painful ones. She would get to be the child I once was, and then the adolescent and young adult I never got to be.

Four years later, when Eden came along, I tried to multiply my good intentions by two, but before long a major flaw began to surface in my plan. My daughters, it seemed, weren't terribly interested in following my lead. They didn't like the games I'd liked as a child. (*"Uno?"* I found myself saying. "What the heck is *that?*") The books I'd once cherished—The Bobbsey Twins series, *Flat Stanley*, and *The Little House*—didn't pull rank against *Captain Underpants* or *I Spy*. And whereas I'd once been obsessive about ice-skating and gymnastics, Maya only wanted swimming, and Eden had an early aptitude for dance.

It was a sobering moment, the day I realized my daughters weren't going to be smaller versions of me. Perhaps this states the obvious, but for a woman who waited half her lifetime to recreate the mother-daughter bond she lost, it is a new and startling observation to be made every day. How can these children who emerged from my body have ideas and desires so different than I once had? How can our relationship be anything other than what I'd planned for so long?

As Daniel Stern reminds us, the desire to repair or redo one's own past vicariously through a child is a strong one. Most parents have unfulfilled wishes, paths not taken, dreams abandoned or deferred. Because raising a child—especially a same-sex child— inevitably causes a parent to revisit similar stages in her own past, motherhood gives us the chance to correct all the unfortunate events or missing pieces of our own childhoods by letting us get it right the second time. By raising our children, we always, to a certain degree, get to re-raise ourselves.

Parents who had unfortunate or difficult childhoods may be especially vulnerable to this phenomenon. When Maxine Harris interviewed sixty-six men and women who had lost a parent during childhood or adolescence for her 1995 book, *The Loss That Is Forever*, she found that, as parents themselves, these individuals had both a great deal of empathy for their children and a strong desire to provide whatever had been missing or taken from their own childhoods. But by making this a primary goal of their parenting, they often lost sight of whom they were trying to take care of: their children or themselves.

"Early loss freezes images in time," Harris explains. "Even when we become chronological adults, we often retain a vivid image of ourselves as children. Looking at one's own young son or daughter, it may be easy to see the face of one's childhood staring back. When this happens, a survivor of early loss risks treating a child as a reincarnation of his or her own childish self."

Parents naturally project a great deal onto their children, seeing in them the wished-for, distressed, or hurt parts of themselves. "Your own past affects your present-day actions most when you become a parent because you are once again dealing with the child in you," Michael Schwartzman explains in his book *The Anxious Parent*. "As a parent you may experience [with your child] something so similar to what once happened to you that you instantly identify with your own child. You feel *empathy*, a kind of connectedness and deep understanding of exactly what your child is going through." When we see our children reliving events similar to ones that we once lived, we naturally assume they're experiencing the same emotions we felt at the time. And our memories of how we once felt then guide the way we respond.

Let's take, for example, a girl with two older brothers, who loses her mother at age eleven and whose father never remarries. When puberty arrives two years later, she has to go through it without the support of a woman in the house. Her first menstruation is a confusing, lonely time, and she vows to herself that one day, when she has a daughter, she'll be there to celebrate the occasion with her and act as a compassionate guide.

Fast-forward thirty years, to a house in a leafy suburb, where the woman (let's call her Susan) is now forty-three, and her oldest daughter is about to turn thirteen. "Mom!" her daughter is shouting from the bathroom. "I need you! Come here! Quick!"

Susan has been waiting for this day for thirty years. She's got the speech planned, the feminine products stacked up in the cabinet under the bathroom sink, and a huge smile planted on her face as she rushes to the bathroom door. As she accompanies her daughter through the next half-hour, she is also guiding the thirteen-year-old version of herself, who went through these motions alone. Thirty years later, she gets to unravel the memory of that lonely day and replace it with the memory of this day, when she gives her daughter the support and guidance she never had. When Susan emerges from the bathroom with her arm around her daughter's shoulder, both women have just gone through a significant, transitional event.

Or, equally as possible, let's roll back the tape and watch the half-hour unfold like this, instead:

Susan rushes to the bathroom door. Opening it just a crack, her daughter asks for a pad to be passed through.

"Honey, can I come in?" Susan asks eagerly.

"It's okay. I can take care of it" is the reply. Or maybe it's "Mo-o-om. No!" Or even "Eeuw! Gross! I don't want *you* in here with me *now*!"

Or maybe Susan's daughter is eleven when it happens, and she's panicked and confused. Or maybe she's fourteen, and it happens at school, and Susan doesn't even hear about it for another three months. When she discovers the box of pads in her daughter's bathroom and responds with a mix of exhilaration and disappointment, her daughter can't understand what the big deal is about.

And why should she? Susan's daughter operates from a point of view that doesn't have to take mother loss into consideration. Her mother has always been there, and there's every reason for her to believe her mother will always be there. Yet for Susan, a motherless point of view is the only point of view there is. She's propelled by memories of growing up without a mother, of managing without female support, of always being the girl who was different from the rest. And this skews her parenting in a direction that constantly tries to make up for the motherless childhood she had.

"When my daughter was a year or two old, a friend of mine was over, and we were playing a game downstairs," remembers fifty-five-year-old Louise, who was six when her mother died. "I was putting my daughter to bed upstairs. She was terrible about going to sleep, and she was crying, 'Mommy! Mommy!' I kept running up there. This friend had five children and was a good deal older than me, and she made some comment like 'She's fine. She can just stay up there and she'll be okay.' And I said, 'I just remember the fear of lying in bed alone and not having a mother.' And my friend said, 'Your daughter *has* a mother.' That was such a shock to me. It really hadn't occurred to me before."

When Louise heard her daughter crying "Mommy!" she immediately traveled back in time to the frightened six-year-old she'd once been, the one who'd cried out at night for a mother who never came. Was Louise responding to her daughter when she went upstairs to comfort her, or was she answering the call of her childhood self? Probably both.

Mother loss may have echoed loudly every time we felt sad, lonely, isolated, angry, or confused as children or teens, but it's not the constant background music of our children's days. Yet we project the same depth of emotion we once felt onto their present-day hurts. A night with a babysitter isn't just a night at home; it becomes a night when the child is left behind, without a mother's comfort. A playground snub is never just a playground snub; it's an occasion, in our minds, for a son or daughter to feel like an outcast, lonely and uncertain and isolated from the rest.

"I react so much on impulse," admits forty-year-old Lisa, the mother of a ten-year-old daughter. "I don't even consider that this is not what my daughter is feeling or thinking. Sometimes, at night, I'll cry, 'Poor baby!' and my husband will be, like, "What are you *talking* about?"

Lisa was eight when her father died suddenly, and ten when she lost her mother. She went to live with an aunt and uncle who, after a year, turned her care over to her maternal grandparents. Although her grandparents gave Lisa adequate physical care and affection, no one in the family was equipped to handle the enormity of a child's grief. "I had nowhere to go but into my shell," Lisa quietly explains. On the one hand, this has motivated her as a mother to act as an advocate for her daughter's emotional well-being. On the other hand, Lisa admits that she spends a significant amount of time afraid that her daughter will feel lonely or sad. Has she confused her daughter with the child inside herself, she wonders, and is she behaving out of proportion to the situation at hand?

"Sometimes I'll look at her from afar, usually when we're out, and she seems so small, and I'll just start crying," Lisa says. "Because I love her so much. My son, it's, like, okay, fine, whatever. I always trust that he'll be all right. But I just have so many fear issues with my daughter. She's petite and she wears glasses and she has very pale skin, and when I see her at school . . . on the second day of school this year, I walked her over to her class line. I stood there with her, but she was, like, 'Bye!,' so I started to walk away. I kept turning around. I was watching her in this little group of kids, and she was just standing there. And I felt so scared for her.

"She was fine. She was, like, 'Oh, I'll go stand on line and wait until my friends come,' but I was, like, '*Oh my God.*' I was just so afraid that she was feeling alone, that she would feel that emptiness I once felt. I went home that day and cried."

Watching her ten-year-old daughter standing by herself gave Lisa direct access to memories of all the times she stood alone, literally and figuratively, after her parents died. Being alone herself, as an adult, doesn't have this effect on her, she says. It's seeing her daughter, and identifying with her as a child, that triggers Lisa's sadness and fear. In that moment, the little girl she gave birth to and the "little girl" inside her fuse into one. Intellectually, Lisa can discriminate between her daughter and herself, even point out that whatever loneliness Ally feels would be small compared to what Lisa once felt, but emotionally, in those moments, she experiences the two of them as one.

That's the difference between identifying and overidentifying, explains Donald Zall, DSW, BCD. "When you empathize, you're actually able to have a sense of what the other person's thoughts and feelings may be, but you know that you are you and they are them," he says. "When you overidentify, the line gets blurred. You may act more like a child, or be so protective and so rigid that there's no room for the child to move."

The single most common parenting behavior among all the women I interviewed was the way their own motherless childhoods served as a sort of reverse parenting guide. They based important parenting decisions on replenishing or resurrecting what they once lost, and on creating what (if not for the loss) might otherwise have been. But by seeing our children primarily as younger versions of ourselves instead of as the unique individuals they are, do we deny them the kind of mothering they deserve?

When we project the vulnerabilities of a motherless child onto our own child, it's difficult to deny him anything at all. We want to fill every emotional need he has, never wanting him to feel abandoned or rejected, not even for a moment, as long as we're here to protect him. So we tip the balance far in the other direction. We overcompensate like mad, engaging in crazy parenting gymnastics to give him every drop of mothering we want him to have. This is why I leave my office at five P.M. every Thursday and drive half an hour uphill to get home just to spend thirty minutes with my daughters before Jillian, our Thursday night babysitter, arrives. Once they're settled, I drive half an hour back down the same exact route and then drive another twenty minutes past my office to meet my husband for dinner.

This makes no sense to him. Granted, it makes sense to no one except me.

"Paula works until six, and Jillian arrives at six," Uzi reminds me almost weekly. "So why don't you just come straight from your office to mine?"

"Because then the girls go twenty-two hours without seeing me."

Well, they go twenty-two hours without seeing him every Thursday, and they seem to be surviving. That's what his expression says. Plus, gas prices being what they are. Plus, they adore Jillian. Parents are pieces of mobile furniture to them when she's around.

So, what's my explanation? Just that I'm the mother. Which means I'm supposed to be around. I'm supposed to be doing, well, *everything*. Until they tell me not to. Which I may or may not ignore.

"I smile sometimes to think of all the overcompensating we do as motherless moms that tends to be overlooked or underappreciated by our children, whose needs are often incompatible with our own," Gina Mireault says. An encounter she had with her school-age son regarding his lunchbox illuminated this point to her. "I'd turned packing his lunchbox into a Martha Stewart event—complete with seasonal napkins and all four food groups, mostly to make up for the substandard lunches I had to take to school after my mother died," she explains. "Packing his lunches actually became thoroughly stressful for me. He magically let me off the hook by asking me to *please* not pack him a special napkin, and also asking that his lunch be the same meal every day. What I thought was a maternal failure—the same ordinary lunch every day—was actually a maternal success in his eyes. Those kinds of moments help release me from the grip of motherlessness, because they force me to confront my fantasies of 'good mothering' with the reality of what my children actually do and don't want from me. One of my friends, a motherless mother, said it well when she mused that 'just being alive for them should be enough!'"

It's important—necessary, even—to imagine what it feels like to be your child and, through this understanding, to determine how to best meet his needs. But any past emotions revived through parenting a child need to be resolved separate from that child. "*Very* separate from the child," emphasizes Michael Schwartzman. "*Very* separate."

Self-healing through motherhood works best when it's a corollary to child-rearing rather than a goal. There's nothing wrong with finding healing through the parenting process. When it happens as a happy accident, even better. There's a problem, however, when a woman deliberately turns to her child, or even gives birth to a child, to meet her own unresolved emotional needs.

"If you have a need to cuddle and you have a small child, and you cuddle her and that's good for her and it's good for you, that's fine," Maxine Harris explains. "But if she's now fifteen and it's not good for her anymore but you still need the warmth and those loving arms around you, you need to find another way to get it. The parenting experience is most wonderful when there's a match between what you need and what your child needs, and you're both getting well nurtured at the same time."

A child who exists to meet a parent's needs, or who is confused with a younger version of the parent's self, is a child denied her own identity. And isn't that exactly the opposite of what we want? Most of us carry the hope that our children will be free to reach their fullest potential. That's what many of us feel *we* lost when childhood and adolescence became years to get through instead of years in which to thrive.

Giving one's child the freedom to be a separate entity and make choices of his own—choices that not only don't heal us but may even hurt us—is a hard yet necessary step. It involves separating the image of one's child from the image of one's younger self. It means reminding ourselves, as many times a day as necessary, that our children are not feeling exactly what we once felt. That they do not always need, or even want, what we once lost and have been trying to recapture ever since.

"You can't expect that what worked for you, or would have worked for you, will work for your children," Michael Schwartzman says. "Even though they may share your genes and a similar environment, they also come from somebody else. They're wired differently than you were, and because of that, they have a different sensibility about things. That's why mothers' groups are so good, and why best friends are so helpful. You need a lot of feedback. You need to be able to walk around what you're doing and look at it from the outside."

That's what forty-three-year-old Suzanne learned last year. Suzanne, who was fifteen when her mother died of an aneurysm, had made elaborate plans for her daughter's sixteenth birthday, involving a weekend for two at a nearby resort and spa. She was hoping the event would be memorable for her daughter, and also healing for her, because this was the birthday she and her mother had planned for but never got to spend together.

But Suzanne's daughter had other ideas. Her school ski club had organized a trip for that week, and she wanted to go with her friends. "I was, like, 'How can you even consider that?'" Suzanne recalls. "We had terrible arguments about it, awful fights where I ended up crying a couple of times. She really couldn't understand why her birthday was so important to me. Finally, I decided I wanted to spend the weekend with her, but I didn't want her memory of her sixteenth birthday to be one of being forced to be with me, just to make me feel better. So I said, 'Okay. You can go on the trip.' But I grieved terribly while she was gone. It felt like such a loss to me. Such a letting go of that dream I'd had all these years. She, on the other hand, had a fantastic time. She got back and said, 'Mom, thank you so much for letting me go.' So, in the end, I was glad that she went."

By giving her daughter the freedom to join her friends, and by not making her daughter shoulder responsibility for her mother's feelings, Suzanne took an important step toward separating her need for emotional healing from her daughter's need for autonomy. Her choice also forced her to recognize a fundamental difference between the two of them. Suzanne had once been a fifteen-year-old grieving for a lost mother, but her daughter had been a fifteen-year-old *with* a mother, a daughter who felt secure enough to leave her mother for a week and return, knowing she would still be accepted and loved.

"The daughter didn't have to deal with having lost a mother, and wanting to rectify that," Therese Rando points out. "The part that's most interesting to me was that this mother was healthy enough to let her child go on the trip. Because there would be many other mothers who would find a way to not let that happen."

I'm not sure I could do it myself. Not yet. My daughters are still young enough to want to spend time with me, and I love the interaction. A day spent with them isn't just a day spent with them. It's an affirmation of our connection, a reminder that I'm here, interested in them, loving them, being with them in the way that only a mother can. A day that I don't spend with them feels like a day in which they might feel abandoned, or cry for me, or have to settle for something less, and the idea of that I cannot stand.

Children give us love, nurturing, and unconditional acceptance. And it's so delicious, so deliriously wonderful to have this connection back again that it can easily cloud our parenting decisions. "I so enjoy being with my kids," says forty-two-year-old Sarah, who was nine when her mother committed suicide and now has a ten-year-old son and an eight-year-old daughter. "And I so enjoy being a mother that, you know what, I just want to be with them all the time. We'll do playdates sometimes, but usually we'll just go by ourselves to the mall. Now I see that this is what they prefer. And I'm not sure that's a good thing. My son would rather stay home with Mommy and play than go out and be with friends. That motherless-daughter need [I have] for constant attention and connection and reassurance that children are so good about giving—well, I've had to start letting go of that and say to them, 'Wait a minute. Go outside and play. Who do you want me to call? When do you want them to come over?' I really have to work at it. And my son has to work at it, too, because he'll say, 'Oh no, Mom, let's you and I have a me-and-Mommy day.'"

As Sarah's children get older, she finds they're acutely aware of her blind spots. By now, they know what to say or ask for to get the results they want. She admits that some of this is because of the way she parented them. Because she was so quick to overcompensate as a mother, she says, she had trouble enforcing consistent boundaries and rules. When her children learned she could be easily swayed by their requests for comfort or attention, they asked for it more often.

"I have to work harder every day to not react to a tantrum, or

to not react to 'But Mommy, I don't feel well. I don't want to go to
school today. I need to be with you,'" she says. "It's so easy for me
to say, 'Oh, you've got a mommy, of course you can stay home with
me.' Versus 'Get your little butt to school. You don't have a fever.'
It's really, really hard to know when to be tough and when to give
in. As they get older and more manipulative, it's becoming a constant game for me, wondering, *Are you or aren't you sick enough to stay
home, or do you need something emotional from me?*"

When Sarah realized her own desire for connection and attention was affecting her children's behavior, she started seeing a
family therapist. "Therapy gives me an opportunity to ask someone,
'What's happening when my child does this?'" Sarah says. "It helps
me keep the focus on 'I'm the adult. He's the child,' and not go into
some of that regression stuff that goes on in a parent's head when
she's still needy. Because then it becomes 'I don't want to attend to
your needs now. I need to get *my* needs met.' And it's also helped
me learn how to be consistent with my kids, and to set boundaries.
If your mother dies, as mine did, from depression and suicide, the
boundaries are blurred. If you have a mother who's sickly for a long
time, you start taking care of her. And then you start creating a relationship where your children take care of you."

Sarah fell into the pattern of letting her own longing for closeness override the decisions she knew she should make. How many of
us would say we, on occasion, have done the same? *It's only preschool,*
I tell myself on a morning when Eden is lobbying to stay home with
me. *And I've been working so hard all week.* But it gets harder to say *it's
only third grade* without feeling a little twinge of guilt, and seriously
difficult to believe *it's only high school* more than once or twice a year.

To keep the focus of parenting on my daughters' unique needs,
instead of on my own lingering desire for comfort, protection, security, and control has been perhaps my biggest challenge as a mother.
Every day I have to remind myself that my job isn't to be the mother
I once had, or the mother I once wanted, but instead to be the
mother my children need me to be. It sounds so easy, but it's so

incredibly hard, to let go of trying to mother myself through mothering my children, and to just allow myself to be the best mother I can be. Not the mother in the mirror. Just the mother I am.

So soon, I know, I'll be replaced by their friends. And then how hard it will be to let them go, knowing that our connection will be replaced, on their end, by their connections to others. And that this is how it has to be, for them to separate and grow. I only hope I can remain clear that I'm the parent when that time comes, and not slide back into being the child who's still looking for love.

Forty-three-year-old Nova felt this starting to happen just a few months ago, and her first impulse was to hold on tight. Nova, who was fourteen when her mother committed suicide, now has a son and a daughter, ages twelve and nine. "Both my sisters have criticized me over the years, saying I'm too involved with my kids," she says. "Every day, part of my day is spent thinking of neat things to do with them." Nova works a thirty-hour workweek, and her weekends are reserved for family time. Her son is already more interested in spending time with friends, but she and her daughter share a passion for crafts. So, a few months ago, Nova made reservations for the two of them to take a weekend felt-making class in their community.

So, Saturday morning comes, and she's, like, "Ugh! Do I have to go? I want to go with a friend!" I know, it's more typical than not for a nine-year-old to want this, but I couldn't help taking it personally. And the timing was bad, too. I'd been feeling really sad and down that week. I said, "Come on, it's going to be fun. You said you wanted to do it, and we signed up." It was just this huge battle. She was in the room, screaming as she got dressed. And I started getting sadder and sadder, and finally I just burst into tears. I felt like I was trying so hard to think of fun things to do, to be a good mother, and she didn't appreciate it at all. It ended up that she was crying, I was crying, and I said, "We have to go. We're going to be late."

So, we got in the car, and we were driving down the road, and she said, "Mommy, I love you." I said, "I love you, too. And no matter how mad we get, we're always going to love each other. I was just looking forward to spending the day with you." She said, "I want to. I want to have fun, but now we can't because we're both mad at each other." I told her, "We can get past this. We can leave it in the car when we get there." We did, and we ended up having a great day.

Mothers are, after all, human. We hurt. We cry. It's impractical to think we can shield our children from our emotions, nor should we. Letting them believe we lead emotionally flat lives sets them up for a standard of stoicism impossible for them to meet. At the same time, seeing us regress to an earlier emotional state can frighten a child. They need to be quickly reminded that we're still in control. They also need to know that they're not the cause of an outburst.

Explaining how we're feeling, in real-time, to children old enough to understand is essential. Even small children can grasp, "Mommy's feeling sad right now, but it's not because of you." And then we have to realign the parent-child power structure. We have to step back, take some deep breaths, and remind ourselves: *I'm the parent here. I'm the one in control.*

By doing exactly this, Nova was able to turn her momentary lapse that Saturday morning into a learning experience for her daughter. We may get mad at each other, she explained out loud, but we will always love each other. The subtext of her message was, Mothers and daughters may get mad at each other, but that won't make a mother leave. This was an important point for Nova to restate for herself, as well. After losing a mother to suicide, she carried with her the fear of others leaving abruptly and without warning. Reassuring her daughter in this manner also reminded and reassured her that she is not a mother who will leave. It reinforced that she can make different choices as a mother than her mother once did.

Our children are not us. We are not our mothers. I feel compelled to say this again. It's such a simple statement, yet, in practice, so hard to accept. I'm reminded of an early interview I did for this book, with a woman named Ruth, who met me at a busy coffee shop in the middle of a weekday afternoon. My babysitter had canceled at the last minute, so I had to bring Eden along. She was sleeping in her infant car seat, and I kept rocking the stroller with my foot throughout the interview, hoping to buy us just a little extra time. Ruth was a stunning, poised woman in her mid-forties, with two sons, ages twenty and seventeen, and an eleven-year-old daughter. She exuded a quiet wisdom about parenting, and I wanted to hear everything she was willing to share.

Ruth was eleven and the youngest of seven children when her mother died of cancer. She speaks of those years in a subdued tone, but her voice brightens considerably when she speaks of raising her sons, in whom she takes obvious delight and pride. Her tone then changes to more thoughtful and introspective when she talks about parenting her daughter. Raising sons was a wholly gratifying experience, she explains, but accompanying her daughter through childhood involves much deeper emotional work for her. She feels a close connection with all her children, but her daughter, Emily, is the one who breaks her heart with regularity. It's hard, Ruth says, much harder than with her sons, to keep her daughter's emotions compartmentalized from her own.

> We're so close. And I feel that my work going through these years with her is to be the adult here, and to check in with myself a lot without making it about me. Because raising her hits these hot spots that I don't have immediate control over. One day I picked up her and another little girl from school to bring them to the girl's house for a playdate. The whole way there, this little girl kept saying, "You know, I don't really want to play with you. I want to play with my neighbor Steffi instead." I could see Emily getting hurt. By the time we got to this girl's house, I thought I was going to throw up. I was *so upset*.

After I dropped them off, I got back in the car and called my husband. The secretary said, "There are twelve people in his office," and I said, "I think you need to interrupt him." So, he picked up the phone with this whole meeting going on and I burst into tears. I was sobbing, "Sophie didn't want to play with Emily!" and he was, like, "Where are you? *Pull over!*" I was practically having a nervous breakdown. So, I pulled over and I said, "I don't know what just came over me" and I burst out laughing. I was okay after that. But it is so funny how in that moment . . . I was sitting there thinking, *How do I go to those places? I'm a grown-up!* It's so complicated.

No Pain, No Gain

The first time it happens, Maya's in kindergarten. When I pick her up at the bus stop, something is obviously wrong. She doesn't want to talk. She sits burrowed in the back seat, solemn and depressed. At dinner, she picks at the food on her plate.

"What's going on?" I ask her.

"Nothing."

"Did you have a hard day? Do you want to tell me about it?"

"No."

Finally, when we're reading a book before bedtime, she's ready to talk.

"Nobody wanted to play with me at school today," she says.

I prop myself up on an elbow. She's always had friends at school. There was a tough time a few months ago, when she missed a week of school and by the time she returned, her best friend had found another, but I thought we'd ironed that one out. Maybe she just *felt* left out today?

"What happened?"

"At recess, I didn't have anyone to play with."

"So, what did you do?"

"I had to play alone."

The image of her wandering the perimeter of the soccer field, trying to interest herself in rocks and sticks until the bell rings, slices deep. I remember the feeling so clearly. Lunchtime. Looking around the cafeteria for a friendly face. Knowing I'd have to sit alone. Spending most of lunch in the bathroom, to avoid it.

"I don't have any friends at school," she adds.

"What about Lucy and Alexis? Aren't they your best friends?"

"They want to play with each other."

"What about Sierra?"

"She only wants to play horses."

"Rory?"

"She's mean to me."

"I'll tell you what," I say to her, kissing the top of her head. I try to think fast. "I'll come help out in your class this week and I'll see what's going on. And if the other kids are being mean to you or leaving you out, I'll talk to the teacher about it. Okay?"

She nods, her head buried in my arm. I kiss her good-night and turn out the light. Then I go upstairs to Uzi, who's working on his laptop in bed, and fill him in on the tragic details.

"So, I guess that's that," I conclude.

"That's what?" he murmurs. He's still tapping away at the keyboard.

"That's *that*. We have to find her another school." Chop-chop. That's how I say it. Like my mind is made up, and nothing will change it now.

"Whoa," Uzi says. This gets him to close his laptop. "Don't you think that's a little premature?"

"No." Well, maybe. So? The thought of Maya marching off to school so bravely every morning, without complaint, into a classroom where no one will play with her, into snack times and recesses she has to spend alone . . . no. We can't allow that to continue. We have to solve this problem. Right now. Another school, with friendlier kids. That's the answer.

Uzi shakes his head. "I just don't get you sometimes," he says. Which is the only understatement of the evening.

Let's take a step back and look at what may have been going on with me that night. For sure, I was empathizing with Maya, having felt excluded as a child, too. That kind of empathy was fine. As I stated earlier, it's important—necessary, even—to empathize with one's child, to imagine that you know what it feels like to be her and, through this understanding, to try to help meet her emotional needs.

I was also identifying with Maya, as my own memories of being left out on the playground and desperately wishing I could attend a different school came flooding back. This is a completely normal process. All parents do it. Watching our children, especially our same-sex children, pass through significant developmental phases reactivates our emotional memory surrounding those events. Fortunately, this kind of identification forges a unique emotional link between parent and child. Unfortunately, this phenomenon doesn't discriminate: we get to reexperience all our childhood events, the exhilarating and the lousy.

If I'd stopped at identification that night, the situation would have been easy to resolve. I might have recognized that I was projecting what I'd once felt as a gawky, shy, overly sensitive first-grader onto my strong-willed, confident six-year-old, and then I could have separated Maya's experience from mine, and gone on to help her solve her current problem rather than a historical version of mine.

But that isn't where the empathy stopped. It kept going, and going, past overidentification, all the way down to the memory of profound loss and pain and all the sadness and confusion that came with it. It went straight to the years I felt unprotected and overlooked when my mother was dying, and after she was gone. And the possibility that my children could ever feel that vulnerable or that sad is completely unacceptable to me. I *had* to act. I had no choice.

You see, my kids aren't allowed to feel emotional pain. Or, to be more specific, emotional pain isn't allowed to find them. I don't want them to ever feel a tenth, not even a hundredth, of the loneliness or grief I once had to face. I can't bear to hear them crying for me. Or to know that they're feeling abandoned, or disappointed, or rejected, or sad, or settling for anything. That's the worst. To watch them bravely trying to make themselves happy with something less than what they'd hoped for or expected, to see them trying to turn a disappointing situation into something acceptable to them, something that's just sort of okay—this cracks my heart in half, every time. It makes me want to saw open my breastbone and wrap my own skin around them as a shield. It makes me willing to do anything, *anything*, to take their hurt away.

It seems I've got a case of what psychologists call "pain intolerance," the inability to withstand a child's sadness, anger, disappointment, loneliness, or grief without trying to deny, minimize, or "fix" the suffering. It's the reason why a mother who can't tolerate her child crying out for her at night struggles with teaching her child to fall asleep alone. It's why a mother will call the parents of the child who snubbed her daughter on the playground that day, trying to extract an apology. And it makes a mother bribe the college student next door to be her son's prom date after two other girls have turned him down, because she can't stand the thought of him spending that night home alone.

"I don't want to baby my kids, because I believe that I am who I am because of having to figure out so much on my own," says forty-two-year-old Alma, the mother of three daughters ages five to fourteen, who was ten when her mother died. "But it's hard, because if they're upset about a typical teenage thing, I want to fix it like this—" she snaps her fingers twice. "It's, like, I need to take care of it, I need to make it right for them. I have a girlfriend who's always telling me, You can't do this. While you're still figuring out how to fix their problems, they've moved on, but you're caught up in "No one fixed my problems, so I'm going to fix theirs." I try not to let my daughters see how I want to take care of things for them, but in my mind, I get kind of depressed and crazy that I can't. I'm always so relieved when a problem is solved. And then, the next hour, there's another one."

It's natural for a parent to want to spare a child pain of any kind, but mothers who lost their own mothers during childhood find a child's distress especially taxing, says Henri Parens, MD, a professor of psychiatry at Jefferson Medical College and a training and supervising analyst at the Psychoanalytic Center of Philadelphia. The reality of a child's pain brings a motherless mother straight back to a time in her life when she was left alone and un-provided for, without adequate tools for coping. It brings her back to the memory of emotions she doesn't want to ever feel again. That's the root cause of pain intolerance. It's not that we can't tolerate these emotions in our children. It's that we can't tolerate reliving these emotions ourselves.

"The pain of a woman's own unresolved mourning invades everything," Parens explains. "It colors everything. So, a child's small hurt on a playground becomes a much bigger thing for the mother, and resonates with the internal, existing pain of mourning. That's a big obstacle for most very good parents: they can't tolerate their own past mourning being revivified, and having to deal with their own child's issues at the same time."

Parens claims that women suffer pain intolerance with both sons and daughters, and from interviews conducted with women who have children of only one gender, this does appear to be true. Women who have children of both genders, however, speak very clearly about having a stronger impulse to shield their daughters, perhaps because they identify with their daughters' experiences to a more specific degree.

"To my son, 'no' meant 'no,'" admits Sarah, who lost her mother to suicide and later suffered from a clinical depression herself. "If he cried, I was never good at tolerating it, but eventually I did learn to tolerate it enough so he had a clear sense of how things would be. With my daughter, 'no' was always 'maybe.' It was 'I want you to have a better childhood than I had.' It was 'I want you to break the pattern so that you can have a happy life. And if it means I have to give you everything, I will.'"

It's human and automatic to want to protect a child from any form of pain. It's unrealistic, however, to think that we can. A life fully lived inevitably includes some hardships, disappointments, and adversity. A child needs to learn how to handle these moments. He needs to learn how to mourn the losses of everyday life: a friend who rejects him, a last-place finish, the death of a pet cockatiel. But a child can't learn how to tolerate the naturally painful events of childhood if his mother won't let him experience any childhood events as painful.

As hard as it may be for us to accept, we who have spent large portions of our lives mourning and wishing this hadn't been the case, the ability to mourn small losses is an essential part of childhood development. Children who learn how to suffer disappointments and anxiety without interference develop the psychic resources for handling larger crises as adults. By disallowing our children to experience sadness or grief—even when we do it out of altruism or love—we block a natural process. And to a lesser degree, we repeat the cycle of what happened to us when our mourning was blocked, ignored, or dismissed when our mothers left or died.

The theory behind homeopathy is to expose the body, over time, to small doses of an irritant, to slowly build up resistance. The same is true for children's tolerance to distress. A child learns how to manage disappointment, loss, and anxiety by facing small stressful events spaced out over time. This is the concept of "optimal anxiety," the idea that children need to be exposed to a certain threshold of distress in order to develop the inner resources they need. But how can we, as mothers, know where that threshold lies? We, who crossed it too fast and so young? It's hard for us to know exactly where, in a comparatively uneventful childhood, such a line would be found.

The "right" amount of optimal anxiety varies with a child's age and temperament, as well as with a family's cultural values, explains

Alicia Lieberman, PhD. "However, even within a particular culture, knowledgeable adults differ in their views of how much anxiety, frustration, or stress are 'just right' for an individual child," she writes. "There is no mathematical formula for calculating exact amounts of optimal anxiety. This is why child rearing is an art and not a science, and why parents need to stay in touch with their personal convictions in deciding how much anxiety their child can tolerate."

A similar theory involves "optimum frustration," which proposes that children need exposure to small amounts of frustration as well. "There needs to be a balance between gratifying and frustrating experiences," explains Benjamin Garber, MD. "A certain amount of frustration has to be experienced in order for a child to move forward developmentally. If a kid isn't ever allowed to soothe himself, then how is he going to learn?"

By engaging in small struggles, and mastering them, children develop feelings of competence and self-confidence. They learn to trust their own opinions and become resourceful. Failures are important, too. Only by testing our own ideas do we learn which ones serve us well and which should be avoided.

"If you never let [a child] try anything on his own, he'll always be sheltered, ruled, and influenced by your opinions," Michael Schwartzman explains in *The Anxious Parent*. "If you never allow him to get close to an emotionally difficult situation, you'll stunt him developmentally and emotionally. How will your son or daughter learn to cope out in the world if you are always holding him, standing behind him, doing for him the things that he must learn to do for himself?

"If you're 'kind' enough to remove all obstacles and strife, your child will never discover the magic of his own potential. Only by giving him the freedom to explore—within appropriate boundaries and limitations—will he be able to develop the emotional skills he needs to check and test and modulate his own feelings."

Sometimes the mother of the playground bully does need to be called about her child's behavior. And sometimes a child does need to be protected from an inappropriately harsh teacher. That's when stepping back to calmly assess a situation, or asking a trusted friend or professional for a reality check, is important. In situations like these, I have to ask myself if my impulse to intervene comes from experience or emotion. Is this an occasion that objectively calls for an adult to step in? Or is my own emotional distress about to make me act in a way I'm going to later regret?

A child's temperament also needs to be factored in. An emotionally resilient child can probably manage more distress or anxiety on her own than one with a timid or highly sensitive personality. One of my daughters struggles hard to accept any small disappointment, while the other shrugs them all off. That's just how they were born.

Psychologists might have different opinions on the amount of distress each individual child can withstand, but all psychologists would agree on this: the optimal amount, for any child, is never zero. When adults stifle a child's grief expressions, hostility may surface in the child. Additionally, children who are taught to hide or suppress their feelings of sadness and loss may grow into adults who have difficulty expressing their feelings or accepting the feelings of others. To that, I'd add that children whose parents quickly rush in to rescue a child, to remove or fix the cause of painful feelings, risk raising children who grow up dependent on others to reassure them and minimize their distress, and never learn how to do it for themselves.

"All kids, all people, like to have things happen to them passively, and also to be active, aggressive, and assertive on their own behalf and to make things happen," Michael Schwartzman says. "When you have a parent who makes all the decisions and runs what goes on because of their own intolerance for the emotional field that's around them, you run into many, many problems." Enormous friction can develop between child and parent, he explains. It also becomes difficult for a child to trust the judgment of a parent who constantly hovers.

Additionally, a child who grows up aware that her feelings of sadness or distress cause upset in the house may start hiding or suppressing them in an attempt to protect her mother. Or, even worse, she may start to believe there's something inherently wrong with these feelings—and, by extension, with herself. Children who are expected to feel happy all the time are robbed of their genuine emotions, and may be set up for a lifelong pattern of anxiety.

Identifying the patterns in our own households and changing them is tough emotional work—slow going, but eminently possible. With help from her therapist, Sarah has been zeroing in on the dynamic that exists between her and her daughter, and is trying to guide her daughter toward different coping skills when disappointments arise.

I've had to start letting go of my own need to pacify her. When she cries over a disappointment, like having had to sit out of recess for five minutes, I want to sit and cuddle and hug her, because it feels so good. Then I'll realize, "I just spent an hour holding my daughter over this disappointment." Yeah, she needs some attention, but I feed into it by making disappointment something so overwhelming that it needs an hour of cuddling with Mommy, to the exclusion of either of us doing anything else.

I'm trying to learn how to say, "You know what? This is a disappointment and I need to hold you, but disappointments, well, we need to get over them. You can cry for as long as you need to. But you really need to find another way to feel better. You want to go bang on the piano? You want to work on the computer? Mommy loves you, but this is no longer making sense."

It's so hard to know these outer limits of appropriate, to know where to set the boundaries, when our own childhoods were crisscrossed with dividing lines that were inappropriate or premature. So we create our own guidelines. Because we once longed for an available mother, we commit to becoming one. Because we had too much pain in our childhoods, we try to give our children lives with minimal distress.

Really, what a child needs most is for his feelings to be heard. The very first step toward getting past pain intolerance is to allow a child to say whatever he needs to say, and to listen with an open heart rather than rushing in to "soothe, fix, advise, criticize, instruct, admonish, and do whatever else we do naturally that shuts down the lines of communication," as Harriet Lerner says. It means staying right in that moment with our child, without letting our thoughts backpedal to the past.

This first step involves letting the child's distress be something that belongs to the child, not to us. And then to treat it as such.

"I'm trying to learn how to let my daughter just talk when she's upset," Lisa says, "because I know it makes her feel better when I'm not always throwing my two cents in or trying to take care of it right away. If a girl at school is mean to her, I let her talk about it, and then I'll explain to her why girls do that, and let her know she's done the right thing in handling it. It doesn't make her feel 100 percent better, but it helps. I still want to go to that girl's house and kick her butt, or to tell my daughter what she should say next time. I'm very opinionated. But I'm trying to be quiet and listen, even when it's hard."

The first trip I took without Maya was in the fall of 2000, when she was three years old. I flew to New York on a Wednesday and planned to stay until Saturday afternoon, three nights, the longest we'd been separated since she was born. Before I left, I read bedtime stories into a tape recorder for her to listen to every night, and I called home Wednesday after I landed, Thursday morning at breakfast time, and Thursday after she got home from school. Late Friday morning, as I was striding north on Leroy Street to catch a taxi to a meeting, my cell phone rang.

"Mommeeee," Maya sobbed. Her voice was barely audible above the honks and screeches of car brakes. "I miss you so much. When are you coming home?"

I skidded to a stop in front of the Italian restaurant on the corner. A tiny, cold hand gripped my heart. I looked at my watch. It was 11:10 A.M. If I called the airline now, maybe I could get bumped up to a 5 P.M. departure that afternoon.

"Soon," I told her. "I'll try to come home soon."

Then Uzi got on the phone. "Sorry," he said. "She wanted to talk to you."

"Look, I think I might be able to get a flight out later today."

"Why?" He sounded genuinely surprised.

"She's so upset."

"Oh, come on. She's fine. She was crying for you last night, too, and then she got over it."

"What happened?"

"I was putting her to bed, and she started crying, 'I miss Mommy.'"

"What did you say?"

"I said, 'Yeah, I miss her, too.' And then we talked about when you were coming home, and she calmed down and fell asleep."

How remarkable, I thought after we'd said good-bye. For all the times I poked fun at my husband's laid-back parenting skills, for all the times I insisted I was the only one capable of getting a task done right, there were ways, I knew, in which he possessed an innate parenting wisdom I did not yet have. I learned something important from my husband that day on Leroy Street—that what a child needs most at a moment of distress isn't necessarily a fast or expensive fix. What she needs most may be validation. Simply being a parent and attending to Maya's feelings, without turning away out of discomfort, went far to help her cope with her anxiety and distress.

"Mothers need to understand that they can't make their children's pain disappear, but that they can alleviate it by comforting the child," Henri Parens says. "They have to allow that children can suffer, and that they, as mothers, can help a suffering child tolerate the pain and work through it. Each time the child is feeling bad, the mother has an opportunity to help her child."

I didn't take a flight home from New York that Friday evening. I knew Maya would be all right. She was learning how to tolerate separation. Uzi was helping her. As for me, well, I had to begin learning how to manage my own distress, at a healthy distance from my child. A street corner 2,800 miles away seemed like as good a place as any to start.

13

Raising Teenagers

THE ZONE OF THE UNKNOWN

My childhood skidded to a stop on a Tuesday afternoon in the middle of my fifteenth year, with my mother's first mammogram results. They showed the jagged gray outline of a three-centimeter-wide tumor in her left breast, an anomaly in a woman of forty-one. "A tumor the size of a peach pit" is how she described it to me, and that was the image that lodged in my mind. In 1980, American cancer patients were flying to Tijuana to have compounds drawn from peach pits injected into their veins, and it seemed horribly ironic to compare the nucleus of my mother's disease to an experimental treatment whose efficacy she didn't believe in and whose cost she couldn't have afforded even if she did.

For the next sixteen months, while traditional chemotherapy sapped her patience and her strength, I lay in bed at night thinking about how to come up with the airfare for two tickets to Mexico. I had about $600 in bat mitzvah savings in the bank, and if I babysat every Friday and Saturday night, I could come up with, I calculated, another $20 per week. But that would mean no nights out with my friends, a privilege I wasn't sure I was willing to give up. And there would obviously be the cost of treatment once my parents arrived. When I factored in the additional expense of someone to watch my siblings every afternoon until I got home from school, the price tag expanded far beyond my means.

Our house, normally a focal point of visitors and mess and noise, took on an eerie core of silence for the next year and a half. In retrospect, it's not surprising that I cut school for the first time a few weeks after my mother's diagnosis, or that, soon after her surgery, I fell in love with a boy straight out of juvenile hall and toppled into a relationship more physically intense than I was ready to handle. I was hungry to lose myself in something beyond the family, something that would transport me outside a house that required me to be silent every afternoon so my mother could sleep off her chemotherapy treatments, and solicitous at the dinner table so as not to upset the precarious balance of normality we were all trying to maintain.

I hated that peach pit in my mother. I hated it. *Hated* it. I would have blown it to microns myself, ripped it out and ground it to shreds with my new wisdom teeth, if only someone would have told me how.

I knew, even then, that these weren't usual thoughts for a teenager to have. But then, I was no longer having a usual adolescence. Driving a mother home from chemotherapy with my learner's permit, comforting her when her eyelashes began to fall out, and leaning over a hospital bed at seventeen to kiss her body good-bye— these weren't experiences my high school friends shared. I'd had a typical mother-daughter relationship up to a specific point in adolescence, a year and a half of limbo, and then an entirely different family life afterward.

When I think now about parenting my daughters through adolescence, my projections extend only so far. I have a fairly clear picture of what fifteen is like. Then sophomore and junior years of high school get fuzzy. Beyond that, I trip over the edge of my imagination into a void. How do mothers and daughters study for the ACT together? Shop for prom dresses? Celebrate a graduation? When I call a daughter at college on a Sunday morning, what will we talk about? Am I supposed to help her choose her classes, or let her figure it out herself? Losing my mother to illness at fifteen and to death at seventeen has made me painfully aware of what teenage daughters emotionally need from their mothers. But it hasn't given me any guidelines for how to act or what to expect from my own daughters during those years.

This sentiment was by far—by *far*—the most common one expressed by the mothers interviewed for this book when the discussion swung around to raising teens. Sixty-three percent of the women surveyed for this book, and 73 percent of those who participated in one-on-one interviews, lost their mothers before turning eighteen. Whether their children were approaching adolescence, in the midst of it, or already on the other side, nearly all of these women spoke of the uncertainty and inadequacy they felt about shepherding their children through a reasonably uncomplicated adolescence if they hadn't experienced one themselves.

These are women like forty-three-year-old Nova, the mother of a nine-year-old daughter and a twelve-year-old son, who was fourteen when her mother died. "I raised my younger brother and sister during my teenage years," she explains. "I worry that my expectations for my kids won't be grounded in reality, because I don't have my own experience to draw from [as a guide]. It's hard enough, once you're an adult, to remember what you did as a teenager. But my experience as a teenager hopefully will be so different from what my children's will be that I'm feeling kind of lost."

Fifty-two-year-old Suzanne, who has two children in college and a fifteen-year-old at home, was sixteen when her mother was diagnosed with breast cancer and seventeen when she died. The lack of experience with a mother beyond that point, Suzanne says, often left her feeling as if she had no relevant history to draw from when her children reached those critical years.

"I felt like I didn't know what to do when my kids hit sixteen, seventeen," she recalls. "I didn't have my mother's model to refer to. Even if I was going to reject it, at least I would have had a starting point. I tended sometimes to be too understanding, too nice. My kids would say, 'You're using the Mr. Rogers voice again. We *don't* need it anymore.' What they needed was, 'Yeah, life is tough. Now get out of bed and go to school.'"

Encouraging her children to become responsible, autonomous individuals was foreign to Suzanne, because she'd never gone through that process with a parent. "I was trying to let go, but I wasn't really geared for it, because I never let go as a teenager," she explains. "I was chopped off too soon."

When I share these stories with friends who have mothers, the response is always the same. All mothers of teenagers feel lost and confused, they're quick to remind me. *All* mothers are mystified by the erratic behavior, the fickle tastes, and the upside-down logic that characterize these years. The message is that no parent really knows what she's doing at this time.

Well, yes. And no. Every mother of a teen does step into the unknown after puberty begins. The parenting strategies that worked so well with school-age children no longer work with teens, and success is maddeningly ephemeral: what's acceptable today may not fly next week, or even tomorrow. In addition, the world in which our children become teens is sufficiently different from the world in which we started dating, or smoked our first cigarettes, or learned how to drive. The type of information teens are exposed to, as well as the manner in which they receive and exchange it—cell phones, wireless networks, instant messaging—has changed so much in the past twenty years that parents today are just as likely to feel clueless as confident. Our children know more than we ever did at their age, and they stand up to us in ways we never would have dared to talk back to our parents. "Ours is a generation of uncertain parents," says Anthony Wolf, PhD, in his book about parent-teenager relations, *Get Out of My Life, but First Could You Drive Me and Cheryl to the*

Mall? "We witness our children's less restrained behaviors and we do not understand and we do not know what to do. *We* would not have behaved that way. In the face of their teenager's insolence, parents feel frustrated, mad, and above all inadequate."

Popular parenting books offer a partial solution to this dilemma: they encourage parents to travel back emotionally in time. "Suspend the worry, the common sense, and the wisdom you have accumulated over the last years," one book suggests. "Think back to what you were like and what was important to you back then." "Remember your own adolescent struggles and use them as reference points and emotional stabilizers when your teens rebel against the limits you've imposed," suggests another.

But what advice exists for those of us whose adolescent "struggles" bear little resemblance to parenting issues at hand, especially when the dominant tasks of adolescence—such as developing a cohesive sense of self, taking on and meeting more mature responsibilities, acquiring a more complex view of relationships, developing new coping skills and decision-making strategies, renegotiating the parent-child relationship, and redirecting energy from the family to one's peers and the larger world—were accelerated, disrupted, halted, or otherwise affected by a mother's absence or untimely death?

Raising teenagers is a significantly different experience for most motherless mothers than it is for other women. When Sol Altschul, MD, and Helen Beiser, MD, both early psychoanalysts at the Barr-Harris Children's Grief Center in Chicago, looked at the parenting behaviors of adults who'd lost parents during childhood, they found that when problems arose, they usually came from one of two sources. The first was an overidentification with either their dead parents, or their children, or both. The second was the lack of experience of being fully parented in the later stages of childhood.

We constantly rely on childhood memories for comparison and guidance when raising our own kids. When a child accuses a mother of being overprotective or intrusive, for example, the mother naturally flashes back to a time twenty or thirty years ago, when she longed for more freedom and chafed against her mother's dominance or rules, and factors that memory into the present-day parenting decisions she makes. When a motherless mother looks back to her teen years, however, she's likely to find strategies she developed to cope with a mother's illness or absence instead. *An overprotective mother?* she might think. *I wish! I spent most of those years mothering myself.* The confusion and uncertainty she feels when parenting a teen comes not so much from a lack of understanding about the adolescent mindset, or a cultural gap, as from a lack of awareness of the role mothers normally play during the teen years.

"Literally, as my son hit the exact age I was when my mother died, I feel like I stalled out," explains forty-six-year-old Dierdre, who lost her mother at fourteen and has a son the same age. "Before that point, mothering certainly had its difficult moments, but I mostly felt competent and able. This fall, I felt lost. I tried to draw on my own experience of being a teen and being parented as a teen, but my memory has such black holes. I virtually received no parenting as a teenager. I find myself second-guessing my decisions, especially around how much freedom to give them. I seem to err on the side of more freedom, which in these times may not be so wise. But that's more of what I knew, since I basically raised myself during my teen years."

Altschul and Beiser observed a similar phenomenon with a patient they called "Mrs. B." Mrs. B.'s mother was sick for most of her daughter's early childhood, but had remained capable of a warm and loving relationship almost until the very end. She died when Mrs. B. was seven. The young Mrs. B. was then raised by a single father, whose behaviors were erratic. He began to impose harsh and sometimes bizarre rules on her activities, yet occasionally indulged her with gifts and outings. Nonetheless, she was popular and did well at school as an adolescent, and, in her twenties, married a man whose personality differed greatly from her father's.

When Mrs. B. became a mother, she again enjoyed a close and loving early mother-daughter relationship. When her daughter turned six, however, Mrs. B. became less confident in her ability to guide and counsel her child except by imposing rules and limits, as her father had once done. As the child entered early adolescence, Mrs. B.'s lack of confidence became even more apparent. The mother "felt helpless and at a loss as to know how to relate to her daughter's struggles with issues of self-esteem regarding attractiveness, makeup, dating, etc.," the authors wrote. "She had had to handle alone such experiences in her own adolescence and she now seemed ignorant as to how to communicate about such concerns with her daughter. While issues of identification were obvious problems for Mrs. B., the lack of experience with her own mother beyond the age of seven deprived Mrs. B. of a model for the mother-daughter interrelation that was so vital for her role of mother to a teenage daughter."

For Mrs. B., as for Dierdre and other motherless daughters like them, the salient issue is not just that the mother-daughter relationship was lost before adolescence, but also that the parenting they received afterward departed dramatically from what had come before. Very often, motherless mothers speak of distant, inconsistent, or punitive parenting styles fathers and stepmothers employed during their teen years, and the adaptations they made to emotionally survive. This kind of role-modeling can teach them how *not* to parent a teen, but doesn't offer much guidance beyond that point.

"I think going through adolescence with Emily is going to be uncharted territory for me," says forty-six-year-old Ruth, who was eleven when her mother died and now has an eleven-year-old daughter. "It'll probably bring up a lot of hard memories, because it was such a lonely time for me. Because my dad was just not available. He remarried when I was fourteen and it was terrible for everybody. My stepmother didn't want to deal with two messed-up teenage girls at home, and she was not nice. My dad was focused on us in kind of weird ways. He thought we were his priority, but he didn't know how to be there emotionally. He was just kind of hanging on, very depressed, but he also had a violent side. You never knew when you walked in the room if he was going to kiss you or smack you. I spent my teenage years kind of hiding or trying to stay away."

To Ruth, ordinary female adolescence is an existential question mark, since her own teen years were marked by such inconsistency and drama. She's anticipating a bumpy road. And expecting to be confused and lonely during her daughter's teen years may in fact lead her right into that state.

When Laurence Steinberg studied 204 Midwestern families with firstborn adolescents, he discovered that parents who had negative ideas about adolescence were the ones most likely to encounter psychological turmoil during their children's teen years. Steinberg calls this a mother's "cognitive set," the collection of images and opinions she holds inside her mind. Typically, these messages come from her own experiences as a teenager; the messages she gets from books, friends, and the media; and occasionally from an individually pessimistic outlook.

A mother's cognitive set is a fairly accurate predictor not of her child's behavior, but of how she'll *experience* the parent-child relationship as her child becomes a teen. That's because we tend to zero in on the aspects of a situation that support our original beliefs. In her thought-provoking book *Girl in the Mirror*, Nancy Snyderman, MD, points out that African-American mothers tend to view their daughters' puberty as an opportunity for a more mature mother-daughter relationship to develop. Unlike Caucasian mothers, who are more likely to focus on keeping their teenage daughters safe, vis-à-vis dating and drugs, African-American mothers emphasize problem-solving with their daughters. As a result, mother-daughter relationships in black families tend to have less conflict and more emotional closeness than in white families, which is exactly what black mothers anticipated from the start.

Mothers who expect to feel lost during their children's teen years, it seems, are likely to find themselves in precisely that state.

Redirecting this chain of events has to begin with changing our expectations. True, most of us don't have memories of uninterrupted mother-daughter relationships to draw from. But we do have countless experiences, some of them sprung from adversity, that can be applied to the job.

Revising one's expectations of adolescence, and finding the confidence to successfully parent children through those years, begins with a commitment to let go of negative stereotypes and learn how to rely on past experience—even when it's not directly relevant to our children's lives—for wisdom and insight. It also helps to educate ourselves about classically "normal" teenage behavior. To do this, we'll examine some of the long-held myths of adolescence, and look at how a motherless mother's history can both complicate and aid her process as a mother, a mentor, and a guide.

Myth #1: Separation is necessary.

For a teen, who's eager to branch out in the world, distancing from parents is an age-appropriate task. But parents don't have the same biological urge. To them, a teen's need for privacy and space can feel like an unnatural and untimely event. "One of the masochistic experiences of motherhood," psychoanalyst Helen Deutsch wrote more than sixty years ago, "arises from the fact that the child's emotions develop centrifugally away from the mother, while the mother remains tied to him and must renounce him."

Unlike the first separation process during toddlerhood, when a child asserts his physical and psychological will but still depends heavily on a parent for comfort and security, this time the child also needs to create emotional distance to cement a sense of self. A mother's job at this time is a challenging one. As her adolescent gradually relinquishes his attachment to family in favor of peer relationships and his own autonomy—a dynamic, inconsistent, ambivalent, and often highly unpredictable process—she needs to remain fairly static and predictable, exhibiting empathy, wisdom, and acceptance even as her child reassigns her to a more peripheral role in his life.

This can be a disorienting and confusing time for motherless mothers, especially those who never distanced naturally from a mother during adolesence. Books and magazines can explain why it happens, but only personal experience can give a woman a full emotional awareness of its importance and its necessity. "When my daughter shuts down, I think, *Gosh, why doesn't she want to share that with me?*" explains forty-two-year-old Alma, the mother of a fourteen-year-old daughter, who was nine when her own mother died. "I ask my girlfriends about it, and they say, 'Don't you remember when you were a teenager, and you didn't even want to go to the mall with your mom?' Well, no. I would have loved to have been able to go to the mall with my mom. So I can't personally relate to those moments. That's the scary part for me."

As a teen, a motherless mother may have separated physically or emotionally from a father, a stepmother, or other caregiver, upon realizing she had developed certain needs the adults in her family could no longer meet. But if her mother died prior to or during her teen years, she probably didn't get the chance to gradually loosen her dependence. And if she was quite young when her mother died, she may never have reached the stage when the mother's imperfections became clear. She may have been left instead with immature or unrealistic ideas of how a mother-child relationship naturally evolves.

"When my youngest was in high school, my menopause was approaching, and both my sons were resisting being connected to me in the way I wanted them to be," recalls fifty-nine-year-old Brenda, who was nine when her mother died. "I was grabbing on for dear life, and thinking I'd failed in a number of ways. That's what came to my mind: that I must not know anything about being a mother, because they didn't care about me anymore. I had no realization that this was a normal teenage phase. I just thought that your children hang on and always want to be with you."

Brenda's perception of what a mother gives a child was stuck in a nine-year-old child's point of view. She believed that mothers should manage every aspect of their children's lives, because after her loss she'd felt unprotected and alone. When her sons started drifting away from her and toward their friends during their teen years, she was stunned and disoriented. It didn't match up with her idea of what the mother-child relationship should be, and she perceived their departure as her failure.

Brenda's sons were doing exactly what high school students do (and it's to her credit that she didn't orchestrate ways to stop them). Multiple studies of adolescent behavior reveal that as children move through the teen years, they almost systematically spend less time at home. In their landmark 1984 book, *Being Adolescent*, Mihaly Csikszentmihalyi, PhD, and Reed Larson, PhD, found that high school freshmen spend about 25 percent of their time awake with their families. This proportion drops to 15 percent by senior year. Furthermore, about half of this home time is spent in routine activities, such as eating, showering, and doing chores. The other half is devoted to leisure activities, such as watching television and playing sports and games.

Home serves mostly as a place for personal maintenance and regeneration during the adolescent years, a site where teens refuel in between school, work, and time with friends. Parents as the pit-stop crew: that's what it can feel like sometimes. This new shift in the family can lead to an array of responses in a motherless mother, ranging from happiness to relief to envy, with elements of excitement, abandonment, or loss tossed into the mix.

Much of a mother's response depends on how she interprets her teen's desire to spend more time among peers. If she experiences it as a personal loss, Laurence Steinberg found, it's usually because she's struggling with the loss of identity, purpose, and self-definition that comes with the mothering role. If she experiences it as an abandonment, it's because she's feeling the loss of the prior relationship. Some mothers, however, experience a child's adolescence as a time of personal rebirth. They're able to take pleasure in their children's maturity and see it as an opportunity for both mother and child to enjoy more individual freedom.

This is how forty-four-year-old Wendy, who was fifteen when her mother died, came to view her daughter Cody's burgeoning independence. When sixteen-year-old Cody first began spending after-school time and weekend hours with her friends, Wendy felt left behind. She had always defined herself by her close and involved relationship with her only child, but now she was spending more time waving good-bye to Cody or waiting for her to come home. "I was feeling a little bit like 'Poor me. What about me?'" Wendy admits. When all this began, her impulse was to hold on. This caused her real discomfort, however, because she didn't want to thwart Cody's development. Then Wendy discovered that by looking at the change in their relationship through a slightly different lens, she could experience it differently.

"I had a moment where I asked myself, 'Do I want to fight this natural thing? Do I really want to guilt her into not enjoying something that's normal for her? Or do I want to look at it a different way and think, *Wow, I got some free time here,*'" she recalls. "I met my husband when I was twenty-one and I married young, so I never lived alone. I never had lots of freedom, and there have been times where I've missed that. And so I thought, *Well, I can get a little bit of that now.*"

Cody and Wendy remained emotionally close throughout this process, which helped Wendy feel connected to her daughter even as their physical time together decreased. In many other families, however, a child's quest for physical distance coincides with the need for emotional privacy as well, and it's the latter part of this equation that's often hardest for a motherless mother to bear.

Fifty-two-year-old Suzanne, who was seventeen when her mother died, says the most challenging part of raising teenagers for her has been accepting her children's need to pull away emotionally. Now the mother of a seventeen-year-old daughter and two sons, ages twenty and fifteen, Suzanne fondly remembers the years when her children were young. "They were an affectionate group," she recalls. "I let them turn the house upside down. We had trampolines and gym mats everywhere. If they wanted to run through the kitchen with Popsicles, it didn't bother me. I wasn't very fussy, and that works well with young kids for a nice, even tempo. But the teenage years, when they go to their rooms, and they don't want to talk, and they decide you have bad shoes and too much gray in your hair, have been very difficult for me. I tend to take all that quite personally. I missed them, and I missed my role."

Suzanne hadn't planned another role for herself, she explains, because she hadn't fully expected to live this long. Her mother died at the age of forty-six, and during early motherhood, Suzanne was focused mainly on giving her children as much as she could before she, too, reached that age. Somewhere in the back of her mind, she says, she felt she'd never make it to the years when her children would grow up and go off on their own.

The more her children tried to pull away, Suzanne recalls, the more anxious she became about maintaining their prior connection. "It was a struggle for me to not bug them emotionally," she admits. "When they'd say 'Just leave me alone!,' I couldn't do that. I'd follow after them, saying, 'What's wrong? Tell me what's wrong.' And it didn't work. I've had to pull back a little and realize this was my own need to be close to them and be involved in their daily lives. Getting that perspective helped. Also, thank God, I became closer to my husband at this time and kind of reestablished a warmer, more fun relationship with him, so I felt that at least we had each other." At a time when her children seemed to retreat, she found comfort in knowing she wasn't being left alone.

Parents are told that we should let our children go, especially our sons, who need to make a clean break from mothers to develop the kind of competent personality structure that creates successful adult males. Recent research, however, has found that this philosophy may be doing a great disservice to our boys. Sons need to find new forms of connection to parents during the teen years, not to lose it entirely. When Susan Shaffer and Linda Gordon interviewed adolescent boys for their book *Why Boys Don't Talk—and Why It Matters*, they found that autonomy was important to boys, but not at the expense of losing emotional closeness with others.

Teenage girls may be (more or less) open to emotional expression and a free exchange of information—the traditionally "female" mode of communication. Maintaining an emotional connection with boys often takes on a different tone. Connecting with our sons, Shaffer and Gordon explain, is more likely to involve brief moments of agreement, short exchanges that reaffirm interest and trust, and long periods of comfortable silence.

"My son and I both love hot dogs," says fifty-one-year-old Rosemary, the mother of a nineteen-year-old daughter and a thirteen-year-old son. "So, we go to the Wiener Factory together, and he'll talk to me a little bit while we're there. I'm allowed to ask him maybe two or three questions, and he'll answer, and then he'll go, '*Mom!*' He's a great kid, but he's just not easily communicative, like my daughter is."

Even when teens assert their own opinions, disregard ours, and head out the door in search of their own lessons to learn, they still need emotional support and guidance from adults. To remove it, Susan Shaffer and Linda Gordon say, is to take away the safety net they unconsciously rely on. "We need to have confidence in our own ability to provide that safety net," they explain, "regardless of our marital status, socioeconomic background, or ethnicity." To that, I add: "And regardless of our past histories."

When we think of the push-pull phase of adolescence as a separation, it's easy to feel hurt and rejected by our children's attempts to liberate themselves from our opinions and guidance. When we redefine the process as "individuation," however, we can start seeing it as a child's silent request to renegotiate an existing relationship, and look for new ways to communicate. "There's no other parenting transition, except for birth or adopting a child, that's as large as this notion that suddenly you're supposed to 'separate,'" Harriet Lerner explains. "That's really a terrible thing laid on mothers. They're told they're supposed to let go and separate, and that makes them even more panicked, because it's the wrong language. The goal is to move on to new kinds of connections, and hopefully, over time, even richer connections."

Myth #2: Conflict, rebellion, and rejection mean I've done something wrong.

"My oldest daughter hated me through her teen years," recalls fifty-year-old Rebecca, a mother of four, who was ten when she lost her mother to cancer. "She's twenty-seven now and loves me, but she hated me then. And it confused me. I didn't know about ugly stages of adolescence, because I never went through that. My mom died a queen. My mom died the most beautiful woman in the world. The holiest. The most spiritual. My memories of getting spanked were because *I* made the mistake, not her.

"I was clueless during this time with my daughter," she continues. "I felt guilty that I was always busy cleaning the house or shopping, and that I didn't get down on the ground with her and play. Now I look back and say, 'I was with her at the market. We picked out cereal together. That's as valuable as doing Play-Doh.' But I always felt guilty about how busy I was, and when the oldest one got so snotty, it just added to my guilt that I hadn't done enough or hadn't done it right."

The conflict Rebecca experienced with her daughter was a heightened version of what many mothers and daughters encounter during the teen years: hurt feelings, power struggles, and nitpicking about responsibilities and chores. Whereas sons tend to withdraw to their rooms, turn on the stereo, and hide from conflict during the teen years, girls are more likely to plant their feet in the living-room carpet and go to battle. Girls are the ones to watch out for.

Or at least that's the warning that mothers of teenagers have been passing down for decades. "Oh-ho," my friends say. "You've got two girls. Wait till you see what you've got coming." The more subtle ones just grimace and murmur, "Boys are easier. But it's hard either way." Their words echo the message behind most popular parenting books on adolescence. Expect conflict, they tell you. A quick scan of titles on the parenting shelf in my neighborhood bookstore yields *Parenting Your Out-of-Control Teenager*; *Don't Take It Personally*; *Are You Losing Control?*; *Rage, Rebellion & Rudeness*; *WHY Do They Act That Way?*; and my personal favorite, *When We're in Public, Pretend You Don't Know Me*. An alarming number of books contain the words "surviving" or "survival" in their subtitles. And don't even get me started about the movie *Thirteen* or the ABC-TV reality show *Brat Camp*. It's almost enough to make me invest in *The Parent's Guide to Boarding Schools* instead.

Do the teenage years have to be filled with parent-child strife? Not necessarily. Although books and films emphasize the conflict inherent in parent-teen relationships, about 80 percent of adolescents actually make the transition from childhood to adulthood without serious upset. Among the families Laurence Steinberg studied, full-fledged conflict between parents and teens was rare. Constant bickering and squabbling over mundane issues was more common, and that alone was usually harmless, since it seems to be the intensity of conflict, and not its frequency, that has adverse mental-health effects on family members.

It's often *parents* who have the harder time during these years. The mothers in Steinberg's study—many of whom were hitting midlife at the same time their children were entering adolescence—described feelings of loss, depression, envy, anger, frustration, regret, and lowered self-esteem as their children matured, especially with same-sex children. Half of the mothers in his study experienced a decrease in mental well-being as their children made the transition. One-third, however, reported improvement in their mental health, suggesting that some mothers experience their children's adolescence as an opportunity for growth.

In the writing classes I teach, I emphasize the difference between conflict and tension. Conflict, I tell my students, arises when two characters disagree. Tension always exists, even when characters agree. It's like a constant form of low-level energy between charged particles. The same principles hold true when parenting teenagers. Most often, parent-teen conflict centers around different ideas of what's important, what matters, and what's true or real. It comes and goes, depending on the situation at hand. But tension is more like a low-level hum in the background of daily life, and it's fueled by the most mundane things: the way a parent dresses or laughs or chews, for example, or a son's perennially low-slung jeans.

The eye-rolling, stony silences and snippy, monosyllabic answers of adolescence—no mother will admit to loving this part of the teen years. Yet some appear to handle it lightly, and with grace. I'm always amazed by mothers who can airily brush off a teen's back talk, or turn a moment of tension into a joke that makes them both laugh, as if they're operating from a place of inner faith that kids eventually get through this stage and turn into loving sons and daughters again. For motherless mothers, who lack the personal experience of having rebelled against a mother as a teen and later returned to her as an adult, such faith is harder earned. "Every time my kids explode at me, I think, *That's it. I've messed up. I've lost them,*" says forty-six-year-old Hillary, the mother of a teenage son and daughter, who was ten when her own mother died. "But then, half an hour later, they're helping me cook dinner, like nothing happened. I just don't understand this kind of ambivalence at all."

To make the situation even more confusing, consider that childish and nasty behavior at home—which may be the only place where teens feel emotionally safe enough to regress—isn't always an attempt to push a parent away. More often, as Anthony Wolf explains, it's an attempt to stay connected. Conflict occurs precisely because teens are conflicted. They want emotional closeness with parents, but they also find it unacceptable to be attached to or dependent on the family. To a teen, arguing with parents meets both needs: to assert his free will, and to capture the parent's attention. "Passionate involvement" from parents, Wolf explains, is what most teens want, even if it's in the form of anger or frustration. A child who battles is nonetheless a child who's maintaining a relationship with her parents, even relying on them for support, though her methods may leave room for improvement.

Forty-one-year-old Francine recently discovered this when her fourteen-year-old daughter Julie began to rebel. At first, Francine was blindsided by the conflict. She had been only eight when her own mother died, and had spent most of her adolescence caring for her younger brother and sister in a household run by an autocratic father. Rebellion hadn't been an option for her. She'd been too afraid of her father's rage.

Francine married young, but the marriage was troubled and ended when Julie was nine. Today, Francine dates the origin of her problems with Julie back to those turbulent years, when she was trying to support her children as a single mother and parent them through the ages when she hadn't been mothered herself.

"I made a lot of mistakes as a mother, because I didn't know how to be," Francine recalls. "I was strict at all the wrong times and lenient at all the wrong times. I spent most of my time working, trying to make ends meet. I eventually met my second husband, and after two years we got married. But the transition to being a family again was difficult." By age fourteen, Julie was blaming her mother for the divorce and her disrupted childhood. She started cutting school, then stopped attending altogether. She failed all her classes. Francine responded the only way she knew how: by cracking down, as her father had done whenever she or her siblings needed discipline.

"I did everything I could do, or so I thought," she recalls. "I tried talking to her, shouting at her, taking away her cell phone and computer, talking to her friends, going to a psychologist with her. I even tried following her, and finally ended up having a physical fight with her. I smacked her around the face and she kicked me in the stomach. That smack and kick were an all-time low for us. I retreated to my room and was depressed for three days. I felt I'd lost my daughter, and then we started talking again. But this time, the talking was different. I wasn't ordering her around, and that's the thing I've learned: being a mother is not ordering your kids around and making decisions for them, except in dangerous situations. It's helping them make decisions for themselves. My father never, ever let me make a decision. He didn't know how to raise me, so he did the only thing he could. He bound me to him with rules, and put the fear of death into me if I did anything wrong."

When conflict erupted in Francine's house, she fell back on the only parental role–modeling she'd received as a teen. At the same time, she knew she didn't want to parent as her father did. Her commitment to breaking the pattern helped her come to a higher understanding of herself as a parent, and of her daughter as an individual with needs and desires of her own.

"My daughter and I are hopefully in a different situation now," she says. "Today we can laugh about what happened, because she knows I love her with all my heart. There are still issues about tidying her room, coming home at a decent hour, dressing appropriately, going to school, and doing homework, but when I get angry about it, she listens and answers me instead of running away. I pick my fights with her. I choose what's important to me and her, and let other things drop. I don't want to lose her again."

Francine responded to conflict first with confusion, then with anger. Some of her rage was a reaction to her daughter's unruly behavior, some of it was the result of losing parental control, and some of it, Colleen Russell says, was probably latent anger bubbling up from her past. As she explains, "You may have had an angry mother or father you vowed never to be like, but these generational patterns come through anyway. We often wind up repeating what our parents did to us, even when we consciously want to do otherwise."

When a mother erupts in anger, Russell suggests, she should try to take a step back and ask herself what's really going on. Sometimes we leap to anger when we're feeling hurt, she explains, because anger covers up hurt and pain. Also remember, she says, that mothers don't have to come up with answers or solutions to conflicts on the spot, especially when emotions are flaring. "You can always say, 'This is difficult for me and I can't talk about it right now. We'll talk about it later, when everyone's calm,'" she advises. "A parent can have a time out, too. I've actually said to my sons on occasion, 'I'm not going to talk to you right now. I need a time out.'"

Above all, Russell suggests, talk to other parents to get reality checks, and to see how they're dealing with similar problems. When you feel you don't know what normal is, trust other people to tell you, and to offer advice.

Dierdre checks in with her husband about changes in her son's attitudes and behaviors. "Fortunately, my husband had pretty normal teenage years, so I can use his childhood as a reference point instead of mine," she says. Suzanne remained close with the members of her first mothers' group over the years, who have offered support and advice about raising teens. "Sometimes I would borrow their mothers," she recalls. "I would literally call up one of the gals and say, 'Would you go ask your mother what she would do about this, and then get back to me?'"

And forty-eight-year-old Millie found reassurance from a psychologist at her daughter's college after a disastrous moving-in episode.

We carted all my daughter's belongings upstairs to her dorm room, and as soon as we got there, she was belligerent with me and had objections about every suggestion I made. I was already beside myself with emotion, because I just didn't know how I was going to handle this separation. Finally, I couldn't stand the pain anymore, so I took a walk around campus just to cry. My husband found me sitting on a concrete wall, sobbing. He said, "You're just gonna have to toughen up." Yeah, right. When I walked back into the dorm room, my daughter said, "Where were you? I needed your advice!"

I never knew my daughter's behavior was normal and necessary until I attended a parents' orientation at her school a
month later. During the daylong session, a school psychologist—
a smart little woman in a dark blue suit—stepped up to give a
lecture about handling your child's absence. She started with "I
have three kids, and when they were your child's age, I don't
know which was worse for them—when I breathed in or when
I breathed out." She then talked with us about teenage development and how it's normal for them to be rebellious and ad-
versarial, staking out their own ground toward independence.
That rebellion is what makes it easier for them to say good-bye
and move forward responsibly in their own lives. I missed all
that when I was a teenager. It wasn't until after that lecture that
I felt better about being a motherless mother. Yet I always continue to question all my moves as a parent, every day. I guess I
always will. And I tell myself maybe—just maybe—that's not a
bad thing.

Myth #3: My child's adolescence is so much easier than mine was.

When we see a teenage son or daughter distraught over the loss of
a two-week romance or a snub from a clique, it's hard not to think,
Oh, honey. This is a major loss? I could tell you stories. Yet, as parents,
we do real damage to our teens by minimizing or dismissing their
experiences, just because they don't measure up—subjectively or
objectively—to the emotional magnitude of what we went through
during those years. It prevents us from seeing what's really going
on in their lives, and from knowing who they truly are. Losing a
championship game or getting a C on a test may seem like a very
small blow to us, but it is no less important or painful to our teens.
And, as their mothers, we need to find ways to offer empathy just
the same.

Teens aren't always looking for prescriptive advice when problems arise. They also need maps to help them find their way out of the tangle. That's where finding an emotional correlative can be useful. Even though we may not have had the exact same experiences as our teens, it still helps a child to hear how a mother felt in various situations when she was young.

Let's say, for example, that a teenage son is furious because his father just took away his IM privileges for a week as a disciplinary measure. And his sister is distressed because the basketball coach just told her she'll be starting every game on the bench. IMing, of course, didn't exist when their mother was a teen, and perhaps she never got to play high school sports because she had to be home every afternoon to take care of her siblings. Still, when she thinks about it, she can remember a time when she felt she was treated unfairly, or had high hopes that were unexpectedly dashed, and she can share the memories of how she felt at those times. Underneath every adolescent experience is always a common human emotion: elation, disappointment, betrayal, desire, outrage, regret. If we can learn to speak to the underlying feelings of an experience, rather than to the specific situation, we'll have an easier time finding common ground with our teens. And we might find we have more useful experiences to draw from than we'd previously thought.

Without empathy, a parent is at risk for sliding into envy or jealousy, both of which can result when a mother compares her teen's life to her own. In Steinberg's study, as in my anecdotal interviews, these parents constituted a notable minority. They reached such feelings, typically, through one of two routes: either by comparing their teens to themselves at the same age, or by comparing their teens' lives to their own lives today.

In the case of the former, jealousy develops from the discrepancy between what an adolescent has or is, and what the parent lacked at the same age. For motherless mothers, this typically involved comparing their teen's life with an involved mother to their adolescence without an engaged mother, or without any mother at all. Such comparisons are all but inevitable, and in addition to inspiring envy, they can also provoke deep sadness by reminding a mother of what might have been.

Comparing a teen's life to one's self in the present can elicit envy for a child's less responsible, more carefree existence, especially when the burden of supporting such a lifestyle weighs heavily on a mother. In addition, a firstborn child's adolescence and a mother's midlife often coincide, especially now that women bear children later and girls reach puberty earlier. For a motherless mother, midlife is likely to be a particularly emotional transition. Most adults in their forties and early fifties are struck by the awareness that time to make radical changes in their lives is dwindling, and many begin thinking in terms of years left rather than in terms of years already lived.

Midlife also characteristically brings with it a heightened vulnerability to any experiences that inspire self-doubt, and an urge to reexamine one's life choices while there's still time left to make a major change. On top of this, midlife is also a common time for a motherless mother to reach her mother's age at time of death (see chapter 11). It's tempting to blame household disharmony on the vicissitudes of adolescence, but a parent's emotional state often weighs heavily into the equation, too. In fact, Steinberg found that when a parent compared herself at midlife to her teen and felt jealousy, it was because the comparison reinforced the mother's unhappiness and regret about choices made or not made up to that point. Sometimes, however, it tempted her to make changes for the better.

Myth #4: Love is all you need.

Martha was barely a kindergartener when her mother died of kidney failure, and when she tries hard, she can recall images of an indulgent, loving parent. "In every picture I have of us together, she's smiling and holding me," says Martha, now fifty-four. "You can just see how much she loved having a baby, a child. It was really special for her. She divorced my father when I was about two and brought me to live with her father in an apartment in New York

City. And I was unbelievably spoiled. The two of them just doted on me. Neither of them worked, so they were both home with me all the time. So, I had a solid foundation, and it was good, because it gave me five years of being loved. Which helped me get through the absence of love for many, many years after that."

After her mother's death, Martha, an only child, went to live with her mother's brother, his wife, and their three children. "I kind of got dropped in their lap," she recalls. "They took me in, but it wasn't something they'd wanted. My adoptive father was okay, but my adoptive mother was very resentful and took it out on me. I was fed and clothed and all of the basics. But there wasn't much love, and there was a lot of emotional and physical abuse. Still, I felt really lucky, because I'd had that good start."

When Martha became a mother at twenty-two, she drew from her scant early memories for guidance. When raising her two children, she tried to give them as much focused attention and positive reinforcement as she could, despite being a single mother on a tight budget for much of that time. Consistent, unconditional love and support were what children needed most, she believed. She was relaxed about rules, and rarely disciplined her kids. "I was a pretty permissive parent," Martha admits. "My kids are grown up now, and they say, 'I wish you'd been a little stricter when we were teenagers.' Who knew? I thought I was doing a good thing, because I was parenting as my mother had. But then, I was only five when she died. Who knows what she would have been like when I was a teenager?"

To establish a maternal identity, Martha had modeled herself after the only positive mother figure she'd known: her biological mother. But because their interaction spanned only the first few years of Martha's childhood, it didn't offer a realistic model for raising a child through adolescence. While love, support, and encouragement are undeniably important to a child's emerging self-esteem, psychologists and psychiatrists alike agree that a tougher, more structured form of parenting—a "love and limits" approach—is more effective during the teen years to help an adolescent feel safe.

The "love" half of this equation refers to giving children affection and emotional support, while allowing them to have their own points of view. The "limits" part requires that parents set boundaries, establish consequences, and enforce those consequences when rules are broken. "It's about empowering another person in a developmentally appropriate way, by setting house rules, guidelines, and expectations and agreeing to stick to them," Colleen Russell explains.

This may feel foreign to mothers who grew up in authoritarian homes where rules were strictly enforced without the slightest nod to democracy, or in homes where rules were so lax—or nonexistent—that teens were permitted to do as they pleased. It may also feel uncomfortable or even threatening to mothers to whom keeping an even keel in the family, even if it means relinquishing authority, is of paramount emotional importance.

As Mihaly Csikszentmihalyi and Reed Larson explain in *Being Adolescent*, "Many parents experience their strongest emotional rewards within the family, and thus come to depend on it to stabilize their personality . . . they are especially threatened by any conflict with each other and with the children." This can lead to a permissive style of parenting where a parent fears antagonizing or losing the stabilizing influence of her child's love. Such parents are typically warm and emotionally invested in their children, but back down from conflict and hand authority over to the adolescent. The result is a household without clear rules or limits, and only a vague sense of who's in charge. Children who grow up in these homes often have close friendships and are confident around their peers but frequently have trouble accepting authority. Underneath their assertions that they enjoy their "freedom" may lie the feeling that they're being ignored—and, lacking adequate parental supervision, they're likely to get in trouble and do poorly at school.

Sometimes mothers have to be willing to risk their own personal security to help their children grow, as fifty-two-year-old Phyllis recently learned. Phyllis, who was fifteen when her mother died from a drug overdose, always tried hard to please her sons and make their teen years easier than hers had been. She'd spent the first half of her adolescence taking care of her mentally unstable mother, trying to prevent her from taking her own life. As a mother, she helped her sons find their way out of any trouble they got into, and played peacemaker in the family to keep parent-child relationships smooth and relatively carefree.

"I thought I was helping to promote their independence, but what happened was in many ways I went in and rescued them too much," she now admits. "And I think that was detrimental to our kids' development, in some ways. On the other hand, when my older son started smoking pot and doing poorly in school, a therapist advised my husband and me to stop rescuing him and to let him suffer his own consequences. Well, that was disastrous, because he slid even further down, and we could have been there to help him. In retrospect, I wish I had been firmer about enforcing consequences myself."

Studies of parenting styles show that the love and limits approach, also referred to as "authoritative" parenting, is the one most likely to produce self-reliant, socially competent, responsible teenagers capable of having good relationships with their parents and others. It may be the mother's willingness and ability to negotiate with her teenager and to remain in authority while giving the teen an increasing amount of psychological autonomy—this elegant two-step so critical for mothers and teenagers to achieve—that brings the most harmony to their relationship during these years. It may also be the most reliable route to an adult relationship built on trust and respect.

When Phyllis's older son wanted to drop out of college, she and her husband supported his decision, but refused to support him financially beyond paying the next month's rent. It was one of the hardest choices she made as a parent, but she's grateful she did it.

"He gave me a Mother's Day card this year, with a poem on it that said, 'Thanks, Mom, for having the courage to let me make mistakes, for having the wisdom to help me learn from them, and for having the heart to love me through it all,'" she says. "And inside he wrote, 'Thank you for always being there through thick and thin.' He's been working now to pay his own bills. Just recently, he told me, 'If you and Dad had continued to support me, I never would have realized that I'm smoking so much dope I can't see straight.' Now he's stopped smoking, and he gets to work on time every day. And I realize that having tough limits and boundaries makes a difference. I learned I had to set limits and then let go, and it's the best thing I could have possibly done."

Myth #5: They've made it to adulthood—my job is done.

Getting a child successfully to adulthood is the surest way for a motherless mother to give her adolescent what she didn't have. While most mothers express elation or sadness when the time comes for a child to step out on his own, the overriding emotion described by women interviewed for this book was relief. *I made it,* they thought. *I got them through childhood. I didn't die.* When their children step into a college dorm, or onto a military bus, or into their first job, these mothers let out the big collective "Whew."

Then, inevitably, comes the big "What next?"

For some women, visions of parenting didn't extend beyond this predetermined goal. They were focused with laser-beam intensity on escorting their children into adulthood, without paying much attention to the years beyond.

"My daughter was a very independent child," says fifty-two-year-old Justine, a single mother who was fourteen when her own mother died. "It was me who would have liked to have kept her my best friend for the rest of my life, and not let her go. But for her own good, I encouraged her to work hard and do well, and then she left when she was seventeen, to go to college. I just hadn't thought about that part. All I wanted was to get her to a certain point without her getting pregnant or getting involved with the wrong guy, or getting into drugs or drinking. I never thought that at seventeen, when she graduated from high school, that meant she was leaving."

The act of releasing a child into the world can be an exhilarating, though emotionally draining task. It's a form of physical separation, no matter how we view it. And it's hard not to think of a child's launching as a test, of sorts. All the effort, investment, and guidance poured into the child is going to serve him well—or not—once he's out on his own.

When the child leaving home is an only child, or the youngest, a mother faces the task of redefining herself. Every other aspect of her life—her marriage, if she has one, her life goals, and how she spends her time—has to be renegotiated. "Divorce rates skyrocket after the last child leaves home, because every issue you haven't been dealing with while you've been focused on your child comes and hits you in the face," Harriet Lerner says. The initial empty-nest stage, she explains, is "a *very anxious* time. You need to appreciate that so you don't wonder, 'What's wrong with me?' The best insurance policy to breathe your way through is always to focus back on yourself. Take it as an opportunity to work on all there is to work on—your relationships, your priorities, whatever talents and abilities you want to develop this week or over the next five years. Ideally, one does this *before* the last child leaves home."

Cynthia, forty-five, learned this two years ago, after her youngest child, a daughter, started military training. Cynthia had been excited to deliver her daughter to boot camp, but almost as soon as she'd said good-bye to Rayanne, she felt herself start to unravel.

"I cried on the plane all the way back home," recalls Cynthia, who was seven when her mother died. "I cried so hard after I got home that I made myself sick. I couldn't go to work for a week. One day, I was lying in bed, thinking, *What am I going to do now?* I had already raised both my kids and I was still so young. And then I heard the Lord say to me, bigger than anything, 'Remember, you thought you weren't even going to live this long.' And it was like a light bulb went off inside my head. Because I'd never expected to get this far, to the point where my kids were raised and on their own. It reminded me that just being alive was a blessing."

Some of Cynthia's response to her daughter's departure was undoubtedly the result of the physical act of separating from a loved one, and some due to the sudden and abrupt realization that she hadn't planned beyond this point and didn't know what would come next. Some of Cynthia's response also, however, may have come from fulfilling the most important mission she'd laid out for herself as a parent: getting her children to adulthood. She may have been grieving for the knowledge that she'd accomplished what her mother had never been able to achieve. She may even have been subconsciously grieving the loss of her old way of thinking, as it was replaced by a new, more expansive view of the future. The reminder that she still had many years to live gave her the strength to pull herself out of bed and reroute the investment she'd been putting into her children into herself.

Today, Cynthia has a full-time job, a happy marriage, and a lovely home. She leads a group for motherless daughters at her church and mentors several young motherless girls. "Here I am," she laughs, as if surprised by the wonder of it all. "Still living."

Our house is so full of life now, with backpacks scattered recklessly across the entry, bath water constantly running, high-pitched laughter, and the constant dull thud of sneakers hitting wooden floors. It's hard to imagine a time when all this will move elsewhere, when the chaos of family life with small children will make way for quiet music and candlelight and long (uninterrupted!) conversations with my husband. Already we know how much we'll miss the activity. Still, I can't help looking forward to the day when I know I've safely escorted my daughters into womanhood. This will be my crowning triumph, the moment when I can raise both fists in the air and say, "I did it!"

But between here and there is more than a decade, and two adolescences to traverse. Will we make it through with minimal upset, or are there major upheavals ahead? Will my mother's absence through my own teen years hinder me as a parent, or will it free me to make choices based only on what's right for my child, without unwanted influences from the past? If a mother's expectations are truly self-fulfilling, I'm going to place my intent on the latter. Check in with me in ten years. I'll let you know how it's going.

Epilogue

*A*nd so, we move forward together, my two girls and I, through the years that will slowly mold them into the women they'll become. The same years will carry me through my mother's age at time of death, and into the years she never got to see. I don't discuss this with my daughters, but the aura of these numbers surrounds us nonetheless.

"How long do you think you'll live?" Maya asked me the other day.

"Oh," I told her. "A long time, I think. A very long time." It's taken me almost a decade to believe this, but I finally do.

"But *how* long?" she pressed.

"I don't know—eighty? Ninety. At least ninety," I said definitively. Ninety is a good number. My grandmother lived until ninety. My cousin Billie is still flying around the country at ninety-five. I'll aim for their examples instead.

Strange, now, how after so many years my mother's model is starting to recede. Before I became a mother, I was a motherless daughter, and "motherless" always overshadowed "daughter" in that phrase. Now I'm a motherless mother, and "mother" is the word that carries most of the weight. Early loss influences me, daily, but it doesn't define me anymore.

"The other day I was talking to my coworkers, one of whom is trying to get pregnant," recalls forty-four-year-old Wendy, the mother of a sixteen-year-old daughter, "and she asked another woman, 'How do you like having boys?' The woman said, 'I just love it,' and then she said, 'But Wendy's so happy she has a girl.' I said, 'That's true. But I think the reason I wanted a girl so badly is because my mother died when I was fifteen.' If my mother's death makes sense in a conversation now, I'll bring it up. Whereas before, it didn't matter if it made sense in a conversation, I made sure people knew it about me, because I felt it symbolized who I was."

During those first, exhilarating, overwhelming years of mother-hood, I frequently wondered, "How did my mother handle this?" and "How must she have felt when that happened?"—constantly looking for clues about how to behave. But the more I mother my daughters without the answers to these questions, the less the an-swers seem to matter. My mother's insights and behaviors once felt like the only key to successful motherhood. Now I've come to think of them as just one person's approach, which I can gratefully accept or politely decline.

Like most motherless mothers, I expected that motherhood would bring me closer to my mother. It has, but it's given me an un-expected forum for differentiating, too. After eight years of mother-hood, I know I'll never be as patient, or as selfless, or as trusting as my own mother was. But neither will I be as innocent or as compla-cent. Her death made that impossible for me. At seventeen, I became a fighter, with an insatiable zest for living. As a mother, I take on a heavy load, too heavy some of the time. I don't want my daughters to remember me as a mother who accepted arbitrary limits, or who shied away from change or growth. Sometimes I worry they're un-witting participants in my own reparative journey. Other times, I believe we're sharing the ride of a lifetime. By the age of four, Maya had more stamps in her passport than I had at twenty-five. When I say I want to give my children the world, I mean that literally, even when it means forgoing material comforts to do so.

And then I wonder if this drive toward being an *über*-mother isn't my way to prove that what I lost at seventeen was irreplaceable and huge. If I become the sun around which my children orbit, the one who strives to meet their every need, it justifies the enormity of the emptiness I feel. *Mothers are essential,* my existence then reaffirms. *That's why I was never the same again.*

Never the same, perhaps, but in some ways stronger. More determined. More resilient. More appreciative of small things, and more grateful for every day we have. About two years ago, I realized I could make a choice: I could obsess about motherhood, or I could experience it. The decision wasn't hard. I chose life. Or, perhaps I should say, life chose me.

In January 2004, when I was in the middle of writing this book, I was involved in a major car accident on the way back to my office one afternoon. The car I was driving hydroplaned in the rain around a tight curve; crossed the oncoming lane in a wide, lazy U-turn; and rolled twice down an embankment, landing upside down. I crawled out the shattered back window, unharmed except for a small bruise where the steering wheel had pressed against my thigh.

It was a miracle, everyone who pulled over said, that anyone climbed out of that car alive. A miracle: people liked that idea. Strangers pulled over to touch me. Someone asked to kiss my hand. For those few moments, I felt papal, saintly, profound. Then the paramedics arrived and asked me to recite my name and age, and I became just another medium-aged mother in a short black raincoat with little pieces of safety glass in my hair.

I wasn't in shock, not by their terms, but that night, I lay in bed staring at the ceiling for hours. Every time I closed my eyes, the car started tumbling sideways down the hill. I hadn't cried after the accident, hadn't broken down when my husband arrived at the scene, or even later, when I got home and rushed through the front door to hug my kids. But in bed, I ran my hands up and down my limbs just for the pure pleasure of feeling my skin alive. If just one variable had been different that afternoon—if a car had been coming in the opposite direction, say, or if the accident had occurred a hundred feet up the road, where the embankment was steeper and ended in a creek—my husband and daughters would have been having a very different night. And that's when the tears came, huge, jagged sobs, because I got it, really got it, how awful and random life can be, and I understood how quickly mine could have been yanked away.

And what if it had? At two, Eden would barely have remembered me. At six, Maya would never have fully recovered. By what grace or chance had I been permitted to return intact to my children that night, when, at forty-two, my mother was taken from hers forever? And how fast it all would have happened. I always thought that in the final moments of her life, a mother would think of her children, and die with their images in her mind. But if my life had ended in the car that afternoon, my last thought would have been *The car is rolling. How strange.* There wasn't time to think about anything beyond the immediate present. I would have left my daughters without any sort of good-bye, and of all the residual effects of the accident, this one is still hardest for me to accept.

As a mother, I think often about what I want most for my children. Safe cities, clean air and water, enough food, good schools— all that, of course. And like any mother, I hope my daughters will one day grow into conscientious, content, generous, well-adjusted citizens of the world. Parents are naturally selfless and expansive in their desires; no dream for a child can ever be too lofty or too big. So, forgive me when I say that what I want most for my daughters is something small and selfish, something that also benefits me.

For three years, I've been living among the stories of hundreds of motherless mothers. Christine's is the one I think of most. Just six years old when her mother died of cancer, Christine is now the mother of two daughters, ages four and one. After her first daughter was born, Christine would place her in the bassinet next to her bed every night and say two prayers. "I would say to myself in my head, 'God, don't let me screw this up. Please don't let me screw this up,'" she told me. "And my other prayer was 'Please, God, don't let me get sick. Please let me see her get married someday. Please let me see her go to college. Okay, okay, not college, God? Then high school. I'll take high school graduation.' You know, I would try to make these *deals*."

What Christine wants most as a mother is the same thing I want, and what nearly every motherless mother wants, too—something so simple, yet so elusive, the one thing our mothers never got. It's the chance to teach a daughter how to use a tampon; to fix a son's tie for the prom; to shriek and applaud from the bleachers at a high school graduation. To walk a child down a flower-studded aisle. To hold a grandchild in our arms. To be there, by our children's sides, experiencing it all.

Take everything else I have. Just leave me with this. What I want most is time. Just time, precious time.

Motherless Mothers Survey

Between October 2002 and June 2005, 1,322 motherless mothers from more than twelve countries participated in an online survey for this book. The results are as follows:[*]

1. How old are you now?

Younger than 20—1%

20 to 29—15%

30 to 39—40%

40 to 49—29%

50 to 59—12%

60 to 69—2%

70 and older—1%

2. Where do you live?

Forty-nine U.S. states, Washington, DC, and more than eleven foreign countries, including Australia, Canada, France, Germany, Israel, Italy, Japan, the Netherlands, New Zealand, and the United Kingdom.

---

[*] The numbers above are calculated based on the percentages of women who answered each question, not necessarily on the total number of women who took the survey. I have rounded the percentages to the nearest whole numbers. For this reason, the sum does not always add up to exactly 100 percent.

3. **Are you**

single—10%

married (first marriage)—58%

married (second or subsequent marriage)—12%

divorced or separated—11%

widowed—1%

cohabitating with male partner—6%

cohabitating with female partner—1%

4. **What is your professional status?**

58% work outside the home

25% homemaker

5% student

3% retired

9% other (part-time work, self-employed, home office)

5. **What is your educational level?**

3% some high school

33% high school graduate

40% college

24% postcollege

6. **What is your race?**

77% Caucasian

7% African-American

7% Latina

2% Asian

2% Native American

5% other (includes biracial)

7. **How many children do you have?**

   35% one

   41% two

   18% three

   6% four or more

8. **How old are they? (mark all that apply)**

   28% ages 0 to 2

   54% ages 2 to 12

   26% ages 12 to 20

   22% ages 20 and older

9. **Do you have**

   27% sons only

   33% daughters only

   40% sons and daughters

10. **Do you have grandchildren?**

    9% yes

    91% no

11. **If yes, are they**

    60% daughter's children

    21% son's children

    19% both

12. **How old were you when your mother died or left?**

    23% 6 or younger

    19% 7 to 12

    22% 13 to 18

    16% 19 to 24

    20% 25 or older

13. If your mother died, what was the cause of death?
   (86% of respondents lost mothers to death)

   49% cancer

   10% heart failure

   7% accident

   4% suicide

   4% aneurysm

   3% infectious disease

   3% progressive disorder (e.g., Parkinson's disease)

   2% stroke

   2% childbirth or abortion

   16% other or unknown

14. If your mother left the family or was unavailable, what were the circumstances? (14% of respondents fit into this category)

   21% mental illness

   16% physical abandonment

   16% alcoholism or other drug dependence

   16% emotional unavailability

   8% divorce

   23% other or unknown

15. Were your mother and father divorced or separated prior to your mother's death?

   26% yes

   74% no

16. How would you best describe your mother's parenting style?

   65% very engaged

   19% somewhat engaged

   9% somewhat disengaged

   7% very disengaged

17. **How would you describe your father's parenting style before your mother's death or departure?**

15% very engaged

31% somewhat engaged

23% somewhat disengaged

20% very disengaged

12% he was deceased or physically absent

18. **How would you describe his parenting after your mother's death or departure?**

18% very engaged

27% somewhat engaged

17% somewhat disengaged

23% very disengaged

15% he was deceased or physically absent

19. **What kind of parenting role model was/is your father to you?**

35% positive

34% negative

31% neutral

20. **Who was your primary caretaker after your mother's death or departure?**

30% father

6% maternal grandmother

6% stepmother

5% sister

4% paternal grandmother

4% aunt

10% other

35% I was already 18 or older

21. Did you have a stepmother?

52% yes

48% no

22. How soon after your mother's death/departure did your father remarry?

11% within one year

15% 1 to 2 years

12% 2 to 4 years

16% 4 years or more

35% he did not remarry

11% he was already remarried when my mother died/left

23. If you have/had a stepmother, please describe your relationship with her.

6% very close

29% somewhat close

65% not at all close

24. Which, if any, of the following behaviors were present in your home during childhood or adolescence? (select all that apply)*

36% emotional abuse to children

30% alcohol abuse

19% physical abuse to children

15% mental illness

9% sexual abuse to children

8% other substance abuse

---

* Of all respondents, 53% indicated that at least one of these behaviors was present in the home.

25. How old were you when you gave birth to your first child?

10% younger than 20

54% 20 to 29

33% 30 to 39

2% 40 and older

26. Did you have a preference for a son or for a daughter?

17% son

36% daughter

47% no preference

27. Who was present at the birth? (mark all that apply)

89% husband or partner

11% friend

10% sister

8% mother-in-law

4% sister-in-law

3% doula

17% other (may include doctors and midwives)

28. Which term best describes your first birth experience?

45% very positive

30% somewhat positive

13% somewhat negative

12% awful

29. Was your first child adopted?

4% yes

96% no

30. If yes, what were the circumstances?

46% infertility

24% single mother by choice

17% chose to adopt rather than give birth

15% repeated miscarriages

15% adopted a family member or friend's child

31. Who helped you (other than a husband or partner) after your first child's arrival?

16% mother-in-law

7% sister

7% friend

4% baby nurse or doula

3% stepmother

11% other family member

52% no one

32. Did you suffer from a diagnosed postpartum depression?

81% no

19% yes

33. Which of the following did you miss receiving from your mother during the postpartum period? (mark all that apply)

88% emotional support (encouragement, shoulder to cry on, etc.)

78% practical support (infant care, babysitting, etc.)

76% information about my own babyhood

76% information about her as a young mother

69% information about her pregnancy and delivery

7% none of the above

34. **How did your opinion of your mother change after you became a mother yourself? (mark all that apply)**

61% more admiration for her

5% less admiration for her

47% more sympathy for her

3% less sympathy for her

66% more awareness of how she must have loved me

14% more awareness of how she should have loved me

8% my opinion of her did not change

35. **Whom do you talk with about being a mother and parenting your children? (mark all that apply)**

80% friends

73% spouse

37% sibling

19% mother-in-law

16% father

6% stepmother

3% father-in-law

5% no one

16% other (includes pediatricians, therapists, other family members)

36. **Where do you go for parenting advice when there's a problem? (mark all that apply)**

65% friend

56% parenting books and/or magazines

55% spouse

24% sibling

23% paid professional

12% mother-in-law

9% father

2% stepmother

2% father-in-law

15% other

24% rely only on myself

37. How supportive and helpful is your husband or partner in raising and caring for your children?

61% very supportive

28% somewhat supportive

12% not supportive

38. How much child-care assistance does he/she provide, relative to you?

11% more than 50 percent

32% about 50 percent

57% less than 50 percent

39. At what age did your children start asking about your mother's absence?

4% younger than 2

43% ages 2 to 6

13% ages 6 to 12

2% ages 12 to 18

38% they did not ask (includes young children who have not asked yet)

40. At what age did you start explaining her death or absence to them?

9% younger than 2

46% ages 2 to 6

20% ages 6 to 12

4% ages 12 to 18

21% I have not/not yet begun explaining it

41. **Do you keep photographs of your mother on display in your home?**

76% yes

24% no

42. **Below are some characteristics of parents (mark the answer that most generally applies to you)**

Fun

47% very much

50% somewhat

3% not at all

Loving/warm

75% very much

23% somewhat

2% not at all

Available

72% very much

26% somewhat

1% not at all

Attentive

66% very much

32% somewhat

2% not at all

Affectionate

74% very much

23% somewhat

3% not at all

Flexible

42% very much

53% somewhat

 5% not at all

Overprotective

42% very much

44% somewhat

14% not at all

Easily overwhelmed

36% very much

41% somewhat

22% not at all

43. **Please mark the answer that best describes the degree to which you have or have had the following thoughts as a mother:**

Life is fragile; our time together may be short

61% often

34% sometimes

 5% never

I need to prepare my children for the possibility of my early death

31% often

43% sometimes

26% never

Keeping my children safe is a top priority

82% often

17% sometimes

 1% never

Keeping myself safe is a top priority

49% often

43% sometimes

8% never

I want to be the mother I didn't have

60% often

20% sometimes

21% never

44. How often do/did you worry about the following:

Getting the same disease or impairment as your mother

50% often

34% sometimes

16% never

Dying young

51% often

40% sometimes

9% never

Not knowing how to be a mother

41% often

36% sometimes

23% never

Leaving children motherless

53% often

38% sometimes

8% never

Losing a spouse or partner

40% often
47% sometimes
14% never

Losing a child

46% often
46% sometimes
 8% never

Not being able to have a child

14% often
19% sometimes
67% never

Control Group Survey

From May 2003 to October 2004, 73 mothers whose mothers are still living participated in a mail survey. Their responses were analyzed alongside the responses of 73 randomly selected motherless mothers whenever a comparison between the two groups was made. The results of the control group survey are as follows:[*]

1. **How old are you now?**

   Younger than 20—0%

   20 to 29—1%

   30 to 39—42%

   40 to 49—27%

   50 to 59—12%

   60 to 69—14%

   70 and older—3%

2. **Where do you live?**

   Thirteen U.S. states and six foreign countries, including Australia, Canada, Denmark, India, Israel, and Grenada.

---

[*] The numbers above are calculated based on the percentages of women who answered each question, not necessarily on the total number of women who took the survey. I have rounded the percentages to the nearest whole numbers. For this reason, the sum does not always add up to exactly 100 percent.

3. Are you

single—10%

married (first marriage)—56%

married (second or subsequent marriage)—16%

divorced or separated—11%

widowed—5%

cohabitating with male partner—1%

4. What is your professional status?

56% work outside the home

22% homemaker

 5% retired

 3% student

11% other (part-time work, self-employed, home office)

5. What is your educational level?

 4% some high school

25% high school graduate

73% college and postcollege

6. What is your race?

81% Caucasian

10% African-American

 4% Asian

 3% Latina

 1% Native American

 1% other (includes biracial)

7. How many children do you have?

29% one

52% two

11% three

 8% four or more

8. **How old are they? (mark all that apply)**

26% ages 0 to 2

53% ages 2 to 12

10% ages 12 to 20

37% ages 20 and older

9. **Do you have**

27% sons only

33% daughters only

40% sons and daughters

10. **Do you have grandchildren?**

23% yes

77% no

11. **If yes, are they**

41% daughter's children

29% son's children

29% both

12. **Were your mother and father divorced or separated during your childhood or adolescence?**

27% yes

73% no

13. **How would you best describe your mother's parenting style?**

53% very engaged

22% somewhat engaged

22% somewhat disengaged

3% very disengaged

14. **How would you best describe your father's parenting style?**

    22% very engaged

    37% somewhat engaged

    15% somewhat disengaged

    18% very disengaged

    8% he was deceased or physically absent

15. **What kind of parenting role model was/is your mother to you?**

    59% positive

    16% negative

    25% neutral

16. **What kind of parenting role model was/is your father to you?**

    55% positive

    30% negative

    14% neutral

17. **Did you have a stepmother?**

    19% yes

    81% no

    If yes, how soon after your parents' divorce did your father remarry?

    27% within one year

    9% 1 to 2 years

    27% 2 to 4 years

    36% 4 years or more

18. **If you have/had a stepmother, please describe your relationship with her.**

    8% very close

    42% somewhat close

    50% not at all close

19. **Which, if any, of the following behaviors were present in your home during childhood and/or adolescence?***

   19% emotional abuse to children

   18% alcohol abuse

   5% physical abuse to children

   11% mental illness

   3% sexual abuse to children

   4% other substance abuse

20. **How old were you when you gave birth to or adopted your first child?**

   5% younger than 20

   47% 20 to 29

   44% 30 to 39

   4% 40 and older

21. **Did you have a preference for a son or for a daughter?**

   10% son

   36% daughter

   54% no preference

22. **Who was present at the birth? (mark all that apply)**

   81% husband or partner

   16% mother

   13% mother-in-law

   13% friend

   6% sister

   3% sister-in-law

   0% doula

   32% other (included grandmother, father, father-in-law, and doctors and/or midwives)

---

* Of all respondents, 33% indicated that at least one of these behaviors was present in the home.

23. Which term best describes your first birth experience?

46% very positive

39% somewhat positive

6% somewhat negative

9% awful

24. Was your first child adopted?

7% yes

93% no

25. If yes, what were the circumstances? (mark all that apply)

60% infertility

20% chose to adopt rather than give birth

20% repeated miscarriage

0% single mother by choice

26. Who helped you (other than a husband or partner) after your first child's arrival?

54% mother

35% mother-in-law

28% baby nurse or doula

10% friend

8% sister

3% stepmother

12% other family member

15% no one

27. Did you suffer from a diagnosed postpartum depression?

90% no

10% yes

28. **Which of the following did you receive from your mother during your first pregnancy and/or postpartum period? (mark all that apply)**

   66% emotional support (encouragement, shoulder to cry on, etc.)

   55% practical support (infant care, babysitting, etc.)

   41% information about her pregnancy and delivery

   58% information about my own babyhood

   38% information about her as a young mother

   11% none of the above

29. **How did your opinion of your mother change after you became a mother yourself? (mark all that apply)**

   54% more admiration for her

    3% less admiration for her

   42% more sympathy for her

    1% less sympathy for her

   53% more awareness of how she must have loved me

   21% more awareness of how she should have loved me

   18% my opinion of her did not change

30. **Whom do/did you talk with about being a parent and raising your children? (mark all that apply)**

   83% friends

   73% spouse or partner

   63% mother

   44% sibling

   30% mother-in-law

   25% father

    8% father-in-law

    4% stepmother

    4% no one

   19% other (includes grandmothers, sisters-in-law, babysitters, and aunts)

31. Where do/did you go for parenting advice when there's a problem? (mark all that apply)

66% friend

59% spouse or partner

59% parenting books and/or magazines

52% mother

37% paid professional

30% sibling

16% mother-in-law

4% father-in-law

3% stepmother

16% other (includes support group leaders, grandmothers, God)

11% rely only on myself

32. How supportive and helpful is/was your spouse or partner in raising and caring for your children?

68% very supportive

26% somewhat supportive

6% not supportive

33. How much child-care assistance does/did he/she provide, relative to you?

4% more than 50 percent

47% about 50 percent

48% less than 50 percent

34. Below are some characteristics of parents. Please mark the answer which most generally applies to you.

Fun

59% very much

41% somewhat

0% not at all

Loving/warm

87% very much

13% somewhat

0% not at all

Available

74% very much

26% somewhat

0% not at all

Attentive

75% very much

25% somewhat

0% not at all

Affectionate

79% very much

21% somewhat

0% not at all

Flexible

53% very much

46% somewhat

1% not at all

Overprotective

22% very much

60% somewhat

18% not at all

Easily overwhelmed

8% very much

47% somewhat

45% not at all

35. **Please mark the answer that best describes the degree to which you have or have had the following thoughts as a mother:**

Life is fragile; our time together may be short

30% often

52% sometimes

18% never

I need to prepare my children for the possibility of my early death

10% often

27% sometimes

63% never

Keeping my children safe is a top priority

84% often

16% sometimes

0% never

Keeping myself safe is a top priority

53% often

40% sometimes

7% never

I want to be the kind of mother my mother was not

35% often

37% sometimes

28% never

36. **How often do/did you worry about the following:**

Dying young

15% often

42% sometimes

43% never

Not knowing how to be a mother

  5% often

42% sometimes

53% never

Leaving children motherless

11% often

52% sometimes

37% never

Losing a spouse or partner

11% often

67% sometimes

22% never

Losing a child

20% often

51% sometimes

29% never

Not being able to have a child

  8% often

25% sometimes

67% never

APPENDIX 3

Resources

The following organizations offer social events, therapy groups, or both for motherless women. Additional resources and news about upcoming groups and events are listed online at www.motherlessmothers.com.

Motherless Daughters of Los Angeles

PO Box 64373
Los Angeles, CA 90064
310-474-2208
www.motherlessdaughtersbiz.com
Contact: Irene Rubaum-Keller, MFT

Motherless Daughters of Orange County (MDOC)

9053 Suva St.
Downey, CA 90242
562-862-6653
MDofOC@hotmail.com
www.motherlessdaughtersoc.com
Contact: Mary Felix

Metro Detroit Motherless Daughters (MDMD)

45333 Kensington
Utica, MI 48317
586-337-3110
metrodetroitmd@yahoo.com
www.metrodetroitmotherlessdaughters.net

Contact: Vicki Waldron

Motherless Daughters of Chicago

Chicago, IL
773-233-5460 (Chicago)
630-424-8081 (western suburbs)
mdofchicago@hotmail.com

Contacts: Ruta Grigola (Chicago)
　　　　　 Dawn Klancic (western suburbs)

Motherless Daughters of New England

Boston, MA
mdonema@yahoo.com
http://motherlessdaughtersofnewengland.intranets.com/

Contact: Linda Mills

Circle of Daughters

4637 Ironwood Dr.
Hamburg, NY 14075 (Buffalo area)
716-627-4934
info@circleofdaughters.com
www.circleofdaughters.com

Contact: Day Cummings, CSW, RN

**Motherless Daughters of Switzerland
(Toechter ohne Muetter)**

   41 (0) 52 213 80 60 (Winterthur)
   41 (0) 43 288 88 88 (Zurich)
   toechterohnemuetter@hotmail.com
   www.geocities.com/prettyswiss/Toechter_ohne_Muetter.html
   (in German)

   Contact: Andrea Allen

**The Motherless Mothers Foundation—Israel
(Imahot L'lo Imahot)**

   c/o Rahav
   Grizim 7, Apt. 2
   Tel Aviv, Israel
   972-54-471-4044
   972-54-442-5856
   motherlessmothers@mail.com
   www.motherlessmother.org.il (Hebrew and English)

   Contacts: Julie Rahav
            Shoshanit Lupo Feigenberg

Notes

Epigraph

Linda Gray Sexton, *Searching for Mercy Street* (New York: Little Brown and Company, 1994), 261.

Introduction

xxiii *When Mireault compared . . . doing as mothers.:* Gina C. Mireault, Toni Thomas, and Kimberly Bearor, "Maternal Identity Among Motherless Mothers and Psychological Symptoms in Their Firstborn Children," *Journal of Child and Family Studies* 11 (September 2000); also personal communication with Gina Mireault, PhD, October 10, 2002.

xxiii *When I surveyed 73 mothers . . . :* Motherless Mothers Control Group survey, question 28 (see Appendix 2).

xxiii *Only 15 percent . . . : Ibid.,* question 26.

xxiii *In a similar survey . . . :* Motherless Mothers survey, question 31 (see Appendix 1).

xxiv *The motherless women were also . . . : Ibid.,* question 44; Motherless Mothers Control Group survey, question 36.

xxv *In the 1970s . . . their firstborn infants.:* "Harry F. Harlow," www.muskingum.edu/~psychology/psycweb/history/harlow.htm; "The Experiment," www.ussers.rcn.com/napier.interport/cwm/experim.html; Michael Lewis, "Rhesus Pieces," *APS Observer* 16 (September 2003).

xxv *As Maxine Harris, PhD . . . :* Maxine Harris, *The Loss That Is Forever* (New York: Plume, 1996), 189.

xxvi *Erna Furman . . . by a different person, afterward.:* Erna Furman, *A Child's Parent Dies* (New Haven, Connecticut: Yale University Press, 1974), 292.

xxvi *At about the same time . . . got in the way.:* Rita Rogers, "The Influence of Losing One's Parent on Being a Parent," *Psychiatry Digest* (May 1968), 29–36.

xxvi *A few years later . . . those of the same sex.:* Sol Altschul and Helen Beiser, "The Effect of Early Parent Loss on Future Parenthood." In *Parenthood: A Psychodynamic Perspective*, eds. Rebecca S. Cohen, Bertram J. Cohler, and Sidney H. Weissman (New York: The Guildford Press, 1984), 175–181.

xxvii *This was a problem with many . . . :* Jennie Long Dilworth and Gladys J. Hildreth, "Long-term Unresolved Grief: Applying Bowlby's Variants to Adult Survivors of Early Parental Death," *Omega* 36 (1997–98), 155; personal communication with Gina Mireault, PhD, October 10, 2002.

xxvii *Far fewer studies . . . :* Dilworth and Hildreth, "Long-term Unresolved Grief," 155.

xxvii *He conducted . . . their experience as parents.:* Donald Zall, "The Impact of Early Maternal Bereavement on Future Parenting," diss., Boston College School of Social Work, May 1993.

xxvii *None of the motherless mothers . . . the fragility of life.: Ibid.*; Donald S. Zall, "The Long-term Effects of Childhood Bereavement: Impact on Roles as Mothers," *Omega* 29 (1994), 226.

xxxii *For many years, I was stuck . . . :* In his *Omega* article, Donald Zall talks about motherless mothers becoming "unstuck" after having children of their own, 228.

Chapter One: Motherhood and Mourning

4 *For these daughters, motherhood . . . :* Harris, *The Loss That Is Forever,* 170.

4 *What was broken . . . : Ibid.,* 187.

5 *This type of emotional . . . "maturational grief.":* Therese Rando, *Treatment of Complicated Mourning* (Champaign, Illinois: Research Press, 1993), 64–65.

6 *One of the biggest paradoxes . . . :* Personal communication, Michael Schwartzman, PhD, November 2002.

7 *Life, they say, is . . . :* Myra Leifer, *Psychological Effects of Motherhood* (Westport, Connecticut: Praeger, 1980), 4.

10 *More than half of all . . . done a better job . . . :* Motherless Mothers Survey, question 34; Motherless Mothers Control Group Survey, question 29.

12 *According to psychoanalysts . . . :* Therese Benedek, "Parenthood as a Developmental Phase: A Contribution to Libido Theory," *Journal of the American Psychoanalytic Association* 7 (1959), 395; Nancy Chodorow, *The Reproduction of Mothering* (Berkeley, California: University of California Press, 1978), 89–90.

17 *Psychoanalyst Therese Benedek was the first to propose . . . :* Benedek, "Parenthood as a Developmental Phase," 397.

20 *Of all the women in the . . . :* Motherless Mothers survey, question 3.

20 *And about half of them . . . : Ibid.,* question 21.

Chapter Two: Pregnancy

33 *Sterile surgical environments, antibiotics . . . :* "Achievements in Public Health, 1900–1999: Healthier Mothers and Babies," *Morbidity and Mortality Weekly Report* 48 (October 1, 1999), 849–858.

34 *What is surprising is . . . :* Leifer, *Psychological Effects of Motherhood,* 4; Sheila Kitzinger, *Ourselves as Mothers* (Reading, Massachusetts: Addison-Wesley, 1994), ix.

34 *They also mark the beginning . . . :* Kitzinger, *Ourselves as Mothers,* 1.

34 *Just one generation ago . . . in most women's lives.:* Susan Maushart, *The Mask of Motherhood* (New York: Penguin, 1999), 61.

34 *And like most major life changes . . . :* Gayle H. Peterson, *Birthing Normally,* 2nd edition (Berkeley, California: Shadow & Light, 1984), 156.

34 *It's not unusual for a pregnant woman . . . :* Shaila Misri, *Shouldn't I Be Happy?* (New York: The Free Press, 1995), 24.

35 *Various studies have found . . . :* "Dealing with Depression and the Perils of Pregnancy," *New York Times,* January 13, 2004.

35 *Pregnancy was once thought to protect women . . . :* Jonathan Evans, Jon Heron, Helen Francomb, Sarah Oke, and Jean Golding, "Cohort Study of Depressed Mood During Pregnancy and After Childbirth," *British Medical Journal* 4 (August 2001), http://bmj.bmjjournals.com/cgi/content/full/323/7307/257.

35 *Now, for some women . . . : Ibid.;* "Dealing with Depression and the Perils of Pregnancy," *New York Times;* Gayle Peterson, "Can Treating Depression Improve Your Fertility?" www.askdrgayle.com

35 *Part of the problem lies with . . . :* Alliance for Health Reform, www.allhealth.org

37 *Pregnancy, like any time of emotional stress . . . :* Peterson, *Birthing Normally,* 131.

37–38 *Back in the 1950s Bibring . . . leading to a new stage of maturation.:* Grete L. Bibring, "Some Considerations of the Psychological Processes in Pregnancy," *The Psychoanalytic Study of the Child* 14 (1959), 113–121.

38 *That's a main reason why . . . : Ibid.,* 116; Miriam Elson, "Parenthood and the Transformations of Narcissism," in *Parenthood, a Psychodynamic Perspective* (New York: The Guilford Press: 1984), 300–301.

40 *Numerous studies on parenting behavior . . . with children of their own . . . :* Michael Rutter, "Intergenerational Continuities and Discontinuities in Serious Parenting Difficulties," in Dante Cicchetti & Vicki Carlson, eds., *Child*

Maltreatment: Theory and Research on the Causes and Consequences of Childhood Abuse and Neglect (New York: Cambridge University, 1989); Avshalom Caspi and Glen H. Elder Jr., "Emergent Family Patterns: The Intergenerational Construction of Problem Behavior and Relationships," in *Relationships Within Families* (Oxford: Hinde & Hinde, 1988); R. L. Burgess & L. M. Youngblade, "Social Incompetence and the Intergenerational Transmission of Abusive Parental Practices," in G. Hotaling et al., *Family Abuse and Its Consequences: New Directions in Research* (Beverly Hills, California: Sage, 1988).

40 . . . *even though their lives are "made more complex . . .":* Kathryn Baker, *Mothering Without a Map* (New York: Viking, 2004), 3.

40 *But the opposite doesn't hold true . . . :* Rutter, "Intergenerational Continuities and Discontinuities in Serious Parenting Difficulties," 321.

40 *True borderline patients . . . :* Phillip W. Long, MD, "Borderline Personality Disorder: Treatment" on www.mentalhealth.com/rx/p23-pe05.html

40 *The majority of women in the Beth Israel study . . . :* Grete L. Bibring, Thomas F. Dwyer, Dorothy S. Huntington, and Arthur F. Valenstein, "A Study of the Psychological Processes in Pregnancy and of the Earliest Mother-Child Relationship," *The Psychoanalytic Study of the Child* 16 (1961), 10.

40–41 *In some cases . . . with so little?":* Ibid., 11–12.

41 *Susan Maushart describes . . . :* Maushart, *The Mask of Motherhood*, 47.

44 *Of all motherless daughters . . . :* Motherless Mothers survey, question 33.

44 *It's easy to label that group . . . :* Control Group survey, question 28.

44 *In fact, this latter group . . . :* Ibid.

45 *Yet for more than half . . . :* "National Survey of Family Growth (NSFG)" Survey Description, http://www.cdc.gov/nchs/about/major/ nsfg/nsfgback.htm; Stanley K. Henshaw, "Unintended Pregnancy in the United States," *Family Planning Perspectives* 30 (1998), 24–29; 46.

50 . . . *("the replacement baby") . . . :* Daniel N. Stern and Nadia Bruschweiler-Stern, *The Birth of a Mother* (New York: Basic Books, 1998), 72.

52 *In 1995, the last year for which . . . :* www.cdc.gov/nchs/fastats/fertile.htm; "Fertility, Family Planning, and Women's Health: New Data From the 1995 National Survey of Family Growth," *Vital and Health Statistics*, Series 23, No. 19, Centers for Disease Control and Prevention/National Center for Health Statistics, Table B, 3. www.cdc.gov/nchs/data/series/sr_23/sr23_019.pdf

53 *About 10 to 20 percent of the time . . . :* "Unexplained Infertility," Advanced Fertility Center of Chicago. www.advancedfertility.com/unexplai.htm

55 *In a Parenthood.com worldwide survey . . . :* "Pink When You Wanted Blue," http://topics-az.parenthood.com/articles.html?article_id=2707&printable=true

56 *In most of the world . . . :* "Preference for Sons Over Daughters," from Joni Seager, *The State of Women in the World Atlas: New Edition* (New York: Viking Adult, 1997).

56 *Not surprisingly, the majority of women . . . :* "Pink When You Wanted Blue," 1.

56 (fn) *Curiously, only one-third . . . :* Motherless Mothers survey, question 26.

56–57 *. . . like 68 percent of the Parenthood.com . . . :* "Pink When You Wanted Blue," 1.

58 *This corresponds with the more . . . : Ibid.*

Chapter Three: Labor and Delivery

62 *"The special events that take place . . . :* Stern, *The Birth of a Mother*, 58.

63 *As Susan Maushart has pointed out . . . :* Maushart, *The Mask of Motherhood*, 88.

67 (fn) *For a full definition of "doula" . . . :* Marshall H. Klaus, John H. Kennell, and Phyllis H. Klaus, *Mothering the Mother* (Reading, Massachusetts: Addison-Wesley, 1993), 4.

69 *Now that Western women . . . :* Maushart, *The Mask of Motherhood*, 86.

69 *One of my favorites . . . on a woman's moods.:* Miriam Stoppard, *Dr. Miriam Stoppard's New Pregnancy & Birth Book* (New York: Ballantine Books, 2000).

70 *This makes them also more likely . . . :* Ina May Gaskin, *Ina May's Guide to Natural Childbirth* (New York: Bantam Books, 2003), 139.

70 *Fear of motherhood, disharmony . . . : Ibid.,* throughout; Peterson, *Birthing Normally*, 11.

70 *Whether the exact biological culprit . . . :* K. Wijma, "Why Focus on 'Fear of Childbirth'? *Journal of Psychosomatic Obstetrics & Gynecology* 24 (2003), 141–143; www.birthsource.com/proarticlefile/proarticle68.html); Peterson, *Birthing Normally*, 11.

70 *Peterson describes labor and delivery . . . :* Peterson, *Birthing Normally*, 4.

70 *"A woman who has developed a style . . .": Ibid.*

73 *Norma Tracey, PhD . . . :* Norma Tracey, "Thinking About and Working with Depressed Mothers in the Early Months of Their Infant's Life," *Journal of Child Psychotherapy* 26 (2000), 185–189.

73 *Because of this, she says . . . : Ibid.*

73 *Fewer than .001 percent of women . . . :* "Deaths: Final Data for 2000," *National Vital Statistics Reports*, Vol. 53, No. 5, Oct. 12, 2004, 13.

74 *On being invited into the birth room . . . :* Gaskin, *Ina May's Guide to Natural Childbirth*, 134.

75 *Acknowledging one's fear . . . :* Peterson, *Birthing Normally*, 19.

75 *Ina May Gaskin believes . . . :* Gaskin, *Ina May's Guide to Natural Childbirth*, 135.

76 *Women in some African countries . . . :* Kitzinger, *Ourselves as Mothers*, 110.

78 *Ina May Gaskin remembers . . . :* Personal e-mail communication with Ina May Gaskin, February 21, 2005.

86 *A woman's subjective experience of childbirth . . . :* Kathleen A. Kendall-Tackett, "The Impact of Negative Birth Experiences on Mother/Infant Relationships," *The APSAC Advisor* 7 (1994), 9–10; 25–26.

86 *Women who had poorly controlled pain . . . : Ibid.,* 2–4; Kathleen A. Kendall-Tackett, "Trauma Associated with Perinatal Events: Birth Experience, Prematurity, and Childbearing Loss," in *The Handbook of Women, Stress and Trauma* (New York: Taylor & Francis, 2004).

86 *"Underlying these feelings are often . . .":* Kendall-Tackett, "The Impact of Negative Birth Experiences on Mother/Infant Relationships," 4.

86 *Of all the motherless women . . . :* Motherless Mothers survey, question 28.

87 *Women whose mothers are still alive . . . :* Control Group survey, question 23.

87 *According to Phyllis Klaus . . . :* Klaus, Kennell, and Klaus, *Mothering the Mother,* 3.

89 *Even a few counseling sessions . . . :* Colette Bouchez, "Therapy Can Help Women Overcome Fear of Childbirth, a New Study Shows," http://adutopia. subportal.com/health/Womens/Childbirth/504641.html; T. Saisto and E. Halmesmaki, "Fear of Childbirth: A Neglected Dilemma," *Acta Obstetricia et Gynecologica Scandinavia* 82 (March 2003), 201–208.

90 *Mother hadn't really told me much . . . :* Sexton, *Searching for Mercy Street,* 244.

90 *From the thousands of births she's witnessed . . . :* Gaskin, *Ina May's Guide to Natural Childbirth,* 138.

90 *Gaskin attributes this to . . . : Ibid.,* 167–173.

91 *If you notice that someone's presence . . . :* Peterson, *Birthing Normally,* 128.

92 *Different women define control . . . :* Bonnie Fox and Diana Worts, "Revisiting the Critique of Medicalized Childbirth: A Contribution to the Sociology of Birth," *Gender & Society* 13 (1999), 328.

92 *Screaming in pain, moaning, crying . . . :* Nina Barrett, *I Wish Someone Had Told Me* (New York: Fireside, 1990), 11.

Chapter Four: Postpartum

100 *When Myra Leifer, PhD . . . from the delivery.:* Leifer, *Psychological Effects of Motherhood.*

102 *Infant care awakens in a mother . . . :* Elson, "Parenthood and the Transformations of Narcissism," 309.

102 *. . . "primary maternal preoccupation" . . . :* D. W. Winnicott, *Babies and Their Mothers* (Reading, Massachusetts: Addison-Wesley, 1987), 36; Kitzinger, *Ourselves as Mothers,* 12.

102 *By withdrawing in this manner . . . :* Winnicott, *Babies and Their Mothers,* 36.

103 *A British study comparing . . . likely to separate or divorce.:* Eva A. Frommer and Gillian O'Shea, "Antenatal Identification of Women Liable to Have Problems in Managing Their Infants," *British Journal of Psychiatry* 123 (1973), 149–156.

104 *Nancy Maguire, PhD . . . than other women did.:* Nancy B. Maguire, "The Impact of Childhood Maternal Loss on the Transition to Motherhood," diss., The California School of Professional Psychology, October 1999.

104 *Another British study, however . . . :* E. S. Paykel, E. M. Emms, J. Fletcher and E. S. Rassaby, "Life Events and Social Support in Puerperal Depression," *British Journal of Psychology* 136 (1980), 345.

104 *My survey results didn't find that . . . :* Motherless Mothers survey, question 32; Control Group survey, question 27.

104 *Those who'd lost a mother before age six . . . :* Motherless Mothers survey question 32 cross-tabulated with survey questions 12, 28, and 31.

104 *Lack of support during the postpartum period . . . :* Paykel et al., "Life Events and Social Support in Puerperal Depression," 339–346; Kathleen A. Kendall-Tackett, *Depression in New Mothers* (Binghamton, New York: The Haworth Press, 2005), 114–116.

104 *. . . along with prior episodes of depression . . . :* Kendall-Tackett, *Depression in New Mothers*, 96–97; Paykel et al., "Life Events and Social Support in Puerperal Depression," 342–343.

104 *. . . social isolation . . . :* Linda Clark Amankwaa, "Postpartum Depression, Culture and African-American Women," *Journal of Cultural Diversity* (Spring 2003).

104 *. . . low feelings of self-efficacy and self-esteem . . . :* Kendall-Tackett, *Depression in New Mothers*, 94–95.

104 *. . . a history of victimization or abuse . . . : Ibid.*, 98–104.

104 *. . . profound sleep deprivation . . . :* KL Armstrong, AR Van Haeringen, MR Dodds, and R Cash, "Sleep Deprivation or Postnatal Depression in Later Infancy; Separating the Chicken From the Egg," *Journal of Paediatric Child Health* 34 (1998 June), 260–262; H. Hiscock and M. Wake, "Infant Sleep Problems and Postnatal Depression: a Community-based Study," *Pediatrics* 107 (June 2001), 1317–1322.

104 *. . . marital stress . . . :* Kendall-Tackett, *Depression in New Mothers*, 116–117; Peter S. Stemp, R. Jay Turner, and Samuel Noh, "Psychological Distress in the Postpartum Period: The Significance of Social Support," *Journal of Marriage and the Family* 48 (May 1986), 271–277; R. Kumar and Kay Mordecai Robson, "A Prospective Study of Emotional Disorders in Childbearing Women," *British Journal of Psychiatry* 144 (1984), 41.

105 *. . . serious doubts about having this particular child . . . :* Kumar and Robson, "A Prospective Study of Emotional Disorders in Childbearing Women," 42.

105 *. . . a complicated emotional relationship . . . :* N. Uddenberg and L. Nilsson,

"The Longitudinal Course of Para-Natal Emotional Disturbance," *Acta psychiat. Scand.* 52 (1975), 161.

105 . . . *a family history of mental illness* . . . *:* personal communication, Shari Lusskin, MD, October 25, 2004.

105 . . . *a baby who cries excessively* . . . *:* Sheila Kitzinger, *The Crying Baby* (London: Penguin Group, 1989), 78.

105 . . . *and a naturally pessimistic or fatalistic* . . . *:* Kendall-Tackett, *Depression in New Mothers*, 91–93.

105 *The blues, characterized by weepiness* . . . *:* Linda Clark Amankwaa, "Postpartum depression, culture, and African-American women"; www.askdrgayle.com/recent8.htm; www.med.umichedu/obgyn/smartmoms/labor/depression.htm

105 *Postpartum psychosis is an extremely dangerous* . . . *:* www.askdrgayle.com/recent8.htm

105 *It's quite rare, affecting fewer than 1 percent* . . . *:* Kendall-Tackett, *Depression in New Mothers*, 8.

108 *Self-sufficiency, as Harriet Lerner, PhD* . . . *:* Harriet Lerner, *The Mother Dance* (New York: HarperCollins, 1998), 125.

109 *Yet the United States is one of the few* . . . *:* Myra Leifer, "Psychological Changes Accompanying Pregnancy and Motherhood," *Genetic Psychology Monographs* 95 (1977), 90.

109 *The high degree of ceremony* . . . *:* Gwen Stern and Lawrence Kruckman, "Multi-Disciplinary Perspectives on Post-Partum Depression: An Anthropological Critique," *Social Science Medicine* 17 (1983) 1033–1040.

109 *Some researchers believe that a new mother's ability* . . . *:* Fox and Worts, "Revisiting the Critique of Medicalized Childbirth: A Contribution to the Sociology of Birth," 344.

110 *For a new mother, such women* . . . *:* Stern, *The Birth of a Mother*, 131.

110 *Of particular importance to this matrix* . . . *: Ibid.*

110 *"The affirming matrix often has* . . .*": Ibid.*

115 *Although a mother-in-law was* . . . *:* Motherless Mothers survey, question 31.

116 *Even more striking, however* . . . *:* Motherless Mothers survey, questions 21 and 31.

116 *Only 6 percent of the women who have stepmothers* . . . *:* Motherless Mothers survey, question 23.

117 *But in truth, hours or days* . . . *:* Maushart, *The Mask of Motherhood*, 87.

118 *Too many women feeling guilty* . . . *: Ibid.*

118 *As Andi Buchanan so succinctly writes* . . . *:* Andrea J. Buchanan, *Mother Shock* (New York: Seal Press, 2003), x.

118 *The taking-hold time of the post-partum period* . . . *:* Holly Richardson, "Drive-Through Deliveries: Are they "Bad Medicine?" www.childbirth.org/articles/postpartum/ drivethru.html

118 *Some women, like my friend* . . . *:* Leifer, *Psychological Effects of Motherhood*, 73.

119 . . . *delayed by the stress of a premature or difficult birth* . . . *:* Stern, *The Birth of a Mother*, 195.

119 . . . *problems connecting with the fetus during pregnancy* . . . *:* Leifer, *Psychological Effects of Motherhood*, 77.

119 . . . *and by the baby's temperament* . . . *: Ibid.*, 95–98.

119 *Mothers of colicky infants and babies* . . . *: Ibid.*, 72; Kitzinger, *The Crying Baby*, 210–213.

119 *Maternal attachment also appears to be related* . . . *:* Leifer, *Psychological Effects of Motherhood*, 72.

Chapter Five: Getting Attached

124 *Studies have shown that first-time mothers* . . . *:* Marja Terttu Tarkaa, "Predictors of Maternal Competence by First-time Mothers When the Child Is 8 Months Old," *Journal of Advanced Nursing* 41 (February 2003), 233.

124 *Mothers who feel socially isolated* . . . *: Ibid.*

126 *The smiling, cooing, and babbling* . . . *:* Kelvin J. Seifert and Robert J. Hoffnung, *Child and Adolescent Development* (Boston: Houghton Mifflin Co., 1987), 271.

126 *These instinctual infant responses* . . . *: Ibid.*; John Bowlby, "The Nature of the Child's Tie to His Mother," *International Journal of Psychoanalysis* 39 (1958), 364.

126 *The nature of a mother-infant bond* . . . *:* Seifert and Hoffnung, *Child and Adolescent Development*, 277.

127 *The first,* secure *children* . . . *efforts to comfort them, or both.: Ibid.*, 275–276; Mary Main and Erik Hesse, "Parents' Unresolved Traumatic Experiences Are Related to Infant Disorganized Attachment Status," in Mark T. Greenberg, Dante Cicchetti, and E. Mark Cummings, eds., *Attachment in the Preschool Years* (Chicago: University of Chicago Press, 1990); Mary Main and Jude Cassidy, "Categories of Response to Reunion With the Parent at Age 6: Predictable From Infant Attachment Classifications and Stable Over a 1-Month Period," *Developmental Psychology* 24 (1988), 415; Robert Karen, *Becoming Attached* (New York: Warner Books, 1994), 158–176.

128 (fn) *It's not unusual* . . . *as long as a few hours* . . . *:* Alicia Lieberman, *The Emotional Life of the Toddler* (New York: The Free Press, 1995), 141.

128 *They gave the impression of wanting comfort* . . . *:* Karen, *Becoming Attached*, 158.

128 *Their mothers also ranked low* . . . *: Ibid.*, 159.

128 *Yet mothers with avoidant . . . the mother's personality.": Ibid.,* 159–160.

129 *She noticed a variety of attachment behaviors . . . :* Main and Hesse, "Parents' Unresolved Traumatic Experiences Are Related to Infant Disorganized Attachment Status."

129 *So, five years later . . . with their own kids.:* Mary D. Salter Ainsworth and Carolyn Eichberg, "Effects on Infant-mother Attachment of Mother's Unresolved Loss of an Attachment Figure, or Other Traumatic Experience," in Colin Murray Parkes, Joan Stevenson-Hinde, and Peter Marris, *Attachments Across the Life Cycle* (London: Routledge, 1991), 160–183.

130 *The ones who talked about their parents . . . :* Marinus H. van Ijzendoorn, "Adult Attachment Representations, Parental Responsiveness, and Infant Attachment: A Meta-analysis on the Predictive Validity of the Adult Attachment Interview," *Psychological Bulletin* 117 (1995), 388.

130 *These adults also spoke about . . .": Ibid.*

130 *They seemed to be still confused . . . : Ibid.*; Lelia Beckwith, Sarale H. Cohen, and Claire Hamilton, "Maternal Sensitivity During Infancy and Subsequent Life Events Relate to Attachment Representations at Early Adulthood," *Developmental Psychology* 35 (1999), 695.

130 *As she expected, secure mothers . . . :* Main and Hesse, "Parents' Unresolved Traumatic Experiences Are Related to Infant Disorganized Attachment Status," 166.

130 *Most important for our purposes, however . . . :* Ainsworth and Eichberg, "Effects on Infant-mother Attachment of Mother's Unresolved Loss of an Attachment Figure, or Other Traumatic Experience," 160–161.

131 *When Main pressed further . . . in the disorganized group.":* Main and Hesse, "Parents' Unresolved Traumatic Experiences Are Related to Infant Disorganized Attachment Status," 168.

131 *Mothers who hadn't mourned their losses . . . : Ibid.,* 174.

131 *Or a mother who felt . . . : Ibid.,* 176.

131 *Main also identified unusual . . . : Ibid.*

132 *"Frightened," overreactive behaviors such as these . . . their source of alarm.: Ibid.*; Carlo Scheungel, Marian J. Bakermans-Kranenberg, and Marinus H. van Ijzendoorn, "Frightening Maternal Behaviors Linking Unresolved Loss and Disorganized Infant Attachment," *Journal of Consulting and Clinical Psychology* 67 (1999), 60.

133 *When the Berkeley researchers revisited . . . :* Main and Cassidy, "Categories of Response to Reunion With the Parent at Age 6: Predictable From Infant Attachment Classifications and Stable Over a 1-Month Period," 415, 422–423.

133 *Children classified as ambivalent at age six . . . : Ibid.,* 423.

133 *Children who had fallen into the D category . . . care from the mothers . . . : Ibid.*

134 *Other studies have found . . . "they're mean.":* Karen, *Becoming Attached* 187–198.

134 *Other studies tracking kids up to age eighteen . . . :* Beckwith, Cohen, and Hamilton, "Maternal Sensitivity During Infancy and Subsequent Life Events Relate to Attachment Representation at Early Adulthood," 697.

134 *But secure attachment in early childhood . . . they received as babies.:* Karen, *Becoming Attached*, 194.

136 *Children seem most able to change . . . :* Ibid., 230–231.

136 *The most striking example . . . developmental or attachment problems.:* Selma Fraiberg, Edna Adelson, and Vivian Shapiro, "Ghosts in the Nursery: A Psychoanalytic Approach to the Problems of Impaired Infant-Mother Relationships," in Selma Fraiberg, ed., *Clinical Studies in Infant Mental Health* (New York: Basic Books, 1980), 167–178.

137 *Alicia Lieberman, PhD, a former student . . . to become more secure.:* Alicia F. Lieberman, Donna R. Weston, and Jeree H. Pawl, "Preventive Intervention and Outcome with Anxiously Attached Dyads," *Child Development* 62 (1991), 199–209.

138 *"Even a mother who has sought therapy . . .":* Karen, *Becoming Attached*, 233–234.

138 *Resolving loss may also . . . better at expressing it.:* Kim Leon, Deborah B. Jacobvitz, and Nancy L. Hazen, "Maternal Resolution of Loss and Abuse: Associations with Adjustment to the Transition to Parenthood," *Infant Mental Health Journal* 25 (2004), 130–148.

139 *Parents need only make an effort . . . :* Karen, *Becoming Attached*, 233–234.

Chapter Six: Zero to Four

143 *Women like me . . . toilet training, or discipline.:* Selma Fraiberg et al., "Ghosts in the Nursery: A Psychoanalytic Approach to the Problems of Impaired Infant-mother Relationships," 165.

143 *Nursery ghosts can make . . . :* Ibid.

146 *In* The Reproduction of Mothering *. . . :* Chodorow, *The Reproduction of Mothering* (Berkeley, California: University of California Press, 1978), 90.

147 *The world he's in . . . :* Michael Schwartzman, *The Anxious Parent* (New York: Simon & Schuster, 1990), 112.

148 *The nighttime scenario . . . without the mother's help.:* Lieberman, *The Emotional Life of the Toddler*, 161.

149 *A British study of first-time mothers . . . a new mother's mood.:* Frommer and O'Shea, "Antenatal Identification of Women Liable to Have Problems in Managing Their Infants," 150–154.

150 *Of all the women surveyed . . . :* Motherless Mothers survey, question 4.

151 *At that age, Rebecca's daughter . . . missed when she's gone.:* Bowlby, "The Nature of the Child's Tie to His Mother," 359–370; Calvin F. Settlage, "Defenses Evoked By Early Childhood Loss: Their Impact on Life-Span Development," in Salman Akhtar, ed., *Three Faces of Mourning* (Northvale, New Jersey: Jason Aronson, 2001), 56–57.

152 *For very young children . . . :* Lieberman, *The Emotional Life of the Toddler*, 153.

152 *Children have a natural anxiety . . . possible onset of illness.:* Schwartzman, *The Anxious Parent*, 228–232.

153 *Norma Tracey, PhD, and her colleagues . . . removed from it altogether.:* Norma Tracey et al., "Who Do I Love When I Love My Mother? Who Do I Love When I Love My Baby? Separation and Attachment Themes in Parent-Infant Groups," Research Paper 5, Gymealily Psychotherapy Centre. www.gymealily.org/resources_paperva5.htm

154 *"A mother's job is to be there . . .":* Erna Furman, *On Being and Having a Mother* (Madison, Connecticut: International Universities Press, 2001), 39.

154 *For a child to master the developmental task . . . : Ibid.*, 39–40.

154–155 *Furman observed two behavior patterns . . . to bear the pain.: Ibid.*, 41–42.

157–158 *They're not an indication . . . Becky Bailey, PhD.:* Becky Bailey, "How Should I Respond When My Child Says, 'I Hate You'?" http://parentcenter.babycenter.com/expert/preschooler/pbehavior/69220.html

159 *They can't quite grasp how . . . : Ibid.*

160 *Mastering self-care, Erna Furman believed . . . :* Erna Furman, *On Being and Having a Mother*, 53.

161 *Most child-development experts agree . . . :* Jennifer Baldino Bonett, "Chores for Toddlers Can Boost Development," www.metrokids.com/september04/choresfortoddlers.html; Susan E. Davis and Robert Needlman, "Chores for Toddlers," www.drspock.com/article/0,1510,5981,00.html

162 *Chores are important, because . . . their own spills and messes.:* Bonett, "Chores for Toddlers Can Boost Development"; Davis and Needlman, "Chores for Toddlers"; Susanne Denham, "When Can My Toddler Start Doing Chores, and What Kinds Are Appropriate?" *Ask the Experts*, www.babycenter.com

163 *But the majority of women surveyed . . . :* Motherless Mothers survey, question 7.

163 *And because the average interval . . . :* Katie Tamony, *Your 2nd Pregnancy* (Chicago: Chicago Review Press, 1995), 153; "Are You Ready for Another One?" www.babycenter.com, June 1, 2005.

163 *Most second-time mothers worry . . . :* Schwartzman, *The Anxious Parent*, 297.

163 *. . . the first child's "dethronement.":* Tamony, *Your 2nd Pregnancy*, 77.

Chapter Seven: The Absent Grandmother

169 *Women are almost always closer . . . :* Gunhild O. Hagestad, "Continuity and Connectedness," in Vern L. Bengtson and Joan F. Robertson, *Grandparenthood* (Beverly Hills, California: Sage Publications, 1985), 40; Hope Edelman, *Mother of My Mother* (New York: Dial Press, 1999), 9.

171 *In virtually every survey . . . :* Ann Eisenberg, "Grandchildren's Perspectives on Relationships with Grandparents: The Influence of Gender Across Generations," *Sex Roles* 19 (1988), 205–210; Boaz Kahana and Eva Kahana, "Grandparenthood from the Perspective of the Developing Grandchild," *Developmental Psychology* 3 (1970); Harald A. Euler and Barbara Weitzel, "Discriminative Grandparental Solicitude as Reproductive Strategy," *Human Nature* 7 (1996).

171 *Mothers' mothers tend to be . . . :* Eisenberg, "Grandchildren's Perspectives on Relationships with Grandparents," 213.

171 *This is mainly because . . . :* Rosalind C. Barnett, "Adult Daughters and Their Mothers: Harmony or Hostility?" Working Paper No. 209, Wellesley College, Center for Research on Women, 1990, 1.

171 *Married adult women tend to live . . . :* Joan Aldous, "Parent-Adult Child Relations as Affected by Grandparent Status," in Vern L. Bengston and Joan F. Robertson, *Grandparenthood*, 125.

172 *And because family characteristics . . . :* Victoria R. Fu, Dennis E. Hinkle, and Mary Ann K. Hanna, "A Three-Generational Study of the Development of Individual Dependency and Family Interdependence," *Genetic, Social & General Psychological Monographs* 112 (1990), 156–157.

173 *Sometimes a grandmother reinforces . . . :* Maurine Boie LaBarre, Lucie Jessner, and Lon Ussery, "The Significance of Grandmothers in the Psychopathology of Children," *American Journal of Orthopsychiatry* 30 (January 1960), 182–183.

173 *Grandmothers can also act as mediators . . . :* Hagestad, "Continuity and Connectedness," 46.

173 *Women in their fifties and sixties . . . :* Carolyn J. Rosenthal, "Kinkeeping in the Familial Division of Labor," *Journal of Marriage and the Family* (November 1985), 969–972.

173 *The rituals that take place there . . . :* Edelman, *Mother of My Mother*, 157–160.

173 *Even grandmothers who don't handle . . . :* Hagestad, "Continuity and Connectedness," 46.

173–174 *They come to understand the general . . . can be fulfilled.:* Fu, Hinkle, and Hanna, "A Three-Generational Study of the Development of Individual Dependency and Family Interdependence," 156.

174 *The presence of an empathic . . . :* Hagestad, "Continuity and Connectedness," 45.

174–175 *Of all the women* . . . : Control group survey, question 36; Motherless Mothers survey, question 44.

175 *Children who grow up under* . . . : Edelman, *Mother of My Mother*, 52.

179 *"Look," he said. "There's Grandma Anne* . . . : Sexton, *Searching for Mercy Street*, 261.

180 *More than three-quarters of the motherless mothers surveyed* . . . : Motherless Mothers survey, questions 40 and 41.

Chapter Eight: The Grandma in Heaven

187 *To truly "get" what death means* . . . : Brenda L. Kenyon, "Current Research in Children's Conceptions of Death: A Critical Review," *Omega* 43 (2001), 68–70.

187 *Kids with high verbal abilities* . . . : *Ibid.*, 75.

187 *Children who have a low tolerance* . . . : Israel Orbach et al., "Children's Perception of Death and Interpersonal Closeness to the Dead Person," *Omega* 30 (1994–95), 2.

187 *Religious beliefs in an afterlife* . . . : C. Randy Cotton and Lillian M. Range, "Children's Death Concepts: Relationship to Cognitive Functioning, Age, Experience with Death, Fear of Death, and Hopelessness," *Journal of Clinical Child Psychology* 19 (1990), 125.

187 *. . . and the specific cause of a death* . . . : Kenyon, "Current Research in Children's Conceptions of Death: A Critical Review," 85.

187 (fn) *It seems that the closer a child* . . . : Orbach et al., "Children's Perception of Death and Interpersonal Closeness to the Dead Person," 8.

187 *To fully grasp them, she'd first need* . . . : *Ibid.*, 2.

188 *To fully understand "died,"* . . . : personal communication, Gina Mireault, PhD.

190–191 *A child who hasn't accounted for* . . . : Phyllis Rolfe Silverman, *Never Too Young to Know* (New York: Oxford University Press, 2000), 44–45.

191 *She might engage in a sort of* . . . : *Ibid.*

194 *I move back from him* . . . : Jennifer Lauck, *Show Me the Way* (New York: Atria Books, 2004), 95.

194–195 *Seventy-nine percent of the women surveyed for this book* . . . *ages six to twelve.*: Motherless Mothers survey, question 40.

196 *Children in this age range* . . . : Silverman, *Never Too Young to Know*, 50.

196 *While kids this age can't understand* . . . : *Ibid.*

197 *They're generally aware that it can happen* . . . : Barbara Kane, "Children's Concepts of Death," *The Journal of Genetic Psychology* 134 (1979), 144–149.

197 *By ages four and five, kids* . . . : *Ibid.*

197 *Because children this age think so literally* . . . : Silverman, *Never Too Young to Know*, 51–52.

198 *The preschool years are the time* . . . : Ibid.

199 *Specific answers to questions like* . . . : personal communication, Gina Mireault, PhD.

200 *Most six-year-olds have started* . . . : Kane, "Children's Concepts of Death," 144–149.

200 *They can put sequential events . . . practical than emotional.*: Silverman, *Never Too Young to Know*, 53–54.

201 *Whereas younger children mostly think* . . . : Kane, "Children's Concepts of Death," 150.

201 *School-age kids are likely* . . . : Terry Tafoya, "Once Upon a Session," *Paradigm* (Fall 2000).

201 *They become slightly less egocentric* . . . : Silverman, *Never Too Young to Know*, 53–54; personal communication, Gina Mireault, PhD.

203 *By age ten, most children* . . . : Kane, "Children's Concepts of Death," 141, 152; Kenyon, "Current Research in Children's Conceptions of Death: A Critical Review," 63.

203 *When talking with older school-age kids . . . complexity of the concept.*: Carol Irizarry, "Spirituality and the Child: A Grandparent's Death," *Journal of Psychosocial Oncology* 10 (1992), 56.

203 *Abstract, "adult" thought* . . . : Silverman, *Never Too Young to Know*, 55–57.

203 *As they develop a greater . . . more sophisticated intellect.*: Kenyon, "Current Research in Children's Conceptions of Death: A Critical Review," 71–81.

203 *An important task of the teen years* . . . : Silverman, *Never Too Young to Know*, 55–57.

205 *As an intellectual concept* . . . : Kane, "Children's Concepts of Death," 150.

205 *When children feel confused* . . . : Irizarry, "Spirituality and the Child: A Grandparent's Death," 47.

Chapter Nine: Protective Parenting

210 *As a general rule* . . . : Gina C. Mireault and Lynne A. Bond, "Parental Death in Childhood: Perceived Vulnerability and Adult Depression and Anxiety," *American Journal of Orthopsychiatry* 62 (October 1992), 518; Neil D. Weinstein, "Unrealistic Optimism About Future Life Events," *Journal of Personality and Social Psychology* 39 (1980), 806; Neil D. Weinstein, "Unrealistic Optimism About Susceptibility to Health Problems," *Journal of Behavioral Medicine* 5 (1982), 441.

211 *Perceived vulnerability is a close cousin* . . . : Mireault and Bond, "Parental

Death in Childhood"; David S. Gochman and Jean-Francois Saucier, "Perceived Vulnerability in Children and Adolescents," *Health Education Quarterly* 9 (Summer/Fall 1982), 47.

212 *Because people rely on past experience . . . :* Neil D. Weinstein, "Effects of Personal Experience on Self-protective Behavior," *Psychological Bulletin* 105 (1989), 41.

213 *Mireault's 1992 survey . . . anxiety later in life.:* Mireault and Bond, "Parental Death in Childhood," 517–524.

213 *Motherless women who feel . . . :* personal communication, Gina Mireault, PhD.

213 *Anxiety is the response . . . :* Elizabeth Zetzel, "Depression and the Incapacity to Bear It," in M. Schur, ed., *Drives, Affects, Behavior, vol. 2* (New York: International Universities Press, 1965), 243.

214 *Some psychologists even argue . . . :* Ibid., 244; personal communication, Gina Mireault, PhD.

214 *Daniel Stern calls these . . . :* Stern, *The Birth of a Mother*, 104–106.

215 *First, the individual regresses . . . actual, external threat.:* Zetzel, "Depression and the Incapacity to Bear It," 246.

215 *"The toughest emotional challenge . . . :* Lerner, *The Mother Dance*, 93.

219 *Eighty-six percent of the motherless mothers . . . :* Motherless Mothers survey, question 42.

219 *I thought that proportion . . . :* Control group survey, question 34.

219 *To them, their behaviors are . . . :* Lieberman, *The Emotional Life of the Toddler*, 88.

222 *Parents who feel particularly vulnerable to loss . . . :* Ibid., 139.

222 *Children who start hearing this . . . :* Ibid., 140.

222 *"A parent who screams 'No!' . . . :* Schwartzman, *The Anxious Parent*, 162–163.

224 *It appears to be a personality characteristic . . . :* Gochman and Saucier, "Perceived Vulnerability in Children and Adolescents," 55.

Chapter Ten: Five to Twelve

233 *The mother's focus shifts . . . :* Carol George and Judith Solomon, "Internal Working Models of Caregiving and Security of Attachment at Age Six," *Infant Mental Health Journal* 10 (Fall 1989), 226.

234 *"Of all the interpersonal . . . ":* Louise Bates Ames and Frances Ilg, *Your Six-Year-Old* (New York: Dell, 1979), 15.

234 *The mother is the one most likely . . . :* George and Solomon, "Internal Working Models of Caregiving and Security of Attachment at Age Six," 226.

234 (fn) *More than half of all American children* . . . : Charlene Giannetti and Margaret Sagarese, *The Roller-Coaster Years* (New York: Broadway Books, 1997), xv.

241 *A mother is typically the recipient* . . . : Frances Ilg, Louise Bates Ames, and Sidney Baker, *Child Behavior* (New York: HarperPerennial, 1981), 208.

241 *Feelings toward a father* . . . : *Ibid.*

241 *"Feeling that you've lost your child's love* . . . : Schwartzman, *The Anxious Parent*, 250.

242 *Some parents will "actually . . . to remain unbroken . . .": Ibid.*, 251.

242 *Sarah is using what* . . . : *Ibid.*, 270.

246 *Six-year-olds can be* . . . : Ilg et al., *Child Behavior*, 208.

246 *It's fairly typical for mothers* . . . : Ames and Ilg, *Your Six-Year-Old*, 97.

247 *Children this age prefer arguing* . . . : Ilg et al., *Child Behavior*, 204.

247 *This new attitude is . . . out the window.":* Donna Corwin, *The Tween Years* (Chicago: Contemporary Books, 1999), 19.

247 *When Laurence Steinberg, PhD . . . eleven to thirteen for boys.:* Laurence Steinberg, *Crossing Paths* (New York: Simon & Schuster, 1994), 118.

248 *Ages ten to thirteen, as she describes them* . . . : Karen Stabiner, "Today Show" interview, May 26, 2005, www.video.msnbc.com

248 *. . . between ages ten and twelve* . . . : Nancy Snyderman, *Girl in the Mirror* (New York: Hyperion, 2002), 10–11.

248 *Most children make up* . . . : *Ibid.*, 11.

255 *At moments when you're uncertain . . . a developmentally appropriate way.:* adapted from Michael Schwartzman, *The Anxious Parent*; and personal communication, Colleen Russell, MFT.

256 *Ninety-seven percent of us* . . . : Motherless Mothers survey, question 42; Control Group survey, question 34.

Chapter Eleven: The Drive to Survive

260 *More than half of the motherless women surveyed* . . . : Motherless Mothers survey, question 44; Control Group survey, question 36.

260 *John Bowlby, the noted attachment theorist, described* . . . : John Bowlby, *Loss: Sadness and Depression* (New York: Basic Books, 1980), 352.

260 *He believed that children* . . . : *Ibid.*

261 *Contrary to what most* . . . : Cynthia P. Galt and Bert Hayslip, "Age Differences in Levels of Overt and Covert Death Anxiety," *Omega* 37 (1998), 199.

262 *"Before I had children"* . . . : Michael Lewis, "Daddy Fearest," www.slate.com, August 13, 2002.

274 *The uneven distribution of domestic labor . . . :* Arlie Hochschild, *The Second Shift*, reissue (New York: Penguin, 2003).

274 (fn) *Forty-eight percent of women . . . :* Control Group survey, question 33, Motherless Mothers survey, question 38.

Chapter Twelve: It's About the Child

282 *Most parents have unfulfilled wishes . . . :* Stern, *The Birth of a Mother*, 75.

282 *When Maxine Harris, PhD, interviewed . . . her own childish self . . .":* Harris, *The Loss That Is Forever*, 178–179.

283 *Parents naturally project . . . :* Lerner, *The Mother Dance*, 214

283 *"Your own past affects . . . :* Schwartzman, *The Anxious Parent*, 30.

299 *It seems I've got a case of . . . :* Henri Parens, "An Obstacle to the Child's Coping With Object Loss," in Akhtar, Salman, *The Three Faces of Mourning* (Northvale, N.J.: Jason Aronson, Inc., 2001), 159–163; Lerner, *The Mother Dance*, 205.

301 *This is the concept of "optimal anxiety" . . . :* Lieberman, *The Emotional Life of the Toddler*, 133.

302 *"However, even within a particular culture . . . :* Ibid.

302 *"If you never let [a child] . . . his own feelings.":* Schwartzman, *The Anxious Parent*, 227.

303 *When adults stifle a child's . . . :* Dilworth and Hildreth, "Long-term Unresolved Grief: Applying Bowlby's Variants to Adult Survivors of Early Parental Death," 155.

304 *Children who are expected to feel happy . . . :* Lieberman, *The Emotional Life of the Toddler*, 140.

305 *. . . rather than rushing in to . . . :* Lerner, *The Mother Dance*, 130.

Chapter Thirteen: Raising Teenagers

310 *Sixty-three percent of the women surveyed . . . :* Motherless Mothers survey, question 12.

311 *"Ours is a generation of uncertain . . . :* Anthony Wolf, *Get Out of My Life, but First Could You Drive Me and Cheryl to the Mall?* (New York: Farrar Straus Giroux, 2002), 4–5.

312 *. . . the dominant tasks of our adolescences . . . :* Snyderman, *Girl in the Mirror*, 124–125; Mihaly Csikszentmihalyi and Reed Larson, *Being Adolescent* (New York: Basic Books, 1984), 8, 30.

312 *When Sol Altschul . . . stages of childhood . . . :* Altschul and Beiser, "The Effect of Early Parent Loss on Future Parenthood," 175–181.

313 *Altschul and Beiser observed a similar phenomenon . . . to a teenage daughter.* *Ibid.,* 180–181.

315 *When Laurence Steinberg studied 204 . . . :* Steinberg, *Crossing Paths,* 231.

315 *Typically, these messages . . . : Ibid.,* 247.

315 *In her thought-provoking book* Girl in the Mirror *. . . :* Snyderman, *Girl in the Mirror,* 100–101.

316 *"One of the masochistic experiences of motherhood . . . :* Helene Deutsch, *The Psychology of Women, Vol. II: Motherhood* (New York: Grune & Stratton, 1945), 21.

316 *Unlike the first separation process . . . :* Steinberg, *Crossing Paths,* 110.

316 *As her adolescent gradually relinquishes . . . :* Elson, "Parenthood and the Transformations of Narcissism," 312.

318 *In their landmark 1984 book . . . :* Csikszentmihalyi and Larson, *Being Adolescent,* 130–135.

318 *Home serves mostly . . . : Ibid.,* 136.

318 *If she experiences it as a personal loss . . . the prior relationship.:* Steinberg, *Crossing Paths,* 101.

321 *When Susan Shaffer and Linda Gordon . . . :* Susan Morris Shaffer and Linda Perlman Gordon, *Why Boys Don't Talk—and Why It Matters* (New York: McGraw-Hill, 2005), 29.

321 *Connecting with our sons . . . : Ibid.,* 22–23.

321 *To remove it . . . : Ibid.,* 26.

321 *When we redefine the process . . . :* Snyderman, *Girl in the Mirror,* 100.

322 *Whereas sons tend to . . . :* Wolf, *Get Out of My Life,* 27–29.

323 *. . . about 80 percent of adolescents . . . :* Snyderman, *Girl in the Mirror,* 46; Steinberg, *Crossing Paths,* 101.

323 *Constant bickering and squabbling . . . on family members.:* Steinberg, *Crossing Paths,* 56, 113.

323 *The mothers in Steinberg's study . . . an opportunity for growth.: Ibid.,* 29, 59, 255.

324 *Most often, parent-teen conflict . . . :* Csikszentmihalyi and Larson, *Being Adolescent,* 140.

324 *They want emotional closeness . . . anger or frustration.:* Wolf, *Get Out of My Life,* 5, 20.

325 *A child who battles . . . : Ibid.,* 35.

329 *Even though we may not have had . . . :* Stanley Greenspan, *Playground Politics* (Cambridge, Massachusetts: Da Capo Press, 1993), 252.

329 *In Steinberg's study . . . :* Steinberg, *Crossing Paths,* 88.

329 *They reached such feelings . . . : Ibid.,* 79–97.

330 *Most adults in their forties and early fifties . . . make changes for the better.:* *ibid.*, 41, 74, 91.

331 *. . . a "love and limits" approach . . . :* Sumru Erkut, "Daughters Talking About Their Mothers: A View from the Campus," Working Paper No. 127 (1984) Wellesley College Center for Research on Women, 14.

332 *As Mihaly Csikszentmihalyi and Reed Larson explain . . . :* Csikszentmihalyi and Larson, *Being Adolescent*, 133.

332 *This can lead to . . . : Ibid.*

332 *The result is a household . . . do poorly at school.:* Steinberg, *Crossing Paths*, 218–225.

333 *Studies of parenting styles.:* Erkut, "Daughters Talking About Their Mothers," 14; Steinberg, *Crossing Paths*, 225.

333 *It may be the mother's willingness . . . :* Leslie Gavin and Wyndol Furman, "Adolescent Girls' Relationships with Mothers and Best Friends," *Child Development* 67 (1996), 384.

Bibliography

Akhtar, Salman, ed. *Three Faces of Mourning*. Northvale, New Jersey: Jason Aronson Inc., 2001.

Altschul, Sol, ed. *Childhood Bereavement and Its Aftermath*. Madison, Connecticut: International Universities Press, 1988.

Barrett, Nina. *I Wish Someone Had Told Me*. New York: Fireside, 1990.

Black, Kathryn. *Mothering Without a Map*. New York: Viking, 2004.

Buchanan, Andrea. *Mother Shock*. New York: Seal Press, 2003.

Csikszentmihalyi, Mihaly, and Larson, Reed. *Being Adolescent*. New York: Basic Books, 1984.

Davidman, Lynn. *Motherloss*. Berkeley, California: University of California Press, 2000.

Furman, Erna. *On Being and Having a Mother*. Madison, Connecticut: International Universities Press. 2001.

Gaskin, Ina May. *Ina May's Guide to Natural Childbirth*. New York: Bantam Books, 2003.

Genevie, Louis, and Margolies, Eva. *The Motherhood Report*. New York: McGraw-Hill, 1989.

Grollman, Earl, ed. *Explaining Death to Children*. Boston: Beacon Press, 1967.

Harris, Maxine. *The Loss That is Forever*. New York: Plume, 1996.

Ilg, Frances L., Ames, Louise Bates, and Baker, Sidney M. *Child Behavior*. New York: HarperPerennial, 1981.

Karen, Robert. *Becoming Attached*. New York: Warner Books, 1994.

Kendall-Tackett, Kathleen A. *Depression in New Mothers*. Binghamton, New York: The Haworth Maltreatment and Trauma Press, 2005.

———. *The Hidden Feelings of Motherhood*. Oakland, California: New Harbinger Publications, 2001.

Kitzinger, Sheila. *Ourselves as Mothers*. Reading, Massachusetts: Addison-Wesley, 1994.

———. *The Crying Baby*. New York: Viking Penguin, 1989.

Klaus, Marshall H., Kennell, John H., and Klaus, Phyllis H. *Mothering the Mother*. Reading, Massachusetts: Addison-Wesley, 1993.

Lauck, Jennifer. *Show Me the Way*. New York: Atria Books, 2004.

Lazarre, Jane. *The Mother Knot*. Boston: Beacon Press, 1986.

Lerner, Harriet. *The Mother Dance*. New York: HarperCollins, 1998.

Lieberman, Alicia F. *The Emotional Life of the Toddler*. New York: The Free Press, 1993.

Maushart, Susan. *The Mask of Motherhood*. New York: Penguin Books, 1999.

Parkes, Colin Murray, Stevenson-Hinde, Joan, and Marris, Peter, eds. *Attachment Across the Life Cycle*. London: Routledge, 1993.

Peterson, Gayle. *Birthing Normally*. Berkeley, California: Shadow and Light, 1984.

———. *An Easier Childbirth*. Berkeley, California: Shadow and Light, 1993.

Piaget, Jean. *The Child's Conception of the World*. Savage, Maryland: Littlefield Adams Quality Paperbacks, New Edition.

Placksin, Sally. *Mothering the New Mother*. 2nd edition. New York: Newmarket Press, 2000.

Schaefer, Dan, and Lyons, Christine. *How Do We Tell the Children?* 3rd edition. New York: Newmarket Press, 2001.

Schwartzman, Michael. *The Anxious Parent*. New York: Simon & Schuster, 1990.

Sexton, Linda Gray. *Searching for Mercy Street*. New York: Little, Brown and Company, 1994.

Shereshefsky, Pauline M., and Yarrow, Leon J. *Psychological Aspects of a First Pregnancy*. New York: Raven Press, 1973.

Simon, Leslie, and Drantell, Jan Johnson. *A Music I No Longer Heard*. New York: Simon & Schuster, 1998.

Snyderman, Nancy L., and Streep, Peg. *Girl in the Mirror*. New York: Hyperion, 2002.

Steinberg, Laurence. *Crossing Paths*. New York: Simon & Schuster, 1994.

Stern, Daniel N., Bruschweiler-Stern, Nadia, and Freeland, Alison. *The Birth of a Mother*. New York: Basic Books, 1998.

Tamony, Katie. *Your 2nd Pregnancy*. Chicago: Chicago Review Press, 1995.

Winnicott, D.W. *Babies and Their Mothers*. Reading, Massachusetts: Addison-Wesley, 1987.

Index

Don't miss Hope Edelman's first book, the beginning of the motherless journey.

Motherless Daughters explores the myriad ways that losing a mother affects almost every aspect and passage of a woman's life.

First published a decade ago, it is still the book that motherless daughters of all ages look to for understanding and comfort, and it is the book that they continue to press into each other's hands.

Building on interviews with hundreds of mother-loss survivors, this life-affirming book is now newly expanded to reflect the author's personal experience with the continued legacy of mother loss. Now married and a mother of young children herself, Edelman better understands how the effects of mother loss change over time, and in light of new relationships.

A work of stunning courage and honesty, *Motherless Daughters* is a must-read for the millions of women whose mothers have gone, but whose need for healing, mourning, and mothering remains. It is a timeless classic.

Da Capo

www.dacapopress.com